STORIES IN STONE

JEFFERSON COUNTY, TENNESSEE CEMETERIES

VOLUME II

Dandridge and
White Pine Sections

Transcribed by

David H. Templin and
Cherel Bolin Henderson

Heritage Books
2024

Dedicated

to

Beulah D. Linn

Sevier County Historian

who first introduced us to
the fascinating record of the
past found in our area's cemeteries

━━━━━━━━━━━━━━━━━━━━

HERITAGE BOOKS
AN IMPRINT OF HERITAGE BOOKS, INC.

Books, CDs, and more—Worldwide

For our listing of thousands of titles see our website
at
www.HeritageBooks.com

A Facsimile Reprint
Published 2024 by
HERITAGE BOOKS, INC.
Publishing Division
5810 Ruatan Street
Berwyn Heights, MD 20740

International Standard Book Number
Paperbound: 978-0-7884-8761-3

FOREWORD

This is the second of three planned volumes of Jefferson County cemetery transcriptions. Volume I, published in 1986, covered the Dumplin Valley and South of the French Broad areas. Volume III will conclude the series and will contain the Strawberry Plains and the New Market-Jefferson City sections.

An effort has been made to locate and transcribe all cemeteries in Jefferson County with the exception of the large, recently-established perpetual care cemeteries. There are cemeteries listed here which have been destroyed, but whose existence has been verified through the use of maps, WPA records, and interviews with area residents.

We plan to eventually combine all three volumes of Stories in Stone into one large book of Jefferson County cemeteries. Therefore, we are carrying the page numbers straight through all three volumes. Volume I ended with page 189, and volume II begins with page 190 and ends with page 367. Volume III will begin with page 368.

Am attempt has been made to avoid errors, but as with any large work such as this, mistakes are unavoidable. We apologize for these and ask that corrections be sent to us. The cemeteries were transcribed, alphabetized, typed, and the lists taken back to the cemeteries and re-checked stone by stone.

In 1937, under the direction of the Works Projects Administratioin (WPA), most, but not all, of the cemeteries in Jefferson County were copied. We have had occasion to compare the names and dates found in these records with the stones and have found them to contain a very high percentage of errors and many omissions. We feel, despite the errors, that the WPA transcriptions were invaluable in reconstructting old cemeteries that have been destroyed, and in identifying stones that have since disappeared. Though the WPA records are helpful, we urge caution in accepting the names and especially the dates listed there.

In contrast, the records made by TVA during the Douglas Dam project have been found to be extremely well done. TVA made an earnest effort to identify and locate next of kin to all graves in the Douglas Dam area. The consent of the next of kin was required to relocate a burial. Thus many unmarked burials were identified. TVA grave removal records are located in Chattanooga and may be helpful to the researcher because they list the name of the person who identified the burial and gave the consent to relocate it. The records are available by writing to TVA Grave Removal Records, 200 Haney Building, Chattanooga, TN 37401. There is a charge not only for a copy of the records but also for research involved in finding them. The prices, while not prohibitive, are rather high, so you may want to ask for an estimate before ordering.

The recording of these cemeteries has, for us, been a labor of love. Jefferson County is rich in the lore of the past as we have been delighted to learn as we explored these graveyards stone by stone. We have not found the stones to be mute, but we have been enthralled by the wonderful, fascinating stories they have told us. In ways great and small, Jefferson Countians have participated in the events that have shaped our nation -- the intriguing State of Franklin period, the War of 1812, the Trail of Tears, the Mexican War, the myriad personal tragedies of the Civil War, onward through history to the present. As we added names and personalities to the participants of the times, both the past and the present took on new meaning for us.

When we began this project we had only a nodding acquaintance with historical figures such as George Doherty and John Seahorn, both of whom were compatriots and friends of John Sevier and strong supporters of the State of Franklin. The Civil

I

War tragedies of Russell Snodgrass and Shale T. Harris were entirely unknown to us. Yet finding these graves and many others has sparked within us an insatiable desire to learn more and has prompted us to spend many hours in research. Sometimes our search has been rewarded with a treasure trove of information just waiting to be discovered, but at other times our efforts were in vain as we found the answers to be lost in the unfathomable darkness of the past.

Huge, expensive monuments speak loudly, proclaiming their messages to all. But the grave marked only by a rose bush, a shrub, periwinkle, or the springtime colors of Easter Flowers and Irises speaks just as eloquently, telling us of the time, the care, the love that went into the planting as an assurance that this loved one's grave would be remembered.

Beautiful and moving in its simplicity is the fieldstone so often found in area cemeteries. Many of these are works of art, beautifully crafted with care and infinite patience. Money can purchase a grand monument, but love created fieldstones.

Equally moving to us are the children's graves. We have found as many as six or seven tiny stones in a row, each marking an infant burial, all of them belonging to the same parents. A young mother and babe dying in childbirth, buried in the same grave, tell of a husband and father's grief as he buried all that was dear to him.

Heartbreaking are the gallant young men who died in our country's wars. We often find these graves decorated with the red, white, and blue of the American flag. But at least, as the flowers and flags testify, these soldiers came home to rest in native soil; others were not so lucky. Scattered across Jefferson County are the graves of countless Civil War soldiers, Blue and Gray, who were felled by battle, disease, and accidents as the tides of war swept through this area. Strangers in a strange land, they were buried in lonely graves beside the roads, in fields, in cemeteries, or often just where they fell. Forever the unknown soldiers, their graves, if marked at all, have small, uninscribed fieldstones.

We sincerely hope that these volumes of **Stories in Stone** will be of help to genealogists and historians. We also hope these written records will stand as a tribute and remembrance of all of those buried in Jefferson County. But as much as we want our work to aid others, we must say, in all honesty, that through the knowledge, interest and understanding gained while working on this project, we feel we have benefited most of all.

We would like to express appreciation to so many friends who helped us with this volume. Special thanks goes to Steve Cotham for taking time out of a hectic schedule to take the photos used here; to D. Morton Rose and to James Messer who advised us as to the possible methods of drawing the maps; to Beulah D. Linn, Sevier County historian, who, in her neat, precise handwriting, lettered the maps; to Tony Hardegree of TVA, Chattanooga, who went the extra mile in helping us; to Fran Allison for the beautiful drawing used on the cover; and to Jim Stinnett of Stinnett Printers, Alcoa, Tennessee, for his patience, advice and help.

David H. Templin

Cherel B. Henderson

INTRODUCTION

To save space, abbreviations were used in compiling the transcriptions of tombstones printed in this book. An attempt was made to list all important information found on the tombstone, slate, funeral home marker, or footstone.

Abbreviations were used in the columns of birth and death dates for the names of the months and to indicate the presence of only one date. NOD ("no other date") indicates that the person appeared to be still living and that the single date given appears to be a birth date. In some cases, it was obvious from the early birth date that the person is now deceased, but the death date has not been added to the tombstone. OD("only date") indicates that the transcriber found only one date, which could have been either birth or death date. The date was arbitrarily entered in the birth or deth column, according to the judgement of the transcriber. In cases where the stone stated"born" or "died," the date is listed in the appropriate column with a notation reading (born) or (died).

Abbreviations frequently occur in the "comments" field. The chief abbreviations used here for words spelled out in full on the tombstone include:

c/o	=	child of
d/o	=	daughter of
fhm	=	funeral home marker
h/o	=	husband of
i/o	=	infant of
M/M	=	Mr. and Mrs.
md.	=	married
s/o	=	son of
Tenn.	=	Tennessee
TN	=	Tennessee
WWI	=	World War I
WWII	=	World War II
y,m,d	=	years, months, days (age)

Multiple names listed on one tomstone (usually husband and wife) are indicated by being linked together on the right with a single parenthesis.

                    Smith, John)
                      Mary   )

Cemetery listings have been alphabetized within each cemetery by surname and then by given name. Multiple names on one stone are alphabetized arbitrarily by the first Christian name listed, usually the husband. Unless "h/o" (husband of) or "w/o" (wife of) appears in the comments field, it should be assumed that the transcriber made a judgement based on matching tombstones, side by side stones, or similar dates.

Surnames are omitted in the "comments" field unless they are different from those under which the deceased is listed alphabetically. Usually these different names are the maiden names of wives. On those rare occasions where there are two stones for the same person with discrepancies in information, this is indicated in the "comments" field. Parentheses around any piece of information should indicate that it was not present on the tombstone itself, but was provided by some knowledgeable person.

INDEXES

The **Primary Index** is the surname index only to those names which were interpreted by the transcribers as the surname of the deceased. These surnames were usually listed in the left hand column, but in a few instances a burial may be listed in the text. Since other surnames were included in the "comments" field, or appear as maiden names of the wives, a **Secondary Index** was created to make that information more readily available to the researcher. A careful search of the page indicated in the **Secondary Index** will be necessary to derive any benefit from the list.

PUBLIC CHAPTER NO. 541

SENATE BILL NO. 1558

By Henry

Substituted for: House Bill NO. 1608

By Naifeh, Tanner, Kisber, Dills, Kent, Gaia
Kerneil, Gill, Crain, Herndon, Davis (Gibson), Stallings,
Murray, Davidson, Mr. Speaker McWherter

AN ACT To protect cemeteries and to impose penalties for violations.

BE IT ENACTED BY THE GENERAL ASSEMBLY OF THE STATE OF TENNESSEE:

SECTION 1. No person shall willfully destroy, deface, move, or injure any grave, gravesite, monument, tomb, gravestone, bronze memorial, statuary, mausoleum, or similar item wherever located or destroy, deface, move or injure any fence or enclosure in or around the same, or injure any tree, plant or shrub therein. Violation of the provisions of this section shall be a felony and any person guilty thereof shall be fined one thousand, five hundred dollars ($1,500.00) or imprisoned in the penitentiary not less than one (1) year nor more than three (3) years, or both, in the discretion of the court. Any act as to each tombstone, monument, or gravestone, bronze memorial, statuary, mausoleum, or similar item shall be a separate offense.

SECTION 2. Nothing in this act, however, shall be construed to prohibit the moving of a grave, gravesite, monument, tomb, gravestone, bronze memorial, statuary, mausoleum, or similar item upon the written authorization of the decedent's personal representative and, if living, his spouse, or as otherwise provided by law.

SECTION 3.   This act shall take effect upon becomoing a law, the public welfare requiring it.

PASSED: April 9, 1984

_____
                           SPEAKER OF THE SENATE

_____
                           SPEAKER OF THE HOUSE OF REPRESENTATIVES

APPROVED this 24th day of April   1984

* *

Remove not the ancient landmark, which thy Fathers have set.....

                           Proverbs 22:28

V

JEFFERSON COUNTY, TENNESSEE

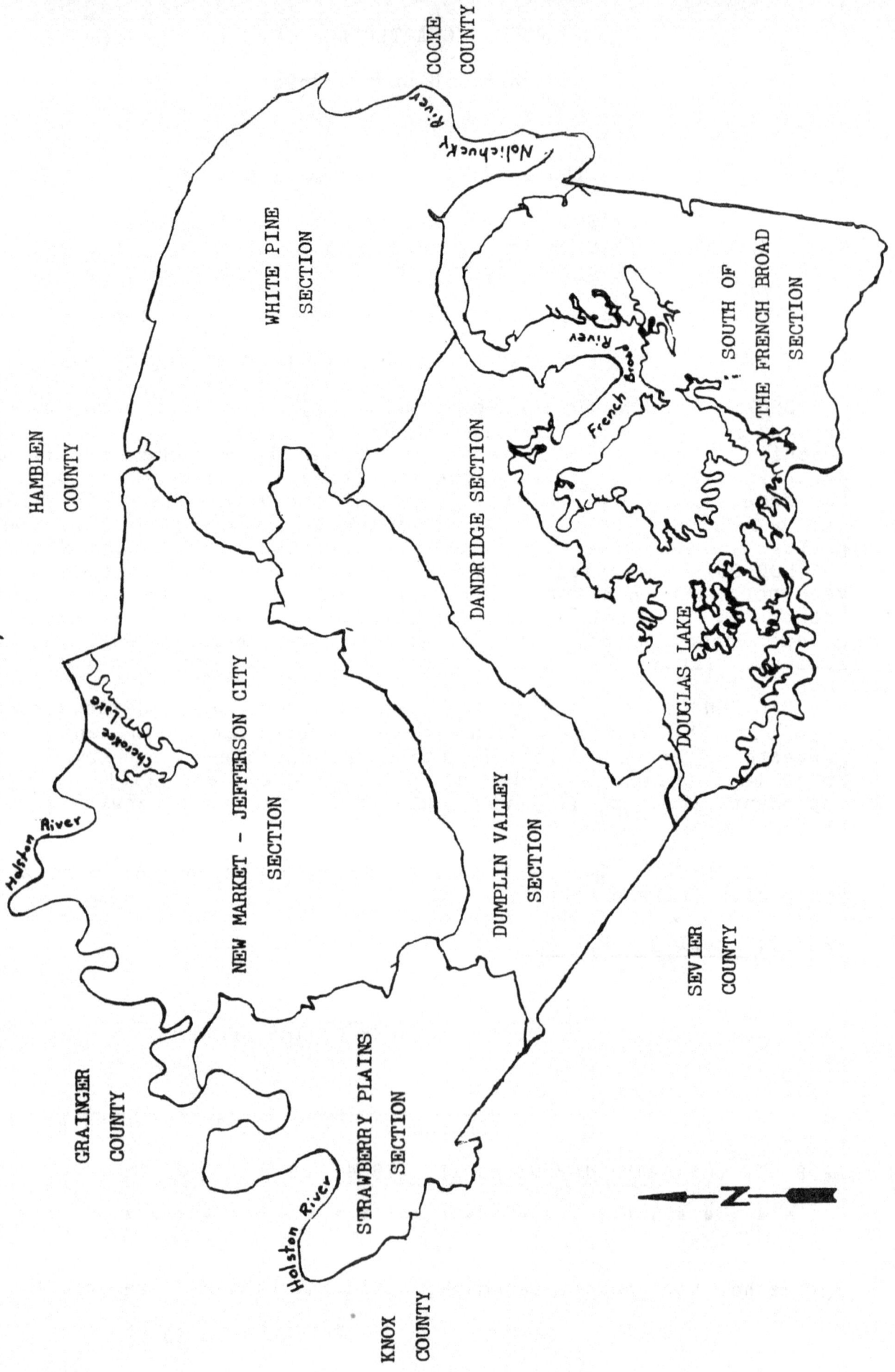

GRAINGER
COUNTY

HAMBLEN
COUNTY

COCKE
COUNTY

Nolichucky River

WHITE PINE
SECTION

SOUTH OF
THE FRENCH BROAD
SECTION

French Broad
River

DANDRIDGE SECTION

Holston River

Cherokee Lake

NEW MARKET – JEFFERSON CITY
SECTION

DUMPLIN VALLEY
SECTION

DOUGLAS LAKE

STRAWBERRY PLAINS
SECTION

Holston River

SEVIER
COUNTY

N

KNOX
COUNTY

TABLE OF CONTENTS

Engraved on this stone is the Civil War saga of Shale T. Harris and the finance who stood by him while he was in a Confederate prison awaiting execution. A last minute reprieve from President Jefferson Davis spared his life.

The French Broad River was the gateway for early settlement into this area, and two of the earliest communities in the county, Oak Grove and Shady Grove, were located on this waterway. The oldest marked grave in Jefferson County is that of Josiah Leith who died in 1787 and was buried in the Old Shady Grove Methodist Church Cemetery. In 1941 the grave was moved to the nearby newer Shady Grove Methodist Cemetery, safe from the floodwaters of Douglas Lake.

Other early churches in the area included Hopewell Presbyterian (1785), and Lower French Broad Baptist (1786), which met at the Coons School House above Dandridge. Many old family graveyards are found in this section, the most notable being the Kelly and the Graham cemeteries, both in the Oak Grove Community.

DANDRIDGE SECTION

DANDRIDGE SECTION

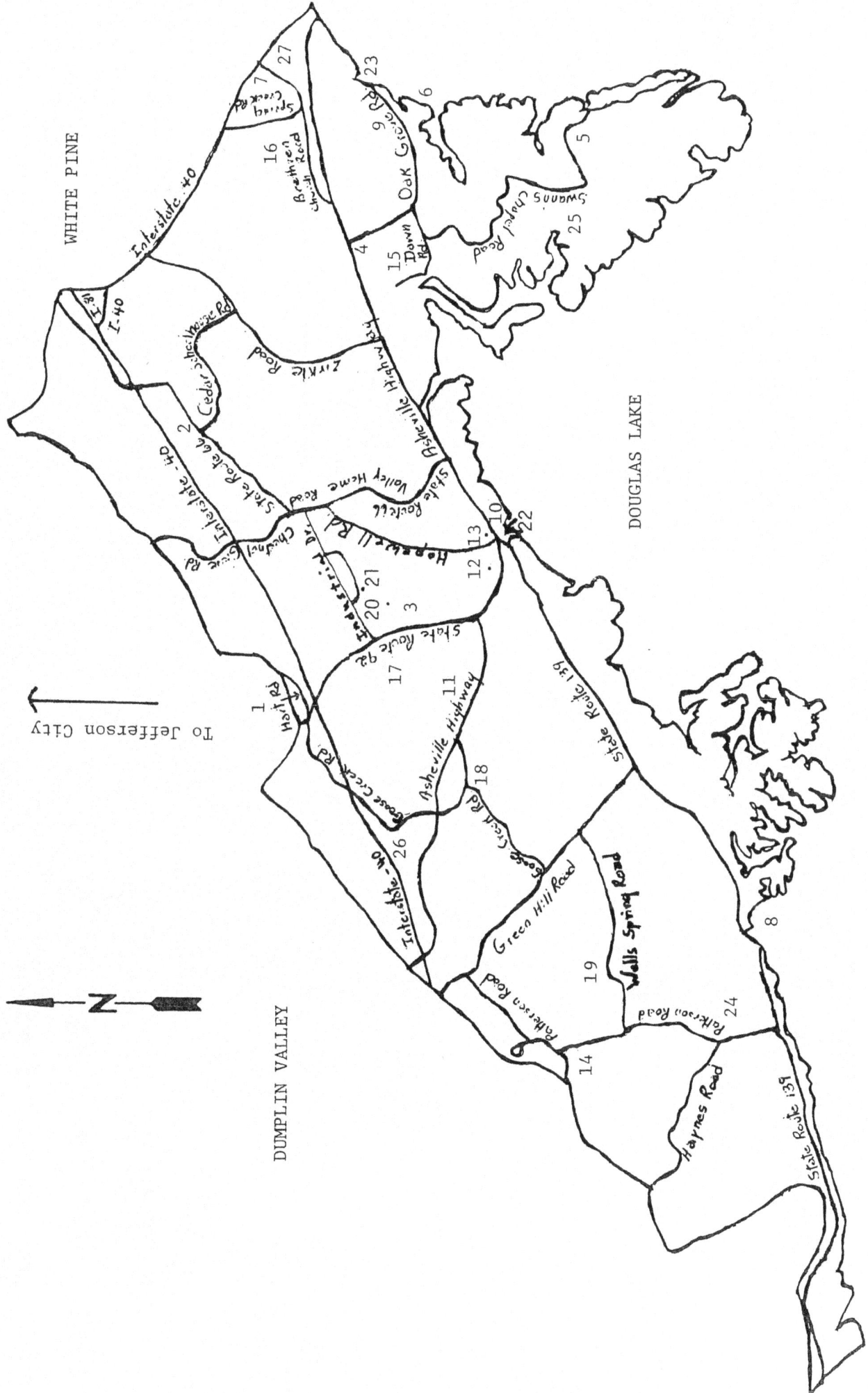

N

To Jefferson City

WHITE PINE

DUMPLIN VALLEY

DOUGLAS LAKE

I-81
Interstate 40
I-40

Spring Creek Rd

27
7
16
Brethren Church Road

23
9
Oak Grove Rd
6

Cedar Schoolhouse Rd

4
15
Down Rd

Zirkle Road

5

State Route 66
Interstate-40

Chestnut Grove Rd

Valley Home Road

State Route 66

Asheville Highway

Swanns Chapel Road
25

Transtrine Dr.

20 21

3

12 13
10
22

Hopewell Rd

Hart Rd

1

Goose Creek Rd

17

State Route 92

11

Asheville Highway

18

State Route 139

Interstate-40

26

Green Hill Road

Patterson Road

19

Wells Spring Road

Patterson Road
24

Haynes Road

14

State Route 139

8

ANNABEL CEMETERY

BROWN-William Arthur	22 Mar 1894	9 Dec 1976	
Ruth Jane	10 Aug 1899	10 Mar 1952	
CASE-Vivian Bernice	OD	17 Sep 1972	Inf twin dau. of Floyd & Beckie
CLINE-Sanford Leon	25 Jul 1912	26 Jul 1912	
FRANKLIN-Albert L.)	21 Mar 1893	8 Dec 1915	
Lettie T.)	24 Aug 1900	31 Dec 1974	
Ben)	OD	27 Feb 1907	
Frank)			
Charlie A.)	6 Jan 1890	30 Mar 1965	
Minnie J.)	2 Dec 1873	23 May 1922	
Kenneth V.	19 Oct 1911	30 Aug 1951	
Lon	8 Aug 1919	10 Mar 1922	
Lottie Ruth	3 Apr 1903	6 Jun 1929	
Luther)	1 Mar 1864	20 Jan 1944	
Cordie Lee)	27 Feb 1864	23 Nov 1928	His wife
Mack B.)	2 Feb 1888	8 Mar 1941	
Annis V.)	9 Dec 1886	1 Jan 1970	
Mary Elizabeth	5 Sep 1861	7 Dec 1917	
Mary V.	3 Oct 1895	5 Jul 1896	
Ora George Etta	30 Nov 1944	10 Dec 1944	d/o M/M G. W.
Ora Hart	6 Nov 1890	18 Dec 1958	
Rue Raymond	3 Sep 1905	27 Oct 1912	s/o George & Minnie
GRANT-David	Died	27 Apr 1885	Aged 84y
Betsy	1 Mar 1803	28 Jun 1889	w/o D.
Elizabeth C.	14 Mar 1840	OD(born)	30y; d/o David & Elizabeth
Isaac	12 Sep 1831	16 Aug 1915	Corp'l Co. B 9th Tenn Cav
Mary	13 Dec 1825	14 Feb 1897	71y 2m 1d
James	16 Jul 1827	4 May 1896	
Betsy Cannon	1832	1892	
John B.)	6 Oct 1865	19 Sep 1919	
Mary L. Gass)	10 Aug 1868	16 Mar 1918	w/o John B.
HART-William D.	1 Mar 1878	23 May 1909	h/o Susie B.
William H.)	23 May 1848	23 May 1925	
Sarah B.)	22 May 1847	27 Sep 1920	
MANN-B. B.	29 Nov 1863	7 Feb 1899	
William T.	22 Jan 1901	20 Jun 1902	
NEWMAN-William H.	17 Feb 1875	22 Dec 1900	
PAINTER-Lebert C.	24 Feb 1895	13 Dec 1955	
Mary Inez	3 May 1926	5 May 1926	d/o Hobert N. & Dixie
Vada E.	22 Jan 1904	28 May 1911	d/o W. S. & Jane
William S.)	16 Nov 1855	25 Mar 1920	
Jennie H.)	20 Jan 1865	21 Oct 1934	
RIMMER-James Albert	16 Nov 1930	18 Nov 1930	s/o Carl & Nona
THORNHILL-Claude Avery	14 Feb 1945	6 Apr 1982	Sp5 US Army Vietnam
Frank A.	23 Jul 1912	24 Jun 1973	
Idra)	15 May 1915	27 Nov 1974	
Blanche)	25 Nov 1921	NOD	
J. M.	23 Mar 1855	25 Aug 1925(?)	
Jos. M.	No dates		Co L 1st Tenn Cav
Thomas Allen)	4 Jun 1865	8 Jan 1936	
Roxie Presley)	3 Aug 1881	18 May 1939	
Thos. W.	No dates		h/o Leah (footstone)
			Co. L 1st Tenn Cav
WHALEN-Thomasin	25 Aug 1825	10 Nov 1909	

This cemetery is fenced and well kept. There are 28 burials marked with

uninscribed fieldstones. To reach this cemetery, begin at Exit 417 from I-40
and turn toward Jefferson City. Drive 0.1 miles and turn right onto Hart Road.
Drive 0.1 mile. The cemetery is on the right.

The graves of John Sehorn (left) and his wife Elizabeth (right), found in
Graham Cemetery near the French Broad River. In our study of over 600 area
cemeteries, the inscription on John Sehorn's stone is unique. It reads "John
Sehorn, 21 Jun 1748 O.S. - 23 May 1831." O.S. stands for "Old Style," a
reckoning of dates discontinued in 1752. (See Graham Cemetery, page 219.)

A fence encloses the
Graham family plot
amid a tangle of vines
and briars. (Graham
Cemetery, p. 219).

BALCH CEMETERY

ACUFF-Pheby Ann	11 Nov 1834	7 Apr 1889	w/o Howard
BAKER-M. E.	22 Jan 1870	15 May 1903	
BALCH-James P.	25 Jul 1798	29 Jun 1879	
Polly R.	8 Apr 1801	21 Nov 1873	w/o James P.
BELL-Sam R.	24 Feb 1885	17 Feb 1890	s/o S. J. & S. E.
S. E.	8 Oct 1850	19 Jun 1898	w/o S. J.
Thula	24 May 1888	5 Jun 1888	d/o S. J. & S. E.
BIGGS-E. C.	28 Apr 1885	3 Aug 1887	
M. E.	18 Oct 1880	21 Jul 1886	
W. L.)	13 May 1844	28 May 1922	
Susan N.)	28 May 1849	8 Sep 1924	
BREEDEN-Edna Cox	1916	1969	(fhm-Farrar)
Ella E.C.	17 Jul 1873	14 Sep 1954	
Harvey L.	28 Apr 1891	15 Oct 1981	
Lula	1 Nov 1895	21 Apr 1956	
John L.	13 Feb 1884	29 Jan 1975	
Martha R.	1863	1925	
BROOKS-Nannie Riley Miller	1902	1982	(fhm-Farrar gives last name as BROOKS)
BROWN-Charles H.	22 Feb 1956	21 Aug 1968	
Eugene)	22 Jun 1900	23 Sep 1961	
Lillie R.)	13 Mar 1916	25 Mar 1966	
Frances R.	5 Nov 1936	17 Feb 1937	
Harrison P.	1892	1976	(fhm-Brooks)
Harvey E.	8 Mar 1945	17 Oct 1982	Pvt US Army
Inez A. Gooch	20 Jun 1899	15 Dec 1935	
James Allen Jr.	30 Jun 1969	18 Feb 1971	
John R.)	28 Feb 1861	1 May 1934	
Rachel B.)	8 Aug 1866	14 Sep 1943	
Walter H.	11 Aug 1952	27 Jun 1980	Sp4 US Army Vietnam
Warren	24 Oct 1920	30 Apr 1977	
William "Bill")	1881	1946	
Hettie Lunsford)	1882	1968	
Wilson C.	8 Aug 1885	14 Mar 1959	
Sarah F.	16 Nov 1890	16 Jan 1959	
CARMICHAEL-R.K.	20 Apr 1889	19 Nov 1913	w/o F. R.
CHAMBERS-Otha	18 Feb 1882	23 Jun 1953	
Julia	25 Oct 1888	11 Jan 1971	
COLLEY-Leatha M.	OD	25 Sep 1923	
Patton K.)	18 Mar 1880	25 Jan 1957	
Kate E.)	14 Aug 1887	25 Mar 1938	
Ruby	OD	17 Jan 1911	
Sevier	OD	14 Feb 1915	
COLLINS-Ann Eliza	1859	1946	
Eldo	6 Sep 1908	14 Sep 1908	s/o W.H. & L.M.
Hillard	1 May 1887	23 Aug 1964	h/o Lizzie
Infant	OD	4 Oct 1912	s/o M/M W.H.
J.A.	16 Jul 1818	19 Dec 1890	Father
Sarah Hartenstine	21 Aug 1827	12 Apr 1903	w/o J.A.
Susan E.	12 Oct 1851	12 Oct 1883	
W. H.)	22 Nov 1879	15 May 1913	
Lula May)	21 Sep 1883	25 Nov 1950	
CORBETT-A. B. "Ted")	6 Oct 1913	20 Apr 1972	
Louise M.)	17 Jul 1911	NOD	
Charles C.	28 May 1897	19 Oct 1966	TN Pvt US Army WWI & II
Earnest M.	6 Oct 1890	13 Jun 1960	

CORBETT-Nellie	6 Mar 1888	23 Sep 1928	w/o Earnest
Eula M.	30 Jun 1905	14 Mar 1914	
Infant	No dates		s/o D.D. & E.D.
J.P.	26 Jun 1862	29 Mar 1920	
Loue H.	26 Aug 1883	19 Nov 1883	d/o D.D. & E.D.
M. E.	15 Dec 1868	12 Sep 1913	
Will H.)	3 Aug 1885	20 Oct 1952	
Love)	24 Dec 1894	NOD	
COX-Infant	17 Dec 1948	18 Dec 1948	
John Raymond)	23 Feb 1907	25 Sep 1945	
Edna Mae)	3 Jan 1912	1 Jul 1984	
Joseph Daniel)	25 Feb 1884	28 Jul 1954	
Ollie Collins)	30 Jun 1883	17 Nov 1967	
Marshall E.)	27 Nov 1909	27 Jun 1976	"Mutt"
Alma B.)	26 Mar 1916	NOD	
Ross R. Jr.	OD	31 Mar 1942	s/o M/M Ross R.
CROSS-Mary A. Rimmer	1 Aug 1855	4 Jan 1908	w/o R.
EDGAR-Infant	Born & died	10 Oct 1879	s/o A.B. & J.C.
Rebecca J.	16 Dec 1837	2 Jun 1888	51y 5m 18d (broken)
W. I. I.	7 Apr 1836	28 Sep 1904	
FOSTER-Lyman M.)	1 Jun 1915	NOD	Married 1 Aug 1948
Ethel Corbett)	4 Aug 1918	NOD	
S. Corbett	10 Dec 1949	14 May 1964	
FOX-Arthur)	25 Mar 1882	23 May 1951	
Lizzie)	14 Jul 1887	28 Oct 1978	
GREEN-Delores	Born & died	1934	d/o Claude & Cora
Jesse A.)	22 Jan 1856	9 Nov 1934	
Ada E.)	3 Nov 1878	2 Jun 1934	
HAMMOND-Hattie M.	14 Dec 1853	8 Jul 1889	w/o N.B.; 35y 7m 24d (broken)
HAYES-Carrie Rimmer	Died	28 Sep 1907	
HUGHES-J. Frank)	1849	1920	
Georgia A.)	1882	1930	
JARNIGAN-Fred)	7 Sep 1920	NOD	Married 30 Aug 1941
Zelma Corbett)	23 Nov 1914	8 Nov 1984	
Infant	OD	25 Feb 1969	s/o Bill & Norma
KNIGHT-Bonnie	5 Jun 1899	2 Aug 1914	
Callaway	21 Nov 1858	11 Oct 1912	
Ollie	2 Nov 1870	18 Aug 1916	
Carah A.	8 Nov 1892	24 Sep 1904	Killed in Railroad Wreck at New Market, Tenn. d/o G.W. & O.C.
LEDFORD-Walter	Died	16 Apr 1956	_y 3m 7d (fhm-Maloy)
LINER-Susie	1946	1982	(fhm-Farrar)
LOVE-Harding	29 Mar 1922	9 Jun 1970	Sgt Co F 39t Inf WWII
James Carl)	10 Dec 1912	27 Mar 1968	
Pauline)	10 Dec 1922	NOD	
Mort H.)	31 Aug 1888	20 Apr 1970	
Nannie Jane)	29 Jun 1892	29 Jan 1979	
PFC William A.	25 Jan 1919	13 Jul 1943	Born Tenn. Died South Pacific Co. I 169th Inf US Army WWII(Military stone gives birth as 24 Jan 1919)
Frank M.)	20 Dec 1934	NOD	
Lola Ruth)	20 Jan 1934	21 Mar 1986	Wed 10 Nov 1967
MANIS-Arnold Mitchell	18 Jun 1893	19 Jul 1893	s/o Grant & Isabella B.
Earl Clifford)	10 Jun 1912	3 Jan 1985	
Bondretta Martin)	27 Apr 1910	NOD	

MANIS-Emma J.	7 May 1897	6 Aug 1898	d/o Grant & Isabella
Eugene	24 Sep 1906	25 Oct 1907	s/o Grant & Martha
James Walter	4 Jul 1894	28 Aug 1895	s/o Grant & Isabella B.
Jeneva B.	16 Sep 1909	14 Jun 1911	d/o A. M. & O.L.
Isabella B.	14 Feb 1866	6 Apr 1898	w/o Grant
T.D.	23 Jan 1839	25 Sep 1919	Co A 9th Tenn Cav
Frances Amanda	8 Feb 1845	26 Dec 1898	w/o T.D. 53y 10m 18d
MARTIN-Carl L.)	31 Mar 1889	15 Feb 1975	
Eva S.)	12 Jan 1889	5 Jul 1978	
E. J.	13 Aug 1869	14 Dec 1921	
Nancy E.	29 Dec 1876	19 Aug 1902	d/o W.C. & Margaret
L. Hearsel)	8 May 1914	NOD	
L. Pauline)	18 May 1917	NOD	
Wanda C.)	21 Mar 1939	NOD	
MILLER-Albert W.)	7 Aug 1860	6 Jan 1936	
Martha E.)	16 Sep 1859	24 Dec 1936	
Marshall H.)	20 May 1900	21 Sep 1926	
Alford	1910	1985	(fhm-Westside Chapel)
Claude	25 Jul 1909	13 Feb 1972	TN PFC 604 QM GRREG Co WWII
Earnest	20 Sep 1891	24 Jan 1966	
Frazier	20 Mar 1914	1 Aug 1923	
George W.)	25 Dec 1855	5 Mar 1936	
Elizabeth Swan)	28 Jul 1858	14 Jul 1933	
J. J.)	30 Sep 1881	5 Jul 1971	
Ethel Corbett)	1 Dec 1887	11 Feb 1959	
Sam)	29 Jan 1880	15 Jan 1963	
Etta Line)	6 Jun 1890	24 Feb 1964	
Sarah	No dates		(handmade)
Tom	15 Aug 1881	28 Feb 1961	
Tom Jr.	25 Oct 1922	11 Apr 1968	
William "Will"	26 Sep 1897	12 Dec 1949	Father
Nannie Riley	24 Dec 1902	16 May 1982	Mother (See Nannie Brooks)
Willie Geraldine)	Born & died	3 Feb 1946	Daughters of M/M William
Elizabeth Ann)	Born & died	1 Dec 1937	"Will" Miller
MOORE-Gladys V.	17 Oct 1920	3 Mar 1973	
W. Mitchell)	23 Jun 1895	1 Oct 1976	
Mae M.)	4 May 1897	NOD	
MORGAN-Edmond H.	12 May 1827	15 Dec 1886	
Sarah R.	14 Oct 1824	11 Oct 1892	w/o Edmond
Emelia Black	6 Oct 1861	16 Feb 1892	
Harvey L.	15 May 1895	20 Jul 1895	
Infant	Died	27 May 1887	d/o J.P. & A.H.
James P.	1 Apr 1856	2 Mar 1935	
Almeda Hasseltine	24 Sep 1857	16 Oct 1928	w/o J.P.
Minda Bell	16 Sep 1880	12 Jun 1893	
William	Died	13 May 18(80?)	91y _m _d
Emelia	3 Nov 1804	9 Feb 1893	w/o W.
RACKARD-Fannie Mae	28 May 1935	28 May 1935	
Robert E.)	27 Dec 1915	23 Feb 1979	
Lucille F.)	2 Sep 1918	NOD	
RICKARD-Eulay Mae	29 Mar 1896	25 Jan 1973	
Junior	6 May 1923	14 Jul 1939	
Paul Henderson	7 Oct 1921	5 Apr 1975	
RIMMER-A. G.)	4 May 1882	25 Aug 1947	
Sarah Z.)	8 Sep 1883	7 Aug 1958	
Arthur Martin Jr.	23 Jun 1963	29 Sep 1976	

RIMMER-Edwin W.	2 Oct 1876	29 May 1895	
Infant	Born & died	26 Mar 1905	s/o A.G. & S.Z.
James W.	20 Apr 1840	6 Jan 1918	
Catherine	17 Mar 1843	15 Jun 1909	w/o J.W.; born in Person Co., N.C.
Joseph E.	10 Mar 1879	3 Feb 1913	
Julia A.	29 Jun 1872	2 Dec 1878	d/o A.S.W. & _.A.(broken)
J. Warren)	14 Mar 1828	4 Jun 1910	
Bettie)	28 Mar 1830	29 Jan 1895	
Mollie Hart	Died	21 Apr 1902	
William	22 Oct 1802	27 Nov 1883	Born in Person Co., NC
William Warren	Died	7 Aug 1923	
ROBERTS-Benjamin	9 Dec 1809	31 Jan 1892	
Anivy	29 Jan 1823	19 Apr 1905	
Ella	18 Mar 1849	25 May 1884	w/o J.W.
SELLARS-Fred	13 Oct 1883	8 Jan 1971	
Ellen	27 Mar 1887	6 Jun 1925	
SHARADER-Luther Pearl	25 Apr 1915	30 May 1943	
Rufus)	28 Jul 1882	20 Sep 1960	
Lucy K.)	11 Aug 1883	2 Jan 1982	
SOLOMON-George Lee	7 Aug 1904	28 Jan 1970	Married 17 Oct 1922
Oney Brown	7 Mar 1904	23 Mar 1964	
Robert Eugene	22 Sep 1926	1 Jul 1965	
TRENTHAM-James E.	28 Jul 1894	24 Sep 1894	s/o L.A. & M.C.
VESSER-Mack	29 Jun 1888	1 Dec 1970	
Mae	2 May 1906	NOD	
Mandy Breeden	20 Mar 1893	20 May 1952	
YOUNG-R. Kyle)	30 Dec 1928	9 Apr 1984	
Fannie S.)	11 May 1925	NOD	
Robert Francis	1897	1986	(fhm-Westside Chapel)
Sharlene Michelle	13 Dec 1970	13 Apr 1971	
(NO LAST NAME)-Oda M.	No dates		

This cemetery is neat and well-kept. To reach it, begin at Exit 417 from I-40.
Turn south toward Dandridge on State 92. Drive 1.7 miles to the intersection with
U.S.25-70. Bear left onto US25-70. From this intersection drive 1.4 miles and
turn left onto Valley Home Road (St.66). Drive 3.1 miles. Turn left onto the
gravel road leading to the cemetery.

Balch Cemetery. Jefferson County
residents still talk about the 1904
New Market train wreck. Shown here is
the stone of one of the victims, 11 year old
Carah A. Knight, d/o C. W. & O. G. Knight.

DANDRIDGE CEMETERY

ALLEN-Charles T.	25 Oct 1928	27 Feb 1974	Tenn Pvt US Army Korea
Ida Neal	19 May 1895	17 Feb 1984	
ATCHLEY-Alvin Eugene	18 Feb 1929	10 Oct 1969	
Dock C.	23 Jul 1896	11 Jul 1950	Tenn Cpl QMC WWI
Lula)	23 Sep 1869	2 Apr 1942	Mother
Emma McCLURE)	23 Jun 1902	28 Oct 1965	Daughter
BALLINGER-Carolyn Pat	Born & died	13 May 1951	d/o Lula Mae & Clarence
Clarence Jr.	26 Aug 1954	1 Nov 1954	s/o Lula Mae & Clarence
Clarence C.	12 Mar 1926	30 Sep 1960	
Elmer J.	19 Sep 1910	16 Aug 1947	
BRADFORD-Baby	Born & died	1914	
Chas. Edwin	Feb 1877	Nov 1931	Brother
Dicie	11 Mar 1843	29 Nov 1932	
Grandma Eliza	No dates		
George)	6 Sep 1881	9 Aug 1946	
Hattie S.)	27 Jul 1875	18 Jul 1929	
Clarence H.)	18 Jan 1903	6 Aug 1966	
Georgia A.	31 Jan 1880	7 Sep 1927	
BRAGG-George E.	2 Feb 1917	5 Jul 1973	TN Pvt US Army WWII
Charlie)	30 Aug 1888	26 Jan 1970	
Addie T.)	11 Dec 1883	10 Aug 1971	
Clay D.	2 Nov 1895	25 Feb 1952	Tenn Pvt 812 Pion Inf WWI
Sarah Nichols	1897	1977	(fhm-Farrar)
BREEDLOVE-Arlunda Rhea	1936	1948	
Robert M.)	1863	1949	
Minnie R.)	1886	1932	
Carrie Marie	1910	1918	
BRIGHT-Carrol	10 Sep 1848	12 Feb 1915	
Lila E.	27 Oct 1873	10 Jul 1922	
CARSON-Lizzie Bradford	14 Mar 1879	18 Feb 1948	
CHANDLER-Julia Peck	8 Mar 1856	26 Feb 1925	w/o Sam
COX-Floyd A.)	14 Aug 1898	NOD	
Lucy Mae Neal)	24 Nov 1911	NOD	
CRESWELL-Henry	2 Nov 1882	29 Dec 1905	
DEWITT-Mamie L.)	No dates		
Charls W.)	No dates		
Annie H.)	No dates		
Ethel J.)	No dates		
DOCKERY-Liller Snapp	23 Feb 1890	7 Jul 1938	
EuDAILEY-Anna	1839	(broken)	
Helen M.	25 Feb 1897	24 Jul 1919	w/o F.M.
Jordan B.	24 Sep 1885	6 Aug 1903	s/o P.U. & A.B.
Phillip)	25 Jan 1856	NOD	
Alice Netherland)	1 Sep 1858	11 Jul 1929	His wife
Selton	21 Jul 1892	2 Feb 1960	
EVANS-William T.)	28 Apr 1888	15 Oct 1976	
Annie L.)	29 Mar 1881	23 Dec 1975	
FAIN-Frank Straton)	23 Dec 1898	1 Sep 1955	
Ina Howell)	5 Dec 1908	13 Aug 1965	
James P.	16 Feb 1896	18 Dec 1973	
Lucy	17 Jul 1858	7 Apr 1921	
Milligan)	1877	NOD	
Jennie)	1878	1931	
Pearl C.	22 Jun 1907	28 Feb 1973	
T. W.)	6 Apr 1867	NOD	
Janie)	8 Sep 1869	7 Jan 1920	His wife

FITZGERALD-James Kelly)	18 Sep 1907	15 Apr 1966	
Willie Gertrude B.)	11 May 19__	19 Jun 1978	
GAMMONS-Walter L.	18 May 1882	23 Aug 1940	
HARGRAVE-Dr. Walter C.)	28 Mar 1874	13 Dec 1946	
Lectia S.)	27 Aug 1894	26 Oct 1957	
Walter Clarence	OD	2 Mar 1928	Inf s/o Rev. & Mrs. W.C.
HELTON-Mary	28 Dec 1862	20 Jan 1920	
HOWEL-J. Thermond	1 May 1878	6 Mar 1911	s/o John & Mary
HOWELL-Edom J. Jr.	27 Jun 1917	4 Aug 1944	
Lucile	9 Nov 1913	4 Oct 1920	
Walter E.)	30 Jun 1920	27 Apr 1983	S/Sgt US Army WWII
Willie A.)	21 Aug 1925	NOD	
Willie Fain	6 May 1888	13 Nov 1940	
INMAN-Old Aunt Sallie (of Col.)		No dates	A faithful servant, supposed to be 100 years old
Wm.	Died	5 Sep 1928	Aged about 75 years, an honest man and a faithful servant
KYLE-Roy R.	8 Mar 1898	6 Jan 1962	
Sadie Mills	25 Dec 1911	30 Oct 1985	(dates from fhm-Dockery)
MILLS-Henry)	16 Jul 1887	NOD	
Sinia)	30 Mar 1888	7 Dec 1952	
Titus T.	6 Sep 1914	14 Feb 1965	s/o Henry Tobe & Sina
MITCHELL-A. N.	Died	26 Feb 1925	63y
Galyon	11 Apr 1896	20 Aug 1918	
Jennie	28 May 1904	9 Jul 1922	
Selina	14 Dec 1884	19 Jul 1918	
NEAL-Baby	No dates		
Jim	No dates		Pappy
Henrietta	No dates		Mammy
Little Jim	No dates		
Luther	No dates		
George Clark	29 Oct 1918	31 Oct 1964	Tenn Tec5 535 Port Co TC WWII
OLDEN-Agnes R. Allen	26 Jun 1933	10 Apr 1981	
PECK-Floyd S. "Jack"	5 Jun 1906	30 May 1974	
Hariet	9 Jun 1885	18 Nov 1911	(broken)
Katie	1 Feb 1888	10 Feb 1941	
Roy	14 Mar 1908	22 Dec 1931	
Sarah	9 Jul 1881	10 Apr 1937	
William B.)	1902	1968	
Frances N.)	1896	1975	
PERRY-Martha	1880	1959	(fhm)
RAMSEY-Mattie P.	No dates		
REDMON-Columbus C.	1 Apr 1895	4 Jul 1941	
RIGGS-Linday	Apr 1866	Dec 1930	
ROBINSON-Hazel Snapp	19 Mar 1905	23 Sep 1984	
Shirley A.	30 May 1946	24 May 1982	
ROGERS-Nellie J.	12 Jan 1896	1 Feb 1896	
ROPER-Emily	Died	14 Aug 1916	Age unknown
SHARP-Ruth A. B.	9 Nov 1922	7 Oct 1966	Tenn PFC 1050 Base Unit AAF WWII
SHERFIELD-Oscar D.	12 Nov 1872	1 Feb 1959	
Laura B.	15 Mar 1906	21 Dec 1935	
SNAPP-Lucy M.	5 Jul 1898	28 Apr 1975	
R. A.)	19 Feb 1874	19 Sep 1954	
Roberta)	2 Jan 1886	18 Sep 1970	
Tincy W.)	2 Feb 1922	28 Oct 1978	TN US Army WWll (military marker
Mahon W.)	11 Nov 1916	NOD	says Tiney L.)

SNAPP-Wesley	Died	5 Jul 1903	
Susan	Died	13 Jun 1929	Aged mother; w/o Wesley
SWAN-Jane	10 Jul 1878	20 Sep 1914	
SWANN-no name	No dates		
TALLEY-T. J.	15 Apr 1870	10 Aug 1924	54y 3m 25d
Mary Ellen	19 Aug 1870	3 Aug 1896	w/o T.J.
TALLY-Susan	1858	19 May 1903	w/o John
TAYLOR-Rosia	4 Nov 1898	7 Mar 1922	
TERRELL-Juanita Peck	25 Dec 1906	6 Jul 1986	
THOMAS-Dow)	1865	1952	
Mary A.)	1875	1958	(fhm-Dockery, says b. 1880)
Harrett	10 May 1856	23 Oct 1919	
Hugh W.)	1900	1977	
Madge K.)	1908	NOD	
Lucy	18 Jun 1822	29 Mar 1892	
Lydia	17 Apr 1877	9 Nov 1954	
Margaret	21 Aug 1887	21 Oct 1898	
Nellie J.	25 Nov 1891	24 Feb 1910	
Tennie	23 Jun 1880	16 Jul 1894	
TINES-Ellen	1830	26 Apr 1930	
TREECE-Anna Snapp	2 Sep 1906	4 Mar 1975	
TURLEY-Pauline Bragg	19 Mar 1911	16 Mar 1964	
WOODRUFF-No Name	No dates		(handmade)

In addition to the above graves, this cemetery contains over 100 uninscribed fieldstones. Grave-sized depressions indicate the presence of many more unmarked graves. When we returned to check the cemetery in June, 1987, we were dismayed to find that several of the largest stones had been overturned. To reach the cemetery, take Exit 417 from I-40 and drive south toward Dandridge on State 92 for 1.3 miles. The cemetery is on the left.

Shady Grove Methodist Church Cemetery. This fieldstone was lovingly crafted to the memory of Anna Rebeca Fry (daughter of John and Susan), who died shortly after her first birthday.

DANDRIDGE MEMORIAL CEMETERY

ARMSTRONG-Grace Black	4 Nov 1898	20 Mar 1978	
BACON-Harriet Jean	14 Jul 1963	14 Jul 1963	
BALES-James R.	1919	1981	US Army WWII
BOWMAN-Nora Jane	14 Jun 1936	13 Oct 1977	
Russel Lary)	8 Apr 1953	18 Oct 1969	
Samuel Taylor)	6 Jul 1956	18 Oct 1969	
BREWER-Loyd C.)	1912	NOD	
Nina T.)	1915	NOD	
BRIMER-Donald T.	1910	1963	
Johnny Thomas	24 Aug 1961	22 Jul 1971	
BRIGGS-Calvin W.)	1911	1971	
Nellie W.)	1915	NOD	
BROWN-Viola Turner	6 Feb 1922	2 Dec 1969	
BUCHANAN-Walter D.	1902	1974	
Roberta R.	1900	1968	
BUTLER-James M.)	1892	1972	
Lee S.)	1895	1976	
BYRD-Brandon Joseph	31 Dec 1975	15 Apr 1976	
CATE-Clyde V.)	1912	1983	
Evaunda M.)	1916	NOD	
Odell	30 Aug 1881	19 May 1970	
COBEN-John M.)	1888	1981	
Maude P.)	1890	1969	
COLLEY-Beldon D.)	1912	NOD	
Blanche M.)	1914	NOD	
COLE-E. Briscoe)	1902	1976	
Laura C.)	1909	NOD	
Mack O.)	20 Aug 1927	1 Jan 1985	TSgt US Army WWII Korea
Betty)	1 Apr 1932	NOD	
COUCH-J. G.)	1905	1983	
Lucille L.)	1903	1984	
DEERING-Ralph H.)	1911	1969	
Marie H.)	1919	NOD	
DOUGHTY-Benjamin	1801	1881	
EVON-Joseph	21 Oct 1914	21 Nov 1983	Tec5 US Army WWII
FRANKLIN-W. Bruce)	1902	1976	
Roberta M.)	1907	NOD	
GALLOWAY-Stewart T.)	1911	1972	
Abigail S.)	1910	NOD	
GEORGE-Kenneth C.)	1917	1982	
Mary B.)	1916	NOD	
GIETEMA-Thomas	1895	1966	
GIFFIN-Robert H.)	1890	1979	
Mary L.)	1895	NOD	
GOFORTH-Kenneth R. "Krow"	22 May 1935	7 Dec 1983	
W. D.)	1933	NOD	
Anna Carolyn)	1934	1982	
HALL-Irvin L.)	12 Mar 1885	30 Oct 1983	
Hester L.M.)	15 Jan 1891	21 Dec 1964	
Lewis)	1924	NOD	
Elon S.)	1922	NOD	
HANCE-Rev. Hugh)	13 Nov 1904	30 Dec 1985	
Lillie)	19 Feb 1905	6 Sep 1972	
HAYNES-Brandon Scotr	11 Jan 1983	11 Jan 1983	
William H.)	1912	NOD	
Edna V.)	1913	NOD	

HELTON–William H.)	13 Aug 1904	28 Mar 1973
Jessie V.)	16 Feb 1904	25 Jun 1980
HODGE–Steve B.	8 Nov 1944	1 Aug 1976
HORTON–Anna Joyce	14 Mar 1912	13 Sep 1984
HUFF–Clyde)	1911	1982
Ruby)	1917	NOD
JONES–Bob L.)	1934	1964
Betty H.)	1935	NOD
KOSAK–Rudolph Jr.	1929	1981
LEE–Victor)	1928	1985
Mary)	1935	NOD
LINDSEY–Lonas C.)	1914	NOD
Anna Ruth)	1916	NOD
LYONS–Jack)	1926	NOD
Pauline C.)	1932	1981
McCOIG–Gilbert W.	1913	1966
MILLER–Paul E.)	1907	NOD
Ethel P.)	1898	1974
Thomas L.	1967	1968
MOORE–James P.)	18 May 1899	28 Sep 1982
Ruth L.)	31 Mar 1905	9 Oct 1982
MORIE–Cynthia	6 Mar 1964	26 Apr 1964
NICHOLSON–Tom H.)	1893	1964
NIELSON–Nils O.)	1919	1987
Frances J.)	1924	NOD
OLLIS–Paul R.)	1931	NOD
Mary T.)	1933	NOD
OWNBY–Guy E.)	1911	1970
Mary E.)	1916	NOD
PATTERSON–Joe S.)	1900	1980
Maud D.)	1900	1962
POTTER–Alma E.	1925	1980
George R.)	1902	NOD
Annie H.)	1900	1973
PRUITT–James H.)	1926	NOD
Lena Mae)	1927	NOD
RAY–Mary J.	11 May 1898	30 Jun 1981
RENEAU–James E.)	1939	NOD
ALICE C.)	1942	NOD
James P.)	1912	NOD
M. Blanche)	1918	NOD
RIMMER–Cecil E.)	1908	1982
Eula W.)	1913	NOD
Dennis E.	20 Jun 1950	26 May 1969
Franklin I.)	1924	NOD
Evelyn W.)	1928	NOD
ROBINSON–Lattie R.	1912	NOD
Ruby H.	1913	1978
RUFFNER–Raymond M.)	1887	1964
Pearl T.)	1906	1971
RUTHERFORD–A. C. "Jake")	1912	1968
Jennie V.)	1916	NOD
SAMPLES–Richard Darrell	21 Jul 1964	23 Jul 1964
Rosh)	1900	1976
Bernice)	1901	1976
SAMS–Tommy C.)	2 Feb 1923	24 Nov 1984 Sgt US Marine Corp WWII
Barbara Hill)	8 Jan 1931	NOD Married 28 Sep 1950
SEAL–Karen Elaine	17 Nov 1981	17 Nov 1981

SEAL-Oscar R.)		1897	1968
Nettie D.)		1904	NOD
Vickie Lynn	9 Jun 1970	19 Dec 1981	
SKEEN-William Arthur)		1882	1963
Etta L.)		1886	1967
SLATON-Alger F.)	4 Dec 1911	NOD	
Mary Ellen)	28 Apr 1913	16 Jul 1983	
SMITH-Fred E.)		1920	1970
Bethel C.)		1920	NOD
Malinda Lee	20 Jun 1961	20 Jun 1961	
SOLOMON-John)		1923	NOD
Blanche P.)		1923	1984
SPOON-Earnest)		1904	1984
Maggie L.)		1912	NOD
SPOONE-James E.	27 Mar 1937	17 Aug 1983	
STEWART-Henry C.)		1899	1978	Pappy
Elizabeth J.)		1911	1986
Jerry R.	12 Apr 1939	10 Sep 1986	
STUART-Carl L.)		1930	1969
Ortha B.)		1928	NOD
Douglas)		1922	NOD
Donna)		1929	NOD
SUTTLES-Maynard O.	26 Nov 1918	8 May 1980	
SWANN-Claud A.)		1911	1971
Hazel R.)		1923	1968
TAYLOR-Albert G)		1832	1922	(Moved from old Taylor Cemetery,
Rachel)		1833	1922	South of French Broad River, see
Sarah Jane)		1838	1879	Vol. I, page 71.)
Eugene)		1921	1986
Aileen M.)		1924	NOD
Infant	11 Nov 1889	16 Nov 1889	i/o A.C.
Nina E.	19 Jul 1885	12 Nov 1885	
THOMAS-Charlie B.		1890	1900
Harold J.)	9 Jul 1962	5 Jul 1982	
Timothy L.)	9 Aug 1963	5 Jul 1982	
Ocie L. Sr.	27 Jun 1908	6 May 1982	PFC US Army WWII
Vhoundes)		1912	1976
Clara V.)		1915	NOD
TROUTMAN-Laura Gwen	27 Sep 1980	7 Oct 1980	
Leslie Ann	27 Sep 1980	27 Sep 1980	
TURNER-Leonard E.)		1910	1974
Emma K.)		1913	NOD
WEST-Gentry A.)	29 Nov 1909	31 Jul 1986	
Frances J.)	6 Sep 1921	NOD	
WILDER-No name	No date		(new grave)
WILLIAMS-Charles M.)		1933	1970
Janice)		1938	NOD
Wailon C.)		1904	1987
Lillian M.)		1904	1979
WILLS-Edgar)		1916	1981
Opal)		1909	NOD
WINE-James F.)		1911	NOD
Lillie F.)		1910	1985
WOODYARD-Quintin)		1908	1976
Susan D.)		1920	NOD
YOUNG-Dorothy H.		1927	1970
Stella B.		1902	1968

To reach this cemetery, begin at Exit 417 from I-40. Drive south on State 92 toward Dandridge for 1.7 mile to the intersection with US25W-70. Bear left onto US25W-70. From this intersection drive 3.3 miles. Dandridge Memorial Cemetery is on the right.

This bench, constructed of massive native stones (left), and the monument (right) dedicated to the Revolutionary soldiers buried here, were erected by the Martha Dandridge Garden Club. Revolutionary Cemetery, Dandridge.

"McCuiston (first name not given), died 24 Sep 1812, 75y." This fieldstone is in the Revolutionary Cemetery in Dandridge.

FAIRVIEW CEMETERY (Black)

ALLEN-Uncle Dave	No dates		age 88
Joseph Cephus	1896	1979	
BEAR-Millie	1820	9 Jan 1896	
BEARD-Lettie Mae	1922	1978	(fhm-Westside)
Wesley W.	1905	1976	(fhm-Westside)
BLACKBURN-Jennie	1848	13 Jun 1898	
BOWENS-Tessie Bragg	1886	1967	
BOYD-Julie Allen	15 Apr 1819	15 Oct 1894	Erected in memory of
			Mother by M/M Rev. William Susong
BRADFORD-Deadrick Branner	16 May 1875	20 Oct 1952	w/o Charles E.
BRAGG-Bernie Augusta	15 Sep 1886	12 Jun 1954	
Edna Vivian	26 Jan 1896	18 Jun 1959	
Cecil A.	OD	21 Feb 1937	TN Pvt 20 Engr.
Charles W.	14 Jul 1879	19 May 1936	
Josie L.	23 Jul 1883	19 Mar 1969	
Charlsie Porter	8 Oct 1918	7 Dec 1979	w/o Bernie A. Jr.
Eugene	16 Feb 1893	18 Jul 1962	
Eugene W.	28 Sep 1928	28 Aug 1929	
Frank	18 Sep 1910	30 Jul 1962	
Howard	18 Apr 1903	24 Feb 1980	
Christine	26 Apr 1904	30 Apr 1984	
James L.	24 Oct 1866	15 Jan 1901	
J. C.	27 Mar 1941	18 Oct 1941	
Lydia J.	26 Feb 1897	26 Oct 1924	
Mary Love	2 Apr 1903	26 Sep 1969	
Raymond C.	23 Jun 1924	11 Dec 1984	US Navy WWII
Roy	11 Dec 1889	28 Jun 1960	
Isabella	21 May 1887	6 Jan 1951	
Rufus M.)	28 Feb 1865	23 Jun 1946	
Josephine)	1 Jul 1872	14 Mar 1966	
Sarah Jane	25 Mar 1850	24 Aug 1894	
Susan	15 Jun 1854	21 Mar 1915	
Tisley A.	28 Apr 1895	23 Oct 1925	
Walter	29 Apr 1891	25 Apr 1921	
William Garrett	10 Aug 1918	19 Aug 1980	
BRANNER-Charles L.	2 Aug 1919	3 Jun 1980	
Geraldine	OD	9 Oct 1983	Age 24 (fhm-Jarnigan)
John	OD	17 Mar 1977	Age 66 (fhm-Jarnigan)
Minerva Webb)	1848	1898	
Horace J.)	1897	1927	
Milton)	1907	1907	
CHANDLER-Minerva A. Bradford	20 Feb 1903	29 May 1948	w/o Samuel
COX-William Elexander)	1874	23 Jan 1957	
Elizabeth Dunwoody)	1878	16 Sep 1960	
CUBBERSON-Frohi Elaine	1898	1967	(fhm-Farrar)
Harrison B.	1861	1975	(fhm-Farrar)
ELLIOTT-Peter	1835	25 Feb 1906	
Mary	1 Feb 1840	24 Jan 1916	w/o Peter
FAIN-James Luther	27 Apr 1886	27 Mar 1951	
Tan Clair Humpary	About 1893	10 May 1920	
GARRETT-Jesse	26 Oct 1889	25 Mar 1962	TN Pvt Co M 802
			Pioneer Inf. WWI
GLAZE-Jackson	No dates		Co F 1st U.S.C.H.A.
GOURLEY-Nekewa	OD	5 Apr 1981	(fhm-Jarnigan)

HARRIS-Maria L.	2 Aug 1888	14 Feb 1913	
JACKSON-Dora	No dates		
William	27 Mar 1901	20 Sep 1966	New York MA 1 WWI
JANAE-Bannikka	OD	4 Dec 1982	Age 2 (fhm-Jarnigan)
KEY-Charlesena	Born & died	4 Sep 1981	(fhm)
Lewis	6 Aug 1911	1 Feb 1973	(fhm-Jarnigan)
LOWER-Carrie	Died	15 Jan 1903	
LYLE-Jesse	Died	2 Jan 1899	Age 79
MARSHALL-Abe)	No dates		
Pearl)	No dates		
Raymond	1 Apr 1899	20 May 1920	
MAYES-Freman	10 Oct 1855	11 Sep 1921	
Millie Swann	OD	7 Jun 1933	About 70 years old
Joe E.)	19 Nov 1926	NOD	Son
Bertie F.)	3 Jun 1900	19 Oct 1980	Mother
Raymond	10 Dec 1921	6 May 1936	s/o Frances
Robert "Bob")	27 Mar 1906	30 Dec 1962	
Blanche Allen)	18 Feb 1896	NOD	
NICHOLS-Benjamin	1888	1969	
Spencer F.)	12 Oct 1871	14 Mar 1954	
C. Nannie)	14 May 1877	13 Aug 1950	
REDMON-Henderson	1827	22 Sep 1898	
RICE-Lida F. Bragg	6 Sep 1873	22 Oct 1895	w/o J. W.
RUFFIN-Bettie Blackburn	6 Jul 1875	1 Dec 1902	w/o Pryor
Cynthia Bragg	1 Feb 1876	19 Jul 1917	w/o Pryor
SEAHORN-Lucy	1850	13 Oct 1896	
STEVENS-James	17 Dec 1913	30 Jul 1973	
TAYLOR-Dare Jr.	1 Apr 1933	28 Jan 1952	
Ellen	Died	2 Aug 1912	Age 65
Elsie Jobe	14 Feb 1898	17 Nov 1967	
James Alfred	17 Apr 1930	4 Jul 1984	US Army Vietnam
J. R.	1950	1980	(fhm-Farrar)
Lelia	19 Jul 1884	29 Jan 1918	
THOMAS-Dowell L.)	1892	1964	
Betty B.)	1899	NOD	
WOODS-James	No dates		Co. K 1st U.S.C.H.A.
(No last name)-Horace	No dates		

This cemetery is located beside a picturesque, white frame church. To reach the site, take Exit 417 from I-40. Turn south toward Dandridge on State 92 and drive 1.7 miles to the intersection with US25-70. Bear left onto 25W-70. From this intersection drive 3.4 miles and turn right. Drive 2.9 miles and turn left at Swann's Chapel Church. Drive 0.2 miles. Fairview Church and cemetery are on the right. (There are several curves with roads leading off. Take care to stay on the main road.)

FRENCH BROAD BAPTIST CEMETERY

ALLEN-J.A.	Died	8 Jul 1915	52y
William A.)	23 Feb 1883	31 May 1959	
Sallie Rogers)	28 Aug 1893	11 Mar 1926	
AUSTELL-William	20 Mar 1777	20 Dec 1849	
Jane	14 Aug 1778	27 May 1851	Consort of William
BALL-Alfred)	24 Dec 1839	7 Aug 1922	Grand Army of the Republic Veteran
Mary McNabb)	19 Jan 1845	27 Feb 1925	His wife
Florence	11 Mar 1871	23 Oct 1962	
J. B.	5 Nov 1935	14 Oct 1936	s/o M/M Rufus
Mertha F.	1871	1962	(fhm-Stetzer)
Vira	14 Aug 1880	6 Feb 1918	d/o M/M Alfred
BALLARD-Mable	2 Jul 1896	1 Sep 1896	d/o Wm. & L.N.
Parlea	16 Apr 1890	15 Jul 1891	d/o Wm. & L.N.
BIGGS-Hattie Ball	4 Sep 1884	28 Oct 1963	
BROWN-Dennis R.	1 May 1958	14 Jun 1973	
BUTTRY-Elbert P.	16 Mar 1853	14 Oct 1930	
Catherin	27 Jun 1859	9 Nov 1929	
BYRD-Audrey Fay	5 Aug 1949	5 Aug 1949	
Clyde)	12 Nov 1918	26 Jun 1982	Pvt US Army WWII
Hester)	21 Jul 1913	1 Oct 1977	Married 20 Jul 1938
CHAMBERS-Irene	Died	26 Nov 1935	75y
R. L.	10 Oct 1863	25 Jan 1911	
CLEVENGER-Hollis	26 Sep 1909	18 Mar 1985	
Lucy	16 Nov 1907	29 May 1955	
Melvin	8 Nov 1883	23 Aug 1916	
COLLINS-Henry H.)	1840	1928	
Bettie)	1841	1912	
Jennie)	1873	1942	
J. T.	24 Apr 1842	25 Jun 1895	Co H 2nd N.C. Mtd Inf
Ira	17 Jan 1836	6 Jul 1889	Co H 2nd N.C. Mtd Inf
CONN-Hershel L.)	11 Feb 1902	25 Sep 1974	
Gladys M.)	1 Jan 1906	20 Apr 1971	
COWAN-Henry C.	9 Nov 1911	18 Jun 1967	
Joe W.	9 Jan 1915	NOD	
Mary G.	26 Aug 1924	12 Oct 1973	
Thomas A.	11 Jun 1864	9 May 1932	
Pearl J.	27 Jun 1877	21 Feb 1948	
Tommie	27 Nov 1900	19 Aug 1903	s/o T.A. I P.J.
DENTON-M. C.)	No dates		
Sallie North)	No dates		
Melvina	10 Dec 1827	18 Jan 1892	
DINSDALE-James B.	23 Jun 1887	6 Oct 1973	
Frances Swann Taylor	1 Dec 1892	21 Sep 1979	w/o J.W.; d/o Col Alfred R. & Frances B.
DRINNON-John I.	1 Apr 1869	24 Jul 1929	
Martha	1 Nov 1877	3 Apr 1932	w/o J.I.
EDDINGTON-Junior Taylor)	14 Jul 1938	21 Mar 1983	
Earlene Large)	26 Jul 1939	NOD	
ELLISON-Eva	18 Mar 1890	28 Jan 1892	d/o J.P. & M.A.
FAIRFIELD-Chas. D.	24 May 1825	17 Feb 1885	
Martha R.	24 Apr 1839	6 May 1891	
C. Dexter	31 Aug 1872	25 Oct 1947	
Martha G.	25 May 1872	22 Aug 1943	
Walter B.	26 Aug 1866	24 Jun 1907	

FAIRFIELD-Walter Burr	30 Apr 1892	30 Apr 1951	
Annie Fine	4 Apr 1896	8 Jul 1982	
FINCHUM-Jane Beard	20 Jun 1835	7 Aug 1915	w/o Thomas
FISHER-Charles H.)	1867	1957	
Josie)	1863	1948	
William Oscar	15 Sep 1892	21 Apr 1893	s/o C.H. & Josie
FOWLER-William J.)	7 Sep 1880	16 Nov 1947	
Kate A.)	10 Sep 1886	8 Jan 1976	
FOX-P. Buford)	27 Jun 1940	NOD	
Nancy Sams)	4 Oct 1941	NOD	
HATFIELD-Robert F.)	12 Apr 1892	23 Apr 1961	
Margaret E.)	25 Sep 1894	30 Jan 1968	
HAWKINS-Lawrence Ray	1965	1985	(fhm-Farrar)
HENDERSON-Mary Jane	9 Oct 1944	19 Feb 1945	
HINKLE-Allie D.	18 Jul 1891	2 Feb 1956	
Walker)	30 Oct 1860	9 May 1938	
Callie)	16 Apr 1863	1 May 1944	
HUGGINS-A. Frank	8 Nov 1899	5 Jan 1975	
Alsie E.	17 Jan 1878	15 Mar 1930	
Andrew J.)	3 Nov 1844	9 Sep 1929	
Sallie A.)	8 Jun 1847	22 Jan 1910	
James Isaac)	14 Sep 1872	17 Nov 1947	
Virginia Dorman)	29 May 1870	5 Nov 1957	
A. Jeter Jr.)	23 Nov 1876	14 Feb 1922	
Ola M.)	2 Dec 1875	3 Mar 1954	
Hal M.	23 Jul 1901	21 Oct 1955	
James Dorman Sr.	29 Nov 1905	5 Feb 1978	
John L.	3 Jul 1874	20 Mar 1904	
JARNIGAN-Howard Thomas	18 Aug 1915	22 Apr 1972	
Howard Thomas)	4 Jul 1940	1 Mar 1985	
Bonnie Jo)	9 Jul 1945	NOD	
James Edward)	27 Apr 1955	4 May 1955	
JENKINS-H. Gordon)	20 Aug 1919	16 May 1983	Married 24 Apr 1938
Irene W.)	5 Nov 1921	NOD	
JONES-B. Cecil	3 Feb 1891	24 Jan 1900	s/o J.F. & A.L.
Eli A.)	16 Jan 1867	29 Jun 1936	
Julia E. Pratt)	12 May 1868	11 Feb 1904	His wife
Hugh R.)	11 Sep 1887	15 Apr 1934	
Cordie Day)	11 Nov 1891	21 Aug 1974	
Infants	31 Jan 1903	11 Jul 1904	Son and Daughter of E.A. & J.E.
Nannie Lynch	6 Oct 1866	17 Oct 1937	
LANE-Clarence R.	2 Jan 1933	20 Mar 1949	
Fene)	12 Apr 1885	7 Feb 1977	
Bessie M.)	29 Sep 1891	28 Mar 1976	
Charlie P.)	6 Sep 1920	24 Apr 1932	s/o Fene & Bessie
LARGE-Alcie C.	4 Jul 1863	6 Jan 1930	
Annie Mae	3 Jan 1926	26 Aug 1946	
Mabel Ruth	17 Jun 1942	11 Mar 1943	d/o M/M W. M.
Margaret Callie	10 Feb 1944	1 Mar 1944	
Mary Frances	6 Oct 1930	23 Oct 1948	
Samuel M.	6 Nov 1857	3 Feb 1952	
LEEPER-Robert Jarnagin)	9 Sep 1884	2 Oct 1961	
Cremora Zirkle)	29 Oct 1886	5 Aug 1971	
LEMONS-Charlie H.	15 Apr 1873	3 Apr 1895	21y 11m 18d
LEONARD-Marion F.)	6 Jul 1906	NOD	
Leona Lee)	22 May 1910	19 Mar 1954	

LOVELACE-Billy Mack)	27 Feb 1933	NOD	
Christine Sams)	23 Nov 1936	NOD	
MASON-Robert Henry	26 Sep 1894	24 Sep 1895	s/o D.H. & N.G.
William H.	19 Oct 1897	4 Jul 1898	s/o D.H. & N.G.
MITCHELL-Alma	28 Dec 1892	6 Aug 1893	d/o J.L. & Ellen A.
Edith	15 Mar 1886	18 Jun 1898	
Elbert H.	30 Dec 1878	29 Aug 1920	
John L.	2 Apr 1858	29 Aug 1922	
Ellena S.	7 Jun 1861	16 Feb 1942	
L.H.	5 Dec 1842	4 Apr 1892	
Lloyd H.	24 Mar 1888	19 Oct 1910	
MURPHY-Ida Bell Cooper	23 Sep 1868	29 Nov 1894	w/o J.H.
NORTH-Infant	16 Aug 1907	17 Aug 1907	s/o J.L. & E.L.
Jerome L.)	30 Apr 1880	23 Feb 1948	
Ethel Hinkle)	22 Jul 1884	12 Jul 1976	
Maude	26 Apr 1875	1 Jun 1898	d/o P.R. & L.C.(broken)
Louise C. Hammer	29 Aug 1848	4 Nov 1922	w/o P.R.
Pauline G.	29 Apr 1905	24 Jul 1905	d/o J.L. & E.L.
PEDERSON-Robert)	6 Nov 1909	NOD	Son
Jessica)	21 Jun 1911	18 May 1973	Wife
Winiferd)	1 Feb 1880	12 Aug 1972	Mother
PHILLIPS-Annie	14 Feb 1907	16 May 1921	
Cal	11 Nov 1897	20 Jul 1933	
Calvin	8 Jan 1866	17 May 1896	
Cloan	15 Sep 1907	25 Feb 1933	
David R.	20 Apr 1856	19 Feb 1892	
Nannie	1854	1941	
Elbert)	1867	1933	
Martha)	1869	1944	
J. M.	20 Dec 1846	27 Dec 1908	
Pearl	Born & died	2 Feb 1894	d/o Calvin & Florence
Rhoda France	10 May 1896	17 Dec 1951	w/o John
PRYOR-Clyde	29 Mar 1906	5 Aug 1907	s/o G.A. & M.J.
J.A.)	24 Aug 1902	15 Oct 1902	s/o H.L. & Amanda
L.L.)	8 Sep 1900	29 Sep 1901	d/o H.L. & Amanda
RANKIN-Charles J.)	1875	1943	
Fannie B.)	1878	1956	
Jessie Swann	14 Oct 1885	26 Sep 1968	
RENEAU-Belle	6 Feb 1884	30 Dec 1917	w/o J.P.
ROBERTS-Holcombe	1 Sep 1897	15 Dec 1897	s/o G.E. & D.B.
J.C.	11 Jul 1880	3 May 1895	s/o J.W.
Walter Royal	25 Apr 1903	27 Jun 1903	s/o C.W. & Alice
ROMINE-Henry	16 Mar 1878	12 Oct 1918	
SAMS-John Stephen)	14 Dec 1956	28 May 1985	
Jack Robinson)	2 Apr 1933	NOD	
Wendy Northcutt)	27 Jul 1937	NOD	
Robert Murray	29 Jul 1921	NOD	
Marjorie Miller	16 Mar 1932	NOD	
Stephanie	Born & died	21 May 1958	d/o M/M R.M.
SEABOLT-Malinda	8 Dec 1813	24 Feb 1884	d/o S. & C. SWANN
SMITH-Clara Mae	1 Nov 1869	20 Dec 1929	
Carrie S.	1887	1953	
David	4 Dec 1822	6 May 1895	
Susan Inman Seahorn	29 Mar 1818	17 Oct 1900	w/o David
Ernest A.)	15 Sep 1908	22 Apr 1975	
Veda A.)	24 Sep 1908	NOD	

SMITH-Francis M.)	3 Sep 1856	26 Oct 1943	
Delia A.)	29 Dec 1859	5 Dec 1928	His wife
Francis Marion	14 Mar 1882	16 Jul 1957	
Manorah Sullivan	28 Feb 1892	29 Jul 1951	
Hannah Jane	1 May 1852	9 Dec 1929	
Jacob W.	20 May 1848	12 Sep 1895	
Virginia E.	17 Feb 1853	17 Jul 1890	w/o J.W.
Jennie L.	25 Oct 1878	23 Apr 1895	
John)	15 Nov 1820	22 Feb 1905	
Caroline Baer)	7 May 1830	24 Apr 1916	His wife
Johnnie H.	29 Aug 1895	17 Jul 1896	s/o W.H. & J.A.
Paul V.	4 Aug 1886	2 Apr 1902	
William Harden)	2 Mar 1852	4 Aug 1934	
Julia A.)	21 Apr 1856	13 Feb 1903	w/o W. H.
SOUTH-Jimmie Rodger	14 Aug 1936	13 Jun 1966	North Carolina SP5
			Engineer Co. Korea
STARNES-Clarence	7 Mar 1876	21 Mar 1931	
Dona Kay	OD	7 Oct 1953	d/o M/M J.C.
Emma	21 Jul 1871	15 May 1930	
Irene	17 Aug 1873	21 Jun 1950	
Jacob A.	16 Oct 1862	10 Jun 1941	
Mollie Helm	16 Feb 1865	16 Oct 1944	
Mary	11 Jan 1856	6 Aug 1940	
Ollie	23 Feb 1897	7 Feb 1938	
Tennie S.	17 Nov 1900	3 Mar 1941	
William B.	6 Jul 1894	27 Jun 1983	
Mary Canode	9 Apr 1899	9 Dec 1960	
SWANN-Alfred Austell	23 Nov 1888	20 Sep 1954	s/o Alfred R. & Frances B.
Edna Sparks	11 Sep 1895	23 Mar 1967	
Alfred Reuben	24 Sep 1843	9 Apr 1926	
Frances Burnett	27 Nov 1862	17 Jul 1952	
Infant	OD	9 Sep 1951	s/o Alfred & Elizabeth
James Terrell	19 Nov 1886	10 May 1953	s/o Alfred R. & Frances B.
Mary C.	28 Jul 1892	9 Dec 1973	w/o James T.
John)	17 May 1796	20 May 1887	
Sarah A.)	22 Jul 1808	18 May 1888	
Elizabeth)	4 Oct 1827	15 Jan 1834	
Susan)	18 Dec 1832	1 Nov 1838	
Jane)	24 Aug 1835	1 Feb 1840	
Catherine)	8 Sep 1848	5 Oct 1851	
John S.	9 Mar 1895	7 Feb 1897	
Mary Frances Judy	8 Aug 1915	1 Jan 1983	d/o James T. & Mary C.
Samuel	14 Aug 1768	22 Oct 1813	45y 2m 8d
Catharine	30 Nov 1770	7 Jun 1862	91y 7m 7d
Sarah	29 Apr 1902	30 Jan 1919	
TAYLOR-Walter	1867	1941	
Texa T.	1871	1938	
THOMAS-Callie	23 Feb 1863	1 Dec 1903	w/o Tolliver
Eliza	16 Dec 1863	16 Feb 1911	w/o J.M.
George A.	14 Jun 1918	24 Oct 1936	
G. F.)	30 Dec 1865	21 May 1934	
Mary)	5 Aug 1871	20 Jan 1937	
James A.)	4 Aug 1872	24 Sep 1892	
Hattie M.)	16 Jan 1876	22 Dec 1896	
J. C.	15 May 1831	27 Dec 1908	
Nancy	24 Nov 1831	11 Mar 1898	w/o J.C.;d/o Toliver SISK

TAYLOR-J. C.)	6 May 1849	7 May 1927	
Susanna)	12 Mar 1849	12 Mar 1920	His wife
Martha	13 Dec 1865	28 Aug 1884	d/o J.C. & N.T. 18y 8m 15d
TURNER-Etta	8 Feb 1892	10 Nov 1903	d/o L.B. & N.L.
WALKER-Gertrude	3 Jan 1935	30 Jun 1936	d/o Frances & Lee
Samuel T.	23 Nov 1835	24 Jul 1898	
WELCH-Cleo)	10 Mar 1918	23 Mar 1964	
Myrtle G.)	20 Nov 1923	NOD	
Hugh M.)	25 Dec 1910	18 Jan 1973	
Bonnie Turner)	17 Sep 1911	NOD	
John M.	20 Jun 1912	3 Dec 1980	
Paul	16 Oct 1906	22 Aug 1973	
Sanford	12 May 1925	11 Jul 1977	
WIDENER-G.W.	1847	1913	
R. C.	Oct 1852	Jul 1927	Mother
Lawrence P.	14 Oct 1893	27 Jun 1911	s/o G.W. & R.C.
WILLIAMS-Charles Fairfield	28 Jun 1890	11 Aug 1895	born Santa Rosa, CA
Samuel Rufus	20 Aug 1862	20 Feb 1894	
Joseph B.	1 Feb 1891	31 Jan 1894	s/o Samuel Rufus & Dollie
Maggie E.	12 May 1908	19 Jun 1909	
Bessie Leota	26 Jul 1893	20 Jan 1897	d/o Samuel Rufus & Dollie
(No last name)-Daughter	OD	1936	

To reach this cemetery, take Exit 424 from I-40 and drive the short distance
to the intersection with US25-70. Cross US25W-70 and drive 0.3 miles. Turn
left. French Broad Baptist Church and Cemetery are 0.2 miles ahead.

This G.A.R. emblem is found on the tombstone of Alfred Ball in the French Broad
Baptist Cemetery. The Grand Army of the Republic was an organization of Union
veterans of the Civil War.

FRENCH BORAD CHURCH OF THE BRETHREN

Name	Birth	Death	Notes
ALLEY-J. A.)	20 Sep 1855	22 Feb 1932	
Electra)	27 Dec 1857	24 Mar 1943	
Willett Cornelous	21 Sep 1880	23 Jul 1973	
BALL-Betty	16 Mar 1883	12 Apr 1966	
Emmett Sr.	1 Aug 1901	25 Nov 1969	
Mary Horner	25 Nov 1902	28 Apr 1976	
Horace G.	15 Aug 1872	11 Nov 1950	
J. A.)	5 Jan 1879	12 Oct 1949	
Florence)	9 Feb 1876	6 Mar 1956	
Marvin M.	26 Aug 1926	10 Nov 1926	Brother
Nell Eldridge	1918	1978	(fhm-Farrar)
Robert T.	5 Jun 1925	7 Jun 1925	Brother
Sarah L.	14 Feb 1936	25 May 1973	
Susie Bell	23 Apr 1919	2 Mar 1939	
Thomas E.)	5 Jan 1934	NOD	Married 27 Mar 1954
Edith Pearl)	15 Sep 1932	NOD	
William J.)	14 Feb 1893	14 Jan 1976	
Mary Garner)	6 Jun 1892	18 Dec 1950	
BALLARD-Felix	25 Jul 1876	27 Nov 1928	
John	16 Jul 1852	12 Nov 1934	
Mary	19 Oct 1852	21 Dec 1931	w/o John
BECK-Anna Mae	26 Sep 1926	28 Sep 1927	
Creed, A.	2 Mar 1898	15 Feb 1968	
Franklin M.)	1853	1926	
Martha E.)	1864	1937	
Jack	1892	1961	
James M.	1905	1925	
Mary Ruth	28 Jul 1924	8 Dec 1926	
BEETS-Robert H.	17 Jul 1903	11 Oct 1983	
BERRIER-William K.	11 Oct 1925	2 Dec 1961	Tenn BM2 US Navy WWII
BISHOP-Harold W.)	22 Aug 1918	17 Mar 1963	Father
Mildred Bishop WILDER)	11 Feb 1920	NOD	Mother
William J.)	1885	1948	
Pearl J.)	1885	1970	
BRADY-James L.	OD	12 Aug 1938	
BURGIN-William A.	17 May 1912	22 Sep 1980	married 10 Sep 1933
Myrtle E.	22 Feb 1916	NOD	
CAMERON-Sarah E.	24 Feb 1868	18 Apr 1911	
CHAPMAN-Fay	2 Mar 1914	9 Oct 1943	
Kathleen	1927	1957	
Fred Oliver	10 Apr 1910	14 Dec 1972	Tenn S1 US Navy WWII
CHENEY-Kenneth R.)	1904	NOD	
Neual Williford)			
CLEVENGER-Lillie Beck	1896	1971	
Ruben R.	1909	1981	(fhm-Farrar)
COX-Frank W.	24 May 1885	1 Sep 1958	
Lucy Mae	27 May 1886	20 Aug 1968	
Helen Mae	12 Apr 1913	22 Apr 1922	
Frank Worth	19 Aug 1916	29 Sep 1916	
DAVIS-J. C.)	19 Oct 1914	NOD	
Muriel S.)	24 Jun 1914	18 Jun 1976	
ELDRIDGE-Faye Aileen	22 Dec 1939	16 Feb 1940	
J. T.)	27 Jan 1841	25 Feb 1918	
Margarett)	12 Mar 1845	13 Mar 1906	
J. P., Sr.)	11 Feb 1889	NOD	
Josie A.)	19 Jul 1896	29 Jun 1974	
ELLER-Charlie B.	6 Dec 1900	6 Mar 1976	

EMORY-Horace Greely	7 Nov 1884	19 Oct 1949	
EVERETT-Clarence E.)	1 Dec 1898	29 May 1955	Tenn Pvt Co D 120 Inf. Regt WWI
Josie H.)	30 Sep 1896	NOD	
FINE-Grace	8 Jul 1895	22 Jul 1895	
FOSTER-Claude)	4 Mar 1908	NOD	married 14 Jun 1931
Ollie Mae C.)	15 Jan 1909	25 Jun 1982	
Doris Faye)	7 May 1935	NOD	
John W.	19 Jul 1872	29 Aug 1945	
Dicie Bell Large	2 Oct 1880	26 Feb 1958	
Mack	22 Jun 1910	23 Feb 1970	
Mattie B. Samples	20 Mar 1915	3 Dec 1947	
Nellie F.	20 Sep 1912	3 Jun 1924	11y 6m 13d; d/o J.W. & D.B.
FOWLER-Betty	1925	1928	
J. D.)	20 May 1886	NOD	
Lilia)	7 Sep 1895	8 May 1937	
FOX-Herbert Sanford	28 Feb 1927	18 Jul 1942	
James Crockett	2 Feb 1903	7 Feb 1970	
FREE-Fannie Shaffer	21 Aug 1888	9 Jan 1953	
GANTTE-George G.	4 Jan 1874	26 Apr 1938	
J. Allen	14 May 1927	5 Nov 1955	
Paul Granville	28 Dec 1925	25 Mar 1926	s/o M/M G.G.
Ruth Anna Cox	8 Mar 1903	24 Mar 1980	
GHANN-Jack A.	5 Aug 1922	25 Jul 1923	
Lon Sherman	1898	1981	US Navy WWII
GILDON-William)	25 Mar 1888	18 Apr 1941	
Josie K.)	17 Aug 1878	13 Sep 1954	
GREER-Laura Emory	5 Oct 1865	9 May 1946	
GRIFFIN-A. P.	24 May 1896	26 Aug 1936	s/o S. H. & Millie
HALL-Hobert)	10 Aug 1924	1977	Pvt US Army WWII
Hazel E.)	3 Apr 1927	10 Nov 1972	
HUSKEY-Lois B.	26 Sep 1941	24 Sep 1965	
Robert Lee)	29 Mar 1895	18 Jun 1957	
Cora Manning)	26 Jun 1904	NOD	
JOHNSON-Richard T.	1928	1928	
Elbert Jay	1927	1985	(fhm-Farrar)
Thulia	25 Feb 1884	26 Sep 1890	
JONES-Joe H.	1892	1976	
Ethel L.	1901	NOD	
KING-Julian Lawrence	1904	1970	
KINTNER-Elgin P., M.D.)	5 Sep 1917	NOD	Wed 4 Apr 1942
Ethel N. Prichett)	28 Aug 1913	NOD	
Evelyn Jean	9 May 1955	13 May 1955	
LANE-Mack L.)	1890	1954	
Agnes C.)	1900	1969	
Robert Allen	8 Nov 1876	10 Sep 1962	
Nancy Charlotte	26 Sep 1884	15 Dec 1952	w/o Robert A.
W. Ray	1936	1981	(fhm-Farrar)
LARGE-Albert	OD	11 Feb 1949	s/o L.R. & R.E.
LEMON-John L.	23 Aug 1904	19 Jul 1925	
LEMONS-Roy	8 Dec 1931	8 Dec 1931	
McCOIG-Mikey	20 Nov 1922	19 Sep 1974	PFC US Army WWII
Mikey	1949	1968	(fhm-Love Cantrell)
Ruby Francis	1929	1974	(fhm-Farrar)
McCRARY-Flora M.	25 Apr 1886	7 Feb 1902	d/o G.W. & E.B.
George D.)	23 May 1898	5 Oct 1935	
Nancy E.)	1 Apr 1899	6 Aug 1934	
George D.,Jr.)	23 Oct 1920	17 Oct 1963	Pvt 1Cl Tenn 117 Inf 30 Div Oct 5 1935

McCRARY-Grover D.	5 May 1892	9 May 1892	s/o G.W. & E.B.
G. W.)	14 Oct 1862	15 Apr 1926	
Eliza B.)	26 Sep 1870	4 Feb 1910	
Joseph N.)	17 Oct 1859	25 May 1909	
Eva Kate Noe)	10 Dec 1867	10 Mar 1965	
Mary Williford	11 May 1851	3 Aug 1893	
Robert J.	23 Jun 1900	10 Dec 1902	
Minnie E.	13 Oct 1887	28 May 1908	d/o G.W. & E.B.
NEWCOMER-S. E.	20 Sep 1869	8 Mar 1888	s/o E. & I. B.
NINE-Ethel	Born & died	1889	
Joseph F.	11 Nov 1831	9 Nov 1901	
PARKER-Eugenia Irene	11 Nov 1925	9 Aug 1927	
Jay Arley	5 Feb 1924	28 Apr 1962	
PHILLIPS-Charles F.	1911	1971	(fhm-Farrar)
Frances C.	4 Apr 1914	9 Dec 1955	
Vernie W.	19 Sep 1880	27 May 1953	
PRITCHETT-Gomer H.	11 Jul 1912	26 Apr 1973	TN SF2 US Navy WWII
Reuel B.)	13 Apr 1884	2 Apr 1974	
Ella P.)	3 Oct 1883	6 Oct 1957	
RODEFER-Effie	7 Jul 1891	3 Feb 1892	d/o I. & S. R.
RODEFFER-A. R.	8 Feb 1885	18 Feb 1958	
Myrtle A.	4 Apr 1886	14 Oct 1976	
John L. Jr.	31 Jan 1940	5 Apr 1940	
Lois M.	7 Oct 1916	23 Jan 1938	
ROMINES-James T.	23 Jun 1922	22 Dec 1976	PFC US Army WWII
Mabel A.	25 Apr 1924	26 Oct 1974	
SATTERFIELD-Clarence H.)	1889	1954	
Lillie B.)	1887	1970	
Joseph W.)	5 Aug 1923	NOD	Married 31 Dec 1947
Ruth McGaha)	27 Aug 1925	12 Dec 1979	
J. R.	23 Jun 1872	22 Jan 1923	
Ida M.	12 Dec 1872	23 May 1908	w/o J. R.
Mollie K.	25 Oct 1875	28 Jun 1948	
Pauline	2 May 1908	22 Feb 1909	d/o J.R. & Ida M.
S. C.	15 May 1838	12 Jan 1898	
Margaret E.	28 Feb 1846	14 Sep 1921	
Walter	1884	1960	
SCHLECTER-Walter Edwin	8 Jul 1932	NOD	Married 24 Aug 1958
Shelby Jean Williford	12 Mar 1938	12 Jul 197	
SHAFFER-Ada Rose	12 Nov 1894	22 Jul 1960	
George E.	19 Oct 1938	10 Jul 1955	
SHANK-Elizabeth Hodge	Apr 1833	4 Jan 1894	
Lula	12 Apr 1871	1902	
SHRADER-Annie Hagg	20 Dec 1891	3 Sep 1957	w/o Palmer
Minervia	15 Oct 1848	28 Feb 1915	
SISK-Claude)	1905	1947	
Eliza D.)	1908	1970	
SMITH-Charles Edward)	14 Jan 1876	31 Mar 1951	
Nelle McCRARY)	17 Feb 1894	20 Dec 1968	
Claude E.)	21 Jul 1914	3 Oct 1977	
Pearl Killion)	30 Dec 1915	25 Jul 1982	
Della K.	1887	1957	(fhm-Stetzer)
Joe	1879	1928	
Lloyd	18 May 1913	1 Dec 1917	s/o C.E. & Nellie
SPANGLE-Warren A.)	13 Jan 1869	31 May 1943	
Sallie W.)	23 Feb 1879	6 Oct 1949	
STRANGE-Clara Lane	14 Dec 1909	28 May 1942	d/o Robert A. & Lottie
Ruth Williford	28 Jun 1902	10 Dec 1928	w/o W. A.

THOMAS-Caully H.)	14 Apr 1886	NOD	
Della)	2 Apr 1888	NOD	
Eugene F.	16 Aug 1910	21 Dec 1978	
Hester	11 Aug 1912	3 Dec 1914	d/o C.H. & D.L.
Reba	20 Aug 1905	5 Sep 1912	d/o C.H. & D.L.
THOMPSON-Z. S.	2 Jul 1825	21 Apr 1908	
Narcissa	9 Jul 1834	8 Jun 1885	w/o Z. S.
TURNER-Guy)	22 Feb 1903	12 Apr 1984	
Edith)	23 Apr 1907	NOD	
J. F.	12 May 1863	16 Jul 1940	
Mary L.	16 Jul 1867	9 Nov 1944	
VESSER-James	10 Mar 1861	20 Jan 1941	
Martha W.	9 Mar 1869	12 Jul 1962	
Lucy	23 Aug 1900	22 Jul 1901	
WALKER-John Luther	22 May 1903	10 Aug 1945	
Joyce M.	17 Nov 1931	23 Aug 1982	
WATKINS-Evelyn C. Pritchett	30 Nov 1919	10 Aug 1942	w/o A. B.
WHITSON-Hester Garland	1862	1944	
WILDER-Mildred Bishop	11 Feb 1920	NOD	
WILLIFORD-Annie	OD	1889	d/o M/M Fielden
Chrischany	14 Sep 1830	13 Jul 1911	d/o Elizabeth & Meridath
Carrie	16 May 1921	10 Feb 1926	
Darcus Ann	6 May 1883	4 Sep 1919	d/o Jacob & Mary
Dewey	8 Mar 1914	21 Jul 1914	
Earnest	29 Dec 1905	22 Jun 1906	s/o W.R. & J.B.
Elizabeth	30 Oct 1805	12 Jan 1888	w/o Meridath
Fielden)	6 Sep 1870	3 Sep 1929	
Eva)	18 Feb 1880	16 Aug 1945	
Mary)	1 Sep 1885	6 Mar 1967	Aunt Charlie
George)	24 Mar 1887	25 Mar 1955	Married 10 Dec 1916
Ora)	No dates		
Hazel R.	12 Jan 1913	19 Jun 1971	
Henry Calvin	7 May 1924	26 Sep 1981	Cpl US Army WWII
Infant	Born & died	23 Apr 1922	s/o Geo. & Ora
Jacob	6 Apr 1904	25 Oct 1904	
Jacob	28 Jan 1843	17 Jan 1926	
Mary E.	9 Oct 1844	22 Jun 1922	
James	No dates		Co A 9th Tenn Cav
Jack)	1876	1952	
Cora)	1883	NOD	
Edith Love)	1928	1952	
James P.)	1936	NOD	
Irma B.)	1938	1964	
James Hobert)	18 Nov 1900	7 Mar 1965	
Pearl W.)	1900	1934	
Trual)	OD	1928	Infant
Harold)	1921	1935	
J. H.	15 Nov 1879	6 Nov 1898	18y 11m 21d
John B.	25 May 1915	19 Feb 1979	
Hazel R.	12 Jan 1913	19 Jun 1971	
Jane Bartley	7 Sep 1942	17 Apr 1945	
Lou G.	1878	1938	
Mary M.	25 Nov 1879	26 Dec 1955	
Merrideth	1872	1932	
Minnie B.	6 Nov 1902	17 Dec 1956	
Naomi Spangler	1911	1985	(fhm-Farrar)
Ralph Edward)	7 Mar 1914	17 Jun 1979	
Flora Belle Haggard)	9 Aug 1913	NOD	
Robert	1906	1915	

WILLIFORD-Samuel	22 Mar 1875	9 Feb 1951	
Wheeler W.	5 Mar 1877	26 Oct 1903	
Rev. William R.)	1873	1938	
Fannie Biggs)	1873	NOD	
Jennie B.	23 Jul 1877	26 May 1906	w/o W.R.
WINE-Frank G.)	17 Nov 1871	16 Aug 1943	
Martha Bashor)	19 Apr 1875	NOD	
Elijah T.)	1888	1966	
Tina Whitson)	1889	1923	His wife
George F.)	1923	1923	
Jacob)	1837	1915	
Julia E.	Born & died	6 Jul 1906	d/o F.G. &M.E.
Elizabeth Bowman	1845	1914	
Mary E.	14 Aug 1903	20 Aug 1903	d/o J.A. & B.E.
Niles E.)	13 Feb 1904	NOD	
Amanda C.)	10 Mar 1899	4 Jan 1960	
Pauline E.	Born & died	25 Oct 1908	d/o F.G. & M.E.
WRIGHT-Lucinda	14 Mar 1816	25 Oct 1896	w/o T.F.

There is a monument which reads:

"MINISTERS:

Jacob Wine - Elder
Sterling W. Noe
Jno. A. Collins
Emanuel Newcomer - Elder
Jno. Satterfield
W. R. Williford
Reuel B. Pritchett - Elder

CHARTER MEMBERS

Jacob Wine - Minister   Birdie H. Finch
Elizabeth Wine   Sabina Hepner
Geo. W. Hepner   Maggie Satterfield
Martha Hepner   William Silvas
William Finch   Betsy Forber
Americas E. Finch   Jno. A. Collins
Thomas Finch   Mary A.B. Sloat
Edward Finch   Mary Steadman
Mollie Finch   J. McClure

Church organized 1875, church built 1885-6, sideroom 1923-4, basement 1935, front annex 1938.

In memory of my father J. Merrideth Williford, erected 1942 by J.H. Williford."

According to Mrs. Beulah D. Linn who obtained the information from Mrs. C. L. Shaffer, the following is buried here in an unmarked grave:

BALL-Mary Garner	6 Jun 1892	14 Dec 1955	w/o Bill

Perhaps owing to the faith of the Church of the Brethern, this cemetery is unique. The church and cemetery sit high on a hill overlooking Douglas Lake in the distance.

To reach the site, take Exit 424 from I-40. Drive toward Dandridge a short distance to the intersection with US25W-70. Turn right onto US25W-70 toward Dandridge. Drive 0.5 miles and turn right. Drive 0.1 miles and turn right onto Brethern Church Road. Drive 0.1 miles. The church and cemetery are on the right.

GAUT CEMETERY

But for a letter written nearly a hundred years ago, we would have no evidence of this Gaut Cemetery. Simon Perry Gaut, a Cleveland, Tennessee lawyer, wrote 28 May 1895 to his first cousin George Moore Gaut in Smith County, Texas. In this letter Simon Perry Gaut relays a great deal of Gaut family information and mentions the graves:

"Last spring, I visited the graves of grandfather, grandmother, your father's first wife and one of his children. The graves are in a country graveyard but well preserved. The names scratched in (illegible) native stones, used as head stones, can still be deciphered. A large tree has grown at the head of grandfather's grave. A rough tomb made of the native rock was built by your father over the grave of his wife and it still stands though overgrown with moss. I had not seen the graves before since I was a small child."

The graves are also mentioned in a Gaut family history compiled by John Morgan Wooten and appearing in Leaves from the Family Tree by Penelope Johnson Allen. Mr. Wooten, writing of John Gaut who married Letitia McAll, said,

"After six years' residence in Washington County, he settled permanently on the French Broad River, near Dandridge, in Jefferson County. He built an unusually good house for the times, two stories, with cut stone chimneys at each end, and a two-story porch in front. The house is still standing and is pointed out to strangers as the old Gaut house. In an oak grove on the farm rests the remains of John Gaut and his wife, marked by plain headstones on which the inscriptions are still legible."

According to information from the above sources, buried in this cemetery are

GAUT-John		1760	5 Mar 1833	
Letitis McAll	25 Sep 1766	25 Oct 1849		
(First name unknown)				1st w/o Matthew
Child				c/o Matthew & 1st wife

Frank Hill, a Gaut descendant, grew up near the old Gaut farm. He remembers the two-story log house that was always referred to as the "old Gaut house," but he does not remember ever seeing the graves or ever being told about them. We have been unable to locate this cemetery and doubt its present-day existence. According to Mr. Hill, the Gaut farm was above where Island View Boatdock is today, on State Route 139 above Deep Springs Road. We can surmise that the cemetery must have been near this area.

GRAHAM CEMETERY

BALLARD-James	Born & died	5 May 1884	s/o John & Mary (broken)
BROWN-Willie	20 Aug 1886	24 Feb 1887	s/o J.F. & M.C.
BURNETT-Infant	22 Dec 1886	OD (Born)	c/o C.T. & E.E.
FAIN-Lizzie P.	21 Jun 1848	22 Jan 1879	d/o J. & C.C. SMITH
			w/o W.A. FAIN
GRAHAM-Eliza Ann	Died	10 Nov 1828	4y 8d; d/o D.R. & M.C.
Elizabeth	Died	6 Dec 1840	1y 6m; d/o D.R. & M.C.
Gabriel	25 May 1809	29 Oct 1833	
George Junier	Died	20 Apr 1834	Aged 23y
George, Sr.	Died	19 Oct 1832	76y
Elizabeth	Died	9 Oct 1817	53y
Mary Emaline	Died	4 Oct 1831	3y 2m; d/o D.R. & M.C.
Sarah Caroline	Died	4 Sep 1840	3y 23d; d/o D.R. & M.C.
William	10 Feb 1786	17 Sep 1857	71y 7m 7d
Mary	2 Mar 1795	23 Aug 1832	37y 5m 21d; w/o William
POTTS-Lucy	11 Oct 1881	5 Nov 1881	d/o J.W. & A. (broken)
SEHORN-John	21 Jun 1748 O.S.	23 May 1831	(fieldstone-broken)
Elizabeth	Died	23 Feb 1819	(fieldstone)
TURNLEY-J.	Died	Oct 1808	(fieldstone)

WPA copied this cemetery in 1937 and listed the following stones which we could not locate in 1985:

GRAHAM-Mary C.	Died	5 Aug 1856	54y 2m 13d
Sarah	Died	8 Apr 1813	
SATTERFIELD-C. M.	7 Nov 1873	27 Jun 1877	

A visit to this cemetery is as a return to another era. Time seems to have stood still here in this forgotten site. Imagine our surprise when we recorded this cemetery and found the graves of three Revolutionary soldiers, none of whom, apparently were known to be buried here. The most exciting find of the day was the grave of John Seahorn, a Revolutionary soldier and a captain under John Sevier in the State of Franklin days! The inscription on his stone is unique because it bears the date of 21 June 1748 and after this is written O.S., which stands for Old Style. In 1752 England, along with her colony the United States, adopted the Gregorian Calendar, which dropped 10 days from the calendar. Those born before that date (such as George Washington) often changed their date of birth to the New Style or added Old Style after the dates! This is the only time in over 500 cemeteries we have recorded, that we have found this written! John Seahorn's stone is broken.

To reach this site, take Exit 424 from I-40 and drive the short distance to the intersection with US25W-70. Cross US25W-70 and drive 0.5 miles. The cemetery is located in a large grove of trees on top of the hill to the right behind the Fox home.

HARRIS CEMETERY

HANES-John	22 Jul 1829	31 Oct 1864	35y 3m 9d
HARRIS-Clarence Eugene)	20 Oct 1867	16 Oct 1925	
Mary C. Lilliard)	3 Mar 1868	15 Nov 1941	
Eliza C.	Born dead	10 Oct 1867	d/o S.T. & S. E.
Fred S.	17 Feb 1869	22 Mar 1893	
George Temple	17 Jul 1893	12 Sep 1948	
Hal Sheridan)	29 Mar 1865	2 Apr 1927	
Nina)	30 Dec 1873	5 Apr 1955	
Infant	Born dead	26 Apr 1870	
Dr. J. A.	30 Nov 1861	11 Jul 1901	
Lula Holtsinger	24 Feb 1863	3 Feb 1928	w/o Dr. James A.
Sarah I.	Died	14 Apr 1858	13y 11m
S. T.)	22 Mar 1842	4 Oct 1923	Grand Army of the Republic - 1861 veteran - 1866. Late Captain Company D 3rd Tenn Cav U. S. Vol., and late prisoner of war sentenced to death 13 Feb 1863 by Confederate Court Marshall. 26 months in Rebel prisons in irons and close confinement. 25 months under sentence of death.
Sallie E.)	8 Jan 1846	24 Oct 1907	w/o S. T. As my affiance she visited me in prison on the day I was to be executed. As a wife she was ever true, faithful and loving to the end.
Temple)	18 Nov 1827	10 Apr 1892	
Margaret A.)	9 Oct 1829	22 Feb 1913	
Tippy J.	2 Apr 1860	10 Dec 1860	s/o Temple & M.A. 8m 8d
William	11 Jul 1873	27 Aug 1873	s/o S. E. & S. T.
Wm.	10 Feb 1814	22 Aug 1884	
Harriett M.	10 Feb 1824	31 Jul 1891	
Wm. F.	4 Apr 1840	16 Nov 1870	
Zena M.	8 Jun 1846	11 Dec 1909	
HOLTSINGER-Samuel M.	5 Mar 1876	1 Jun 1954	
Nita	27 Jan 1874	1 Nov 1965	
LYLE-J. Flora	1 Jun 1880	28 Aug 1963	
Doct. J. Nat	7 Nov 1843	5 May 1881	
Lavenia	16 Nov 1848	25 Apr 1898	w/o J. Nat
Mary E.	25 Aug 1879	15 Jul 1897	w/o W. C.
MILLARD-Nina A.	30 Dec 1875	17 Sep 1877	
RAGSDALE-Albert Sidney	30 Jun 1862	20 Aug 1921	
Gertrude Harris	31 Jan 1870	6 Jun 1928	w/o Albert Sidney
REEVES-Nola Harris	19 Nov 1854	12 Dec 1911	w/o Thomas Reeves; d/o Temple & Margaret Harris
RUSSELL-Infant	2 Apr 1876	9 Apr 1876	s/o W. T. & Josie
Josie A.	7 Mar 1852	31 Aug 1889	w/o W. T.; d/o Temple & Addie Harris

This small, well-kept family cemetery is located at the corner of Graveyard Alley and US25W-70 in Dandridge. It is immediately behind the Old Revolutionary Cemetery.

HILLCREST CEMETERY

AIKEN-Bertie L.	26 Jun 1890	24 Oct 1981	
AILEY-Eva	15 Nov 1900	12 Mar 1940	
Infant	Born & died	6 Feb 1925	
ALLEN-Albert Watson)	17 Sep 1879	27 Feb 1967	
Lynn Saffell)	3 Jul 1887	18 Sep 1965	
Paul T.)	25 Dec 1907	27 Dec 1975	
Hazel G.)	14 Aug 1913	NOD	
ANDERSON-Dale William	10 Nov 1921	29 Jun 1979	Lt JG US Navy WWII
ATCHLEY-Fred E.	24 Jun 1915	13 Oct 1980	
Robert H.)	12 Oct 1894	11 Oct 1966	
Zema E.)	22 May 1891	5 Feb 1973	
William D.)	6 Dec 1878	27 Jan 1957	
Belva C.)	5 Oct 1884	10 Sep 1970	
BAKER-Alfred A.	29 Nov 1871	22 Mar 1946	
Lou Burchfiel	9 Oct 1874	24 May 1943	
Jacob R.)	23 Mar 1899	23 Sep 1966	
Mattie P.)	10 Jan 1908	NOD	
J. Richard)	11 Sep 1930	28 Jan 1940	
Charles M.)	2 Oct 1927	12 Oct 1927	
John M.)	1879	1963	
Melvina Ailey)	1875	1949	
BARBEE-Ben Carl)	16 May 1923	NOD	
Beulah P.)	6 Apr 1929	NOD	
Carl)	19 Jun 1895	10 Jul 1968	
Annie Z.)	23 Aug 1900	5 Jun 1983	
BARRETT-Charlie C.	11 May 1919	3 Mar 1971	TN Pvt US Army WWII
BARTON-John Riley "Buck"	4 Feb 1907	22 Aug 1969	(See Robert SHEPHERD)
BAXTER-James Ritchie	11 Jul 1962	21 Oct 1982	
BAYLESS-Jerry W.	25 Apr 1947	14 Nov 1969	
BEARE-Burgess J.	12 Oct 1921	9 Jul 1979	h/o Betty Rainwater BEARE
BEAVER-Minnie Rimmer	2 Oct 1893	12 Nov 1975	(See Shade H. RIMMER)
BERRIER-Clifford	20 Jul 1917	4 Dec 1980	
BETTIS-Chas. Pete)	10 Jul 1888	11 Apr 1961	
Viola)	6 Jun 1881	11 Oct 1951	
BLACKBURN-Lynn N.)	7 Jun 1911	2 Mar 1985	
Dorothy C.)	30 Dec 1916	27 Jun 1982	
BLAIR-Robert F.)	13 May 1923	3 Feb 1978	
Willie H.)	11 Jun 1920	NOD	
BOLDEN-W. Horace)	9 May 1893	8 Dec 1966	
Hazel Rather)	7 Jan 1895	11 Jan 1972	
W.H. Bill, Jr.)	24 May 1928	28 Feb 1974	
BRIMER-Ada D. Layman	8 Mar 1874	20 Dec 1965	(See H.M. LAYMAN)
George "Joe")	13 Apr 1889	19 Apr 1962	
Lela E.)	4 Aug 1903	19 Jun 1981	
Harrison W.	24 Jan 1895	1 Jul 1959	
Thomas Rhoten	14 Jul 1866	28 Jul 1941	
BROOKS-Martha A.	22 Mar 1894	28 Jun 1971	
Samuel Saffell	22 Feb 1918	26 Mar 1962	
BRYAN-George Lee	13 Sep 1912	21 Dec 1970	TN S2 US Navy WWII
BRYANT-James E.)	13 Aug 1905	6 Aug 1978	
Lavaughn)	7 Jun 1911	26 Dec 1963	
Martha Ann)	13 Mar 1945	14 Mar 1945	d/o M/M J.E.
BULL-F. Reed, Sr.	23 Dec 1899	27 Oct 1967	
Floyd Reed, Jr.	10 Jul 1924	12 Jun 1982	M/SGT US Army WWII

BURCHFIEL-Artice O.)	1 Apr 1895	18 Feb 1962
Mabel H.)	17 Apr 1895	NOD
James Hill)	12 Feb 1919	10 Dec 1938
James C.)	6 Nov 1864	19 Jan 1958
Margaret Shults)	13 Jul 1869	7 Nov 1958
John W.)	15 Mar 1875	23 Sep 1895
Elizabeth J.)	24 Mar 1859	29 Aug 1860
Rachel A.)	OD	4 Sep 1869
Thomas D. A.)	OD	6 Sep 1869
Robert)	9 May 1809	30 Mar 1881
Anna E.)	19 Jan 1804	14 Aug 1874
Jacob W.)	13 Oct 1872	29 Jul 1889
Rev. John)	27 Jun 1831	13 Jan 1901
Mary A.)	15 Dec 1835	1 Nov 1895
BUSH-Ben W.)	20 Nov 1898	2 Mar 1986
Glenna Mae S.)	13 Apr 1918	NOD
BUSLER-Darius)	27 Sep 1884	16 Feb 1958
Sophia P.)	29 Sep 1888	18 Feb 1956
Ulyss)	14 Mar 1912	11 Apr 1947
Infant	Born & died	3 Nov 1947
Infant	Born & died	7 Feb 1947
CANTRELL-Ervin	15 Dec 1931	29 Dec 1976
CARMAN-Mack Alger)	29 Jan 1923	1 Nov 1972
Trula M.)	13 Jul 1924	NOD
U. H.)	5 Oct 1879	22 Jan 1966
Nancy T.)	4 Oct 1879	13 Dec 1956
Will M.)	5 Mar 1901	20 Sep 1973
Hattie R.)	7 Nov 1899	2 Aug 1957
CARMICHAEL-Manley F.)	20 Mar 1887	29 Mar 1936
Anna S.)	19 Feb 1887	20 Jun 1968
Jake W.)	15 Feb 1912	11 Apr 1982
Evelyn R.)	9 Dec 1917	7 Apr 1974
CARTER-George W.	14 Sep 1894	18 Jun 1973	TN PFC US Army WWI
CASE-A. A. "Stimp"	24 Nov 1896	6 Jan 1949
Jennie M. Gaddis Scarlett	24 Feb 1906	NOD
CHAMBERS-Addie M.	10 Mar 1896	13 Oct 1973
Mollie RAINWATER)	5 May 1896	22 Oct 1969
Pearl Lee)	28 Jan 1889	6 May 1972
Raye H.	15 Oct 1908	9 Aug 1982
CHANDLER-Hezekiah)	28 Sep 1902	28 Feb 1974
Pauline)	13 Apr 1910	NOD
CHESTEEN-Jonathan F.	29 Oct 1895	21 Aug 1973	TN Cpl US Army WWI
CHRISMAN-Tamy Loree Hughes	19 Nov 1962	29 Jan 1982
CHURCHWELL-Rev. L. G.)	26 Jan 1904	16 Jun 1980
Jo S.)	15 Feb 1924	NOD
CLEVENGER-Kenneth W.	23 Feb 1924	3 Nov 1978
CODY-Mack)	14 Nov 1894	26 Apr 1967	TN Cpl US Army WWI
Roxy H.)	2 Feb 1906	23 Jul 1970
COLLINS-Sam H.	28 Jan 1878	28 Feb 1959
COPE-Eugene Herman)	19 Jun 1907	1 Jan 1984
Julia Mae)	6 Aug 1914	22 Dec 1961
CORBETT-Horace C.)	8 Feb 1886	9 Feb 1962
Alice Martin)	15 Jun 1884	25 Oct 1966
Thomas A.)	8 Feb 1888	24 Jul 1964
Frank)	20 Sep 1895	14 Feb 1980
Josie R.)	14 Apr 1901	NOD

CORBETT-Roy F.)	24 Dec 1910	10 Sep 1983	
Beulah L.)	28 Oct 1911	NOD	
Walter)	22 Dec 1912	29 Dec 1982	
Lettie S.)	26 May 1913	NOD	
COX-William Vern)	16 Sep 1926	NOD	
Effie A.)	7 Dec 1925	NOD	
CURRY-Bruce C., Sr.)	13 Dec 1892	11 Apr 1965	
Callie Hale)	6 Jan 1892	16 Oct 1962	
DALTON-Billy Bruce	14 Oct 1934	25 Mar 1979	
Clarence J.	23 Sep 1927	22 Aug 1972	
Thomas T.)	10 Jan 1898	3 Dec 1973	
Josie Ray)	7 Sep 1904	3 Sep 1969	
Thomas W.)	18 Mar 1923	1 Mar 1985	
Frances I.)	11 Sep 1927	NOD	
W. J. Bryant)	8 Mar 1913	17 May 1985	
Clara J. Humphrey)	16 Apr 1921	NOD	
DANCE-Loy E.)	16 Feb 1903	NOD	Married 15 Apr 1972
Ruth Denton)	7 Sep 1936	NOD	
DAVIS-John	10 Jan 1916	16 Apr 1963	
DAWN-W. Frank)	25 Dec 1881	8 May 1961	
Minnie J.)	23 Dec 1889	6 May 1957	
DEAN-David Harold	19 Jul 1948	18 Oct 1969	
Sanford N.	1 Sep 1915	21 Apr 1978	
DENTON-Buford Floyd	1906	1975	PFC US Army WWII
Charlie D.)	25 Aug 1881	17 Aug 1970	
Mattie V.)	29 Jan 1885	18 Nov 1980	
David R.	28 Feb 1959	1 Mar 1959	
David White	2 Aug 1940	3 Nov 1983	
Earl)	5 Sep 1910	23 Nov 1964	
Mildred Phillips)	5 Dec 1914	19 Nov 1984	
Herbert R.	5 Jul 1898	15 Jul 1956	TN Tec5 Engineers WWII
J. C.)	30 Sep 1870	14 Mar 1922	
Sarah R.)	12 Mar 1866	7 May 1905	
John A.)	11 Nov 1902	23 Apr 1964	
James W.)	18 Apr 1905	17 Aug 1905	
Gertie R.)	14 Oct 1901	31 Dec 1901	
Roy)	22 Sep 1890	15 Dec 1953	
Josie Hill)	6 Mar 1892	9 Dec 1977	
Paul E. "Preacher")	12 Mar 1915	11 Dec 1977	
Leota D. JONES "TAB")	23 Feb 1917	18 Feb 1972	
DOCKINS-Mode	26 May 1887	6 Apr 1906	
DOCKERY-Wrex Lando	3 Jul 1892	27 Jul 1967	TN Wagr Sup Co 114 Field Arty WWI
DOCKREY-Carl S.)	22 Jul 1895	6 May 1948	
Burvellee T.)	23 Feb 1896	13 Dec 1961	
DOUGLASS-Joe H.)	1 Feb 1880	28 Mar 1955	
Adra H.)	16 May 1880	9 Jun 1959	
EDMONDS-Christopher C.)	30 Aug 1874	24 Jul 1943	
Nancy M.)	11 Jan 1872	26 Nov 1935	
Clyde	8 Dec 1923	24 Apr 1964	TN Pvt US Army WWII
Helen R.	24 Jul 1946	21 Jun 1962	
Herbert L.)	23 Oct 1919	18 May 1978	
Helen H.)	28 Apr 1920	NOD	
James W.	28 May 1873	14 Jun 1961	
Lockie A.	7 Sep 1885	24 Dec 1961	
William Austin)	8 Mar 1888	3 Aug 1969	
Beulah Newman)	12 Aug 1896	22 Mar 1979	

ELDER-John M.)	30 Sep 1887	7 Jul 1954	
Zula H.)	26 Oct 1888	5 Jan 1966	
Roy S.)	28 Sep 1920	27 Jul 1969	
ELLISON-John T.)	23 Aug 1886	12 Oct 1968	
Minnie W.)	17 May 1889	5 Jan 1961	
ESTES-Paul P., Jr.)	7 Jan 1924	29 Jul 1981	
Betty Jo)	24 Jun 1931	NOD	
EZELLE-Herbert L.)	16 Mar 1902	2 Apr 1977	
Hazel W.)	27 Dec 1916	NOD	
FAIN-George W.)	15 Dec 1891	16 Dec 1982	
Cenia Ownby)	12 Sep 1894	1 Nov 1958	
FIELDS-Charles "Shorty"	22 Jan 1892	26 Mar 1969	
FINCHUM-Ollie M.	28 Sep 1900	NOD	(See Roy J. FOLAND)
FINE-Rufus H.)	26 Dec 1902	24 Jan 1978	
Lillie S.)	18 Jan 1908	NOD	
FOLAND-Billy	21 Apr 1932	18 Dec 1971	
Charlie R.	18 Aug 1903	16 Sep 1979	
Garland Lynn	OD	9 Jul 1977	
Roy J.)	25 Feb 1913	12 Feb 1980	Brother
Ollie M. FINCHUM)	28 Sep 1900	NOD	Sister
FOX-Charles W.)	26 Mar 1897	20 Jul 1976	
Neta Gass)	25 Jun 1909	NOD	
Hascal R.)	29 Sep 1896	7 Mar 1970	
Nola Ruth)	11 Oct 1899	15 Sep 1984	
James E.)	5 Oct 1860	26 Oct 1929	
Hattie Snapp)	2 Feb 1861	15 Dec 1928	
Ashley E.)	17 Apr 1895	22 Jan 1897	
James Swann	18 Nov 1914	23 May 1972	
James Taylor)	10 Nov 1890	30 Jan 1959	
Alma Swann)	4 Jul 1891	20 Dec 1983	
Marshall Eugene)	25 Jun 1899	28 May 1981	
Willie McMahan)	29 Mar 1904	29 Jan 1982	
Tom	27 Apr 1922	7 Nov 1966	Cpl USMCR WWII
Willie French)	8 Nov 1905	23 Nov 1976	
Wilma Swann)	6 Dec 1911	26 Jan 1963	
FRANCE-Richard)	21 Oct 1926	NOD	Married 17 Nov 1955
Della K.)	27 Apr 1924	4 Oct 1980	
FRENCH-Angela L.	27 May 1964	2 Oct 1980	Grandmother (See Walter A. Loveday)
Martin C.)	14 Nov 1889	18 Jan 1977	
Willie V.)	20 Sep 1890	28 Nov 1964	
Michael K.)	4 Sep 1951	NOD	
Ruby J.)	19 Jan 1950	NOD	
Rex L.)	28 Nov 1886	7 Dec 1971	
Nancy Frye)	22 Mar 1889	9 Jun 1971	
Robert Edwin	28 Aug 1968	11 Dec 1968	
William J., Sr.)	16 Jul 1928	11 Mar 1972	
Mattie Bible)	26 Nov 1926	14 Jan 1979	
FRYE-Ernest L.)	22 Nov 1921	3 Mar 1985	
Ruth Hart)	24 Apr 1919	NOD	
GADDIS-Florence C.	29 Mar 1908	31 Mar 1930	
David R.	23 May 1912	29 Jan 1919	
Hugh T.	18 Sep 1914	25 Jan 1919	
J. J.)	21 Mar 1977	25 Dec 1947	Father
Dora Reece)	8 Nov 1880	25 Dec 1947	Mother
GANN-Walter Clabe	1 Oct 1915	9 Mar 1967	TN PFC US Marine Corps Res WWII

GASS-William P.)	6 Sep 1863	17 Aug 1951	
Addie)	14 Nov 1876	25 Nov 1960	
Wm. Raymond)	24 Dec 1899	30 Jan 1976	
Cora B.)	9 Nov 1899	15 Apr 1971	
GAUT-William A.)	23 Jul 1947	26 Mar 1983	Sp6 US Army
Jessie W.)	4 Jul 1919	9 Oct 1980	
GAYLOR-William E.	29 Nov 1917	5 May 1972	TN PFC US Army WWII
GIBSON-Haskell Ray)	14 Apr 1890	14 Dec 1977	
Susan Mae Fox)	6 Oct 1894	3 Jul 1964	
James B.	15 Dec 1921	21 Jan 1975	US Army WWII
GODDARD-James Swann	3 Jan 1951	10 Sep 1974	s/o Paul & Ruth
GOFORTH-Charles Hubert	28 Oct 1928	26 Apr 1983	Sgt US Army Korea
GOULD-Irene Reese	4 Nov 1912	9 May 1983	
GREGORY-Luther "Tip"	3 Feb 1883	4 Aug 1978	
Nancy Lou	15 Feb 1887	3 Oct 1962	
GRIFFIN-Anna R.	7 Apr 1905	17 Mar 1977	
HALL-Dorcas Anne	16 Dec 1901	7 Apr 1967	
HAMMER-F. Earl	1888	1950	
HARRIS-Hal E.)	5 Nov 1886	1 Jun 1936	
Pearl Mathes)	22 Jun 1889	4 Mar 1973	
HARRISON-Emett	23 Apr 1882	17 Apr 1960	
Pressley G.)	13 Oct 1889	11 Jun 1958	TN Cook Sup Co 120 Inf 30 Div
			WWI
Ruth Marie)	24 Sep 1896	7 Nov 1962	
HART-Oliver M.)	22 Jun 1880	24 Nov 1971	
Orpha C.)	28 Nov 1882	1 Sep 1958	
HARTSELL-Jeffery Wade	1 Jul 1959	5 Jul 1959	
HARVEY-Aleck J.	12 Apr 1946	26 Jun 1977	
HEIDECKER-Herman H.)	14 Sep 1895	31 Aug 1980	
Alberta L.)	9 Jul 1907	NOD	
HEMSWORTH-Floyd C.)	1905	1969	
Fanchion D.)	1909	1977	
HENDERSON-Bruce W.)	13 Mar 1921	13 Jan 1986	Married 10 Feb 1946
Gladys C.)	29 Jun 1925	NOD	
J. R.	26 Dec 1948	23 Dec 1973	
S. F. "Bess")	5 Apr 1915	NOD	
Viva J.)	26 Mar 1916	NOD	
T. W.)	13 Sep 1886	4 Nov 1969	
Lula Cox)	5 Jul 1889	21 Sep 1983	
Johnny T.)	15 May 1934	8 Dec 1958	
HENSLEY-Curtis E.)	15 Mar 1933	22 Jul 1980	Married 28 Apr 1954
Anna Mae)	27 Apr 1938	NOD	
HICKMAN-Andrew J.)	2 Feb 1891	27 May 1955	
Georgia R.)	18 Sep 1891	21 Oct 1984	
HICKS-Harry C.)	4 Mar 1907	22 Oct 1961	
Betty L.)	25 Apr 1901	8 Feb 1975	
HILL-Claude E.)	30 Apr 1887	6 Oct 1960	
Katie Miller)	21 Sep 1889	5 Sep 1977	
E. F. "Scott"	11 Sep 1892	16 Dec 1971	
Herbert H.)	11 May 1912	26 Apr 1956	
Rubye S.)	OD	30 Apr 1965	
Infants)	OD	15 Feb 1911	s/oW.C. & A.A.
			d/oW.C. & A.A.
John W.)	28 Apr 1854	20 Dec 1910	
Frances E. Nichols)			
James B.)	1884	1933	
Josie B.)	1884	1950	

HILL-Lon C.)	13 Mar 1882	12 Apr 1939	
Josie Fox)	30 Oct 1888	30 Aug 1932	
James Asbury)	6 Sep 1913	3 Mar 1914	
Mary Helen Harris	14 Oct 1919	24 Sep 1975	
Sarah H.	29 Nov 1909	23 Aug 1983	
William Carroll)	1 Jul 1873	25 Dec 1943	
Alberta L.)	4 Oct 1877	11 Dec 1964	
William F.	30 Oct 1914	12 Nov 1980	
William M.)	25 Aug 1842	26 Sep 1918	9 Tenn Cav Civil War
Margaret M. Nichols)	15 Jun 1856	15 Aug 1914	w/o William M.
HODGE-Clyde N.	9 Jul 1911	11 Jan 1972	TN Pvt Co K 137 Inf WWII
Frank M.)	4 Oct 1889	13 May 1971	
Hattie E.)	16 May 1887	13 Sep 1981	
J. Perry)	15 Apr 1886	23 Apr 1963	
Pearl J.)	30 Jan 1897	29 Apr 1973	
HOLBERT-Ted	6 Mar 1913	8 Dec 1959	S/Sgt 811 Base Unit AAF WWII
W. D. "Don")	2 Jan 1909	25 Feb 1960	
Edna S.)	16 Nov 1915	NOD	
HOOPER-Carl M.	17 Jul 1920	11 Jun 1944	TN PFC 142 Inf 36 Inf Div WWII
HORTON-Harry	22 May 1931	23 Jul 1972	
HOWELL-Eunice French	1913	1984	(fhm-Farrah)
HUDSON-Donald Ray)	1 Apr 1914	15 Mar 1984	US Army WWII
Viola B.)	4 Apr 1922	NOD	
HUGHES-Jesse T.)	16 May 1909	21 Oct 1982	Married 10 Feb 1929
Myrtle H.)	22 Feb 1914	14 Apr 1975	Children: Verna, James,
			Adam, Evenell, Betty, Ruby, Jimmie, Doris,
			Allen, Howard, Kathy
HUMPHREY-Jasper M.	11 Jan 1898	6 Oct 1963	
HUNTER-James Richard	3 Jan 1958	26 May 1976	s/o James Hugh & Robbie June
HURST-George W., Jr.	21 Nov 1955	13 May 1976	
INMAN-Ray H.	22 Aug 1924	7 May 1966	TN Pvt Co A 27 Armd Inf BN WWII
JACKSON-Johnnie Thomas, Jr.	1947	1977	
JARNAGIN-Thomas Barton	Born & died	28 Sep 1952	
JENKINS-Lloyd)	9 Dec 1894	7 Oct 1970	
Paralee C.)	25 May 1898	21 Jun 1969	
Kyle J.)	1 Oct 1922	22 Sep 1944	TN PFC 314 Inf 79 Inf Div WWII
Lemuel)	27 Oct 1845	28 Aug 1926	
Christeen)	21 Feb 1849	12 Dec 1919	
J. N.)	20 Apr 1868	26 Oct 1947	
D. J. Lewis)	23 Aug 1869	26 Jul 1922	w/ J. N.
Milissa)	1 Apr 1912	25 Apr 1912	d/o J.N. & D.J.
Leonard)	7 Aug 1889	23 Aug 1961	
Selma P.)	14 May 1893	21 May 1969	
JOHNSON-K. Douglas)	17 Oct 1915	25 May 1965	Pvt T5 38 Engineers
N. Ruth J.)	11 Sep 1921	27 Mar 1968	
Frank F.	8 Dec 1874	25 Sep 1953	
Sherman Carroll	5 Aug 1960	28 Jun 1982	
JONES-Chester E., Jr.	3 Sep 1935	19 Oct 1964	
George E.)	13 Oct 1895	8 Oct 1974	
Thelma N.)	4 Sep 1900	29 Apr 1954	
Donald J.	30 Aug 1917	28 Dec 1947	
Gartha Mc	6 Dec 1916	NOD	
Herman A.)	3 Oct 1898	9 Aug 1963	
Mary G.)	25 Apr 1902	20 Dec 1985	
Ray Leon)	7 Mar 1918	26 Dec 1977	Cox US Navy WWII
James Paul	1 Oct 1927	1 Feb 1973	TN Cpl US Army Reserve Korea

Name	Birth	Death	Notes
JONES-Pvt. Mark)	2 Aug 1894	14 May 1963	Co A 328th Inf.
Iva Vandyke)	12 May 1900	16 May 1972	w/o Pvt Mark
Mary Eva	24 Mar 1892	3 Jul 1975	
Leota D. "Tab"	23 Feb 1917	18 Feb 1972	(See Paul E. DENTON)
Ralph E.)	4 Jun 1906	4 Mar 1970	Married 12 Jun 1927
Alice J.)	17 Apr 1910	NOD	
Sam H.	17 May 1892	20 Nov 1951	
Blanche	28 Mar 1898	30 Mar 1962	
JUSTICE-Charles E.)	1897	1981	US Army WWI
Elizabeth R.)	1 Nov 1921	NOD	
KANE-Arthur F.)	1902	1950	
Mildred B.)	1895	1971	
KERR-W. O. "Bid")	15 Mar 1910	4 Jul 1982	
Georgia E.)	5 Jun 1909	NOD	
KILLION-W. H.)	25 Feb 1880	27 Jul 1963	
Alice M.)	19 Jun 1880	1 Jul 1961	
Georgia)	OD	13 May 1968	Sister
KYKER-Earl W.	14 Nov 1903	29 Nov 1982	
KYTE-Gregory Edward	7 Apr 1960	20 May 1960	s/o M/M Byrl
James Haskell)	26 Feb 1899	28 Nov 1963	
Dicy Ellison)	21 Jan 1898	23 Apr 1982	
Chas. Anthony	21 Aug 1949	16 Sep 1949	
Peggy Sue Rainwater	1952	1972	w/o Timothy R.
LACKEY-Wm. Harvey)	1 Feb 1909	28 May 1983	
Willie D.)	8 Sep 1911	NOD	
LAFOLLETTE-Elizabeth Lewis	11 Jul 1880	30 Nov 1954	
LANE-Amy	23 Feb 1983	13 Dec 1983	
Justin	17 Jan 1982	13 Dec 1983	
LARGE-George C.	9 Oct 1912	15 Jun 1985	PFC US Marine Corps WWII
LAYMAN-George A.)	20 Aug 1894	2 Apr 1973	
Mary Eva Jones)	24 Mar 1892	3 Jul 1975	
Harry E.	16 Nov 1920	25 Nov 1977	
Betty Bolden	26 Nov 1923	NOD	
W. L.)	5 Nov 1869	21 Nov 1913	
Ada D. Layman BRIMER)	8 Mar 1874	20 Dec 1965	
H. M.)	18 Oct 1896	9 Mar 1947	
Nelle M.)	13 Nov 1896	5 Dec 1968	
LEEPER-Charlotte K.)	1 Nov 1877	14 Nov 1962	
Mary Jane)	20 Feb 1876	12 Jan 1960	
LEWIS-Earl B.	27 Jul 1924	15 Apr 1965	
Hubert)	14 Feb 1909	17 Nov 1954	
Elsie P.)	8 Mar 1899	17 Apr 1967	
Pearl Martin	12 Sep 1911	10 Dec 1977	
Preston W.)	6 Aug 1926	NOD	
Fannie M.)	9 Jul 1935	NOD	
Darrell Preston)	19 Nov 1957	30 Nov 1957	
W. Earl)	20 Aug 1906	20 Jan 1954	
Sarah Martin)	3 Apr 1907	1 Apr 1983	
LINDSEY-Harley	28 Jan 1907	10 Jun 1964	
James A.)	24 Jan 1912	3 Jul 1971	Married 23 May 1935
Thelma S.)	13 Apr 1913	NOD	
Norman E.	2 Feb 1943	18 Jul 1972	
Walter Gordon, Sr.)	27 Feb 1903	1 Aug 1967	
Zella Webb)	21 Jan 1910	NOD	
Wm.)	23 Nov 1919	NOD	
Violet R.)	18 Mar 1919	NOD	
Joseph Ray)	29 Jan 1918	29 Nov 1973	TN Pvt US Army WWII
Edith M.)	8 Apr 1917	NOD	

LOVEDAY-H. M.)	22 Nov 1897	3 Sep 1973	
Martha P.)	17 Sep 1902	4 Dec 1973	
Walter A.)	12 oct 1923	NOD	
Johnnie A.)	18 Dec 1923	NOD	
Angela L. FRENCH)	27 May 1964	2 Oct 1980	Granddaughter
LUCKE-Mary Sue	1930	1986	(fhm-Northcutt & Son)
McCARTER-David J., MD)	1882	1964	
Gertrude Hill)	1888	1939	
McGEE-Paul W.)	5 Oct 1905	16 Dec 1979	
Juanita M.)	28 Apr 1908	9 Nov 1976	
McKENNY-Andy)	17 May 1883	8 Apr 1979	Father of Mrs. Forrest Wilson
Arrowyia B.)	8 Aug 1900	11 Nov 1971	
Howard Payton)	1931	1977	US Army
McKOY-William G.)	1894	1979	Sgt US Army WWI
Gladys M.)	2 Aug 1899	2 Feb 1970	
McMAHAN-Clenn	9 Oct 1901	19 May 1964	TN 155 Field Arty WWII
G. W., Jr.	27 Mar 1919	1 Dec 1984	US Inf WWII
Frank	10 Feb 1916	10 Jun 1920	
Grant W.)	19 Apr 1881	14 Nov 1920	
Minnie H.)	24 Aug 1882	11 Apr 1968	His wife
McMILLAN-Lloyd W.	31 Jan 1898	10 Sep 1966	TN Pvt US Army WWII
McSPADDEN-Vera Rainwater	5 Feb 1919	8 Jun 1961	
MAJHOR-Walter John	17 Dec 1915	27 Nov 1959	Montana M/Sgt 302 Base Unit USAF WWII
MANIS-Arthur M.)	8 Sep 1886	27 Mar 1950	
Ollie L.)	2 Mar 1888	21 Oct 1974	
Grant))	1866	1927	
Martha M.)	1887	1971	
Eugene)	1906	1907	
MARTIN-Blanche S.	23 Sep 1926	9 May 1969	
Ernest)	25 Sep 1903	NOD	
Dorothy D.)	7 Jul 1912	17 Dec 1982	
Harold Tony	1943	1982	Sp5 US Army Vietnam
Isaac N.)	23 Jul 1877	22 Oct 1953	
Edith N.)	1 Sep 1881	1 Jul 1961	
Lacy F. "Butch"	11 Jul 1914	29 Oct 1983	T/Sgt US Army WWII
Viola Ailey	8 Feb 1917	NOD	
Mack Preston)	11 Jun 1912	9 Sep 1973	
Genevieve Riley)	6 Sep 1909	NOD	
Ronald G.	7 Dec 1947	20 Feb 1986	"Ron"
Wiley R.)	7 Jan 1890	3 Feb 1966	
Ollie Fine)	6 Aug 1896	15 Jun 1954	
Wirt A.	5 Jan 1884	3 Apr 1969	
MAXEY-Mary Charlotte Crowe	8 Feb 1934	20 Oct 1975	
Wm. Carson)	31 Mar 1899	22 Sep 1973	
Teddie B.)	21 Dec 1903	NOD	
MAYES-Dora	1983	1984	(fhm-Farrar)
MESSAMORE-Lon)	5 Apr 1900	22 Mar 1984	
Ida S.)	6 Apr 1906	NOD	
MILLER-Charlie G.)	12 Jan 1890	5 Aug 1976	Married 11 Feb 1916
Minnie G.)	14 Jun 1895	14 Aug 1983	
John Calvin,Sr.)	13 Nov 1886	9 Mar 1974	
Elizabeth C.)	10 May 1896	NOD	
Jimmie H.)	6 Nov 1915	NOD	
Elizabeth R.	22 Aug 1923	30 Jun 1984	
John H.)	8 May 1869	13 May 1951	
Margaret Moore)	17 Sep 1871	27 Nov 1964	
Mary Ann)	17 Nov 1898	2 Jan 1899	

MILLER-Mitchell	4 Sep 1910	4 Dec 1916	
Charles H.	26 Nov 1894	16 Mar 1895	
Loyd E.)	21 Sep 1906	13 Jan 1976	
Mildred C.)	3 Jan 1908	10 Feb 1983	
Hugh M.)	1 Oct 1914	11 Mar 1975	
Pauline B.)	25 Nov 1908	24 Jan 1969	
Moses)	22 Mar 1844	25 Feb 1924	Co F 49th Tenn Cav
Catherine)	22 Mar 1842	21 Jan 1888	w/o Moses
M. A. Ketner)	Died	28 Mar 1902	w/o Moses; 68y
Bennie)	No dates		
MILLS-Little Eloise	23 Jan 1952	21 Mar 1976	d/o M/M H.L. (See Benjamin Henry ZIRKLE)
Ennis)	6 Jan 1907	29 Nov 1983	
Nellie L.)	1 Jan 1921	NOD	
Fred Tinsley)	27 Mar 1913	NOD	Married 3 Jul 1940
Mary Finchum)	22 Nov 1912	NOD	
Hubert N.)	29 Feb 1892	22 Sep 1924	
Nelle R.)	15 Dec 1892	2 Jul 1982	
Nealie A.	1894	1970	Aunt
MOORE-Albert H.)	22 Jan 1865	10 May 1948	
Louvenia Reneau)	24 Apr 1872	8 Mar 1949	
Ray E.)	20 Jul 1911	4 Jun 1962	
Madelle)	9 Jul 1902	15 Jun 1961	
George)	11 Mar 1900	13 May 1985	
Ollie Kate Hudson)	20 Oct 1900	23 Jul 1949	
G. Eugene)	30 Aug 1904	NOD	
Daisy Sims)	12 Apr 1902	7 Apr 1984	
J. Hobert "Pat")	10 Aug 1896	24 Sep 1977	
Lucille S.)	27 Aug 1900	NOD	
J. Sam	29 Jun 1904	17 Jan 1967	
J. W.)	24 Aug 1874	23 Jan 1974	
Lydia Harrison)	10 Dec 1874	5 Mar 1964	w/o J.W.
Troy R.)	7 Feb 1907	24 Sep 1965	
Marion F.)	7 Mar 1918	27 Nov 1983	
Wanda P.)	25 Sep 1921	NOD	
Vickie Gail	OD	27 May 1961	Infant d/o Louise & Victor
MOREE-J. LeVonne	28 Feb 1937	20 Jul 1967	
Naomi S.	19 Dec 1905	11 Nov 1975	
MORIE-Arthur T.	28 Aug 1900	30 Jun 1971	
Charles A.)	1877	1966	
Martha E.)	1880	1956	
Thomas O. "Ott"	9 Apr 1902	19 Dec 1978	
PFC T. Spencer)	23 Aug 1917	20 Feb 1945	HQ Co 3BN 376 Inf APO 94
J. Herman NICHOLSON)	15 Aug 1922	16 Apr 1985	HQ Co Sig C 287 Sig Co Aus
MURRY-Faye)	1965	1965	
Kaye)			
NAPOLITANO-Jane Ella			
Patterson	25 Oct 1916	18 Apr 1973	(See Paul L. PATTERSON)
NELSON-Ira David	23 Aug 1902	29 Jan 1977	
NEWMAN-Clarnce R.)	Born & died	30 Dec 1941	
Reba M.)	8 Sep 1942	9 Sep 1942	
Ruby L.)	16 Mar 1944	23 Mar 1944	
NICHOLS-Eunice E.	16 Sep 1918	16 Dec 1922	
Joe H.)	20 Oct 1921	21 Jul 1984	Pvt US Army WWII
Edith C.)	26 Aug 1923	NOD	
John H.)	4 Jul 1854	21 Aug 1942	
Susan S.)	22 Aug 1852	19 Nov 1939	
Donald M.)	16 Jan 1890	9 Apr 1920	

NICHOLS-Gussie   15 Feb 1883   30 Jul 1930
    Kenneth C.   7 Nov 1893   6 Dec 1918
    Katie P.   2 Jan 1888   8 Jul 1889
    Wyatt F.   )   1 Dec 1828   14 Feb 1903
    Marodah Hill   )   1 Nov 1836   12 Oct 1908   w/o Wyatt F.
    James G.   )   6 Dec 1864   27 Dec 1942
    Ida Jane Clabough)   21 Mar 1876   29 Apr 1947   w/o James G.
    Capt. Hollis L.   )   19 Mar 1870   19 Feb 1942
    W. Randal   )   13 Feb 1867   10 Jul 1927
    Martha C.   )   17 Feb 1872   23 Sep 1874
    Catherine M. Hill)   7 May 1871   18 Jan 1940   w/o W. Randal
NICHOLSON-J. Herman   )   15 Aug 1922   16 Apr 1985   HQ Co Sig C 287 Sig Co Aus
    PFC T. Spencer MORIE)   23 Aug 1917   20 Feb 1945   HQ Co 3 BN 376 Inf APO 94
                                                                Born Tenn.; Died Germany

    Robert M.)   24 Aug 1889   25 Nov 1967
    Bertha B.)   14 Jan 1907   NOD
O'DELL-Horace W.   20 Mar 1903   21 Feb 1968   s/o M/M Joe
OWEN-James L.   6 Apr 1912   19 Aug 1983   Maj US Marine Corps WWII
OWENS-Chalres B.)   28 Aug 1877   25 May 1964
    Florence N.   )   29 Nov 1900   6 Oct 1969
PACKARD-Lynn George)   1 Jun 1908   21 Apr 1979   Pvt US Marines WWII
PAINTER-Margaret Lee Lethco   11 Dec 1901   25 Jun 1952
PARKER-Caro L.   18 Jun 1921   12 Aug 1963
    Charlie H.   )   20 Mar 1892   12 Aug 1983
    Addie Lindsey)   26 Apr 1897   9 May 1979
PARROTT-Doris Ann   14 Oct 1943   4 Jul 1944
    Jess B.   19 Feb 1898   12 Nov 1952
    Alice E.   14 Dec 1888   NOD
PATTERSON-Callie)   29 Sep 1887   6 May 1950
    Sallie   )   4 Apr 1890   3 Jan 1923
    Johnny R.   6 Sep 1947   17 Sep 1960
    Leonard L.)   6 Jun 1886   14 May 1944
    Josie E.   )   8 Aug 1888   15 Nov 1970
    Paul L.   31 Dec 1918   28 Mar 1947
    Jane Ella Patterson NAPOLITANO
                                    25 Oct 1916   18 Apr 1975
    Ralph R.   )   22 Aug 1900   20 Jun 1983
    Chloe   )   14 Aug 1900   5 Aug 1972
    Barbara Lou)   5 Aug 1932   25 Mar 1947
    Ralph J.)   23 May 1915   30 Nov 1984   Married 17 Jul 1937
    Gladys R.)   27 Aug 1921   25 Jun 1979
    Silas   )   14 Mar 1900   NOD
    Julia H.)   5 Aug 1899   29 Jun 1980
PHILLIPS-Alfred A.   1893   1932
    Gypsie Carter   1901   1984
    George F.   )   30 Jan 1892   27 Feb 1958
    Fannie Brown)   1 Aug 1892   22 Jul 1964
POE-Buford   )   9 Dec 1900   16 Jan 1938
    Florence M.)   26 Apr 1900   17 Mar 1983
PRICE-Infant   OD   12 Dec 1966   d/o Glen & Margaret
    William Lee)   9 Sep 1896   19 Jul 1958
    Ola Branum)   9 Aug 1898   20 Aug 1979
PUCKETT-Henry C.)   29 Sep 1906   21 Jul 1973
    Altha V.   )   21 Apr 1912   NOD
QUINN-Raymond)   15 Nov 1918   3 Nov 1968
    Gertrude D.)   30 Nov 1921   25 Nov 1980
RAINWATER-Sara H.   16 Jul 1898   17 Dec 1966   w/o Chester S.
RAMSEY-W. Claude)   10 Apr 1910   NOD
    Ina Ruth E.)   9 Oct 1914   28 Jan 1970

RAMSEY-Jack E.)	2 Jan 1939	10 Feb 1984	Married 4 Jul 1963
Frances I.)	18 Jul 1939	NOD	
REDDEN-William L.)	11 Feb 1901	22 Mar 1981	
Hazel J.)	31 Dec 1905	27 Apr 1981	
REESE-James Robert	28 Dec 1905	1 May 1980	
Jesse Lee)	1 Jul 1894	16 Nov 1960	
Della V.)	11 May 1897	14 Nov 1963	
Josie	18 Feb 1899	11 Feb 1964	
Lester)	2 Mar 1895	11 Aug 1979	
Hudie F.)	26 Oct 1898	4 Aug 1977	
Mabel Manning	7 Aug 1917	1 Dec 1979	
RENEAU-Clare N.)	19 Jan 1926	NOD	
Mildred H.)	3 Nov 1931	NOD	
Claude	8 Feb 1912	22 Sep 1955	
George W.	20 Jun 1904	16 Jul 1980	
John N.	15 Nov 1888	4 Apr 1962	
Willie M.)	21 Nov 1915	7 Aug 1981	
Agnes W.)	19 Mar 1916	NOD	
REYNOLDS-Earl Joseph)	21 Jan 1896	15 Apr 1971	
Betty Brodgen)	24 May 1896	21 Oct 1976	
RICKARD-Burnice S.	19 Apr 1916	4 Oct 1977	Tec 4 US Army WWII
RILEY-George Henry, Jr.))	26 Jan 1878	3 Aug 1962	Father
Anna Laurabell Newman)	14 May 1877	24 Feb 1953	Mother
RIMMER-Hugh K.)	16 Oct 1914	NOD	
Emma S.)	8 Jun 1930	NOD	
Shade H.)	4 Mar 1875	20 Dec 1954	
Minnie Rimmer BEAVER)	2 Oct 1893	12 Nov 1975	
RINEHART-Charles H.)	29 Feb 1896	NOD	
Callie C. Strange)	19 Mar 1900	NOD	
ROBERTS-C. E.	1 May 1903	13 Dec 1964	
Earl E.	5 Oct 1935	1 Sep 1984	SSgt US Air Force Vietnam
RODERICK-Daniel A.)	31 Oct 1881	14 May 1966	Tn Pvt Co D 26 Inf Spanish-American War
Jennie B.)	10 Mar 1885	24 Feb 1973	
ROMINES-A. Clyde	26 Apr 1899	NOD	
Elsie F.	1 May 1899	8 Feb 1970	
Zola Mae	14 Jan 1912	NOD	
RUSSELL-Florence	1904	1960	
SCAGGS-A. C.)	20 Sep 1872	20 Mar 1947	
Lonie)	27 Mar 1880	10 Mar 1962	
Fred)	11 May 1901	7 Apr 1983	
Jessie W.)	26 Mar 1903	15 Jun 1927	
Ralph Louis)	28 Aug 1903	1 Aug 1984	
SCARLETT-Arthur)	24 May 1883	23 Aug 1955	
Nora Mae)	14 Oct 1894	9 Feb 1969	
Clyde H.	21 Mar 1910	29 Jun 1942	
Mary Ruth	26 Apr 1932	6 Oct 1932	
SCHEAN-Dennis Sidney	9 Sep 1956	30 Sep 1982	
SCOTT-Carrie K.	5 Jun 1881	3 May 1947	
SHAW-Rev. Kyle L.)	15 Sep 1912	12 Sep 1980	
Mary I.)	16 Oct 1920	NOD	
SHELL-Belle S.	9 May 1908	12 Jun 1965	
SHEPHERD-Robert "Bob"	4 Feb 1907	22 Aug 1969	Known as John Riley "Buck" Barton, a true friend and faithful helper for 23 years
SHERROD-Robert Lincoln	8 Aug 1893	17 Dec 1982	PFC US Army
William M. II)	13 Jun 1949	26 May 1966	
Robert Anthony)	OD	11 Jul 1968	Infant

SHURBUTT-William S.	28 May 1870	10 Mar 1953	
Nancy Houser	4 Dec 1882	15 Jun 1947	w/o William S.
SIMMS-James T.)	24 Jun 1945	NOD	
Joyce E.)	25 Jul 1944	NOD	
SLOVER-Benj H.)	Died	17 Mar 1909	
Malinda)	Died	27 Feb 1928	
Isaac B.)	Died	24 Dec 1921	
Isaac B., Jr.)	Died	19 May 1900	
SMELCER-Alfred B.)	2 May 1907	12 May 1972	
Trula)	No dates		
SMITH-Lloyd W.	31 Aug 1909	12 Mar 1974	
SNODDERLY-James E., Jr.	23 Sep 1948	24 Sep 1948	
SOLOMON-Sanford J.C.)	8 Sep 1916	18 Apr 1982	PFC US Army WWII
Katie Lee)	17 Sep 1907	26 Jul 1979	
W. L. "Buss")	21 May 1909	17 Feb 1975	
Martha Ray)	7 Dec 1913	13 May 1974	
STONE-Robert E.	15 Jul 1908	18 Jul 1981	
STRAND-Alfred B., Sr.)	25 Sep 1895	1 Oct 1982	
Margaret Boynton)	20 Oct 1905	23 Sep 1978	
STRANGE-Leon C.)	24 Jan 1919	NOD	
Reva E.)	23 May 1919	18 Sep 1977	
Mack S., Jr.	5 Jun 1940	16 Apr 1985	
Mack S.)	2 May 1904	1 Aug 1980	
Mae H.)	5 Nov 1909	24 May 1957	
Perry)	4 Sep 1894	10 Aug 1971	
Helen)	14 Jul 1919	22 Jun 1971	
William H.)	5 Nov 1878	3 Jul 1946	
Edie B.)	22 Dec 1889	17 Nov 1978	
James Murphy)	4 Nov 1905	22 Feb 1978	
Mollie J.)	4 Apr 1911	1 May 1966	
SWAFFORD-Rev. Robert Garth)	28 Aug 1921	7 Oct 1982	
Mary Kathleen)	20 May 1933	NOD	
SWANN-C. L. "Judge")	20 Apr 1884	7 Feb 1960	
Flora)	28 May 1886	28 May 1950	
Hollis L.)	19 Nov 1881	4 Dec 1903	
James Edward)	12 Feb 1873	8 Aug 1968	
Josie Lyle)	28 Jan 1874	8 Jan 1952	
Edward Lyle)	7 Feb 1900	5 Jan 1939	
Frances Swann TRIGG)	2 May 1909	3 Aug 1957	
Irene Allen)	26 Sep 1906	27 Sep 1983	
Sarah Miriam)	6 Mar 1906	10 Aug 1983	
John C.)	13 Oct 1874	13 Jan 1944	
Lara Ellis)	22 Oct 1874	3 Nov 1941	
Lucille H.)	8 Sep 1896	13 Jan 1957	
John L.	8 May 1927	16 Sep 1977	
Mack)	24 Nov 1890	23 Apr 1953	
Lula L.)	15 Feb 1889	31 Jan 1969	
Ray	4 Dec 1909	9 Jan 1977	
Robert)	22 Oct 1845	27 Jan 1928	
Nancy E. Nichols)	31 Mar 1858	29 Oct 1944	His wife
Will M.)	14 Apr 1878	1 Mar 1962	
Lula Henderson)	24 Jan 1889	10 Nov 1971	
TAYLOR-Joe E.	2 Oct 1920	29 Jan 1977	EM2 US Navy WWII (See Benjamin Henry ZIRKLE)
THOMAS-Charles J.)	18 Jul 1887	17 Sep 1956	
Elizabeth Houser)	21 Jun 1892	25 Apr 1951	w/o Charles J.
Hubert E.)	1911	NOD	
Leta Harrell)	1914	NOD	

THORNTON-Katherine Reese	7 Dec 1905	18 Jun 1983	
Lillie N.	9 Jun 1890	21 Jan 1974	
TIPTON-Rex	25 May 1930	4 Feb 1978	s/o Holbert & Nora
TODD-Mildred Mills	5 Jan 1920	31 Dec 1976	
TOMLINSON-Charles)	13 Nov 1877	15 Jul 1961	
Hassie R.)	16 Oct 1878	25 Apr 1978	
Robert L.)	18 Jun 1903	12 Jan 1975	
Ollie P.)	12 Nov 1903	6 Sep 1971	
TOMPKINS-James A.	1896	1952	
TOWNSEND-James M.)	31 Jul 1883	11 Feb 1974	
Francis M.)	29 Jan 1893	18 Apr 1971	
Lem B.)	28 Mar 1894	2 Feb 1948	
TRIGG-Frances Swann	2 May 1909	3 Aug 1957	(See James Edward SWANN)
VANCE-Daisy C. Slover	No dates		
VANDERGRIFF-Tarence H.	13 Jul 1921	14 Feb 1981	Cpl US Army WWII
VANDYKE-Robert J.	12 Apr 1910	19 Jun 1954	
WALKER-Alfred L.)	30 Jul 1917	NOD	
Inez Landrum)	15 Jul 1916	25 Jan 1980	
Edward Sharp)	6 Jan 1941	17 Jul 1981	
Ella Mae Vest)	24 Sep 1937	NOD	
James C.	Died	10 Feb 1921	
Josie L.	Died	4 Mar 1972	
Mary Ellen	Died	29 Mar 1952	
Louise Solomon	21 Sep 1918	18 Dec 1981	
M. Janice	9 Apr 1942	30 Apr 1950	
WARREN-Mrs. Mary	Died	16 Apr 1984	Age 56y (FHM-McCarty)
WEBB-James R.	22 May 1926	16 Mar 1968	TN PFC 53 BN 18 Rein Depot WWII
John A.)	26 Sep 1883	3 May 1945	
Anna B.)	27 Oct 1896	18 May 1978	
Thomas Lane	8 Jan 1922	18 Sep 1978	Sgt US Army WWII
WHALEY-Lenora Messer	10 Sep 1897	25 Oct 1983	
WHEELER-Virgil L.	29 Oct 1922	14 Feb 1967	
WILLIAMS-Bruce)	10 Nov 1892	28 Jul 1975	
Josie P.)	10 Jan 1898	29 Oct 1979	
Lon H.)	18 Mar 1908	15 Jan 1971	
Edna B.)	8 Dec 1908	NOD	
Glenn Edward)	30 Jan 1937	4 Apr 1980	A2C US Air Force - Korea
WILSON-Charles A.)	9 Dec 1918	4 Oct 1983	
Forriest M.)	12 Jan 1919	NOD	
WISHART-Jessie M.	12 Oct 1914	12 Mar 1966	
WIX-Thomas H., Sr.	29 May 1883	19 Sep 1974	
Thomas Haynes, Jr.	7 Mar 1916	14 Jul 1972	
WOODS-Cathy Ann	26 May 1954	29 May 1954	
Wayne Leslie)	1 Mar 1917	22 Mar 1979	
Gladys D.)	No dates		
WOODY-Nancy C.	20 Dec 1895	16 Apr 1958	
WORKMAN-James T.)	15 Jul 1916	26 May 1967	
Bertha M.)	9 Jun 1923	NOD	
Clancie E.)	17 Dec 1949	17 Aug 1968	
YATES-Otie Lester)	3 Feb 1888	9 Mar 1969	W. VA., Pvt US Army (2nd
Ollie B.)	6 Feb 1898	21 Feb 1984	stone says died 8 Mar 1969)
ZIRKLE-Benjamin Henry)	26 Jun 1894	1 Dec 1972	
Maggie Belle)	21 Feb 1892	26 Apr 1969	
Joe E. TAYLOR)	2 Oct 1920	29 Jan 1977	EM2 US Navy WWII
Eloise MILLS)	23 Jan 1952	21 Mar 1976	d/o M/M H. L. MILLS
George Campbell)	29 May 1899	25 Jan 1975	
Elsie Jane Potts)	11 Oct 1902	NOD	

This large cemetery began with the reinterment of graves moved from Douglas Dam
by TVA about 1941-42. To reach the site, take Exit 417 from I-40. Turn south
toward Dandridge on State 92 and drive 1.7 miles to the intersection with
US25W-70. Turn right onto US25-70 and drive west toward Knoxville for 1.3 miles.
The cemetery is on the right.

This massive monument in Old Hopewell Cemetery marks
the grave of Margaret P. Mitchell, 17 Mar 1818-11 Nov 1848.

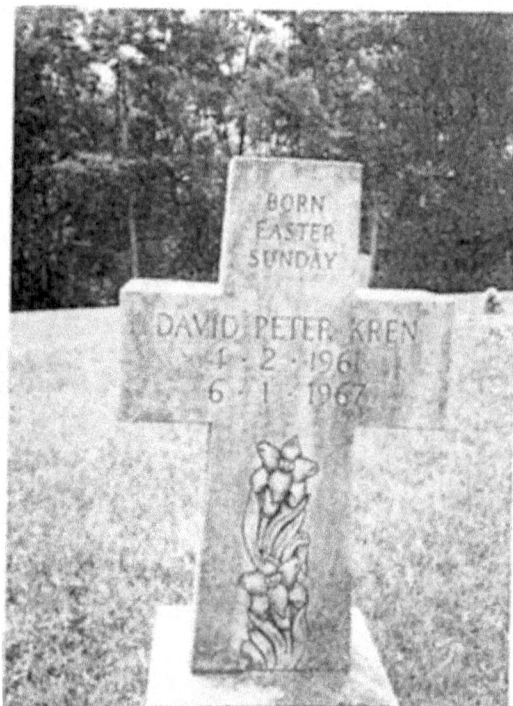

Born Easter Sunday
David Peter Kern
4-2-1961
6-1-1967

AILEY-Jacob)	19 Apr 1847	30 Mar 1924	
Catharine)	24 Feb 1854	26 Nov 1934	
ALEXANDER-Margaret M.	Died	15 Nov 1838	2y 15d
Mary P.	Died	13 Nov 1851	48y ----; Consort of J.
Thomas J.	Died	3 Apr 1858	53y 4m 20d
BACON-Darcas	Died	1 Feb 1851	59y 3m 16d
James	Died	16 Mar 1853	6ty
Rebecca	Died	14 Dec 1851	25y 11m 13d
BAILEY-John R.	13 Dec 1858	27 Sep 1859	
Joseph H.	13 Dec 1858	18 Oct 1859	
L. C.	Died	9 Sep 1860	26y 1m 19d; consort of James H.
William E.	Died	13 Nov 1860	s/o J.H. & L.C. 3m 27d
BALCH-John	Died	21 May 184(9?)	88y 6m
BAER-A. I.	24 Jan 1825	27 Sep 1848	
Poley	12 Jul 1795	26 Jan 1872	Consort of John
BARE-John	24 Oct 1792	13 Oct 1846	
BETTIS-Isabel H.	4 Aug 1801	26 Apr 1872	w/o J.W.
Martha J.	15 Apr 1834	15 Aug 1869	w/o P.J.
Rufus E.	20 Aug 1869	17 Aug 1869	s/o Martha & P.J.
S. W.	21 Sep 1810	1 Nov 1849	39y 1m 11d
William H.	26 Sep 1866	10 Apr 1870	s/o Martha & P.J.
BEST-Dr. F. P.	OD	9 Feb 1912	Father
E. S.	OD	11 Nov 1934	Mother
BIRDWELL-A. R.	Died	16 Jul 1845	wy (illegible)
Harriett M.	Died	14 Jun 1851	
Twin Boys	Born & died	29 Jan 1847	
BLACKBURN-Andrew	3 Dec 1770	1 Nov 1844	
Catharin	20 Jul 1779	20 Feb 1837	Consort of Andrew
Edward	3 Jan 1780	26 Sep 1853	
Peggy	19 Oct 1779	1 Oct 1850	Consort of Edward
Harriett E.	22 Feb 1846	17 May 1871	w/o W.W.
John)	24 Mar 1778	28 Feb 1868	
Elizabeth McGuirk)	19 Jul 1782	3 Apr 1867	w/o John
Martha M.	Died	22 Jun 1875	d/o B.A. & Isabella M. 35y
Mary A. D.	Died	23 Jan 1838	2y 3m 3d
Sarah M.	Died	8 Jul 1854	2y 2m 6d
William I. I.	26 Jul 1822	4 Dec 1852	
BOWMAN-Virginia	Died	22 Jun 1853	2m18d;d/o Griffith M. &_
BRADFORD-Infant	Born & died	14 Sep 1848	d/o W.M. & E.K.
Charles H. N. B.	17 Jan 1831	6 Feb 1837	6y 20d
James	25 Dec 1777	20 Jun 1839	61y 5m 25d
James K.	Died	6 Oct 1839	s/o Alexander K. & Jane 1y 6m
Jos. W.	21 Jan 1833	10 Sep 1856	23y 8m 11d
Kitty L.	Died	10 Feb 1837	d/o Alexander K. & Jane 1y 2m 19d
Manassa	Died	17 May 1864	2y 9m 14d
Napoleon B.	Died	Aug 1833	26y 11m 20d (worn)
N. B.	Died	11 Sep 1857	3y 9m 15d; s/o A.K. and Margaret
Rachel M.	6 Dec 1857	15 Jan 1858	
Sarah Inman	Died	19 Dec 1852	d/o W.M. & E.K.;8m
BRANNER-Annie Lila	Died	15 Apr 1868	d/o M.T. & A.; 13m 22d
Casper	Died	22 Nov 1867	79y 6m

BRANNER-Mariah	8 Jan 1793	18 Nov 1847	w/o Casper
Mary Darthula	5 Jan 1856	14 Sep 1857	d/o M.T. & A.
BRAZELTON-J. G.	Died	29 Jan 1852	34y 11m 11d
CARSON-Infant	Born dead	30 Oct 1845	d/o James & Ataline
Which never had a name because it never breathed			
Juliet H.	7 Jan 1816	10 May 1839	23y 4m 3d
CARTER-Mrs. Elizabeth	1797	1835	38y 5m 11d (broken)
H. C.	Died	15 Nov 1844	
M. J.	Died	25 Aug 1833	(broken)
Presley	Died	1840	
R. H.	Died	7 Apr 1846	
COCKE-Capt. Stephen M.	Died	27 Apr 1864	
COGSIL-C.W.	30 Sep 1825	3 Mar 1853	of Carrollton, O., Teacher in Maury Academy
COOK-Thomas A.	Died	17 May 1855	8y 2m 10d; Erected by his brother Robert 1902; s/o A.B. & N.T.
CORBET-Cztherine J.	25 Jun 1853	28 Nov 1853	5m 3d
James	Died	10 Oct 1855	71y 17d
Mary Gresham	No dates		w/o James; about 96y
COX-Margaret	Died	4 Feb 1853	
CROOKSHANKS-Isabella Ann	7 Dec 1848	7 Oct 1850	
Isabella White	Died	1 Jul 1850	49y; consort of Dr. G.M.
Sara E.	2 Feb 1831	7 Aug 1848	
DAUBINS-S. H.	Died	14 Feb 1846	3y 9m 28d
Margaret Jane	Died	10 Feb 1849	2y 3m 20d
Wm. C.	Died	3 Feb 1853	20y 6m 10d
DENTON-George I.	22 May 1866	22 Dec 1871	s/o J.W. & M.
DEWEY-Joel A.	20 Sep 1840	17 Jun 1873	
DICK-James H.	11 Feb 1857	22 Jul 1859	s/o H.J. & S.A.
Mary E.	10 Dec 1848	2 Aug 1850	d/o H.J. & S.A.
Roena M.	10 Dec 1859	9 Jun 1860	d/o H.J. & S.A.
DICKEY-James	10 Feb 1789	13 Sep 1847	(very worn)
DOGGETT-Florence Swann	Died	11 Feb 1904	w/o Goyne O.; d/o James P. & Victoria SWANN
James Preston	17 Aug 1902	6 Sep 1904	s/o Goyne O. & Florence
DRAKE-Charlotte M.	1913	1984	(fhm-Farrar)
DUNKIN-Mary E.	27 Nov 1814	24 Oct 1859	
DUNWODY-Easther B.	Died	20 Nov 1857	64y 9m 14d
Patrick	31 Jan 1789	-- Feb 187-	(broken)
EDGAR-Andrew	7 Nov 1769	1 Apr 1849	
Elisebeth	23 Dec 1836	25 Oct 1869	w/o W.I.I.
Geo. D.	Died	24 May 1844	
John H.	Died	12 Feb 1849	55y 3m
Sarah T.	19 Mar 1812	9 Apr 1870	58y 20d
EVANS-Eva A.	Born & died	8 Apr 1863	(broken 11 pieces)
James	24 Dec 1818	22 Dec 1864	45y 11m 29d (broken)
John N.	Died	17 Feb 1837	s/o Thomas L. & Letitia M.; 1y 5m 3d
Lucy	Died	14 Sep 1847	67y 4d
Nancy C.	Died	26 Mar 1848	46y 8m
FAGALA-David)	16 Dec 1811	28 Jul 1866	
Penelope F.)	26 Jul 1819	25 Aug 1902	His wife
Jessie Lee	20 Jun 1876	(OD born)	10d; d/o G.W. & M.C.
FAIN-Miss Elizabeth	Died	22 Nov 1876	90y
Hannah E.	16 Feb 1855	17 Mar 1871	
Infant	No dates		d/o T.W. & N.D.
Isabella C.	9 Aug 1862	17 Jul 1878	

FAIN-James H.	31 Aug 1817	20 Aug 1836	
John	20 Apr 1778	11 Oct 1852	
Amelia S.	14 Feb 1794	24 Feb 1864	
Josiah	1 Jan 1802	9 Mar 1872	70y 2m 9d
Maria L. E.	1 Feb 1837	25 May 1860	w/o John N.;d/o Col. Wm. & M.A. Moore; died at Cypress Cottage near Osceola, Arkansas
Mattie C. Moore	No dates		w/o John N.; erected by her loving daughter Flora
Mattie Stephen	8 Sep 1865	16 Dec 1867	d/o Geo. A. & Eliza R. 2y 3m 8d
Thomas G.	22 May 1815	4 Mar 1890	74y 9m 12d
Elizabeth C.	5 Nov 1823	20 Jul 1847	Consort of W.D.
Samuel N.	8 Oct 1858	10 Aug 1859	
FOLAND-Emaline	24 Feb 1825	5 Sep 1848	
FRANKLIN-Owen	Died	21 Feb 1831	(part of stone remains)
Elizabeth	Died	22 Nov 1852	Consort of Owen
Robert	Died	10 Dec 1837	35y 4m 23d (broken)
FREE-Arthur	1908	1985	(fhm-Farrar)
GARDNER-Agnes	21 Jan 1872	6 Nov 1876	d/o J.E. & C.K.
GASS-Rev. Andrew	Died	8 Jul 1859	66y 2m; of Holston Conf.
Mary P.	Died	26 Jan 1850	71y; consort of Rev. Andrew
Daniel P.	2 Jun 1851	14 Apr 1852	s/o Daniel P. & Elizabeth 10m 12d
Florence Iowa	22 Jul 1853	31 May 1855	d/o Elizabeth A. & D.P. 1y 10m 9d (lying on stump)
Ida J.	17 Oct 1872	9 Oct 1873	d/o ___ & Mary A.(broken)
Infant	Born dead	3 Nov 1851	s/o Andrew W. & Mary Ann
John J.	Died	1 Aug 1838	s/o James T. & Elizabeth; ry 9m 20d
John W.	Died	27 Dec 1855	s/o John C. & M.H.; 5m
Letitia H.	17 Dec 1820	1 May 1875	w/o J. A. (broken)
Martha I.	21 Jan 1843	16 May 1882	d/o J.A. & L.H. (broken)
Martha J.	Died	12 Jan 1856	d/o Martha M. & J. Cox; .10m 22d
Mary E.	Died	18 Jan 1861	d/o J.A. & L.H.; 12y 4m 2d
Nancy	24 Jul 1798	9 Jul 1851	52y 11m 15d
Nancy S.	Died	26 Jun 1854	d/o A.T. & F.A.; 1y 5m 3d
William B.	29 Aug 1822	5 Mar 1865	
William H.	Died	10 Dec 1854	s/o Andrew W. & Mary Ann 1y 6m 12d
GENTRY-Darthula Ann	Died	15 Dec 1854	27y 20d
Rhoda	23 Oct 1807	22 Oct 1870	
Charles	10 Apr 1794	16 Sep 1946	52y 5m 6d; (broken)
GOOCH-J. H.)	30 Mar 1872	19 Aug 1924	
Rachel)	21 Aug 1872	26 Sep 1928	
GRAHAM-Cynthia	21 Dec 1798	4 Aug 1881	w/o Wm.; 82y 7m 14d
HALE-William	Died	31 Mar 1851	
HAMILTON-Col. Joseph	Died	3 Nov 1874	79y 11m
Nancy	No dates		46y 15d
Robert)	No dates		
Dorcas Cowan)	No dates		
HAMMER-Louisa E.	7 Nov 1853	1 Apr 1874	w/o J.F. 20y 5m 24d; She was a consistent member of the M.E. Church
S. F.	18 Feb 1873	15 May 1874	

HARRIS-Infant	No dates		s/o H.M. & W.
Isaac F.	Died	7 Jan 1851	s/o M.A. & T.; 13d
HAYS-Alexander	Died	May 1845	62y 10m 20d
Alexander	4 Mar 1842	7 Nov 1852 or 3 (broken)	
Jessie M.	20 Feb 1839	30 Jun 1862	(broken)
Margaret	20 Feb 1766	23 Oct 1848	82y 8m 3d
Margaret	29 Jan 1837	26 Aug 1852	
HEDRICK- Infant	No dates		d/o Luisa J. & Benjamin
Louisa J.	Died	21 May 1859	Consort of Benjamin 22y 1d
HELM-Ruth	29 Dec 1814	18 Jun 1836	
Ruth N.	18 Jun 1836	22 Feb 1838	
HENDRICK-Vanerson	29 Jan 1828		(broken)
HENKLE-George	Died	8 Dec 1852	84y
Susannah	Died	10 Dec 1852	82y
HENRY-Eastier J.	Died	20 Feb 1860	Consort of Silas; 58y 3m 19d
Joseph Ray	27 May 1902	25 Apr 1978	Cpl. US Army WWII
Joseph R. Jr.	14 Jan 1934	31 May 1975	PFC US Army
Ralphine Swann	1910	1934	
HILL-Edward N.	2 Sep 1822	11 Feb 1849	26y 5m 9d
Flora V.	1 May 1881	19 May 1902	
J. P.)	1 Jan 1844	29 May 1920	
Mary L.)	15 Dec 1853	17 Jan 1944	His wife
Mary F.	25 Mar 1845	25 Oct 1866	
Ollie Mae	26 Nov 1883	10 Sep 1901	
S. E.	No dates		d/o R.D. & A.P.; 2y 4m
HINKLE-Solomon	4 Feb 1822	11 Oct 1847	
Francis M.	5 Jul 1827	21 Jul 1872	
William	12 Oct 1790	14 Feb 1838	
HYNDS-Ann B.	8 Dec 1819	2 Feb 1892	Born in Alderton, England; Her last Prayer was for her Thousand Pupils
Daughter	8 Feb 1861	30 Apr 1863	d/o Geo. H. & E.K.
Hon. Robert H.	6 Apr 1802	16 Jul 1856	54y 3m 10d
Mary Jane W.	4 Dec 1810	19 Nov 1850	
HOOD-Nathe. E.	21 Jun 1842	28 Jun 1862	s/o Rev. N. Hood
_____ella W.	28 Apr 1807	30 Jun 1849	Consort of Nathiel (broken)
HOSKINS-Charles C.	Died	29 Oct 1846	42y 8m 29d
James J. P.	Died	3 Apr 1857	17y 2m 23d
HOTSENPILLER-Athy	Died	23 Jan 1855	Consort of John; 39y 9m 28d
HUNTER-Hugh H.	6 Jan 1889	31 Oct 1972	
Hugh H.	1891	1986	(fhm-Farrar)
INMAN-Catherine Bradford)	20 Mar 1817	1 Apr 1857	
Jane Martin	9 May 1811	3 Aug 1852	
KING-Elizabeth J.	26 Feb 1826	23 Jul 1858	w/o John
LANCASTER-Nancy Ivy	23 Sep 1822	5 May 1873	Consort of J.M.; died in Knoxville (broken)
LAWLESS-Agness H.	Died	12 Nov 1848	20y 7m 19d
William	Died	16 Aug 1851	s/o T.H. & E.; 16 7m 23d
LAYMAN-Mary Catherine	Died	4 Feb 1852	d/o Griffith W. & Timanda S.; 7m 23d
LITTLETON-Thomas Herbert	9 May 1886	12 Sep 1887	s/o George H. & Nena G.
LYLE-Amanda E.	12 Jan 1842	17 Jan 1872	30y 5d
Miram	Died	12 Nov 1850	40y 4m 12d
Samuel A.	29 May 1840	2 Jul 1862	
Samuel R.	28 Jan 1806	2 Aug 1848	42y 6m 5d
Samuel	27 May 1847	9 Aug 1834	

McCAMPBELL-Rev. John, D.D.	8 Apr 1781	28 Sep 1859	
Katarin	23 Jun 1798	14 Aug 1872	w/o Rev. John (broken)
McCORD-Robert	Died	1 Feb 1853	25y 9m 11d
Samuel H.	Died	16 Mar 1853	33y 2m 24d
Ann Elizabeth	Died	11 Feb 1853	22y 3m 9d; w/o Samuel H.
McGUIRE-James M.	Died	2 Dec 1859	s/o Eli & Rebecca A.; 2y 8m 8d
Michael	Died	28 Jun 1855	67y 1m
Harriett	Died	24 May 1878	w/o M.; 79y 2m 9d
McSPADDEN-Archibald L.	15 Apr 1798	Aug 1830	
Isabella	1 Jan 1802	26 Sep 1837	
Mary Caroline	7 May 1812	1 Dec 1852	Consort of ___l; (worn)
Mary J.	6 Apr 1848	5 Sep 1857	
Milton H.	Died	13 Mar 1846	39y 10m 9d
Robert Whiteside	17 Oct 1838	26 Apr 1849	
Samuel Alexander	1831	24 Oct 1840	(very worn)
MANARD-William R.	Died	30 Nov 1910	68y
MARSHALL-Infant	Born & died	15 Apr 1850	s/o I.C. & R.A.
MARTIN-Andrew R.	20 Apr 1823	4 Sep 1847	
Hugh	Died	15 Dec 1839	69y 11m 8d
Lemuel B.	10 Sep 1875	23 Aug 1930	
Josie Ethel Cannon	15 Sep 1879	17 May 1952	
R. M.	27 May 1853	5 Jul 1916	
Mary F.	29 Aug 1848	7 Oct 1922	w/o R. M.
MATHES-Alexander W.	19 Sep 1833	22 Nov 1863	30y 2m 3d
James T.	15 Jul 1823	9 Aug 1850	
Luther M.	Died	30 Dec 1844	15y 1m 20d
Milton H.	Died	25 May 1845	19y 5m 17d
Rachel P.	12 Jan 1791	19 Jul 1877	w/o Wm.; 86y 6m 7d
William	Died	25 May 1844	56y 10m 5d
MATIN-Mrs. Sarah	Died	9 May 1830	In the 41st year of her age
MEEK-A. W.	2 Apr 1843	22 Jun 1844	
John Beecher	12 Dec 1848	13 Mar 1881	
MEEKE-James P.	Died	22 Aug 1840	29y 3m 5d
MILLER-C. C.)	22 Jun 1840	21 Jan 1908	
Martha E.)	7 May 1843	7 Jan 1912	His wife
Chas. M.)	Died	31 May 1876	80y 5m
Sarah)	Died	14 Nov 1876	89y 10m
George W.)	Died	7 Nov 1876	57y
Frank A.	8 Jul 1872	18 May 1915	
Maurice C.	25 Oct 1874	5 Aug 1902	
MITCHELL-Berry	27 Oct 1787	28 May 1868	(broken)
Elizabeth	26 Jun 1784	3 Jun 1861	
Berry	17 May 1813	7 Jan 1889	
Elizabeth D.	8 Jan 1809	24 Sep 1899	
Hannibal Bruce	2 Feb 1852	6 Sep 1874	22y 7m 4d
James)	11 Jan 1812	30 Nov 1872	
Elsie)	22 Feb 1818	5 Mar 1890	His wife
James H.	10 Apr 1844	14 Nov 1864	s/o Berry & Elizabeth D.
John C.	7 Feb 1836	18 Sep 1858	s/o Berry & Elizabeth D.
Joseph N.	21 Apr 1852	23 Oct 1853	Youngest s/o Berry & Elizabeth
Lon B.	26 Apr 1847	19 Aug 1927	
Margaret P.	17 Mar 1818	11 Nov 1848	30y 6m 24d
Mattie E.	21 Jun 1851	24 Sep 1869	Youngest d/o W. M. & Penelope; 18y 3m 3d

MOORE-Aurther W.	3 May 1863	31 Jan 1864	s/o W.B. & A.A.; 8m 28d
Joseph G.	15 Oct 1828	15 Jan 1912	
Lonie	No dates		
Lutetia	16 Jan 1868	14 Dec 1868	d/o W.B. & A.A.; 10m 28d
Mary A.	20 Jul 1811	5 Jan 1874	Born Greene Co., TN;
	Fell asleep in Jesus at Rome, Georgia		
Dr. Wm.	Died	14 Sep 1838	55y 3m 19d (broken)
MORT-Cyrenius M.	22 Aug 1832	15 Jul 1869	Born Shenanadoah Co, VA
Sarah C. Rankin	2 Oct 1835	1 Feb 1899	w/o Cyrenius
Noah W.	29 Dec 1836	19 Nov 1854	
NEWMAN-Sinea	Died	23 Mar 1833	Consort of Aaron; 27y 10m 17d
NICELEY-Emma A.	14 Jun 1863	30 May 1867	d/o J.J. & A.R.
Mary V.	Died	26 Aug 1855	d/o J.J. & A.R.;8m 14d
NICHOLS-E.W.C.	21 May 1819	5 Dec 1867	
Wyet Manson	27 Sep 1865	10 Sep 1867	s/o E.W. & P.P.; Born in Sevier County (broken)
NICHOLSON-C. H.	7 Jun 1839	27 Feb 1864	Eldest s/o W.M. & P.
Infant	Stillborn	28 Jun 1844	d/o A. M. & Malinda
James M.	1 Dec 1801	6 Aug 1886	84y 8m 5d
Rachel	Died	4 Oct 1872	w/o J.M.;aged abt. 56y
John W.	Died	8 Dec 1843	s/o A.M. & Malinda 14m 5d
OWENS-Alexander	29 Jul 1845	29 Oct 1869	24y 3m
PARK-William F.)	9 Aug 1845	16 Jun 1921	
Cordie)	17 Jul 1845	11 Aug 1920	His wife
PENNIGON-Don	OD	1980	(fhm-Farrar)
PIERCE-Eliza J.	10 Jul 1827	2 Oct 1845	
RANKIN-Caroline M.T.	14 Feb 1800	24 May 1833	(broken)
James D.	3 Apr 1809	9 Jun 1878	69y 2m 6d
Margaret	Died	17 Mar 1895	w/o James D.; 82y 10m 7d
Sally	Sep 1796	3 Apr 1888	
Thomas	6 Jan 1794	-- --- ----	(broken)
__ eris___ (broken)	Died	25 Jan 1860	d/o J.D. & M.
REYNOLDS-Mary	4 Sep 1906	27 Sep 1906	d/o Henry & Ethel M.
RIMMER-Hugh	19 Aug 1905	24 Jun 1906	s/o G.W. & N.E.
John H.)	15 Sep 1834	22 Jan 1913	
Susan D.)	25 Mar 1847	1 Jun 1943	His wife
ROSS-Martha G.	26 Feb 1824	14 Feb 1863	
SANDRIDGE-Happy Jane	Died	2 Jul 1860	Consort of J.D.;22y 8m 13d
SARTAIN-David Alexander	Died	16 Dec 1854	15y 10m (broken)
John R.	23 Oct 1851	7 Jul 1869	(broken)
Mandy E.	26 May 1846	18 May 1867	
Mollie J.	27 Oct 1856	19 Apr 1873	16y 5m 22d
Nancy I.	25 Jan 1841	22 Sep 1868	
Pryor L.	9 Jul 1818	1 Jan 1871	
Elizabeth	14 May 1818	25 May 1868	w/o Pryor L.
Samuel M.	3 Apr 1849	1 Jul 1868	
Sarah M.	18 Feb 1845	28 Mar 1876	Was a member of M.E. Church and died in sweet peace
SCOTT-Nancy A.	17 Sep 1850	26 Dec 1871	w/o W. G.
Rachel Isabella	Died	14 Mar 1847	d/o P. & R.H.; 3m 12d
Robert H.	Died	12 Mar 1856	60y 28d
Prudence	Died	3 May 1850	Consort of R.H.; 41y
SEBOLT-Diana	17 Jan 1812	28 Oct 1865	w/o John; 53y 9m 11d

SEHORNE-Samuel L.	23 Feb 1842	23 Nov 1864	s/o J.P. & J.C.
SENTER-William Tandy	29 Apr 1904	19 Apr 1905	s/o Dr. W.T. & Elizabeth
W. T.	2 Feb 1874	3 Nov 1905	Father
SHADDAN-Elizabeth J.	Died	9 Aug 1854	d/o E. & W.;1y 4m 18d
Twin Infants	Born & died	17 Sep 1846	i/o E. & W.
SHEDDAN-Amos A.	1 Mar 1823	26 Aug 1847	24y 5m 25d
James	Died	22 May 1833	aged about 58y
John H.	19 May 1842	2 Apr 1853	
John H.	10 May 1805	5 Sep 1842	37y 3m 25d
Margaret W.	5 Mar 1807	25 Jul 1838	31y 4m 20d
Margaret A.	24 Mar 1835	21 Feb 1853	
Mary M.	Died	15 Sep 1860	37y 4m
Thomas A.	31 Mar 1824	27 Sep 1851	27y 5m 27d
William	10 Jul 1778	17 Aug 1841	63y 1m 7d
Elizabeth	Died	27 Jul 1856	Consort of William; 75y 11m 8d
Wilson)	2 Dec 1810	11 Aug 1873	
Eliza)	10 Aug 1816	22 Oct 1902	
William P.	16 Jan 1831	5 Aug 1851	
SHEDDEN-James S.	24 Sep 1801	31 May 1871	(broken)
Mary L.	3 May 1812	21 Jan 1878	w/o James S.
Willson	2 Dec 1810	11 Aug 1873	
SHEPHARD-James W.)	12 Jul 1870	26 Mar 1940	
Mattie)	15 Oct 1868	23 Jan 1932	
SHEPPARD-Calvin)	14 May 1843	20 Apr 1932	
Mary Payne)	3 Sep 1840	2 Mar 1881	His wife
Inez	14 Mar 1896	11 Jul 1905	d/o Walter & Mattie
SIMPSON-James B.	Died	28 Jul 1842	s/o G.W. & M.E.; 17d
Margaret E.	Died	7 Sep 1855	Consort of G.W.;36y 6m 15d
SMITH-William Tempel	Died	21 May 1861	s/o D. & S.J.;11m 2d
Eva P.	16 May 1891	3 Jun 1907	d/o J.H. & Mary D.
SNAPP-Martha L.J.	20 Mar 1828	10 Aug 1885	
STEEL-(broken)	27 Oct 1809	3 Sep 1841	Consort of ___ am H.
			(broken; footstone reads M.S.)
STERN-Amanda C.	Died	6 Dec 1854	d/o J. & C.;1y 7m 1d
SWANN-Cynthia	Died	21 Sep 1911	d/o the late James P. & Victoria C.
James Preston	Died	13 Mar 1884	65y
Victoria C. Graham	OD	8 Apr 1923	w/o James P.
Ralph L.	1875	1937	
Victoria Hill	1871	1951	
SWORD-Infant	Died	1 May 1854	d/o C. & J.; 2d
TUCK-James H.	9 Oct 1852	5 Aug 1855	
VANCE-Adeline	6 Jul 1842	12 Jun 1878	
Lydia	Died	24 Jun 1841	1y 5m 4d
WALKER-George W.	Died	10 Feb 1876	s/o W. & E.;21y 7m 16d
Louiza C.	Died	10 Nov 1874	d/o W. & E.;16y 10m 9d
William	Died	16 Dec 1874	47y 6m 18d
Elizabeth H.	30 Jun 1829	21 Jan 1900	
WEST-John D.)	28 Nov 1862	30 Jan 1888	s/o Dr. T.A. & S.B.
Thomas James)	28 Jan 1886	21 Jul 1886	s/o John D. & Neta P.

To reach this cemetery, begin at the Jefferson County Courthouse in Dandridge.
Drive 1 block north to US25W-70 and turn right. Drive 1 block and turn left
onto Hopewell Street. The new section of the cemetery and the church are on the
right. On the left is the old section.

HOPEWELL CEMETERY

ALEY-Arthur	9 Dec 1877	25 Apr 1917	s/o Jacob & Katie; killed by lightning
Lula J.	7 Apr 1886	26 Jan 1918	w/o Arthur
ALEXANDER-Winnie	1808	1889	
BELL-Florence	1880	1897	d/o S. J.
BENTON-Menda Jane	5 Aug 1855	10 Jan 1886	
BETTIS-Anna Grace	21 May 1878	28 Jun 1878	
Chas. M.)	12 Aug 1862	6 Mar 1903	
Alda C.)	24 Jun 1858	12 Mar 1910	His wife
Cordelia	2 Nov 1835	18 Sep 1909	
D. L.	1837	1920	
E. A. H.	3 Jan 1839	9 May 1896	
Emma W.	24 Mar 1881	8 Jun 1967	
Frank Eugene)	5 Jun 1884	17 Jun 1963	
Lana Morgan)	14 Oct 1884	2 May 1964	
Ina A.	4 Jun 1916	4 Nov 1948	
Infant	Born & died	12 Jan 1923	
James William	3 May 1913	13 Dec 1921	
John E.	15 Feb 1872	20 Jan 1939	
John Eugene	23 Apr 1907	30 Oct 1976	MUS2 US Navy WWII
John W.	3 Mar 1801	15 Jul 1879	
Lina J.	30 Jun 1842	15 Jun 1878	
Mattie B.	5 Jul 1874	19 Oct 1960	
P. J.	6 Apr 1835	3 Mar 1912	
Samuel O.)	8 Feb 1865	21 Jan 1935	
Maude R.)	10 Jul 1873	16 Nov 1963	
Sarah Porter	29 Oct 1915	13 Nov 1915	
Sarah Naomi	17 Apr 1889	15 Jan 1923	
BISHOP-Logene	5 May 1916	5 May 1916	d/o W. J. & P.J.
BLACKBURN-Carrie	Born & died	20 Jun 1887	d/o W. W. & H.R.
Charles A.	20 Jul 1878	25 Mar 1962	
Edith R.	27 Dec 1880	27 Nov 1965	
Horace Edmond	28 Apr 1876	17 Jun 1919	
Hugh H.	26 Sep 1895	9 Nov 1915	s/o Will & Ida
Infant	23 Mar 1905	OD (Born)	s/o M/M C. A.
William W.)	15 Nov 1869	24 Dec 1927	
Ida A. Harrison)	22 Nov 1872	23 Nov 1942	His wife
William Wirt)	9 Apr 1838	31 Dec 1915	
Harriet Roxanna Miller)	13 Jun 1846	2 Aug 1921	
BOLINGER-Annie Gass	17 Jul 1855	12 Aug 1912	w/o G. W.
BOWEN-Mary J.	18 Jul 1818	17 Feb 1891	(See J.R. Colvin)
BRADLEY-Judson T.	21 Jan 1854	28 Oct 1888	s/o W. & E.
Lou F.	13 Jan 1862	18 May 1881	d/o Wilson & E.F.
Wilson)	11 Oct 1829	OD (Born)	
Elizabeth)	26 Nov 1818	OD (Born)	w/o Wilson
BREEDEN-pat	1930	1930	
BRYAN-Andrew F.)	1865	1939	
Mary F.)	1875	1935	
CALDWELL-Mollie E.	13 May 1856	25 Aug 1921	
CARMICHAEL-George H.	18 Nov 1872	13 Oct 1953	
Mary H.	21 May 1875	23 Jul 1921	
CARSON-James H.	20 Nov 1801	25 May 1880	78y 6m 5d; a true friend of education, one of the founders of Carson Newman College

CARSON-Mrs. Lavina T.	7 Nov 1803	21 Oct 1879	7ty 11m 14d; w/o James H.
W. C.)	13 Mar 1818	12 Apr 1885	
Susan P.)	15 Jun 1825	28 Dec 1885	w/o William C.
COLBOCH-Jacob L.	24 Apr 1861	26 Nov 1916	
John M.	17 Mar 1883	15 Jan 1884	s/o Noah & Susan
COLVIN-J. R.)	9 Nov 1820	9 Jan 1899	
Mary J. Bowen)	18 Jul 1818	14 Feb 1891	
S. F.)	23 Sep 1824	14 Jun 1882	
Hattie M.)	9 Mar 1837	10 Jan 1918	
CORBETT-John A.	4 Nov 1880	16 Dec 1918	
Bertha Fuller	16 Oct 1883	30 Apr 1936	
John O.	20 May 1851	16 Jun 1900	49y 26d
Susan Rimmer	2 Dec 1857	29 Nov 1935	w/o John O.
T. R.	17 May 1860	23 Apr 1933	
Mary A.	17 Jun 1853	27 Mar 1891	w/o J.T.
COWAN-Harris	20 Jan 1897	4 Jan 1899	s/o A.W. & Eva
Dr. Joel W.)	22 Dec 1855	23 Feb 1946	Father
Ellen O.)	9 Jan 1876	14 Nov 1968	Mother
J. B.)	26 Sep 1898	10 Oct 1958	Son
Charles)	25 Apr 1901	28 Jan 1958	Son
Rue	3 Dec 1902	4 Jul 1904	s/o A.W. & Eva M.
COX-Naomi	10 Oct 1891	7 Feb 1917	d/o W.C. & L.E.
W. C.	11 Jul 1865	15 Jan 1939	
Lou Ella Carmichael	10 Jan 1869	13 Feb 1929	w/o W.C.
Wm. Thomas)	21 Oct 1881	21 Aug 1924	
Ollie Mae)	16 Jul 1879	7 Dec 1940	
CRAWFORD-J.S.	23 Oct 1862	17 Sep 1887	
William	7 Mar 1819	8 Mar 1890	
Elizabeth J.	1 Aug 1829	6 Jun 1914	
Susan M.	12 Oct 1870	4 Jun 1893	
CROWLEY-Jack M.	9 Aug 1929	20 Nov 1976	US Army
DANIELS-Mattie Hill Newman	3 Nov 1880	14 Sep 1957	
DENTON-Hugh W.)	30 Apr 1858	28 Mar 1940	
M. F.)	27 Jul 1860	7 Mar 1937	w/o H.W.
Jake E.)	9 Aug 1880	25 Aug 1951	
Mattie Hill)	16 Aug 1882	21 Sep 1931	
J. J.	Died	13 Oct 1922	Age 67y
Joe L.	7 Jun 1900	30 Jul 1930	
Lelia Annis	5 Jul 1892	16 Nov 1894	d/o H.W. & M.F.
Menda Jane	5 Aug 1855	10 Jan 1886	
Worley)	15 Jun 1897	20 Sep 1936	
Mary)	23 Apr 1892	23 May 1972	
ECKEL-Silas McRoy	12 Sep 1882	9 Jul 1884	s/o M. & E.R.
EDGAR-Elizabeth	1 Aug 1805	5 Jul 1887	w/o John H.
Darthula H.	3 Mar 1837	9 Oct 1882	45y 7m 6d
Margaret I.	28 Jan 1839	9 Aug 1879	40y 6m 12d (broken)
Samuel J.	19 Apr 1836	7 Jan 1892	55y 2m 18d
Wm. Martin	22 Apr 1844	10 Jul 1903	59y 2m 18d
ELLIS-James A.)	4 Dec 1855	8 Nov 1930	
Nancy C. Ward)	4 Jul 1858	8 Nov 1928	His wife
ELLISON-Stella Hayes	17 Apr 1897	20 Nov 1920	
FAGALA-James H.	12 Jan 1881	18 Jul 1882	s/o G.W. & M.A.
Mattie C.	23 Feb 1852	5 Apr 1879	w/o George W.; 27y 1m 13d
FAIN-Frank Bachman)	16 Feb 1906	10 Jun 1979	
Edna Dalby)	10 Dec 1912	NOD	

FAIN-George A.)	12 Nov 1832	4 Jan 1902	
Eliza Ruth Moore)	10 Nov 1834	18 Nov 1900	Beloved wife of George A.
Julia Maude	10 Oct 1886	28 Jul 1891	d/o W.A. & D.A.
Mrs. Lucy E.	No dates		
Margaret Ruth	4 Dec 1897	14 Jul 1980	
Samuel Clark, MD)	25 Jul 1902	31 Oct 1981	
Virginia Hunt)	3 Jul 1903	NOD	
Dr. Sam W.)	24 Mar 1868	17 Sep 1910	
Mary Clark)	5 May 1875	7 Mar 1952	
W. A.	29 Aug 1843	5 Feb 1920	Co K, E. Tenn Cav. C.S.A. 1861-1865
FAULKNER-John J.)	22 Nov 1830	28 Dec 1907	
Sarah C. Hall)	1 Jul 1836	25 Dec 1902	w/o John J.
Mary A.)	22 May 1862	30 Mar 1940	
Nancy E.)	4 Mar 1860	22 Jun 1878	
FELKNOR-Adrian E.	16 May 1891	7 Sep 1927	
Andrew M.)	4 Sep 1859	14 Oct 1928	
Lucy R.)	25 Oct 1867	27 Sep 1969	
Anne	26 Feb 1899	19 Oct 1982	
G. Ross	18 Apr 1884	8 Dec 1944	
Gus L.	20 Dec 1877	16 Feb 1943	
John H.	13 Apr 1905	13 Aug 1974	
Mary D.	8 Jan 1913	NOD	
John L.	18 Apr 1846	4 Aug 1929	
Darthula Shadden	12 Mar 1846	11 Jan 1923	w/o John L.
M. C. W.	8 Sep 1880	19 Jun 1883	s/o J.L. & D.J.
FINE-Katie	12 Sep 1885	7 Feb 1924	d/o E.H. & Martha
FOUST-Tomie Rainwater	12 Nov 1869	20 Jan 1902	w/o L.C.
FRANKLIN-Mac Calvin)	18 Sep 1880	6 Feb 1962	
Effie B.)	10 Mar 1880	11 Feb 1970	
FRENCH-Conrad)	27 Apr 1904	5 Jan 1962	
Reba H.)	25 Feb 1916	NOD	
Elmer Baxter	11 Feb 1906	6 Nov 1927	
Dr. T. R.)	7 Oct 1870	5 Oct 1855	
Mary Emma)	16 Jul 1878	1 Dec 1959	
FRAME-John H.)	1 Dec 1828	5 Jul 1879	Born Sevier County, died at Mossy Creek
Matilda J. Keeler)	1 Mar 1830	8 Jun 1919	
FRYE-Cora Swann	1902	1948	
FULLER-J. H.	13 Dec 1877	19 Mar 1932	
GALLION-No Name	No dates		
No Name	No dates		
Lila J.	No dates		
GAMBLE-Anna Mae French	10 May 1913	24 Sep 1932	
GASS-Baby Blanche	Born & died	31 Oct 1905	d/o F.L. & H.F.
Frank Lee)	1 Apr 1872	23 Sep 1943	
Hattie Fox)	25 Jun 1876	8 May 1957	
James A.)	20 Jun 1845	10 Dec 1911	
Emma M.)	4 Apr 1850	24 Nov 1926	His wife
James A.)	4 Oct 1818	6 Jul 1893	
Frances WRINKLE)	27 Aug 1855	11 Feb 1886	She sleeps beneath her native earth and near the spot that gave her birth.
James Myrle	20 Aug 1901	7 Mar 1903	s/o F.L. & H.F.
Jim Berry			
Lettie Kate	30 Aug 1903	21 Apr 1904	d/o F.L. & M.F.
Ma-----	1 Dec 1824	31 Jan 1883	28y 2m;w/o J. Cox Gass(broken)

GASS-Martha Malinda	1 Dec 1824	31 Jan 1883	58y 2m (2 stones)
Rettie T.	1 Jan 1857	18 May 1882	w/o J.A. (broken)
GAULT-John	28 Dec 1793	1 Nov 1880	
GAUT-Jane McAmash	18 Dec 1806	5 Jan 1896	
GORDON-Frank S.	14 Dec 1878	30 Jun 1949	
Dr. Joseph E.	16 Sep 1880	14 Mar 1941	
GREGG-Nellie	4 May 1901	24 Feb 1924	w/o J.H.
GROTH-Dr. J.H.	29 Mar 1893	30 May 1975	
Clara Rimmer	8 Aug 1903	15 Nov 1982	w/o Dr. J.H.
GWINN-Napoleon B.	6 Aug 1832	13 Jan 1880	47y 5m 17d
Mary L.	15 Jan 1834	23 Feb 1918	
HALE-Ann Holtsinger	30 Oct 1870	25 Jan 1943	
HARRIS-Charley M.	22 Aug 1877	9 Sep 1879	s/o Henry & Emma J.
Emma J.	20 Feb 1838	15 Jul 1916	w/o Henry
HART-Eva M.	15 Apr 1901	9 Dec 1984	
Hobert I., Sr.)	12 May 1897	10 Apr 1966	
Mae H.)	9 Mar 1900	NOD	
Joe M.)	9 Jul 1851	22 Jun 1944	
Julie C.)	10 Jan 1872	28 Apr 1937	
Joseph Bryan	16 Apr 1958	31 Aug 1958	s/o Mae & LeRoy
HAVIS-Katie L.	Died	15 Nov 1878	18y 5m 7d
HAYES-G. E. "Hugh")	2 Dec 1854	24 Jun 1917	
Sue Smith)	4 Aug 1859	21 May 1925	w/o Hugh
HAYROW-Henry Herbert	23 Feb 1890	4 May 1957	NY PFC Med Dept WWI
Lucile Lyle	16 Feb 1892	29 Mar 1960	
HEDRICK-Joe L.	19 Sep 1851	4 Apr 1907	
Margaret Hendrick	26 May 1864	13 Sep 1940	w/o Joe L.
HENDRICKS-Lawson H.)	1824	1899	
Mary E.)	1831	1899	
Izorah)	1849	1924	
Willie S.)	1868	1894	
HENRY-Elizabeth	9 Oct 1831	14 Apr 1887	w/o S.H.
John Formwalt	4 mar 1903	28 Apr 1967	
Virgie Conway	8 Sep 1908	23 May 1956	w/o Formwalt
Ruth Conway	8 Oct 1904	15 Mar 1934	w/o Formwalt
Kathleen Ray	23 Dec 1891	7 Dec 1902	d/o J.R. & Lucy F.
			10y 11m 15d
Silas H.	25 May 1839	31 Jan 1915	76y 8m 6d
Catharine E.	22 Jan 1842	26 Oct 1896	54y 9m 4d; w/o S.H.
HICKS-Emily Jane	OD	14 Jan 1939	Infant
Gladys R.	19 Mar 1910	15 Mar 1979	
Infant	No dates		
J. C.)	1 Apr 1869	27 Nov 1939	
M. E.)	23 Sep 1868	NOD	
Sammie	OD	23 Oct 1939	Infant
Tommy	OD	6 Sep 1937	Infant
William M.)	1896	NOD	
Neta	1898	1941	
HILL-Amanda P.	29 Jan 1824	27 Mar 1883	w/o R.D.
John Martin)	1826	12 Sep 1903	Born Knoxville, TN
Eliza Mitchell)	20 Sep 1834	11 Jun 1904	His wife
HOLTSINGER-Arthur)	5 Dec 1881	2 Apr 1954	
Alma C.)	16 Jun 1882	4 Dec 1963	
George W.	11 Aug 1836	27 Sep 1906	
Loretta A.	4 Jan 1844	24 Jan 1931	
Grace	30 Dec 1885	20 Nov 1943	
John D.	5 Mar 1878	16 Nov 1960	

HOLTSINGER-George Arthur   29 Jun 1913   3 Jul 1928
    Wallace   27 Dec 1883   12 Dec 1959
HOSKINS-Martha Evaline   8 Dec 1859   7 Oct 1882   w/o I.H.
    Louisa E.   28 Jun 1843   23 Aug 1878   w/o I.H.
    Martha Lucinda)   19 Jan 1845   7 Mar 1881   w/o I.H. (broken)
    James Martha)   3 Nov 1880   7 Mar 1881   d/o I.H. & M.L.
HUTSELL-Jimmie Seabolt   11 Sep 1860   21 Nov 1904   w/o R.L.
HYNDS-Alberta   23 Dec 1906   2 Jul 1917   d/o Alex & Annie
    Alexander   8 Nov 1853   11 Aug 1916
    Anne Duncan   26 Dec 1865   5 Oct 1947   w/o Alex; known and
                                                             beloved as "Mis Ann"

JACK-M.J.   1823   1879
NO LAST NAME-F.H.J.   1876   1879   (These two stones are field-
    J.J.   1853   1879   stones with initials only.
                                                             They are in the row with M.J. Jack)

JOHNSON-Clinton Powell   28 Oct 1935   NOD
    Ann Sherrod   23 Dec 1935   NOD
    Samuel P.   6 Sep 1813   12 May 1883
JONES-Adeline McGuire   26 Jul 1831   26 Jun 1912   w/o David
    Cecil Clark   14 Dec 1917   23 Nov 1967
    Eliza   10 Jun 1817   13 Feb 1889   Consort of G.W.
KILLIAN-Rebecca Fuller   6 Jun 1883   27 Apr 1971
KREN-David Peter   2 Apr 1961   1 Jun 1967   Born Easter Sunday
LETHCO-Dorothy R.   1914   1956
    Infant   OD   22 Feb 1927   d/o M/M Frank
    James A.   14 Oct 1934   14 Dec 1934
LEWIS-Jane   24 Oct 1842   5 Oct 1913
LICHLYTER-Aaron   13 Jan 1845   29 Jan 1927
    Lula   17 Aug 1865   18 Jul 1916
    Martha   20 Oct 1843   30 Oct 1900
LOWE-Mrs. Ed   19 Aug 1826   6 Jan 1902   Formerly Widow of J.M.
                                                             THOMAS (See J.M. THOMAS)

LYLE-Rev. Hubert Samuel, D.D. 1 Mar 1873   21 Mar 1931   s/o W.H. & S.P.; died
                                                             while president of Washington College
    Millicent Candee Robinson 18 Jul 1880   14 Aug 1958   w/o Hubert, DAR 198898
    Jas. Lamar   1 Dec 1865   14 Jan 1936
    Clementine Blackburn   18 Dec 1868   19 Apr 1951
    Lura Jane   20 Aug 1870   26 Jan 1948
    Sara Porter   19 Jan 1894   28 Oct 1969
    William Alexander   16 Apr 1868   13 May 1940
    Ruth Harris   22 Oct 1870   9 Apr 1936
    Rev. William Harris)   2 Oct 1838   11 Aug 1905
    Sarah Porter Mathes)   15 Jun 1843   15 May 1878   His wife
    Harriet L. Mathes   )   10 Dec 1840   2 Jan 1907   His wife
    Rose Mariam   )   9 Jun 1876   29 May 1903   d/o W.H. & S.P.
McCRARY-Hallie McGuire   1 Aug 1862   18 Dec 1940
McCUISTON-Maj. S.S.   Died   13 Jan 1893   75y almost. For many
                                                             years a county official

McGUIRE-Belle)   8 Feb 1870   13 Oct 1929
    David   )   12 Apr 1910   10 Mar 1929   Her son
    Eglantine I.   1 Aug 1832   14 Jun 1916
    George H.   13 Jan 1857   19 Feb 1940
    John   )   15 Aug 1822   13 Nov 1881   Ruling elder of the church
    Catharine)   21 Sep 1816   5 Mar 1892   Wife
    Tip Maze   23 Nov 1890   2 Sep 1894   s/o Geo. H. & Belle

McLAIN-Earl	1 Dec 1892	19 Oct 1894	s/o Geo. J. & Della
MANN-Lucinda	3 Oct 1821	14 May 1902	
William	Died	30 Mar 1885	65y 5m 21d (broken)
MARTIN-Lucy Ray	11 Jul 1914	15 Aug 1914	d/o I.N. & N.E.
W. B.)	10 Apr 1857	6 Dec 1925	
Julia Ann)	12 Mar 1863	12 Feb 1944	
William T.)	30 Jul 1905	22 Sep 1943	
Reva P.)	11 Nov 1917	NOD	
MATHES-Rev. Wm. A.	28 Sep 1814	25 Sep 1899	
Margaret M.	14 May 1818	20 Dec 1881	63y 7m 6d; w/o Rev. W.A.
Harriet Edgar	18 Sep 1831	15 Oct 1905	2nd wife of Rev. W.A.
MILLER-Margaret J. Dobson	24 Oct 1817	23 Apr 1885	w/o Edwin B.
Tinsley J.)	1896	1941	
Nannie E.)	1900	NOD	
MITCHELL-Bruce H.)	11 Dec 1874	21 Dec 1919	
Nelle R.)	14 Oct 1876	23 Feb 1920	His wife
John	3 Jan 1815	13 Dec 1900	85y 11m 10d
Vaughn	16 Apr 1901	24 Oct 1908	s/o B.H. & Nellie
Wm. H.	8 Mar 1817	18 May 1885	
Lucinda C.	5 Sep 1820	28 Jun 1885	
MOORE-John A.	30 Jun 1845	24 Feb 1885	
Mollie A.	27 Dec 1849	20 Aug 1884	w/o John A; d/o J. & C.C. Smith (broken)
Jud	No dates		
Ida M.	31 May 1884	29 Aug 1884	d/o J.A. & M.A.(Broken)
William A.)	28 Aug 1842	7 May 1912	
Louisa Lewis)	31 Mar 1849	10 May 1914	
NEWMAN-Auther U.	21 May 1916	27 May 1916	s/o N.D. & Dollie
Carl Lafayette	25 Dec 1918	5 Mar 1937	
Fred William	1 Apr 1928	11 May 1946	
James	1 Jun 1917	1 Jun 1917	s/o N.D. & D.M.
John T.)	22 Dec 1850	28 Feb 1917	
Sarah Sadie)	14 Jul 1851	1 Feb 1936	
J. L.)	5 Sep 1885	3 Feb 1938	
Margaret E.)	24 Jul 1862	27 May 1944	
Mack	26 Jul 1857	22 Dec 1939	
Samuel Rankin, Sr.	8 Mar 1880	25 Dec 1939	
Della Byerley	21 Dec 1879	21 Mar 1966	
W. L.)	15 Jul 1874	5 Feb 1953	
Jennie)	10 Feb 1875	17 May 1927	
Pearl C. Bales	1 Nov 1887	26 Oct 1956	w/o W.L.
NICELEY-Charles P.	4 Jan 1868	22 Nov 1886	
Laura J.	19 Jun 1861	11 Mar 1883	d/o J.J. & A.R.; 2y 8m 22d
NICHOLS-Adam Stone)	20 Nov 1869	24 Jan 1961	
Sarah Frances)	7 Sep 1871	2 Dec 1956	
Hollis H.)	5 Aug 1907	2 Jan 1983	
Martha F.)	8 Jan 1915	NOD	
NICHOLSON-Penelope	3 Apr 1816	26 Sep 18(91?)	w/o J.M. (broken)
NORTH-Andrew J.	18 Apr 1866	18 Apr 1923	
Willie B.	16 Apr 1869	5 Mar 1905	w/o A.J.
Anna Lee	2 Jul 1927	3 Jul 1927	d/o Ray & Daisy
Connie F.	2 Mar 1905	12 Jul 1905	s/o A.J. & M.B.
Cora M.	8 Feb 1900	3 Mar 1921	
George M.	18 Apr 1859	29 Jun 1911	s/o John & E.C.
Jesse B.)	22 Jan 1874	6 Feb 1955	
Nannie A.)	16 Jan 1872	17 Aug 1952	

NORTH-John C.	1 Jan 1825	19 Apr 1901	76y 3m 19d
Elizabeth C.	3 Jul 1836	29 Apr 1916	w/o John
Julia A.	10 Feb 1855	10 Aug 1878	
Reid	7 Jun 1892	17 Apr 1915	
OWENS-Elizabeth	12 Dec 1830	23 Jun 1880	49y 5m _d
Frank Eugene	1919	1921	
Oscar O.)	1880	1952	
Bessie T.)	1884	1934	
PARRIS-James S.	20 Mar 1895	2 Jul 1908	s/o E.M. & L.M.
PATE-Walter B.	16 Nov 1878	15 Feb 1916	
PATTERSON-Wm. C.	14 Oct 1861	30 Aug 1931	
Cumile	29 Jan 1868	5 Nov 1947	
POTEET-Louise F.	18 Aug 1893	4 May 1947	
PRYOR-Eva Barnes	26 Jun 1875	8 Oct 1965	
J. Jackson	21 Aug 1907	26 Sep 1939	
William G.	4 Feb 1862	15 Jul 1940	
RAINWATER-Dr. Brad)	27 Jan 1861	25 Feb 1947	
Nancy Moore)	10 May 1869	10 Mar 1941	
C. c.	21 Jun 1853	28 Oct 1926	
Elizabeth H.	1851	1913	
Floyd	1898	1973	(fhm-Farrar)
Ralph M.)	16 Jan 1875	25 Sep 1947	
Jessie F.)	10 Aug 1889	29 May 1975	
RANKIN-Arthur	1877	1914	s/o Robt. A. & Orill S.
Geo. T.	14 Nov 1844	30 Dec 1896	
Horace M.)	Died	29 Jan 1936	
Josephine Swann)	15 Dec 1870	24 Oct 1931	w/o H.M.
Mary Kate)	Died	23 Jun 1951	
Robert A.	15 Nov 1837	25 Jun 1900	
Orrill S.	19 Aug 1844	20 Aug 1906	w/o R.A.
RENEAU-Margie Lou	0D	25 Apr 1938	inf d/o Claude & Dee
RICHARDSON-Rev. James McGovack	16 Mar 1860	15 Dec 1933	For 50 years a Presby-terian minister
Katherine R.	24 Oct 1870	26 Jun 1913	w/o J. McG
RIMMER-Alexander)	3 Mar 1830	10 Jan 1899	
Sarah A.)	17 Aug 1843	29 Jan 1882	
C. B.)	10 Oct 1879	30 Mar 1962	
Mattie Smith)	1878	1952	
Fay E.	1 Sep 1896	13 Jul 1984	
Frank T.)	30 Aug 1885	4 Oct 1944	
Lillie A. Tomlinson)	2 Dec 1889	21 Sep 1945	w/o F.T.
G. W.)	13 Dec 1870	16 Aug 1931	
Nora E. Smith)			
Harris Webb, Sr.)	11 Aug 1875	10 Jun 1924	
Victoria G.)	30 Apr 1885	22 Feb 1980	
Howard Ray	1912	1955	
Hugh	19 Aug 1905	24 Jun 1906	s/o G.W. & Nora
Infant	Born & died	18 Sep 1905	s/o G.B. & M.E.
John A.	1923	1973	
Margaret Louise	3 Jul 1910	24 Dec 1914	d/o F.T. & L.A.
Martha A.	13 Jan 1849	16 May 1914	
Stephen Dean	28 Mar 1950	1 Jul 1971	
Theodore	8 Nov 1892	5 Mar 1977	Sgt. US Army WWI
ROBERTS-Leander	1883	1942	
Minnie W.	1876	1944	
SANDERS-Grace E.	1 Nov 1927	12 Nov 1927	

SANDERS-James C.)	22 Jul 1880	21 Feb 1931	
Alicia K.)	26 Jul 1892	29 Apr 1970	
Nahum)	12 May 1848	27 Apr 1931	
Grace)	11 Feb 1842	29 Oct 1913	His wife
Sallie E.	18 Nov 1873	7 Nov 1933	
SARRETT-Miss Elizabeth	Died in	Dec 1896	
SARTAIN-Sarah E.D.	31 Mar 1859	15 Mar 1883	w/o John R.; 23y 11m 15d
SCOTT-James (name from WPA)	Died	25 Apr 1827	in 81st year (broken)
Lavinia	Died	25 Jun 1830	in 76th year
SCRUGGS-James	1 Oct 1794	12 May 1850	56y 7m 11d
SEABOLT-George W.)	4 Mar 1835	27 Apr 1907	
Nannie A. Spears)	22 Dec 1837	2 Mar 1909	
John	25 Dec 1811	30 Jan ----	(broken)
SEAHORN-H. H.	22 Feb 1861	12 Sep 1895	
James Hodges	12 Mar 1859	7 Dec 1898	
J. P.)	29 Mar 1816	17 Feb 1893	
Jane Camel)	1 Apr 1819	13 Jan 1894	His wife
SEAHORNE-Susan E.	22 May 1844	28 Oct 1884	d/o J.P. & J.C.
SETLIFFE-James Alvin	22 Feb 1907	25 Jul 1966	
Geneva Bettis	24 Aug 1905	26 Dec 1957	
SHADDEN-Eliza	17 Feb 1839	9 Oct 1892	
G. M.)	14 Nov 1850	7 Apr 1911	
Hannah Seahorn)	19 Jan 1852	7 Dec 1918	His wife
J. A.)	17 Jun 1860	31 May 1937	
Lucy S. Bettis)	22 May 1869	25 Oct 1925	w/o J.A.
T. C.	24 Jan 1833	22 Jul 1913	
Emeline	14 Feb 1833	3 Jan 1905	w/o T.C.
Willie	No dates		
SHADDON-Joe	No dates		
SHEDDAN-Eliabeth	8 Aug 1812	22 Nov 1890	
George W.	7 Jan 1837	16 Oct 1900	
Malinda	6 Sep 1802	21 Mar 1893	
William	3 Jul 1813	6 May 1883	
SHEPARD-Ethel B.	7 Mar 1877	18 Jun 1972	
W. H.	9 Jul 1874	27 Jan 1938	
SHERROD-J. Howard	22 Apr 1873	23 Aug 1942	
Birdie M.	27 Apr 1877	25 Aug 1951	
Lawrence Ray	11 Sep 1907	12 Feb 1985	
Rhea Fox	22 Jun 1911	NOD	
W. Ivan	1 Apr 1904	29 Aug 1966	
James Roy)	OD	27 Aug 1937	
William Robert)	OD	27 Aug 1937	
SHRADER-George Hale	8 Aug 1904	6 Oct 1979	
Blanche Sherrod	10 Jan 1902	NOD	
SLOAT-Mary Ann (broken)	15 Dec 1842	8 May 1881	w/o Rhoten; 38y 6m 23d
SNODGRASS-Albion Wilson)	26 Nov 1857	27 Jun 1892	
Charles Russell)	3 Oct 1890	24 Oct 1895	
Mrs. Lida Pryor	10 Nov 1864	19 Jul 1937	
SPRINKLE-John W.	15 Dec 1914	28 Sep 1983	US Army
Robert L.)	20 Feb 1889	18 Apr 1966	
Margaret Ray Fox)	30 Jul 1892	4 Feb 1928	
SWANN-Della A.	1880	1946	
Little Dan	6 Aug 1893	19 Aug 1897	s/o J.B. & Nannie J.
Harold E.)	6 Jun 1890	14 Jan 1959	
Thula T.)	10 Apr 1892	2 Dec 1981	
H. R. "Hovie"	1928	1929	

SWANN-James J.	Died	30 Sep 1924	70y
J. Bedford)	24 Feb 1850	24 Apr 1911	
Nannie J.)	24 May 1853	12 Jan 1924	
John E.)	20 Mar 1881	4 Jul 1933	
Eva M. Denton)	6 Jul 1883	30 Jan 1939	
Kate	OD	12 Jun 1980	
Kate V.	Died	4 Dec 1922	
Mary A.	1855	1925	
Mary E.	1933	1933	
Pet	25 Nov 1882	20 Apr 1960	
Rachel	Died	21 Mar 1895	
Reuben	Died	11 Sep 1889	
Roscoe C.	Died	20 Aug 1945	Age about 67y
Mrs. Roscoe	Died	21 Apr 1940	
R. R.	1886	1937	Father
William Arthur	5 Aug 1870	6 Nov 1932	
Nina Gwinn	31 Oct 1877	5 Feb 1963	
W. Scott	Died	17 Jan 1880	
TAFF-John D.)	1874	1943	
Martha B.)	1876	1939	
TAYLOR-Nelle Kate	20 Jul 1888	15 Aug 1972	
Rufus M.)	20 Oct 1858	13 Mar 1943	
Amanda Fagala)	29 Oct 1857	7 Apr 1932	
William Rule	3 Dec 1892	7 Feb 1948	
THOMAS-Claude H.	2 Jun 1901	21 Jan 1928	
D. Bernice)	15 Nov 1905	1 Jul 1975	
Ruth F.)	25 Dec 1907	3 Nov 1984	
J. A.)	17 Mar 1875	29 Jan 1931	
Maggie)	24 Dec 1874	NOD	w/o J.A.
James L.	13 Jul 1892	11 Apr 1946	
Jerry M.	14 Dec 1825	22 Jan 1886	60y 1m 8d
J. M.)	L& Dec 1825	22 Jan 1886	
Mrs. Ed LOWE)	19 Aug 1826	6 Jan 1902	Formerly widow of J.M. THOMAS
Milburn W.	27 May 1882	3 Nov 1939	
Susie Fine	12 Dec 1883	14 Jul 1966	
TINSLEY-Hettie	14 Oct 1908	17 Oct 1908	d/o Dr. P.A. & R.A.
Dr. P.A.	1866	1946	
Rebecca	1869	1918	
Ralph	1891	1920	
Walter L.	30 Dec 1889	23 Aug 1934	
TOMLINSON-Joyaecume	22 Mar 1913	25 Mar 1913	
W. F.	4 Apr 1845	24 Feb 1912	
M. M.	3 Dec 1865	13 Dec 1913	w/o W.F.
TOWNSEND Hellen Imigene	5 Jul 1927	6 Jul 1927	
VANCE-Emma Kate	6 Nov 1894	28 Nov 1894	
James W.)	20 Sep 1853	30 Jul 1921	
Nancy Emma)	14 Apr 1858	11 Nov 1894	
Lucy A.	4 Dec 1866	4 Nov 1950	
T. W.	18 FEb 1824	8 Aug 1896	
VINCENT-Bert)	4 May 1896	26 Sep 1969	
Ellen Hynds)	19 Feb 1898	14 Aug 1979	w/o Bert
WACASTER-Josie	18 Nov 1898	20 Feb 1926	
WALKER-John T.	16Feb 1862	26 Sep 1901	
WATKINS-Elven E.	3 Apr 1834	21 Apr 1881	
WEBB-Andrew)	23 Sep 1841	2 Apr 1902	60y 6m 9d
Jane)	24 May 1853	13 Jul 1925	

WEBB-Dorothy Jane	1933	1933	
George C.)	1873	NOD	
Nola S.)	1876	1953	
James S.	20 Mar 1895	2 Jul 1908	s/o E.M. & L.M.
John Waltor	28 Sep 1915	15 Jul 1916	s/o W.H. & M.W.
Richard	24 Jul 1917	23 Sep 1924	
Stella Elizabeth	3 Apr 1904	11 Apr 1904	d/o Geo. E. & Ora
Walton H.	28 Dec 1887	23 Dec 1922	
Willie W. H.	21 Jul 1872	5 Aug 1885	s/o Andrew & N.J.
WEBSTER-Arthur H.	29 Dec 1848	14 Oct 1916	
Cora Bettie	25 May 1893	2 May 1894	d/o A.h. 7 l.w.
Malinda	31 Jul 1831	4 Jul 1895	w/o Jas. C.
WELDON-Lavina	9 Nov 1800	19 Feb 1885	w/o Harvey; 84y 3m 10d
W. E.)	16 Sep 1825	11 Mar 1907	
Kate)	5 Mar 1831	27 Oct 1888	w/o W.E.; 57y 7m 22d
WELLS-James B.	25 Sep 1804	15 May 1882	77y 8m 20d
James Bedwell	26 Jan 1887	30 Jan 1907	s/o J.A. & M.E.
John M.	14 Jul 1879	8 Oct 1879	s/o John S. & Mary E.
J. S.	6 Aug 1847	16 May 1914	
WILLIAMS-Ed S.)	4 Mar 1869	5 Feb 1944	
Sallie H.)	10 May 1884	12 Feb 1970	
Hayes	24 Jun 1906	11 Sep 1908	s/o E.S. & S.H.
Hugh Hayes	10 Mar 1909	7 Oct 1939	
Inez	28 Apr 1912	29 Jan 1916	
George S.	14 Nov 1886	10 Feb 1913	s/o J.C. & Nannie I.
James	26 Jan 1916	6 Feb 1916	
James C.)	25 Mar 1857	19 Oct 1928	
Nannie I. Henry)	20 Apr 1861	17 Oct 1903	
Jesse D.	10 Jun 1893	11 Sep 1893	d/o N.I. & J.C.
Melvin R.)	22 Oct 1903	2 Oct 1971	
Isabel F.)	3 Nov 1907	24 Jul 1985	
WOODSIDE-J.A.	20 Jul 1832	16 Oct 1898	
Margaret E. Fain	4 Jul 1832	21 Jul 1908	w/o James A.
WRINKLE-Frances Gass	27 Aug 1855	11 Feb 1886	

To reach it, begin at the Jefferson County Courthouse in Dandridge. Drive 1 block
north to US25W-70. Turn right and drive 1 block and turn left onto Hopewell St.
The old part of the cemetery is on the left and the new section and the church are
on the right.

MILES JONES CEMETERY

| JONES-M. | Died | 29 Feb 1869 | 65y |
| M. J. Quarls | Died | 19 Jul 1883 | w/o M.; 72y |

In addition to the above, there is one uninscribed fieldstone in this small family cemetery. According to Clyde Jones who now owns the property and is a descendant of Miles Jones, the following is buried here in an unmarked grave:

JONES-Joe Cyrus   s/o M.

To reach this site, begin at the Jefferson County Courthouse in Dandridge. Drive west on St. 139 for 4.9 miles. Turn right onto Patterson Road and drive 2.6 miles. Turn left onto Ralph Jones Road. Drive to the end of this road. There is a barn on the left. Follow the fence to the right and behind the barn. The cemetery is on a hill in a small grove of trees about 450 yards from the barn.

KOONTZ CEMETERY

Though the old, uninscribed fieldstones protruding from a thick carpet of leaves offer evidence of this woodland cemetery, they remain mute as to the identity of those buried here. Koontz descendants, among them Billie McNamara and Ruth Cate, believe this to be the old burial ground of the Michael Koontz family. Fieldstones and depressions indicate the presence of about 25-30 burials in this spot. A TVA survey of the graveyard about 1941 indicates 32 graves -- 16 adults and 16 children. Their records refer to it as the Frank Dawn Cemetery.

This cemetery is difficult to locate. Begin at Exit 417 from I-40. Turn south toward Dandridge on State 92 and drive 1.7 miles to the intersection with US25W-70. Bear left onto US25W-70. From this intersection drive 3.4 miles and turn right. Drive 0.9 miles and turn right onto Dawn Road. Drive 0.4 mile to the last house on the lane. You will need to walk from here. Follow the road for about 100 yards beyond the house. You will pass a white barn and then a red barn, both on the left. Turn right at the red barn and follow the edge of the woods for about 500 yards. You will pass the heads of two large gullies on the way. Turn into the woods to the right. The cemetery is about 25 yards from the edge of the woods.

LOVE CEMETERY

LOVE-Dorothy	Died		27 Apr 1823	Age 73y
Eleanor	Died		27 Jul 1852	72y 9m 23d
John	Died		14 Dec 1854	
Mary		2 Dec 1851	7 May 1853	d/o Joseph & Manerva
William	Died		18 Oct 1847	76y 7m 17d

There are two additional burials in this small cemetery, both marked with uninscribed fieldstones. This cemetery is lucky in that it is cared for by Mrs. Faye Lane, wife of Oliver Lane on whose property it is located. When we visited in October, 1986, each grave was marked with a chrysanthemum ready to burst into bloom. To reach the cemetery, take Exit 417 from I-40. Turn south toward Dandridge on State 92 and drive 1.7 miles to the intersection with US25W-70. Bear left onto US25-70. From this intersection, drive 4.2 miles and turn left. Drive 0.4 miles and turn left onto the drive leading to the house of Oliver and Faye Hall Lane. The cemetery is 0.2 miles ahead on the left at the end of the lane. It is behind the Lane home and beside a farm shed.

Faye Hall Lane doesn't consider the small Love Graveyard in her back yard a nuisance. She regularly tends the graves and has planted chrysanthemums at the base of each stone (left). "William Love, died 18 Oct 1847, 76y, 7m 17d" (right).

MAYNARD BURIAL

MAYNARD-And'w.   No dates   Co. F 9th Tenn Cav

When we visited this cemetery in April, 1986, 6 or 7 fieldstones were still visible, but only the above stone was inscribed. The site is in a pasture field. This cemetery was recorded by the WPA in 1937, at which time they copied only the above stone, but noted that there was evidence of 10-15 burials.

You won't find this cemetery without a guide. To reach the site, begin at Exit 417 from I-40. Turn south toward Dandridge on State 92. Drive 0.8 miles and turn right onto a farm lane beside a brick home. The cemetery is about one mile out the farm lane in a pasture field.

MOUNT ZION
(Shraders Chapel)

ALEWINE-Henry F.	8 Aug 1850	15 Dec 1913	62y 4m 5d
Frances R.	No dates		w/o Henry F.
Samuel Rufus	Died	5 Jul 1952	
ALLEN-Harlie	16 Jan 1899	11 May 1900	s/o W.A. & Sarah M.
Sarah M.	15 Dec 1876	9 Mar 1900	w/o W.A.
BENSON-Abbie	24 Feb 1872	28 Sep 1946	
James Marshal	1 Dec 1881	21 Mar 1907	s/o C.L. & S.L.
Sarah	20 Nov 1859	8 Dec 1914	w/o C.L.
BRYAN-Dama Lee	OD	21 Nov 1921	infant d/o Frank & Stella
CHAMBERS-E. M.	10 Jan 1911	9 Dec 1913	d/o I.J. & I.V.
Frank D.	28 Jun 1906	26 Nov 1929	
Isaac J.)	1881	1942	
Ida W.)	1878	1947	
Jessie Mae	18 Mar 1896	31 Dec 1918	d/o W.P. & M.P.; 22y 9m 13d
William P.)	1850	1934	
Margaret)	1862	1930	
Wm. Roe	25 Feb 1878	8 May 1935	
COX-Anna L.	16 Sep 1913	27 Aug 1923	d/o Jno. & Mary
Fay Gladys	16 Jun 1909	28 Jun 1911	
George M.	15 Jun 1919	21 Nov 1924	s/o John & Mary
J. H.)	8 Oct 1870	28 Jan 1958	
Ola Cline)	19 Jan 1878	15 Sep 1918	
John F.	15 Feb 1929	10 Sep 1929	
Ollie E.	18 Nov 1921	20 Dec 1922	s/o Jno. & Mary
R. Elmer)	14 Mar 1901	12 Nov 1981	married 10 Aug 1919
Ethel B.)	25 Feb 1902	NOD	
Roy Lee)	17 Oct 1893	NOD	
Lillian Howell)	1 Apr 1900	30 Jan 1978	
Vaughn Meridith	2 Aug 1912	2 Mar 1913	
W. N.)	31 Jul 1868	10 Jan 1939	
Ella Cline)	30 Nov 1867	26 Jan 1942	
DENTON-Nannie S. Miller	1 Feb 1891	21 Feb 1982	(see Nannie S. Miller)
ELLISON-Fred	24 Sep 1920	20 Oct 1920	s/o M.E. & J.N.
Lettie	31 Jul 1913	13 Aug 1913	d/o M.E. & J.N.
FAIN-Jessie B.	18 Dec 1901	24 Jun 1978	
Ray	1931	1982	(fhm-Farrar)
FINE-Walter	1 Apr 1881	14 Aug 1953	
FOX-Caswell	No dates		Co. A 9th Tenn. Cav.
Caswell	No dates		Co. K 9th Tenn. Cav.
GALYEAN-Clara Mae	9 Dec 1905	27 Jun 1906	d/o W.T. & M.B.
W. F.)	3 Apr 1876	8 Aug 1930	
Belle Hicks)	9 Sep 1874	19 Dec 1941	His wife
GANN-Mary Z.	2 Oct 1899	8 Mar 1971	
HOOPER-Pauline	3 Feb 1926	5 Nov 1935	
HOWELL-John O.	14 Jun 1844	10 Mar 1917	
Joseph Clyde	30 Apr 1906	18 May 1906	
Mattie A.	27 Nov 1960	23 Nov 1954	
HURST-Otha	10 May 1823	23 Dec 1928	
LANCASTER-George J.)	1866	1947	
Martha J.)	1880	NOD	
George Martin	1923	1981	(fhm-Farrar)
MATHEWS-Levie	26 Mar 1932	16 Jan 1959	
MESSER-Andrew L.)	3 Mar 1923	NOD	
Anna M.)	5 Nov 1929	NOD	
James I.)	30 Jul 1899	18 Feb 1974	
Nola M.)	26 Apr 1898	28 Sep 1966	

MILLER-Fred A.)	5 Jul 1890	31 Jan 1928	
Nannie E.)	1 Feb 1891	NOD	(see Nannie Denton)
MOORE-Will E.)	15 Jul 1892	5 Aug 1956	
Minnie)	25 Aug 1899	1 Feb 1959	
MOREE-John C.)	1866	NOD	
Martha B.)	1869	1941	
MORIE-Harry Roscoe	7 Jan 1895	2 Apr 1979	PFC US Army WWI Co L 119 Inf
RAULERSON-Mattie E.	9 Jul 1880	5 Sep 1909	
RENEAU-Gerald E.	28 Feb 1938	3 Mar 1938	Infant
RICKARD-Arthur M.)	23 May 1872	6 Jan 1931	
Victoria V.)	10 Jan 1872	18 Dec 1925	
Sergt. Wm.	No dates		Co. A 9th Tenn Cav.
RIKARD-Lucy A.	9 Mar 1829	25 Apr 1900	
RIMMER-Claude E.)	21 Sep 1890	28 Jul 1948	
Flora B.)	27 Oct 1896	8 Jan 1921	
ROBERTS-Arthur	10 Jul 1910	6 Nov 1910	
Charlie F.)	28 Jul 1882	14 Aug 1961	
Mary Hicks)	10 Jul 1880	9 Sep 1960	
Claud	13 Jun 1906	25 Nov 1908	
Francis	24 Nov 1908	2 Feb 1909	
Julie Fine	20 Feb 1887	29 Nov 1929	
Veatrice	20 Jul 1914	6 Aug 1914	
SCHRADER-Bettie Maude	16 Nov 1886	30 Mar 1958	
Ersia	15 Sep 1898	29 Apr 1922	
Eugene B.	24 Feb 1897	10 Apr 1943	
Harry S.	20 Oct 1892	16 Jan 1970	
H. C.	5 Mar 1893	28 Mar 1922	
J. P.	21 Feb 1870	6 Apr 1924	
M. E. Williams	22 Dec 1866	4 Oct 1915	w/o J.P.
Maud	6 Jan 1900	16 Jan 1900	d/o J.P. & M.E.
Paul M.	27 Sep 1920	17 Dec 1946	
Roland	11 Oct 1917	15 Aug 1933	
Verne T.	17 Aug 1917	4 Sep 1984	
William A.)	3 Dec 1889	26 Aug 1922	
Jessie C.)	9 Jan 1895	NOD	
SHRADER-Daniel W.	12 Mar 1887	27 Dec 1895	s/o S.B. & Mary A.
George M.	8 Jan 1878	17 Mar 1907	s/o S.B. & Mary A.
J. Blaine)	10 May 1888	17 Oct 1981	
Lydia Finchum)	20 Nov 1888	13 Jun 1952	
S. B.)	28 May 1844	12 Jun 1925	
Mary)	10 Feb 1856	18 Dec 1928	
SLATON-Joseph Porter)	20 May 1884	3 Dec 1954	
Minnie Ann Cox)	2 Oct 1885	20 Oct 1964	
STRANGE-Rufus M.)	25 Nov 1853	21 Jan 1922	
Nancy H.)	22 Jun 1869	10 Apr 1911	
WEBB-James M.	20 Feb 1865	1 Jul 1917	
John W.	11 May 1868	12 Dec 1948	
Dicy	11 Jul 1866	17 Mar 1951	
Josie	25 Jul 1898	(26?)Mar 1898	
J. T.	2 Jul 1897	25 Feb 1911	
WELLS-Ben H.)	1 Jan 1881	28 May 1951	
Ida J.)	7 Dec 1881	8 Jan 1919	
George W.)	14 Aug 1889	1 Oct 1954	
Edna S.)	13 Sep 1895	13 Mar 1985	
Mary C.)	19 Aug 1917	18 Nov 1917	
Harry T.	1895	NOD	
Iva Lindsay	1907	1955	
Mary Wanda	29 Sep 1927	23 Nov 1927	d/o M/M Harry T.

WILDER-Walter G.	22 Jul 1926	17 Feb 1974	Pvt US Army
WILLIAMS-A. I.	6 Sep 1917	18 Apr 1918	d/o T.J. & Z.J.
Carl)	15 Dec 1911	NOD	
Norma S.)	18 May 1922	21 Jan 1983	
D. V.	26 Nov 1903	16 Dec 1903	d/o J.W. & M.C.
Earl	12 Jun 1914	1 Dec 1914	d/o J.W. & M.C.
E. H.	Dec 1842	24 Dec 1923	
Sarah	13 Jul 1851	9 Jul 1906	w/o E.H.
Gracie	9 Jul 1893	16 Jun 1921	
Glenn A.	31 Jul 1934	5 Mar 1935	
John W.)	25 Jun 1872	2 May 1922	
Mary C.)	14 Mar 1882	22 Dec 1945	
L. L.	11 Aug 1912	12 Dec 1913	d/o R.N. & G.G.
Mahaley	2 Aug 1861	28 Jul 1929	
Oliver M.)	1875	1951	
Rebecca J.)	1882	1948	
R. N.	19 Jan 1887	7 Jul 1948	
Thomas J.	21 Sep 1891	26 Feb 1948	
Wilburn	20 Sep 1910	30 Jul 1921	

NO LAST NAME:

Claude	No dates		(These are in line with
Joe	No dates		and match the stone of
Lucy	No dates		Dana Lee BRYAN.)
Roy	No dates		
William	No dates		
Henry C.	1898	1927	(These two stones are in
Jessie Mae	1925	1929	line with and match the
			stones of George J. & Martha
			J. LANCASTER.)

To reach this small, well-kept cemetery, begin at Exit 417 of I-40. Turn south toward Dandridge on State 92 and drive 1.7 miles to the intersection with US25W-70. Turn right onto US25W-70 and drive west toward Knoxville for 1.8 miles. Turn left onto Goose Creek Rd. Drive 0.4 miles. Mount Zion Cemetery is on the right, opposite a church.

The old inscribed fieldstone of Priscilla Goforth Doherty and the new marker added by her descendant A. G. Campbell of Chattanooga. Mr. Campbell has located the grave of George Doherty and will soon place a marker for it. These graves were moved from the old Shady Grove Methodist Church site which is now covered by Douglas Dam.

PATTERSON CEMETERY

JONES-Adam)	20 May 1870	20 Dec 1920	
Ida Van Dyke)	24 Nov 1869	5 Jun 1931	His wife
Clyde D.	24 Aug 1917	17 Dec 1917	s/o R. H. & L. A.
G. H.	10 Jan 1869	26 Jan 1940	
Harit L.	24 Apr 1877	27 Sep 1917	
Rex	26 Jan 1889	29 Jan 1889	
Roy H. Jr.	28 May 1930	16 Apr 1931	
LINDSEY-Lee N.)	1890	1973	PFC WWII
Nora Bell)	1890	1959	
LUTZ-Flora S.	1895	1958	
MILLS-Walter S.	6 Mar 1889	26 Apr 1916	
OWENS-Edward Eulas	17 Jul 1925	14 Mar 1978	
Grace Layman	9 Apr 1937	14 Jun 1975	
Infant	OD	1972	
PARROTT-Daisy	19 Sep 1893	25 Feb 1950	
Infant	OD	17 Aug 1925	s/o M/M Oscar
Infant	OD	25 Jul 1927	d/o M/M Oscar J.
John	14 Sep 1873	7 Feb 1945	
Emily	30 Apr 1879	22 Apr 1954	
Oscar J.	30 May 1886	19 Dec 1967	
Mary V.	18 Jun 1889	5 Sep 1973	
PATTERSON-Harold	24 Feb 1899	24 Sep 1952	
Robert I.)	28 Oct 1869	29 Jul 1948	
Minnie B.)	8 Oct 1876	9 Nov 1958	
William Harold	8 Aug 1924	23 Jun 1958	
RILEY-J. P.	3 Oct 1876	18 Mar 1960	
STINNETT-James R.	OD	1965	(fhm-Farrar)
VANDYKE-C. F.)	28 Nov 1849	4 Mar 1920	
S. J.)	4 Dec 1852	2 Jul 1918	w/oC.F. 65y 6m 28d
G. Ruben	28 Jul 1882	11 Feb 1933	
Henry C.	17 Jan 1800	7 May 1884	
Lucy Cate	12 Feb 1812	2 Apr 1884	w/o H.C.
Lana	7 Oct 1874	3 Apr 1903	
Lucy	8 Dec 1883	17 Aug 1892	d/o C.F. & S.J.
Nellie	29 Nov 1872	15 Nov 1874	d/o C.F. & S.J.
VAN DYKE-A. F. "Free")	7 Nov 1876	23 Jan 1948	
Drocus W.)	14 Nov 1884	12 Mar 1936	
Andrew F.	20 Jul 1861	10 Aug 1904	
Conel C.	1926	1928	
Flossie M.	4 Apr 1899	18 Jan 1924	
Junior	1923	1923	
M. E.	25 Jan 1911	12 Jun 1913	d/o W.A. & B.M.
Rosella	Born & died	5 Jan 1886	d/o C.F. & S.J.
Roy H.	31 Aug 1889	29 Aug 1890	s/o C.F. & S.J.
William M.)	5 Dec 1863	30 Nov 1914	
Emma Jones)	16 Nov 1871	22 Jun 1924	

To reach this cemetery, begin at the Jefferson County Courthouse in Dandridge. Drive west on St. 139 for 4.9 miles. Turn right onto Patterson Road. Drive 1.5 miles and turn right onto Wells Spring Rd. Drive 0.3 miles. The cemetery is on the left.

POOR HOUSE CEMETERY

Death is the "great equalizer" but those buried here are as anonymous in death as they were in life. Not a single grave is identified. Only small, uninscribed fieldstones and rusty funeral home markers identify the site as a cemetery. According to George "Dick" Eslinger, an employee of Jefferson County, this was a graveyard for inmates of the Jefferson County Poor Farm. He remembers assisting in the burial of a man here many years ago, but he does not remember his name. For those interested in burials here, a close reading of county court minutes will often yield many names of those the county paid to have buried. This cemetery is fenced, but is overgrown.

To reach this cemetery, begin at Exit 417 from I-40. Turn south toward Dandridge onto State 92 and drive 0.9 miles. Turn left and drive 0.4 miles. Turn right and drive 0.1 miles. The cemetery is in the overgrown, fenced area on the right.

POOR HOUSE CEMETERY

George Eslinger also recalled hearing that another site had served as a cemetery for the poor farm. Perhaps this was an earlier burial site or a graveyard for the colored poor. The exact spot cannot be pinpointed, but it is west of the Jefferson County Justice Center. When the plans were being made to construct the Center, an effort was made to locate the cemetery, but no trace was found.

To reach this site, begin at Exit 417 from I-40. Turn south toward Dandridge and drive 0.9 miles. Turn left and drive 0.2 miles. The cemetery is said to be in the woods to the right.

REVOLUTIONARY CEMETERY

(OLD HOPEWELL)

BLACKBURN-Benjamin A.	18 Jun 1805	20 Sep 1877	He was a ruling elder in the Presbyterian Church; 72y 4m 12d
Isabell M.	1 Sep 1806	7 Aug 1887	w/o B. A.
HAMMON-S.	Died	18(21?)	84y (fieldstone)
S.		18_1	8m (fieldstone)
I.S.	No dates		(fieldstone)
McCUISTON-No Name	Died	24 Sep 1812	75y (fieldstone)
McSPADDEN-Alvah	21 Jan 1808	13 Dec 1882	74y 10m 22d
Catherine E.	22 Oct 1821	2 Jun 1894	73y 7m 11d; w/o Alvah
MORROW-R.	Died	18 Aug 1820	(stone under building)
NEWMAN-Martha A.E.	22 Aug 1842	5 Mar 1844	Eldest d/o B.F. M.A.
Nancy	Died	6 Nov 1822	45y
TAYLOR-S.	Died	29 N. 1809	(fieldstone)

INITIALS ONLY:

B.B.	Died	28 Jun 1828	(fieldstone)
C.C.	OD	1834 or 36	(fieldstone)
C.C.D.	No dates		
T.R.	OD	1821	(fieldstone)

MONUMENT: Erected by Martha Dandridge Garden Club in memory of Revolutionary Soldiers buried here.

John Blackburn	1741-1808
Abednego Inman	1752-1831
Samuel Lyle	1747-1834
Richard Rankin	1756-1827
Samuel Rankin	1738-1828

Burial Ground at the site of the original Hopewell Presbyterian Church, first church in Jefferson County, 1785

Notes taken from a TVA field survey book indicate that the following stones were found in the 1941 survey. These stones were not found in 1987.

INMAN-N.H.	Died	1822	Age 10
A.D.	Died	1833	Age 6
Shadrack	Died	1857	Age 69
Sarah K.	Died	1841	Age 43
A. (possibly H)	No dates		

This old cemetery is located one block east of the Jefferson County Courthouse in Dandridge. The above are the only inscribed stones we were able to find in November, 1985. In addition to the above, there are at least 60 burials marked with uninscribed fieldstones.

SEAHORN'S CHAPEL METHODIST

ALLEN-Adam	30 Nov 1809	8 Sep 1883	
Charlie	10 Sep 1869	25 Jul 1941	
Clara	10 Jun 1895	12 Jan 1898	d/o L.H. & Flora I.
Claude E.)	14 Mar 1893	17 Oct 1972	
Naomi Corbett)	1 Jul 1895	26 Jun 1985	
Eddie C.	18 Jun 1887	10 Nov 1969	
Ernest L.	26 Jan 1882	25 Oct 1882	s/o J.W. & S.L.
Eugene Raymond)	23 Apr 1903	NOD	
Ida Brewer)	20 Mar 1910	11 Oct 1977	
Floyd H.)	7 Oct 1883	11 Dec 1936	
Katherine H.)	1 Nov 1885	21 Mar 1968	
Infant	OD	26 Aug 1916	s/o C.E. & N.E.
James W.	14 Apr 1846	13 Sep 1922	
Sarah Louise Pless	6 Mar 1860	27 Jan 1924	w/o James W.
Lemuel H.	7 Dec 1858	10 Apr 1932	
Flora I.	1 Dec 1862	8 Jul 1921	w/o L.H.
Nina H.	19 Mar 1894	18 Jan 1973	
ANDERSON-Jacob C., M.D.)	4 Nov 1864	23 Dec 1959	
Dora A.)	19 Jan 1873	18 Aug 1912	
Dola N.)	25 Sep 1887	8 Jan 1966	
AREHART-George)	19 Feb 1831	7 Jan 1900	
Sallie Bowman)	19 Jul 1833	15 Jan 1910	w/o George
J. C.	23 Sep 1865	7 Feb 1894	
Margaret	20 Feb 1874	9 Feb 1904	d/o Geo. & Sarah
Mary Catharine	2 Apr 1863	2 Oct 1946	
BALL-John M.	15 May 1843	21 Dec 1918	
Catherine	10 May 1841	17 Aug 1893	
BIDDLE-Mattie I. Fagala	2 Apr 1880	28 Jul 1922	w/o William R.
BRAIN-A. M.	28 Nov 1848	14 Jun 1923	
Laura F.	16 May 1853	24 May 1928	
BRITT-Riley)	4 Oct 1857	23 May 1938	
Jula)	31 Dec 1865	12 Nov 1932	
BROWN-Charlie L.	2 May 1890	17 Dec 1952	
James F.)	9 Jan 1864	28 Jan 1947	
Minerva C.)	12 Apr 1865	3 Jan 1942	
Minnie May	20 Dec 1896	4 Jun 1906	
CAMERON-Bell	2 Apr 1871	7 Dec 1946	
J. H.	17 Feb 1867	1 May 1931	
Stewart)	1825	1900	
Elizabeth)	1834	3 Jul 1906	
CLINE-Walter V.	15 Jun 1872	18 Aug 1950	
Cora Brown	20 Mar 1881	7 Feb 1949	w/o W.V.
Pearl E.	20 Sep 1903	22 Jul 1985	
CORBETT-James M.	8 Jan 1818	15 Jun 1898	
Wm. B.	3 Mar 1900	26 Sep 1923	
William E.	3 Oct 1868	18 Aug 1899	
Victoria Link	1 Oct 1869	10 Aug 1950	
DENTON-Audrey Mae	1903	1986	(fhm-Farrar)
Charlie L.)	2 Jan 1883	4 Feb 1945	
Rebecca A.)	5 Oct 1889	25 Aug 1973	
David L.)	11 Jul 1830	7 Feb 1915	
Mary Jane)	29 Dec 1835	6 Nov 1905	
Robert D.	27 Jan 1875	6 Feb 1952	
William Eli }	9 Nov 1873	16 Dec 1939	
Rhoda Priscilla Brimer)	25 Aug 1877	30 Oct 1957	

FAGALA-Rev. George W.	6 Dec 1853	15 Jan 1916	
Mary A.	1 Apr 1847	6 Aug 1887	w/o Rev. G.W.
Sallie J.	12 Nov 1856	5 Apr 1890	w/o G.W.
Infant	Died	12 Feb 1894	s/o Rev. G.W. & J.R.
W. F.	28 Jun 1873	20 Feb 1916	
FELKNOR-Lewis	20 Jul 1886	25 May 1923	
Pearl Allen	14 Dec 1885	27 May 1963	
FOX-Homer Robert Jr.	25 Aug 1959	21 Oct 1982	s/o Homer & Sara
FREE-Mary F.	31 Dec 1894	25 Jul 1897	d/o J.H. & R.
GAMMON-Charles Lee)	28 Oct 1892	17 Aug 1966	
Marguerite H.)	2 Jun 1898	NOD	
GLADDING-1st Lt. James W.	1834	1922	Co. B 2nd Mich Cav
Kate	1844	1925	
HALL-Claude W.	17 Aug 1907	28 Sep 1971	
Freida B.	10 Apr 1910	NOD	
HAMMER-Daisy Rachel	25 Dec 1890	2 Jun 1892	d/o M.B. & L.E.
James C.	19 Jun 1853	3 Jun 1931	
Julia Alice Smith	9 Feb 1859	7 Jan 1929	w/o James C.
J. F.)	19 Feb 1851	24 Nov 1916	
Emma Reeves)	28 May 1863	4 Nov 1936	
Rev. John W.)	13 Aug 1890	18 Sep 1979	
Anna Margaret)	27 Mar 1924	30 Mar 1924	d/o Rev. J.W. & Myrtle E.
Myrtle Jones)	13 Aug 1898	7 Feb 1986	
Melville B.	28 Jun 1865	16 Apr 1939	
Lillie E.	16 Oct 1865	27 Apr 1923	
Ralphe S.	3 Aug 1891	11 May 1913	s/o W.S. & Ada
Paul S.M.)	17 Oct 1888	21 Jan 1984	Wed 17 Aug 1927
Nellie Trundle)	1 Apr 1906	NOD	
Roy F.	18 Mar 1882	21 May 1962	
Lula Seahorn	10 May 1883	10 Nov 1962	
S. B.)	24 Jun 1816	8 Jun 1902	
Elizabeth R.)	20 Jan 1820	22 Oct 1905	
Sarah Elizabeth	5 Mar 1868	7 Dec 1903	d/o W.P. & M.A.
Walter S.	6 Nov 1858	8 Sep 1941	
Ada H.	4 May 1860	9 Feb 1953	
William P.)	10 Feb 1843	4 Mar 1927	
Mary Ann B.)	13 Feb 1849	2 May 1925	
HEADRICK-Benjamin	15 Jul 1820	11 Aug 1892	
HENRY-Wiley)	15 Dec 1867	NOD	
Sarah Wood)	11 Jul 1861	29 Oct 1946	
HENSON-Julie Carol	OD	17 Jul 1967	Infant
HODGES-Nellie H.	4 Sep 1888	17 Jul 1970	
JAYNES-Donald L.)	27 May 1926	NOD	
Hannah C.)	11 Sep 1926	NOD	
Donald Roy)	20 Mar 1956	19 Jan 1978	
Joseph Luther)	20 Mar 1956	NOD	
Lt. Roy T. Jr.)	4 Aug 1922	2 Feb 1945	
Roy T.)	13 Feb 1896	4 Oct 1947	
Sarah E.)	23 Oct 1897	10 Nov 1980	
KINCER-Mary L. Britt	5 Jun 1900	18 Feb 1923	w/o A.L.
LAND-Charles Lee, Jr.	1956	1979	(fhm-Farrar)
LENNON-Infant	OD	6 Mar 1921	d/o J.M. & A.P.
J. M.	23 Aug 1894	4 Jun 1926	
McCOIG-Marshall Getter)	9 Mar 1901	19 Feb 1985	married 26 Sep 1925
Myrtle Strange)	8 May 1907	NOD	
McMURRAY-Samuel D.)	1873	1962	
Jane Love)	1875	1954	

MALOY-Homer C.	5 Sep 1917	31 May 1969	
MARTIN-Martha E.	4 Nov 1866	27 May 1899	
NOE-Grace Pearl)	9 Mar 1902	12 Jun 1902	
Willie Kate)	30 Mar 1903	5 Aug 1903	
Lillie	30 Oct 1879	27 Sep 1903	2/o J. W.
NORTH-Fred B.)	1877	1933	
Vinnie S. Seahorne)	1877	1950	
OWENBY-Elmer C.)	15 Aug 1907	17 Jul 1956	
Mayme A.)	1 Mar 1906	NOD	
PHILLIPS-Allie C.	14 Mar 1890	1 May 1971	
James R.	1849	1924	
Locaddie	25 Dec 1850	7 Aug 1913	w/o James
POOLE-William C.	14 Jun 1933	16 Aug 1984	US Navy Korea; wed 29 Jan 196
RENEAU-Alice F. Chapman	May 1875	22 Nov 1957	
RODGERS-Susan J.	28 Aug 1858	2 Sep 1889	
ROGERS-Charles C.)	14 Feb 1896	14 Feb 1980	
Zettie M.)	27 Aug 1911	8 Jan 1979	
Annie R.	24 Nov 1932	23 Jan 1933	
Elijah M.)	17 Apr 1849	17 Nov 1927	
Adda C.)	5 Jan 1867	15 Nov 1903	
Hugh C.	9 Jun 1884	8 Oct 1969	
John H.)	24 Feb 1880	25 May 1956	
Lula M.	14 Jun 1890	7 May 1969	
SATTERFIELD-Eugene	7 Apr 1911	3 Oct 1912	s/o George & Alma
George S.)	15 Feb 1880	11 Mar 1955	
Alma S.)	29 Aug 1882	4 Oct 1970	
Frank Joseph)	1878	1947	
Myrtle Allen)	1879	1924	
Clytie M.)	1888	1974	
SEAHORN-Benjamin Ponder)	9 Sep 1914	NOD	
John Franklin)	8 Aug 1908	27 Jan 1984	US Navy Veteran
Mary Nell B.)	12 Jul 1914	NOD	
Charles W.)	24 Aug 1899	25 Jul 1983	
Mary Yetta Steger)	11 Oct 1905	12 Aug 1979	
Frank H.)	4 Sep 1904	16 Dec 1978	
Louise Allen)	20 Jun 1906	NOD	
Hugh S.)	18 Feb 1907	23 Jul 1977	
Nora Lee Denton)	12 Apr 1921	NOD	
Shirley Kay)	19 Jun 1948	2 Feb 1970	d/o Hugh & Nora Lee
Infant	2 Jan 1898	11 Jan 1898	s/o J.H. & Jessie
James H.	15 Jun 1874	15 Feb 1902	s/o J.P. & D.J.
Janie	22 Mar 1898	2 Oct 1899	d/o W.R. & A.P.
John Ponder	13 Sep 1846	30 Apr 1887	
Dorcas J. Hays	20 Oct 1852	4 Oct 1927	w/o J. Ponder
John Ponder)	22 Mar 1894	22 Jan 1962	
Daisy Birchfield)	30 Sep 1897	4 Mar 1974	
John William)	27 Jul 1879	23 Nov 1962	
Ann Franklin)	1 Apr 1877	2 Aug 1958	
Mary Eloise	Born & died	21 Apr 1926	d/o John Ponder & Daisy
Nelle C.	7 Jun 1885	26 Sep 1904	d/o J.P. & D.J.
Sam W.)	23 Feb 1900	4 Mar 1973	
Faye Denton)	2 Feb 1902	26 Apr 1966	
William R.)	11 Mar 1854	21 May 1933	
Annie Sartain)	15 Feb 1871	19 Apr 1937	w/o Robert R.
William Robert	27 Apr 1902	14 Apr 1964	
SHAFFER-Betty June	30 Nov 1941	6 Jan 1942	

```
SHAFFER-Carroll Lee)           28 Apr 1898    7 Dec 1971
   Kate R.        )           11 Feb 1898    1 Dec 1981
   Carroll Lee Jr.            24 Jul 1930    7 Sep 1930
   Charles William           13 Oct 1918   17 Jan 1920
   Roger Carroll              9 Jan 1932   11 Jan 1964
SHELL-James                   17 Sep 1892   24 Dec 1920
   J. M.                   Born & died   19 Nov 1930    s/o M/M Curtis
   William)                          1860          1919
   Ida    )                          1870          1955
SMITH-William                 25 Feb 1819   11 Nov 1889
   Mary Jane                  7 Jan 1821   22 May 1896    w/o William
SNODGRASS-William R. )         6 Jul 1856   24 Feb 1934
   Harriet J. McGuire)       11 Feb 1858   29 Jul 1937
TAYLOR-Juliet A.              12 Jul 1839   11 Mar 1911
THORNTON-George B.)            9 Sep 1901    3 Feb 1983
   Nellie D.      )          12 Sep 1907   NOD
TILLETT-George C.              5 Dec 1854    3 Apr 1915
   Nora Lee                   2 Jul 1897   13 Jun 1898    d/o G.C. & M.M.
TURNER-Harry M.)              28 Nov 1869   11 Sep 1947
   Alice Trent )             21 Nov 1879    4 Nov 1949
TURNLEY-Dorcas R.              7 Feb 1812   14 Jun 1893
VAUGHT-Frank P.)              13 Aug 1903    2 Feb 1984
   Ruby J.      )            14 Feb 1922   NOD
   James E.        )          6 Aug 1870    3 Aug 1938
   Josephine H.   )          10 Aug 1871   24 Jul 1937
   Minerva J. Atkins          5 Jan 1840   17 Jul 1901    w/o N.T.
   Sidney D.                 16 Nov 1908    3 Sep 1975    PFC US Army WWII
   William Cameron            2 Jan 1881   11 Mar 1906    Born Wythe Co, Va. Died
                                                         Maryville College, Tenn.

VERPLANK-Andrew B.                   1836          1925
   Emma A.                    7 Dec 1838    4 Dec 1900    w/o A.B.
WEBB-Abraham                  15 Dec 1837   23 Dec 1905
   Margaret E.             Died             14 Nov 1902    66y; w/o Abraham
   Mary L.                    6 Jul 1874   14 Jan 1895    d/o Abraham & M.E.
WILLIAMS-Maggie E.             9 Oct 1871    6 Dec 1904    w/o B.M.
```

INITIALS ONLY:

J.M.C.
W.E.C.

According to Mrs. Frank (Louise) Seahorn, the following are buried here in unmarked graves:

```
CAMERON-Jim                Died        ca.    1845
   Minnie                                                w/o Jim
```


This cemetery is well-maintained. To reach the site, take Exit 424 from I-40 and drive the short distance toward the intersection of US25-70. Cross US25W-70 and drive 0.3 miles. Drive 0.1 mile and turn left onto the drive leading to the church and cemetery.

SHADY GROVE CEMETERY

ALLEY-David	11 Jan 1816	26 Nov 1901	
ANDES-L. D.	Aug 1828	Dec 1900	
Nannie C.	26 Feb 1831	15 Jun 1885	
BETTIS-Carl	22 Dec 1902	8 Mar 1941	
Kimbrough A.)	18 Aug 1875	2 Jul 1906	
V. E.)	14 Oct 1875	NOD	
Verdie	14 Oct 1875	19 Dec 1960	
BLACK-Margaret Elizabeth	OD	10 Feb 1833	(fieldstone)
BLACKBURN-Lois Eledge	15 Aug 1898	21 Dec 1929	w/o Wert
BOLDEN-Florence	23 Sep 1895	3 Jul 1904	d/o H.G. & Emma
Thomas C.	16 Nov 1903	6 May 1904	s/o H.G. & Emma
W. H.	11 Nov 1915	1 Mar 1916	s/o Geo. & Grace
Willie Kate	16 May 1906	24 Jul 1906	
BOLIN-Lester	19 May 1907	17 Jan 1925	s/o W.H. & Thula
Sanford	16 Mar 1911	23 Feb 1912	s/o W.H. & Thula
Thula Cross	7 Sep 1879	21 May 1928	
BRABSON-Patsy Lavaughn	OD	22 Jun 1946	Inf. d/o Parrott & Agnes E.
BRANSON-Jane	4 Dec 1818	1 Jan 1883	
Lutisha	16 Apr 1846	24 Jan 1931	
BREEDEN-Roberta Patterson	15 Oct 1920	26 Aug 1944	w/o Thomas W.
BRIMER-Infant	Died	6 Feb 1914	s/o W.O. & M.H.
Maude	12 Nov 1891	21 Feb 1914	
BROOKS-Amantha	1858	1917	
Charles Arthur	26 Dec 1880	26 Jan 1897	
BROWN-Infant	OD	16 Jun 1894	d/o W. & M.E.
John S.	25 Jun 1833	14 Jul 1912	
Martha J.	8 Jan 1834	23 Aug 1905	w/o J.S.
Mrs. Lou	20 Apr 1860	2 Jan 1938	
CASE-John M.)	27 Mar 1886	30 Aug 1903	
Florence D.)	16 Mar 1889	6 Apr 1946	
John W.	16 Aug 1915	9 Sep 1948	
Ruth I.	1911	1932	
CHAMBERS-Chester T.)	18 Jun 1887	16 Oct 1953	
Ollie M.)	13 Dec 1886	27 Jul 1972	
Edna Earl	28 Jul 1917	6 Aug 1918	d/o C.T. & O.V.
Henry	8 Mar 1827	8 Mar 1895	
Matilda	15 May 1817	23 Apr 1900	w/o Henry
Henry C.)	3 Mar 1859	4 May 1939	
Julia M. Fry)	23 Sep 1866	17 Mar 1927	His wife
Jerry "Boss")	19 Feb 1898	13 Dec 1963	
Hassie Pauline)	13 Dec 1906	11 Dec 1970	
Jake H.)	7 Aug 1852	10 Aug 1935	
Elizabeth)	3 Mar 1855	10 Jul 1938	
Jessie Roy	23 Sep 1892	7 Jul 1949	
John	6 Oct 1822	7 Aug 1915	
Betsey	20 Feb 1841	29 Jul 1910	
Paul	13 Feb 1913	16 Oct 1972	TN Pvt US Army WWII
Rosa	5 Jul 1908	5 Jul 1908	d/o S.J. & C.M.
Wm.	1853	1918	
Biddy J.	30 Oct 1857	5 Sep 1903	w/o W. M.
CHEATHAM-Louis Franklin	8 Apr 1919	17 Jan 1985	Sgt US Army WWII
COX-Arthur Paul	18 Sep 1902	13 Feb 1962	TN S/Sgt US Army WWII
John Woodrow	7 Nov 1912	13 Feb 1962	TN Tec4 3 Engr Sp Brigade WWII
CROSS-Samuel Ransom	1808	1902	Feezell's Co 1 Tenn Inf.
			Indian Wars

DENTON-Calude C.)	1 Oct 1886	24 May 1968	
Dora C.)	2 Sep 1886	5 Aug 1964	
Oscar J.)	28 Feb 1888	18 May 1952	
Amanda H.)	22 Apr 1904	3 Oct 1979	
James P.	10 Feb 1864	18 Jul 1890	
John)	1 Sep 1844	28 Mar 1923	
Mahala Zirkle)	2 Mar 1845	8 Oct 1930	His wife
DOHERTY-George	18 Jan 1749	27 May 1833	Maj Gen, East Tenn Militia
			Revolutionary War
Priscilla	Died	21 May 1819	(fieldstone)
William H.	Died	2 Oct 1819	(fieldstone)
DOUGLASS-And'w	No dates		Co B 9th Tenn Cav
DUNCAN-Isaac A.	25 Mar 1828	11 Feb 1908	
Nancy C.	14 Nov 1832	30 Mar 1891	w/o I.A.
Fannie M.	Died	19 Feb 1892	70y
Powel W.	Oct 1846	29 Apr 1904	
DUNKIN-John	Died	22 Jun 1850	72y
Mary L.	Died	4 May 1846	56y 24d, consort of John
John H.	25 Dec 1815	25 Apr 1864	
Sarah Cassandra	26 Sep 1829	30 Oct 1900	w/o John H.
ELEDGE-Carl)	29 Apr 1892	3 Mar 1962	
Nita)	25 Mar 1896	17 Apr 1978	
Charles R. L.	4 Sep 1887	29 Oct 1960	TN Pvt 2 Co Dev. Bn WWI
Chester H.	28 Apr 1886	9 Nov 1967	
Clarence E.	10 Oct 1890	8 May 1913	s/o W.M. & M.E.
Mamie Cora	30 Sep 1899	27 Oct 1901	d/o W.M. & M.E.
W. M.	21 Oct 1859	10 Aug 1921	
Martha Thurman	30 Oct 1859	21 Jan 1925	w/o W.M.
ELLISON-Edward E.	14 Aug 1892	8 Mar 1958	
Jimmie	29 May 1890	29 Aug 1896	s/o J.N. & M.R.
Joseph Newton)	29 Nov 1862	21 Jun 1934	
Mary Rebecca)	18 Oct 1856	6 Aug 1932	
Liny)	8 Jun 1891	10 Jun 1896	Infants of J.N. & M.R.
Lucy	14 Aug 1892	24 Aug 1892	
O. R.)	4 Jul 1894	19 Sep 1921	
Lillie Parrott)	25 Sep 1894	23 Feb 1963	
ESLINGER-Cromwell	23 Dec 1889	1 Oct 1966	
Elizabeth Brown	24 Oct 1881	20 May 1925	
Viola M.	30 Sep 1893	18 Mar 1961	
FAIN-Clifford R.	2 Jun 1942	24 Oct 1942	
John R.	3 Feb 1906	15 Feb 1968	
Katie Fay	4 Oct 1913	24 Feb 1953	
FELKNOR-Joe Hill	13 Sep 1925	27 May 1971	
Leon C.	29 Jan 1922	11 Jan 1976	
Nelle Zirkle	29 Dec 1889	30 Jan 1962	
FINE-George Paul)	4 Nov 1895	18 Feb 1977	Father
Jessie Rimmer)	2 Mar 1900	1 Jul 1970	Mother
Charles Edward)	7 Oct 1942	9 Nov 1962	Son
William Ferd)	3 Oct 1921	26 Oct 1921	
FOLAND-Arthur	12 Aug 1910	19 Aug 1955	
Maymie C.	7 Feb 1913	NOD	
Nora	8 Oct 1903	1 Jun 1906	
Rufus)	15 Apr 1875	25 Feb 1937	
Nancy)	21 Jul 1872	4 Feb 1937	
William "W.L."	1830	12 Jun 1884	Co E 9th Tenn Fed Cav;54y
Emly J.	1838	1901	
William	5 Jan 1870	9 Jan 1948	
Delia J.	21 Jun 1883	NOD	

FOX-Alonzo Eli	18 Oct 1881	6 Jun 1944	
Viola Seahorn	19 Sep 1881	22 Jul 1935	w/o A.E.
America C.	22 Dec 1875	7 Jul 1903	d/o Cam & R.J.
Arthur G.)	31 Oct 1878	20 Mar 1880	
George W.)	17 Sep 1881	19 Aug 1883	s/o Campbell L. & R.J.
William C.)	31 Jan 1869	7 Sep 1869	s/o C. & R.J.
Bessie M.	26 Aug 1888	5 Sep 1888	d/o W.C. & M.E.
Campbell)	24 Oct 1839	24 Oct 1922	
Rebecca J.)	26 Jan 1848	25 Feb 1929	
Cecil)	19 Apr 1903	8 Mar 1975	
Mae West)	5 Mar 1906	NOD	
Eli	12 Nov 1898	20 Aug 1983	
Dicy M.	4 Nov 1900	10 Oct 1977	
Eli)	3 Aug 1870	14 Dec 1874	
Infant)	Born & died	10 Apr 1868	
Sarah A.)	13 Nov 1873	17 Dec 1874	
William)	9 Aug 1867	14 Aug 1867	
Ernest Walter)	26 Mar 1896	24 Nov 1959	
Laura N. Thornton)	18 Feb 1897	2 Oct 1953	
Florence Grider	19 Apr 1888	9 Jul 1917	w/o A.E.
George L.	7 Jan 1841	17 Apr 1881	40y 3m 10d
D. A.	27 Sep 1849	7 Mar 1891	w/o G.L.
George Lafayette	17 Aug 1894	8 Jan 1979	Pvt US Army WWI
Herbert H.	23 Apr 1929	25 Mar 1967	PFC US Marine Corps
Ida)	31 Aug 1873	28 Oct 1953	
Nora)	16 Dec 1883	21 Nov 1956	
Infant	OD	21 Mar 1890	s/o M.S. & D.V.
James Carroll	28 Jun 1872	14 Sep 1950	
Mary Mort	22 Oct 1874	25 Sep 1945	
James M.)	18 Nov 1870	31 Mar 1914	
Bertie L.)	6 Jul 1879	7 May 1955	
James Norma	15 Sep 1913	3 May 1934	d/o J.M. & B.L.
John C.)	11 Feb 1911	12 Feb 1981	
Gladys L.)	2 Jul 1916	NOD	
Kenneth Lee	OD	17 Sep 1937	s/o A.E. & Mabel
Lora Blanche	21 Oct 1883	21 Jun 1899	d/o W.C. & M.E.
Marshall S.	30 Oct 1858	14 Mar 1901	
Flora D.	12 Jul 1862	16 Oct 1882	married to Marshal Fox 3 Sep 1882; d/o Dow Trotter
Thula Fry	20 May 1862	16 Dec 1948	
Maude S.	6 Aug 1886	12 Jun 1948	
Murphy)	24 Apr 1897	10 Jan 1973	
Mary)	9 Jun 1902	23 Dec 1974	
Nina	16 Oct 1909	13 May 1910	d/o J.C. & M.E.
R. K.	14 Aug 1911	12 Aug 1912	s/o J.C. & M.E.
Thurman	27 Aug 1878	OD(Born)	Died same day;s/o G.L. & A.M.
Virgil Eugene	24 Oct 1923	13 May 1941	
Walter	6 Dec 1904	11 Dec 1904	s/o J.M. & Bertie
William C.)	2 Jan 1852	5 Jun 1928	
Ellen Z.)	25 Dec 1855	4 Oct 1943	
William M.	28 Dec 1877	15 Oct 1892	s/o W.C. & M.E.
William Seahon	OD	22 Jul 1922	s/o Lon & Viola
FRANKLIN-James A.)	25 May 1888	2 Nov 1951	
Nellie A.)	9 Jun 1890	5 May 1969	
FREE-Rebecca	13 Nov 1870	21 Feb 1901	w/o J.H.
Robert T.	7 Jan 1901	27 Apr 1901	s/o J.H. & R.

FRY-Anna Rebecca	14 Sep 1868	5 Dec 1869	d/o John & Susan (handmade)
Curtis R.	8 Oct 1888	23 Apr 1965	
Cyrenious	3 Feb 1864	12 Sep 1865	
John)	13 Aug 1829	6 Jan 1896	
Susan)	6 Feb 1838	28 Dec 1901	
John L.	Born & died	22 Jun 1910	s/o M.B. & M.J.
John N.	1860	1940	
Mary	1864	1937	
Letta L.	28 Apr 1896	21 Aug 1902	
Mack B.	28 Sep 1883	11 Aug 1956	
Mollie J. McSpadden	28 Sep 1881	5 Jan 1946	
FRYE-Annie	4 Jan 1886	21 May 1933	
Chad Lewis	31 Jan 1978	21 Aug 1978	s/o M/M Terry
James N.	19 Jun 1915	27 Mar 1945	TN Sgt 251 Engr Combat BN
			Born Tenn; died Germany WWII
W. A.)	1859	1915	
Dicie Denton)	1857	1927	His wife
GAUT-Margaret	3 Aug 1801	27 Apr 1831	(fieldstone)
GLENN-Andrew J.	20 Jul 1920	28 Nov 1941	
Nancy C.	1866	1940	
William R.)	12 Aug 1891	30 Jan 1957	
M. Cordelia)	3 Aug 1895	13 May 1980	
GOLLADAY-Gadbihl	15 Oct 1834	17 Jan 1872	
GRYDER-Jesse L.)	17 Oct 1857	23 Aug 1935	
Lucretia Farthing)	24 Mar 1852	29 May 1931	
Nettie E.)	12 Apr 1890	24 Jan 1976	
HAMILL-Robert	Died	Dec 1858	(fieldstone)
HARMON-Dicy Smith	10 Nov 1876	15 Sep 1913	
HARPER-Donald Q.)	1916	NOD	
Leila J.)	1914	1982	
HARRISON-Annie Frye	4 Jan 1886	21 May 1933	
Arabella	5 Nov 1866	10 Jan 1953	
Arthur Early	20 Jun 1877	10 May 1953	
Cordelia N.	15 Mar 1868	2 Oct 1868	d/o John & Mary
George W.	29 Oct 1907	26 Dec 1907	
Jake W.	13 Sep 1905	12 Apr 1975	
John)	1835	1921	9th Tenn Co C
Mary Emily Rankin)	1835	1919	His wife
John David	9 Nov 1877	14 Sep 1954	
Lillie M.	7 Sep 1885	20 Mar 1965	
John Marshal	10 Apr 1879	23 Feb 1899	19y 10m 13d
Joseph)	13 Aug 1840	19 Oct 1911	
Susan)	31 Jul 1846	4 Aug 1920	His wife
Mary Francis	22 Aug 1873	4 Jul 1894	d/o Joseph & Susan
Sarah Ellen	26 Jul 1869	25 Apr 1962	
Thomas D.	19 Nov 1870	1 Oct 1874	s/o John & Mary E.
W. A.	Mar 1884	Aug 1949	"Uncle Alex"
HARTLEY-Ben	1888	1956	
HAYNES-Amanda Moore	11 Jan 1888	21 Jan 1930	w/o Raymond
Elijah	18 Mar 1886	NOD	
Mae	11 Sep 1894	21 Mar 1970	
Paul Moore	27 Dec 1908	1 Mar 1909	s/o M/M Raymond
Raymond E. Jr.	26 Nov 1913	13 Jan 1974	TN Sgt US Army WWII
Pvt. Roy A.	7 Apr 1918	11 Feb 1945	TN 152 Inf 38 Div WWII
			Killed in action on Luzon Island
Rush)	19 Feb 1884	19 Feb 1969	
Elizabeth)	16 Feb 1854	1 Oct 1932	
HEARTLEY-Willie E.	26 Apr 1900	20 Nov 1901	

HENDERSON-John F.)	25 Sep 1890	25 Feb 1918	
Zelma Lou V.)	9 Dec 1896	28 Mar 1918	
John Jr.)	Born & died	9 Jan 1918	
HENRY-Dedrich T.	Died	26 Nov 1860	7m; s/o H.A. & N.E.
Elizabeth	11 Nov 1791	15 Dec 1838	(fieldstone)
Ethel	10 Sep 1896	20 Nov 1921	w/o Harry
Hugh	31 Mar 1798	14 Mar 1855	
Hugh L.	25 Nov 1855	27 Jan 1923	
Jane	Died	7 Jan 1835	57y (fieldstone)
J. M.	19 Feb 1819	27 Sep 1837	(fieldstone)
John N.	2 Feb 1885	23 Sep 1886	s/o G. W. & S.E.
Johnnie	Born & died	16 Feb 1889	s/o J.N. & M.E.
Margt.	11 Jun 1832	23 Nov 1837	(fieldstone)
Oliver	6 Mar 1824	28 Jun 1878	54y 3m 22d
Nancy A.	18 Apr 1824	27 Jun 1897	73y 2m 9d; w/o Oliver
S. E.	14 Feb 1864	2 Aug 1901	w/o G.W.
Silas	1797	Oct 1837	(fieldstone)
W. J.	17 Dec 1853	18 Apr 1904	
HICKS-Flora	13 Nov 1892	15 Jul 1893	
James B.	30 Nov 1872	5 Nov 1890	
Jennie	No dates		Our Sister
Maggie E.	23 Jun 1867	5 Apr 1883	
Wm. H.	No dates		Co L 9th Tenn Cav
Rebecca	7 Mar 1851	13 Jan 1913	w/o W.H.
HILL-Charlie W.	27 Mar 1888	28 Mar 1891	s/o G.W. & M.E.
Gergie I.	22 Jul 1893	27 Feb 1895	d/o G.W. & M.E.
George W.)	9 Feb 1866	25 Nov 1937	
Martha E.)	19 Mar 1869	7 Nov 1906	
Infant	27 Sep 1894	25 Oct 1894	d/o G.W. & M.E.
Infant	18 Oct 1906	19 Oct 1906	s/o G.W. & M.E.
James R.	21 Sep 1895	9 Oct 1896	s/o G.W. & M.E.
John)	17 Jun 1889	1 Aug 1975	
Malinda Moore)	28 Apr 1890	23 Nov 1940	
Lula M.	6 Nov 1890	12 Sep 1893	d/o G.W. & M.E.
HINKLE-Lloyd E.	29 Jan 1902	1 Jul 1984	
Martha J.	26 Aug 1869	19 Jan 1875	d/o S.M. & Lavina
Rexey	24 Jul 1884	OD(Born)	s/o W.M. & M.A.
Sylvenes Maberry	17 Oct 1829	25 Sep 1892	
Lavina Bible	17 Sep 1834	20 Jun 1908	married S.M. Hinkle 5 Oct 1855
William	4 Jan 1857	11 May 1938	
Martha Ann	9 Sep 1861	24 Oct 1942	
HOLBERT-Betty Chambers	31 Oct 1889	22 Jul 1925	w/o Palmer
Ernest M.)	31 Jul 1908	26 Mar 1982	married 8 Apr 1968
Blanch W.)	8 May 1921	NOD	
Caldonia (Aldon?)	Died	30 Sep 1891	(fieldstone - very faint)
HORNER-Cpl. Jack A.	3 Nov 1933	19 Sep 1951	Missing in action in Korea
Ida Joe)	19 Mar 1930	2 Feb 1931	
Ruth C. Patterson)	31 Oct 1899	8 Apr 1983	
HUFFAKER-Ellen Henry	1860	1952	Sister; w/o E.U. Huffaker (See Ollie Reece stone)
JEFFERS-Fay Gladys	5 Nov 1911	31 Mar 1913	
Mae	13 Sep 1902	17 Oct 1932	
Shannon)	25 Sep 1875	11 Apr 1945	
Annie M.)	4 Feb 1878	7 Dec 1956	
Wayne	29 Mar 1900	13 Jan 1955	

JEFFERS-Edith F.	24 Feb 1898	4 Aug 1962	
Wm.	No dates		Co A 9th Tenn Cav
JENKINS-Sedette F.	20 Jun 1914	14 Dec 1972	
JOHNSON-H.E.	16 Feb 1870	15 Apr 1916	
M. A.	28 Feb 1833	28 May 1905	w/o F.M.
T. H.	12 Jun 1909	24 Nov 1912	s/o F.M.
W. H.	30 Aug 1866	8 Jul 1905	s/o R.M.
JONES-C. L.)	23 Jul 1870	23 Mar 1934	
Cordie E. Bettis)	19 Jun 1870	9 Mar 1958	
Mary Nelle)	6 Jan 1913	30 Sep 1927	Daughter
David V.	12 Nov 1831	22 Feb 1904	
Barbara A.	1836	28 Jul 1891	w/o D.V.
Floy Artie May	19 Jun 1903	19 Nov 1906	
Hal C.)	30 Jan 1896	24 Aug 1968	
Leora F.)	17 Nov 1902	28 Aug 1970	
Isaac H.	11 May 1838	11 Apr 1914	Grandfather Co M 2 Tenn Cav
Hannah	31 Dec 1844	18 Jun 1920	Grandmother
James Rufus	25 Apr 1870	13 Mar 1945	
Mollie	20 Jun 1878	21 Jul 1916	w/o J.R.
Georgie	30 Aug 1874	30 Aug 1912	w/o J.R.
Joseph A.	20 Feb 1856	27 Mar 1882	
Lawn D.	20 Mar 1875	28 Jul 1883	s/o D.V. & B.A.
Link D.)	21 Feb 1894	6 Dec 1965	
Daisy E.)	19 Nov 1895	3 Feb 1973	
Martha M.	19 Aug 1835	21 Jul 1883	w/o Isaac M.
Ray V.)	11 Jun 1904	7 Feb 1970	
Pate)	19 Jan 1895	23 Jul 1949	
Sam R.)	24 Jul 1871	17 May 1946	
Alice Fry)	9 Jun 1872	8 Nov 1913	
Anna Gass)	22 Apr 1891	1 Jun 1947	
Vena	26 Feb 1873	5 May 1902	
KELLEY-Fanny	8 Feb 1861	30 Jan 1907	
Nellie Agnes)	5 Mar 1893	26 Jul 1893	
Ellen May)	31 May 1895	8 Nov 1896	
Zebedee E.	13 Aug 1850	23 Sep 1921	
KITE-Granville	Oct 1818	4 Nov 1891	
Martha J.	Died	23 Jun 1914	
Sarah	24 Apr 1849	OD(Born)	
LEEPER-Anna B.	5 Dec 1881	5 Dec 1906	d/o J.M. & S.V.
Donna Beryl	10 Dec 1911	12 Oct 1912	d/o L.L. & M.C.
Henry M.	27 Jan 1817	27 Dec 1843	26y 11m
John M.)	2 Jun 1841	10 Aug 1908	
Susan V.)	15 Jan 1853	1 Feb 1916	w/o John M.
Julia Alma	20 Sep 1886	3 Feb 1889	d/o J.M. & S.V.
LEETH-Atsey	Died	26 Aug 1827	(fieldstone)
Jos. H.	Died	Aug 1787	(fieldstone)(two stones)
Josiah, Sr.	ca. 1746	26 Aug 1787	s/o George & Miriam of Va.
LEWIS-Elihu T.	10 Oct 1907	22 Jun 1969	
Robert L.	27 Feb 1883	4 Dec 1944	
Lizzie Walker	17 Nov 1887	15 Jul 1916	
LICHLYTER-Ervin A.	26 Jul 1868	3 Mar 1963	
LINDSEY-Andrew J.)	29 Aug 1899	19 Aug 1958	
Paralee L.)	19 May 1900	17 Jan 1971	
Arthur	23 Jan 1897	19 Sep 1951	
Ida Scarlett	12 Aug 1897	30 Apr 1934	

LINDSEY-Frances E.	11 Mar 1887	1 Feb 1969	
Ellen Louvina	16 May 1875	8 Oct 1900	w/o W.J.
Henry P.)		1885	NOD
Cora L.)		1888	1919
Horace O.	8 Nov 1895	24 Apr 1913	s/o W.J. & E.V.
Howard Frank)	11 Jun 1924	NOD	
Bertha Hodges)	12 Feb 1924	18 May 1981	
I. C.)	21 Dec 1863	27 Jun 1958	
Bettie Rinehart)	10 Mar 1861	19 Jan 1923	His wife
Infant	No dates		d/o W.J. & E.L.
Isaac Floyd)	1 Jan 1897	16 Oct 1959	TN Pvt Co E 383 Inf WWI
Mattie)		1901	NOD
J. D. "Jim")	24 Aug 1888	22 Jul 1957	
Alice M.)	3 Feb 1885	29 Dec 1965	
Joseph W.)		1872	1955
Martha E.)		1883	1951
Mary	Born & died	16 Apr 1916	
Otha C.)	27 Apr 1912	6 Jan 1976	
Vida F.)	27 Jul 1909	NOD	
P. H.	16 Jul 1841	14 Jul 1915	
Thelma R.	28 Apr 1922	17 Oct 1923	d/o I.F. & Mattie
Triplets	OD	14 May 1946	Triplets of M/M Howard
William B.)		1882	1936
Essie M.)		1888	NOD
LINDSY-C. A.	Died	12 Aug 1886	d/o P.L. & E.
LINZY-Nancy A.	15 May 1844	5 Sep 1902	w/o Wm.
LYLE-Luther W.	30 Apr 1871	22 Sep 1874	s/o J.W. & E.
LYNCH-Tom D.)		1890	1950
Neta)		1893	1931
William H.	26 Jul 1920	20 Nov 1973	TN Tec5 US Army WWII
McSPADDEN-Frank Wilburn		1938	1938
Claud)	15 Aug 1880	22 Aug 1965	
Paralee)	14 Apr 1880	5 May 1965	
Georgia A.	2 Jan 1882	6 Mar 1921	w/o B.C.
James W.	1 Aug 1873	6 Oct 1874	s/o S. & M.
Joseph A.	30 Jul 1875	4 Sep 1894	s/o M.W. & S.E.; 19y 7m 5d
Marshall	25 Jan 1883	15 Feb 1883	s/o M.M. & L.E.
Mary Ruth	7 Jun 1911	27 Mar 1913	d/o B.C. & Paralee
Robert	4 Jul 1869	14 Jul 1869	s/o Rufus & Ellen S.; 10d
Milton F., Sr.)	7 Sep 1913	25 Jun 1970	TN Pvt Co C 787 Mil Pol BN WWII
Lorene M.)	9 Aug 1916	NOD	
Milton P.	16 Apr 1892	17 Apr 1892	s/o M.M. & L.E.
M. M.)	17 Jun 1858	1 Mar 1921	
Ellen)	15 May 1856	14 Mar 1925	His wife
Mollie E.	24 Sep 1848	3 Nov 1895	d/o M.V. & Sarah E.
Nora)		1894	1896	Daughter
Infant)	OD	1891	Son
Rufus	19 Aug 1836	8 Feb 1879	42y 5m 19d
Ellen S.	20 Dec 1843	22 Jan 1903	
Sam E.)	14 Jan 1890	23 Mar 1959	
Ersie)	12 Jan 1891	18 Jun 1966	
Samuel D.	21 Feb 1871	19 Jun 1891	20y 3m 28d
Sarah E.	3 Jan 1841	17 Nov 1891	w/o M.W.; 50y 10m 14d
Stephen D.	20 Jul 1942	8 Aug 1942	
MANARD-C. B.	6 Jan 1888	11 Apr 1914	26y 3m 5d
Infant	Born & died	15 Apr 1855	s/o S. & E.

MANARD-J. W.	25 Oct 1873	19 Dec 1890	17y 1m 24d
Rev. N. E.)	2 Apr 1869	8 Mar 1923	
Addie L.)	5 May 1871	NOD	His wife
Nora	14 Mar 1879	8 May 1893	14y 1m 24d
Shadrack	18 Nov 1810	3 Sep 1882	71y 9m 15d
S. M.)	3 Apr 1851	30 Mar 1923	
Bell)	5 Mar 1851	19 Jan 1917	
MARIE-Mary E.	19 Dec 1871	6 Mar 1927	w/o T. N.
MAYNARD-Ernest N.	1893	1983	Co K 46 Inf
Addie L.	1871	1959	
MIDDLETON-Otis F.	20 May 1893	13 Jul 1896	s/o Ulysses & Mary
MINK-Maude A.	4 Oct 1893	2 Aug 1964	
MOORE-Ester H.	19 Jun 1903	14 May 1940	
Frank	12 Feb 1921	20 Jun 1923	s/o Sam & Annie
Frances Ellamae	25 Apr 1918	23 Oct 1922	d/o M/M Arnold
H.H.)	7 Feb 1829	3 Oct 1910	
Rebecca E. Cate)	14 Aug 1835	13 Jul 1895	
Ina Grace	12 Mar 1933	28 Nov 1935	
James W.	3 Feb 1881	1 Jul 1900	s/o Walker & Laura
John Robert)	10 Jan 1879	27 Dec 1943	
Hattie S. Harrison)	2 Aug 1886	28 Aug 1943	
S. Walker	16 Apr 1855	9 Feb 1917	
Lanra Webster	4 Oct 1859	18 Jun 1925	w/o S.W.
MOONAHAM-Ransom	Died	29 Dec 1879	54y 8m 1d
MOREE-Isaac)	31 Dec 1793	23 Dec 1881	
Syddie)	10 May 1783	10 Apr 1878	
MORIE-Earnest B.)	8 Feb 1897	1 Jan 1955	
Artie M.)	19 Sep 1893	21 Nov 1972	
Frank R.	24 May 1917	23 Jul 1918	s/o R. C. & Clara
Hollis C.	25 Oct 1898	14 Jun 1966	
Leona Lindsey	1 Sep 1908	24 Oct 1954	
Howard G.	7 Jan 1899	11 Oct 1901	s/o T.N. & M.E.
I. A.)	1 Apr 1863	1 Apr 1954	
Dorthula)	10 Aug 1863	10 Jun 1921	
Isaac)	28 Nov 1833	NOD	
Mary)	27 Feb 1836	27 Feb 1911	His wife
Jessie B.)	3 Jan 1894	NOD	
Leona E.)	14 Sep 1903	16 Dec 1977	
Milton Ray	20 May 1923	2 Jun 1923	s/o John E. & Ida; 13d
Robert	18 Dec 1891	18 Oct 1950	
Rhoda	Born & died	3 Aug 1936	d/o M/M E. B.
Stella Frances	1922	1983	60y (fhm-Atchley)
Thomas C.)	25 Jun 1865	NOD	
Ethel F.)	23 Apr 1873	10 Sep 1940	
T. N.	6 Mar 1849	5 Feb 1938	
Catharin J.	1 Feb 1856	11 Aug 1882	w/o Thomas N.
W. C.)	5 Nov 1856	NOD	
Sarah A.)	16 Nov 1865	27 Aug 1898	His wife
Wilma B.	20 Jan 1921	27 Nov 1927	
MORT-Arthur	25 Mar 1876	25 Mar 1895	
Conley A.	12 Feb 1902	7 Aug 1904	s/o G.A. & M.L.
George A.	18 Nov 1861	17 Jun 1923	
G. R.	1869	1938	
Callie	2 Jun 1873	5 May 1911	w/o G.R.
John	7 May 1800	17 Nov 1886	
Henrietta	21 Sep 1802	19 Jan 1866	w/o John

MORT-John L.	11 Jan 1847	26 Oct 1931	
Sarah J.	11 Sep 1843	16 Dec 1920	w/o John
Mahala	1821	1868	
MOTT-John)	28 Aug 1870	23 Sep 1931	
Lottie Newman)	8 Mar 1867	20 Aug 1956	His wife
MURPHY-M. J.	16 Mar 1830	3 Jul 1902	
NELSON-J. Wesley	Died	14 Sep 1856	s/o W.M. & L.A.; 2m 2d
PARKER-Freeman M.	1860	1950	
Lucinda B.	1872	1952	w/o F. M.
M. H.	8 Dec 1824	26 Sep 1900	Co B 9th Tenn Inf
Theodore S.	29 Sep 1895	2 Apr 1962	TN Pfc Co G 46 Inf 9 Div WWI
PARROTT-Edgar L.	29 Jul 1898	27 Oct 1978	
Hollis	13 Dec 1896	4 Aug 1934	TN Co L Pvt 327 Inf WWI
Infant	17 Oct 1900	17 Oct 1900	s/o J. R. & A. E.
Infant	28 Jan 1898	28 Jan 1898	s/o J. R. & A. E.
Isaac)	29 Nov 1868	13 Sep 1933	
Nancy Lindsey)	6 Mar 1871	3 Mar 1952	
Isaac V.	27 Aug 1905	20 Mar 1976	
James R.)	30 Jan 1867	17 Jun 1944	
Amanda Lethco)	28 Dec 1856	1 Dec 1925	
William M.	18 Nov 1890	25 Dec 1965	
PATTERSON-Fernando Court	7 Feb 1974	13 May 1962	
George A.)	1876	1958	
Josie M.)	1892	1980	
Harold)	22 Feb 1840	17 Oct 1923	
Suzen)	16 Nov 1842	17 Oct 1877	His wife
A. P. C.	17 Sep 1838	23 Jun 1886	47y 7m 6d
John H.	23 Jan 1924	29 Feb 1924	s/o G. A. & Josie
John S.	5 Aug 1964	17 Aug 1964	
Kenneth C.	24 Aug 1939	31 Oct 1957	
Lefford J.)	17 Feb 1917	1 Dec 1963	
Frances L.)	7 Mar 1922	NOD	
Permilia	Jan 1811	19 Jan 1891	w/o George
Texas Jane	1 May 1873	20 May 1961	
PLUMLEE-Minnie Morie	8 Oct 1889	21 Jul 1975	
REECE-Joseph)	24 Oct 1853	15 Nov 1926	
Hannah J.)	12 Apr 1855	21 Oct 1926	
M. B.	4 Mar 1916	25 Mar 1916	d/o Lee & D.V.
REESE-James)	19 Jan 1871	5 Oct 1941	
Cordie)	11 Feb 1871	5 May 1933	
Ollie	1863	1949	w/o William Reese (See Ethel HUFFAKER) Sister
Ralph D.	9 Mar 1908	12 Apr 1955	
Raymond	22 Jul 1922	28 Jan 1924	s/o J.L. & D.V.
RENAU-Nip.	1843	1930	
RENEAU-Catherine	16 Sep 1838	7 Jul 1906	w/o N.B.
Katie M.	15 Feb 1881	25 Sep 1905	d/o N.B. & Catherine
Stanley E.)	26 Jun 1907	26 Aug 1964	
Callie Mae)	14 Mar 1912	NOD	
Willie E.	Born & died	24 Oct 1934	
Willie R.)	22 Nov 1874	15 Oct 1948	
Mrs. W.R.)	15 Mar 1889	10 Jul 1953	
RHINEHART-John	6 Mar 1888	5 Oct 1922	
RIMMER-Carl S.)	18 Jun 1905	11 Dec 1974	
Eleanor F.)	22 Apr 1907	21 Nov 1974	
Charles B.)	31 Mar 1870	1 Sep 1925	
Lettie M. Denton)	7 Aug 1876	24 May 1945	His wife

RIMMER-Infant	Born & died	28 Mar 1896	d/o J.H. & Hattie
John Henry	13 Sep 1870	14 May 1943	
Nell Walker	9 Mar 1889	17 May 1959	w/o J.H.
Hattie Fry	26 Sep 1877	1 Oct 1909	w/o J.H.
ROACH-Robert Henry	8 May 1904	20 Feb 1970	"Shorty"
ROBERTS-Flora Marie Morie	1928	1947	
ROMINE-J. I.	7 Jul 1872	16 Nov 1951	
Abbie G.	2 May 1867	3 Dec 1943	w/o J.I.
Mattie L. Burchfield	22 Jun 1877	10 Jun 1903	w/o J.I.
ROMINES-Annie R.	13 Sep 1894	26 Sep 1894	d/o M/M J.T.
Joseph Earl)	26 Sep 1897	23 Aug 1962	
Grace Zella)	28 Jun 1897	NOD	
Nora Florence	25 May 1897	3 May 1961	
Quentin E.	21 Dec 1918	8 Jun 1980	
RUSSELL-Mary M.	6 Feb 1844	19 Feb 1873	w/o Simeon P.
SAFFELL-Carl D.	30 Jan 1885	31 Mar 1958	
Gertrude Frye	31 May 1887	7 Apr 1924	w/o Carl D.
SAMPLES-Charley	1 May 1896	27 Mar 1907	s/o W. H. & L. T.
W. H.)	20 Oct 1859	27 Mar 1929	
Laura T.)	6 Oct 1861	27 Aug 1938	
SELF-Louisa Lesly	Died	8 Apr 1869	3y 6m 2d
SELLARS-John	18 Dec 1821	7 May 1900	78y 4m 19d
Harriet	18 Oct 1827	26 Jan 1880	w/o John
SHULTS-Eddie Doyle	OD	25 Oct 1957	Infant s/o Nancy & Fred
SIMES-Gemima M.	7 May 1909	22 Dec 1910	d/o G.G. & D.E.
SIMPSON-Anna Bell L.	17 Jul 1913	23 Nov 1974	
SMITH-Robert A.	6 Apr 1846	24 Mar 1884	Leaving a wife and 2 children; m. to R.M.J. Bettice 27 Feb 1879
Charlie A.)	11 Jan 1880	7 Apr 1955	
Mattie D.)	19 Jul 1883	26 Jun 1951	
Mary M.	4 Aug 1821	OD(Born)	w/o Haral; age 53y
Mollie	10 Jul 1881	14 Aug 1920	
T. H.)	31 Dec 1854	2 Sep 1882	
Nancy)	23 Jul 1855	13 Dec 1913	
SOLOMON-Holland	7 Mar 1889	21 Sep 1909	
John W.)	7 Dec 1870	12 Jul 1945	
Rebecca Harrison)	1 Nov 1874	4 Aug 1938	
J. W.)	25 Sep 1850	22 May 1897	
Sarah C.)	25 Jun 1844	3 Mar 1908	w/o J.W.
Lester F.	16 Mar 1895	6 May 1907	s/o J.W. & R.R.
Nancy	22 Feb 1824	20 Aug 1877	w/o Sterling
Rufus Walker)	2 Sep 1882	7 Apr 1954	
Della Chambers)	14 Sep 1883	6 Jul 1939	
Twin Boys)	Born & died	14 Mar 1922	
Ruby Eugenia)	6 Apr 1912	9 Nov 1921	
Loraine)	Born & died	18 Jan 1921	
SLATON-A. L.	19 Feb 1893	16 Aug 1913	d/o F.M. & M.A.
F. M.)	31 Jan 1843	10 Apr 1919	Co C 9th Tenn Cav.
Mary A.)	2 Oct 1852	4 Dec 1922	w/o F. M.
Corp's J. A.	No dates		Co D 9th Tenn Cav.
Roscoe M.	17 Jul 1891	4 Feb 1919	Sgt AM Casual Det Group One
Thomas)	1 Mar 1818	26 Jan 1899	h/o Rebecca
Rebecca)	7 Mar 1816	5 Jan 1892	w/o Thomas
SWAN-Maggie	Died	22 Dec 1903	50y
SWANN-Amos E.	9 Jan 1882	12 Oct 1882	s/o J.C. & M.J.
Bertha E.	20 Feb 1892	22 Jan 1921	d/o J.A. & M.J. LINE; w/o C.B.
Charlie B.	22 Dec 1879	18 Aug 1942	

SWANN-John C.	3 Dec 1821	13 Jun 1904	
Sarah	(broken)	20 Apr 1895	w/o John C.
Maggie J.	12 Jun 1851	30 Nov 1882	w/o John C.
Lettie Rhinehart	30 Jun 1887	19 May 1980	
Mrs. Lou Tittsworth	13 Jun 1878	11 Apr 1913	
Rhoten	24 Jan 1849	5 May 1930	
Rachel	15 Jan 1851	12 Jan 1930	
Roy T.	23 Feb 1908	25 Feb 1908	s/o G.W. & J.N.
TITTLES-Rose Case	No dates		
TITTSWORTH-E.	5 Mar 1842	22 Apr 1899	
Maria Elizabeth	15 Nov 1848	2 Jul 1904	w/o E.
Harley	26 Jun 1890	18 Dec 1908	
Oren T.	9 Jan 1886	22 May 1905	
Walter	17 Mar 1873	22 Jul 1875	s/o Elihu & Elizabeth
VANDYKE-Calvin E.	24 Apr 1927	27 Mar 1951	
Harley R.)	29 Mar 1895	4 Jul 1949	
Lestie L.)	11 Aug 1899	11 Aug 1984	
James H.	1892		
Jason C.	7 Apr 1933	17 Jun 1978	"Dick"
Julia	No dates		d/o M/M Pate
Margorie	1903	1903	
Martha Jane	21 Nov 1849	15 Oct 1890	40y 10m 24d
Lester R.	11 Sep 1908	11 Sep 1951	
Raymond H.	26 Sep 1924	3 Feb 1983	
Robert A.)	1863	1926	
Catherine Foland)	1865	1913	w/o Robert A.
Samuel W.	25 May 1880	13 Jan 1884	s/o D.C. & M.J.
Shelby Jane	Born & died	19 Apr 1933	d/o Alonzo & Elizabeth
William Robert	17 Jun 1928	21 Jun 1929	s/o Alonzo & Elizabeth
WALKER-Carroll A.	Died	24 Apr 1913	
John A.)	16 Dec 1881	3 Jul 1958	
Florace)	1 Mar 1887	4 Feb 1946	
WATERS-H. W.)	Died	24 Jun 1910	
Nancy)	2 Mar 1842	30 Nov 1908	w/o H.W.
WILKERSON-Charlie)	2 Sep 1884	4 Aug 1966	
Ollie Burchfield)	23 Dec 1888	26 Dec 1983	
Clyde	14 Sep 1912	24 Aug 1922	
John	23 Dec 1882	8 Dec 1946	
John	8 Nov 1853	12 Aug 1934	
Mary	29 Jul 1852	1 Dec 1917	w/o John
Ralph Charles	23 Jul 1910	13 Sep 1976	
Steven Craig	5 Aug 1959	1 Aug 1965	
Zada	28 Feb 1911	20 Apr 1912	
ZIRKEL-James R.	29 Jul ----	4 Dec 1879	s/o W. & M.A. (broken)
ZIRKLE-Reubin	4 Oct 1815	28 Oct 1888	
Matilda	29 Mar 1812	2 Sep 1878	66y 5m 3d
Robert M.	26 May 1872	18 Aug 1956	
Maggie E.	9 Nov 1861	16 Feb 1932	
R. T.)	29 Nov 1859	9 Nov 1939	
Hattie M.)	20 Jul 1867	31 Dec 1943	
William)	12 Dec 1832	22 Feb 1920	
M. A.)	10 Jan 1830	21 Dec 1892	

Inscriptions on the following stones were illegible or incomplete.   They are
included here because they may be of help to someone.

(broken), Susan			w/o --------
(broken),-------	died	21 Dec 1892	62y 11m 11d
M.M.		1882	s/o W.T.M. (fieldstone)

NO LAST NAME - Ollie   No dates
    Herman   No dates
    Aileen   No dates

Cherel Bolin Henderson obtained the following list of unmarked burials from her grandmother Allie Mae Bolden Bolin, the daughter of Elijah Bolden and Catherine Cross and the granddaughter of Samuel Ransom Cross and his second wife Betsy Jane Taylor. She was a babe in arms when Ransom died and she was always told she "was the prettiest baby on the hill" the day of the funeral.

BOLDEN-Catherine Cross	1877	1911	d/o Samuel Ransom and Betsy Jane Taylor Cross; w/o Elijah BOLDEN
CROSS-Faitha Harris	1816	ca. 1855	1st w/o Ransom
Betsy Jane Taylor		1880's	2nd w/o Ransom
LOWERY-Alex			
Emily Cross			w/o Alex
Walter			s/o Alex & Emily

To reach this cemetery, begin in Dandridge at the Jefferson County Courthouse. Drive west on St. 139 for 4.9 miles. Turn right onto Patterson Road and drive 0.1 mile. Turn right onto the drive leading to the cemetery.

As a soldier in Feezell's Co., 1 Tenn Inf, Samuel Ransom Cross participated in gathering the Indians for the "Trail of Tears."

This lovely fieldstone is in Shady Grove Methodist Cemetery.

Name	Born	Died	Notes
BAILEY-George Fain)	14 Jun 1937	21 Sep 1979	SN US Navy Korea
Martha E.)	15 Jul 1943	NOD	
BALLANCE-Amy Beth	1 Jun 1969	3 Jun 1969	
BANKS-Joseph H.)	1893	1978	
Callie R.)	1903	1974	
BENSON-Helen Byrd	4 Mar 1933	8 Mar 1946	
.BOHANAN-Sherrie Lyn	27 Oct 1958	30 Oct 1976	
BREEDEN-Hobert	4 Sep 1915	5 Feb 1974	Married 1 Dec 1937
Artie W.	27 Sep 1911	22 Jul 1983	
BRIGGS-Charles W.)	30 Jul 1928	NOD	
Willie Hurst)	25 Jul 1926	17 Jan 1969	
Edith Hall	18 Nov 1952	20 Jul 1972	
BUCKNER-Mary Jane	1943	1985	(fhm-Farrar)
No name	No dates		
BYRD-Alvin Leon	10 Aug 1957	13 Aug 1957	s/o Bonnie & Troy
Ben	31 Mar 1927	17 Feb 1970	
George	1 Mar 1934	3 Dec 1976	
Oliver Neil	28 Nov 1895	10 Jan 1961	
Effie Williams	20 Oct 1898	27 Jan 1960	
Troy D.)	10 Jun 1919	NOD	
Bonnie Ruth)	13 Apr 1921	NOD	
DOBBINS-Genie Sue	13 Nov 1949	7 Jun 1969	
EDDINGTON-Jesse)	16 Jun 1910	27 May 1983	
Ola W.)	2 Feb 1909	NOD	
EDMONDS-Morton R	1911	1984	(fhm-Westside Chapel)
FRITZ-Robert L. III	28 Aug 1955	5 Dec 1972	
HAMMER-James William	25 Sep 1902	4 Mar 1980	Pvt US Army
Cloella	11 Feb 1907	28 Dec 1974	
HANNAH-Arville W.)	20 Aug 1900	NOD	
Scottie S.)	12 Jul 1905	18 Jul 1966	
Arville William Jr.	18 Mar 1936	25 Feb 1979	SP 4 US Army Korea
Charles E.)	20 Apr 1933	NOD	
Ruby L.)	9 Feb 1928	19 Feb 1984	
HODGE-Rella Christopher	Born & died	25 Jan 1978	
HURST-James H.)	10 Nov 1890	13 Oct 1977	
Maudie Thomas)	6 Feb 1896	NOD	
Vickie Lee	27 Sep 1952	27 Sep 1952	
Warren H.)	23 Mar 1922	4 Jun 1976	
Agnes L.)	1 Nov 1932	NOD	
KERR-J. Pinkney)	5 Sep 1897	11 Feb 1971	
Grace M.)	3 Oct 1901	NOD	
KING-Glenn)	22 Apr 1907	12 Jun 1985	
V. L.)	22 Jun 1922	NOD	
KESSINGER-Archie M.)	21 Jun 1903	24 Jun 1980	
Mannie A.)	2 Jan 1920	NOD	
LANE-Holland A.)	1 Aug 1924	21 Oct 1984	
Elizabeth L.)	1 Jun 1927	NOD	
Noah A.)	26 May 1890	11 Jan 1967	
Delia P.)	2 Feb 1892	9 Mar 1960	
LINDSEY-Ruth Haynes	22 Dec 1935	21 Apr 1980	
LOVEDAY-Green)	20 Feb 1875	20 May 1949	
Bethene)	15 May 1877	16 Mar 1958	
Jess J.)	6 Aug 1900	13 Aug 1976	
Rosa W.)	19 Mar 1899	27 Dec 1973	
Otha Lee)	15 Aug 1910	6 Feb 1981	Wed 1 Jan 1928
Rosie Lee Ward)	16 Apr 1912	NOD	
Race T.	17 Dec 1907	21 Nov 1977	
LOVELL-Patty Russell	6 Mar 1961	14 Nov 1979	

McALPIN-Krista Lynn	30 May 1978	27 Feb 1979	
MADDRON-Ralph G.)	29 Nov 1933	24 Jun 1970	
Ina Ruth W.)	16 Jul 1935	NOD	
MANNIS-William L.)	20 Jun 1922	NOD	Wed 24 Dec 1941
Pauline Banks)	12 Mar 1925	16 Nov 1983	
MATTHEWS-Neppie E.	1925	1978	(fhm-Farrar)
PROFFITT-Phillip R.	15 Jan 1963	19 Dec 1973	A Happy Christian Cowboy
REECE-Hannah E.	23 Nov 1870	22 Mar 1957	
Jim G.)	5 Sep 1898	NOD	
Lonie M.)	28 Apr 1899	16 Jan 1983	
Troy C. "Criss"	29 May 1963	29 Apr 1985	
RILEY-Hazel Geneva	1935	1956	
Laura Mae	1932	1954	Sacrifice to Motherhood
Pamela Geneva	OD	1955	
Treeva H.)	1898	NOD	
Miney N.)	1900	1971	
RIMMER-Daron A.	20 Oct 1970	21 Oct 1970	
Jeffrey Lynn	25 Jun 1973	24 Aug 1973	
RUSSELL-Jessie Willard Jr.	1959	1985	(fhm-Farrar)
Willard)	5 Jun 1926	2 Aug 1983	
Helen)	16 Jun 1931	NOD	
SARTAIN-James "Bud")	4 Feb 1916	NOD	
Addie R.)	14 Dec 1925	NOD	
STRANGE-L. Carl)	16 May 1892	12 Dec 1965	
Daisy)	20 Aug 1901	NOD	
WALKER-Arvilla B. Maddron	7 Jul 1911	2 Feb 1955	
WHALEY-Jerry M.	31 Jan 1881	5 Dec 1971	
WILLIAMS-Grady Sr.)	23 Nov 1907	15 Jan 1969	
Gracie Shrader)	17 Jan 1913	NOD	
Jackie Ray	14 Jun 1953	18 Oct 1969	
Phyllis Ann	1 Aug 1955	14 Jul 1975	
Sanders)	3 Jun 1897	8 Jul 1964	TN Pvt 305 Ammo Tr WWI
Jessie E.)	25 Dec 1896	28 Jan 1972	
WISE-F. L.)	28 Feb 1927	NOD	Father
Lois M.)	23 Apr 1928	NOD	Mother
Gary)	16 Jun 1953	21 Jul 1977	Son
Hubert F.)	18 Mar 1903	NOD	
Aunt Nell)	15 Jul 1909	28 Dec 1984	
Janet Gail	6 Apr 1964	5 Oct 1978	
Lewis Dempsey	5 Mar 1922	13 Nov 1975	US Navy
WOODS-James P.	8 Aug 1928	26 Sep 1966	
John G.)	28 Aug 1882	7 Jun 1964	
Myrtle L.)	10 Oct 1885	14 Sep 1960	

To reach this cemetery, begin at Exit 417 from I-40. Turn south toward
Dandridge on State 92 and drive 1.7 miles to the intersection with US25W-70.
Bear left onto US25W-70. From this intersection drive 3.4 miles and turn
right. Drive 2.6 miles. The cemetery is on the right. There are several
curves with roads leading off. Take care to stay on the main road.

WHALEN CEMETERY

WHALEN-Gideon Guyle   19 Jun 1897   19 Dec 1971

This cemetery sits just behind a large billboard, atop a knoll only yards from
heavily-traveled Interstate 40. Although there is evidence of at least 22 other
burials marked with uninscribed fieldstones, the above is the only marked grave
in the cemetery. Mrs. Thelma Franklin Lindsey of Dandridge, Tennessee advised
that most of those buried here were of the Whalen connection.

To reach this cemetery, begin at Exit 417 from I-40. Turn south toward Dandridge
on State 92 and drive 1.7 miles to the intersection with US25W-70. Bear left onto
US25W-70. From this intersection drive 1.8 mile and turn right onto Goose Creek
Road. Drive 0.6 mile. The cemetery is on a knoll to the left, right up against
the interstate and behind a large billboard.

UNIDENTIFIED

Perhaps the greatest mystery cemetery in this section is the graveyard described
by Rev. Reuell B. Pritchett in his 1975 book CENTENNIAL BOOK of the French Broad
Church of the Brethern as "a large graveyard on the land near the location of the
North School House site near where Tommy Sams is now [1975] building a new restaurant
Southeast of highway 25-70. THis is now covered with a heavy growth of timber."

We have interviewed several people in this area, but can find no one who remembers a North School. One person did recall a North who taught a school on Spring
Creek, but whether or not this is the North School referred to by Rev. Pritchett,
we do not know. Tom Sams is now deceased, but we have interviewed both his wife
and his brother, neither of whom remembers any plans Tom ever had to build a
restaurant.

DOUGLAS DAM REMOVAL SECTION

JOSIAH LEATH SR.
BORN C. 1746 DIED AUG. 26. 1787
SON OF GEORGE AND MIRIAM LEATH OF VA.

The old and the new existing side-by-side. When he placed this new stone, Leeth descendant A. G. Campbell wisely left the hand carved field-stone. The stone of Josiah Leeth is the oldest marked grave in the county.

Volume II of Jefferson County Cemeteries lists only those cemeteries in the Dandridge and White Pine sections which were affected by the floodwaters of Douglas Dam.

In the entire Douglas Dam project, forty-four cemeteries were involved in three counties -- Cocke, Sevier, and Jefferson. Of these 44, only 32 were moved by TVA. TVA took advantage of the fact that several of the graveyards were old and had been abandoned for many years. Since no relatives of those buried in these cemeteries could be found, TVA left them to be flooded or to have access routes cut off. At the request of kin, 104 graves in affected cemeteries were left undisturbed.

From April, 1942, to January, 1943, 2449 graves were relocated. A total of 1379 monuments were moved, ranging in weight from a few pounds to seven tons!

Burials were reintered in 95 different cemeteries. Some, at the request of relatives, were moved to the opposite side of the river from their original locations.

TVA attempted to identify all graves, even unmarked ones, affected by Douglas Dam. This was necessary because the consent of the next of kin was required prior to moving burials.

In 1937, a transcription of Jefferson County cemeteries was made by the Works Progress Administration (WPA). These records have been used in this section as a supplement to the TVA records. We have found these WPA transcripts to be extremely unreliable and we urge that they be used with care and checked against other sources whenever possible.

DOUGLAS LAKE REMOVAL SECTION

DOUGLAS DAM REMOVAL SECTION

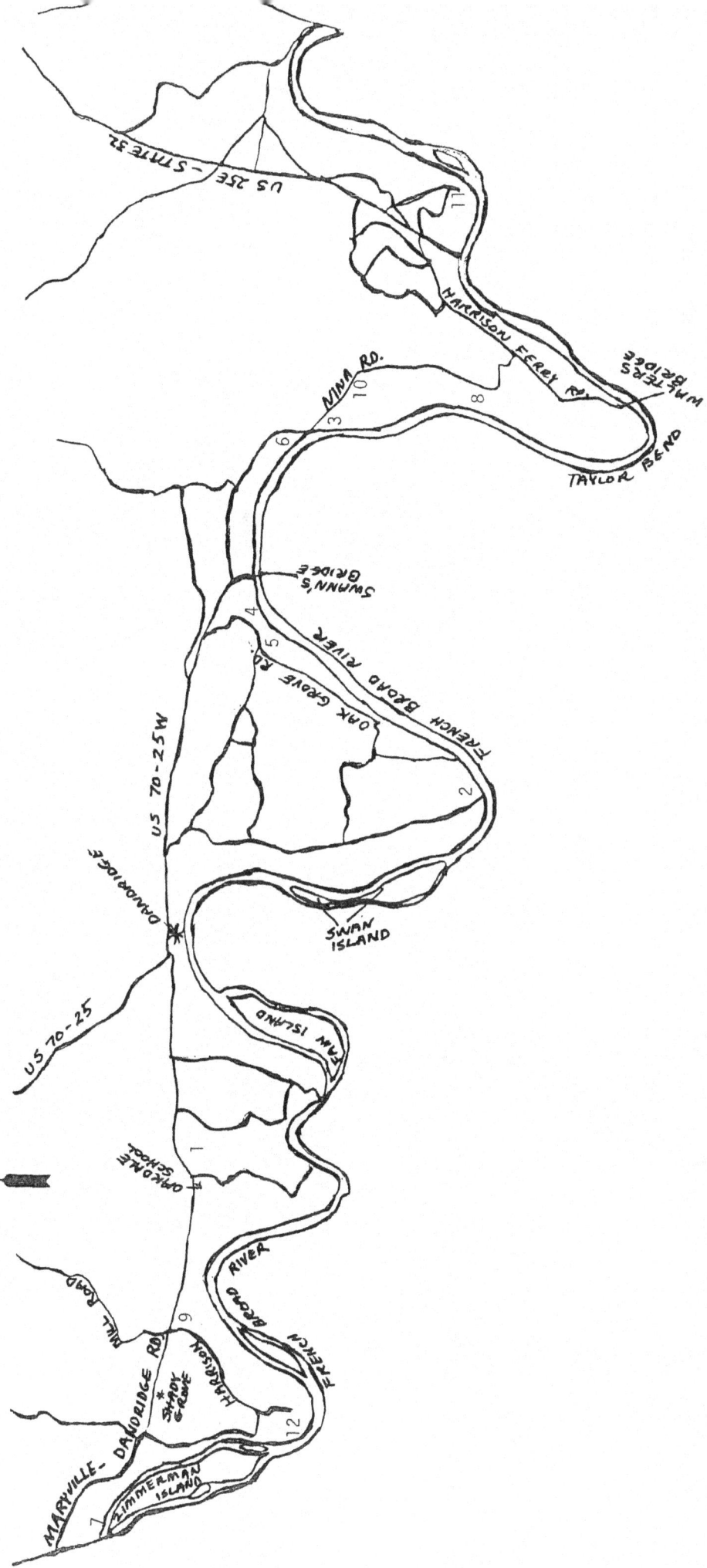

N

US 70-25

US 70-25 W

OAKDALE SCHOOL

1

FAW ISLAND

SWAN ISLAND

2

OAK GROVE RD.

FRENCH BROAD RIVER

5

4

SWANN'S BRIDGE

DANDRIDGE

6

3

10

NINA RD.

8

TAYLOR BEND

HARRISON FERRY RD.

WALTERS BRIDGE

11

US 25E - STATE 32

MARYVILLE - DANDRIDGE RD.

MILL ROAD

HARRISON

SHADY GROVE

9

ZIMMERMAN ISLAND

7

FRENCH BROAD RIVER

12

DENTON CEMETERY

(TVA REMOVAL LIST)

Name	Died	Age	Reinterment Cemetery
DENTON-Lelia Annis	1894	2	Dandridge Cemetery
George G.	1896	29	Lawson Chapel Cemetery
J. B.	1911	85	Lawson Chapel Cemetery
TAYLOR-Deborah	1897	34	Lawson Chapel Cemetery

DENTON CEMETERY

(WPA List)

DENTON-Rev. John B.	26 Aug 1836	6 Jan 1911
George C.	25 Dec 1867	22 Jan 1898
Lelia Annis	5 Jul 1892	16 Nov 1894
TAYLOR-Debie Denton	5 Jul 1892	16 Nov 1894

According to TVA records, the above were the only burials in the cemetery.

ELLIOTT CEMETERY

(WPA List)

ELLIOTT-Anna	Died	9 Sep 1849	70y 2m
Elisa	10 Mar 1820	6 Sep 1906	
George M.	13 Nov 1807	7 Sep 1872	
John	Died	19 Aug 1833	54y 19d
Margaret M.	11 Jan 1820	6 May 1898	

ELLIOTT CEMETERY

(TVA Removal List)

Name	Died	Age	Reinterment Cemetery
ELLIOTT-John	1833	54	Chestnut Hill
Anna	1849	70	Chestnut Hill
Margaret M.	1898	78	Chestnut Hill
George M.	1878	71	Chestnut Hill
Eliza	1908	88	Chestnut Hill

Between the TVA Removal List and the WPA List you will note a discrepency in the death dates for George M. and Elisa. We copied these stones in our transcription of Chestnut Hill Cemetery and can verify that the death dates given in the TVA Removal List are correct. According to the WPA records, there were six additional graves in this cemetery, all of them unmarked.

ELDRIDGE CEMETERY

(TVA Removal List)

```
ELDRIDGE-J. T.          27 Jan 1841   -- --- ----
    Margaret            12 Mar 1845  12 Mar 1905
```

ELDRIDGE CEMETERY

(WPA List)

The following list of Edridge Cemetery was prepared by TVA prior to removing the cemetery in 1942. All burials not otherwise noted were moved to the French Broad Church of the Brethern.

Name	Died	Age	Reinterment Cemetery
BRITT-Ray	Unknown	7 months	Ray's Chapel
Ruby	Unknown	Unknown	Ray's Chapel
ELDRIDGE-Ham	Unknown	Unknown	
Infant	Unknown	Unknown	
Infant	Unknown	Unknown	
Infant	Unknown	Unknown	
J. T.	1841	Unknown	
Margaret	1906	61 years	
Mollie	1918	40 years	
JOHNSON-Lizzie	Unknown	Unknown	Swannsylvania Cemetery
LAWLESS-Infant	Unknown	0	Ray's Chapel
SHULTS-Infant	Unknown	Unknown	
STEWART-Infant	Unknown	Unknown	Phillips Cemetery
TUCKER-Infant	Unknown	0	Ray's Chapel

The Elliott graves from the Elliott family cemetery were moved across the river from their original location to Chestnut Hill Methodist Cemetery.

FRENCH BROAD BAPTIST CEMETERY

(TVA Removal List)

Name	Died	Age	Reinterment Cemetery
ALLEN—Eula	1926	3m	
George	1907	35	
J. A.	1915	52	
Sallie	1926	36	
BALL—Alfred	1918	83	
James E.	1937	1	
Mary W.	1925	80	
Vira	1917	30	
BALLARD—Mable	1896	2m	
Parlea	1891	1	
BROWN—Vinnie Mae	1906	10	Seahorn Chapel Cem.
CHAMBERS—Irene	1935	75	
R. L.	1911	48	
CLEVENGER—Melvin	1921	34	
Reba	1941	27	
COLLINS—Bettie	1913	72	
Henry	1928	88	
I. R.	1889	53	
Jennie	1942	64	
J. T.	1895	53	
DENTON—Melvina	1892	65	
Sallie N.	1910	53	
W. C.	1913	61	
DODSON—J. H.	1913	47	Mt. Airy M.E. Ch. Cem.
William E.	1907	79	Mt. Airy M.E. Ch. Cem.
ELLIS—Ben H.	1898	1	Witt Baptist Ch. Cem.
Callie	1897	2	Witt Baptist Ch. Cem.
Lucy	1895	0	Witt Baptist Ch. Cem.
ELLISON—Eva	1892	2	
FINCHUM—Jane B.	1915	80	
FOSTER—Nellie F.	1924	11	French Broad Ch. Brethern
HASH—Ollie	1932	40	
HENDERSON—Robert L.	1936	25	Shiloh (Sevier County)
HINKLE—Wink	1938	71	
JOHNSON—Mary C.	1932	7	
Mary L.	1936	0	
JONES—B. Cecil	1900	9	
Eli A.	1936	69	
Hugh	1934	47	
Infant	1904	5m	
Nancy L.	1937	71	
LANE—Charlie P.	1932	12	
Peggie J.	1911	0	
LARGE—Alice C.	1930	67	
LEMONS—Charlie H.	1895	22	
MASON—Robert H.	1895	1	
William H.	1898	1	
PHILLIPS—Annie	1921	21	
Calvin	1896	30	
Claon	1933	26	
Col.	1934	28	
David H.	1892	36	
Elbert	1934	55	

PHILLIPS-J. M.	1908	62	
Nannie	1941	87	
Pearl	1894	0	
PRATT-Julia H.	1904	36	
PRYOR-J. A. P.	1902	1m	
L. L. P.	1901	1	
Clyde	1907	1	
RENEAU-Belle	1917	33	
Carolyn	1940	3d	
Infant	Unknown	Unknown	
Infant	Unknown	Unknown	
J. Port	1940	62	
Lizzie	1934	52	
Mary	1920	Unknown	
ROBERTS-J. C.	1895	15	
Holcombe	1897	2m	
SMITH-Amanda	Unknown	Unknown	
Carolyn	Unknown	Unknown	
STARNES-Clarence	1928	55	
Emma	1930	57	
J. A.	1941	79	
Jennie	1940	40	
Mary	1939	89	
TAYLOR-Tex	Unknown	65	
Walter	1941	74	
THOMAS-Eliza	1911	48	
George A.	1936	18	
George	1916	53	Swansylvania Church Cem.
G. F.	1934	69	
Hester	1915	2	French Broad Ch. Brethern
J. C.	1908	77	
Lucy	1902	2m	Swansylvania Church Cem.
Mary	1934	66	
Nancy	1898	67	
Jacob A.	1930	50	Westview
Reba	1912	7	French Broad Ch. Brethern
TURNER-Etta	1903	11	
WALKER-Samuel T.	1898	63	
WIDNER-G. W.	1913	66	
Lawrence P.	1911	18	
R. C.	1927	75	
WILLIAMS-Bessie Leota	1897	4	
Maggie E.	1909	1	
Joseph B.	1894	3	
Samuel Rufus	1894	32	
WOODS-Julia	1911	2m	Relocated Antioch Ch. Cem.

TVA records list the following description of the French Broad Baptist Cemetery at the time it was moved: "A special agreement was entered into between the TVA and the Trustees for the church and cemetery whereby a protective dike was to be constructed around the church and a fill to be made covering the cemetery between the 900 and 1006 contours. This cemetery contained 167 graves, 126 being affected by the fill covering a portion of the cemetery. 114 removal agreements and 12 remain agreements were executed by the nearest surviving relatives of the deceased for the 126 graves which were affected. We moved the 114 graves and 56 monuments to 10 reinterment cemeteries. All monuments were cleaned, repaired when necessary and reset. All reinterred graves not monumented were marked with standard metal grave markers."

FRENCH BROAD BAPTIST CEMETERY

(WPA List)

ALLEN-ELI A.	Died	8 Jul 1915	52y
J. A.	Died	8 Jul 1915	52y
BALL-Alfred	24 Dec 1839	9 Aug 1922	
Mary McNabb	19 Jan 1845	27 FEb 1925	
Vira	4 Aug 1880	6 Feb 1918	
CHAMBERS-R. L.	10 Oct 1863	25 Jan 1911	
COLLINS-Henry	1840	NOD	
Bettie	1841	1931	
J. F.	24 Apr 1842	5 Jun 1895	
COOPER-Ida BEll	23 Sep 1868	29 Nov 1894	
COWAN-Thomas A.	Jun 1864	9 May 1932	
Tommie	27 Nov 1900	19 Aug 1903	
DENTON-M. E.	No dates		
Melvina	10 Dec 1827	18 Jan 1892	
DODSON-J. H.	8 Jun 1866	28 Oct 1913	
William E.	28 Nov 1828	13 Nov 1907	
ELLIS-Ben H.	19 Nov 1897	24 Oct 1898	
Callie	2 Nov 1895	11 Dec 1897	
Lucy	Born & died	3 Feb 1923	
ELLISON-Eva	14 Mar 1890	28 Jan 1892	
Mabel	2 Jul 1896	1 Sep 1896	
FAIRFIELD-Walter Burns	25 Aug 1866	24 Jun 1907	Born Newport, Tenn.
FINCHUM-Jane Beard	20 Jun 1835	7 Aug 1915	
FOSTER-Nellie F.	20 Sep 1912	5 Jun 1924	
HENDERSON-Robert Lee	25 Jun 1911	23 May 1936	
HUGGINS-John L.	31 Jul 1874	20 Mar 1904	
Sallie A.	8 Jun 1847	22 Jun 1916	
JONES-Eli A.	16 Jan 1867	29 Jun 1936	
Infant	31 Jan 1903	11 Jul 1904	Son
Julia E.	12 May 1868	11 Feb 1904	
LANE-Charlie	20 Sep 1920	24 Apr 1932	
LARGE-Alex C.	4 Jul 1863	6 Jan 1930	
LEMONS-Charlie	15 Apr 1873	3 Apr 1895	
MASON-Robert Henry	26 Sep 1894	24 Sep 1905	
William H.	19 Oct 1897	4 Jun 1898	
MITCHELL-Alma	28 Dec 1892	6 Aug 1893	
Edith	15 Mar 1886	18 Jun 1898	
Elbert	30 Dec 1874	29 Aug 1920	
L. H.	5 Dec 1842	4 Apr 1892	
Loy I.	24 Mar 1888	19 Dec 1910	
NORTH-Infant	16 Aug 1907	17 Aug 1907	Son
Louis C. Hammer	29 Aug 1848	4 Nov 1922	
Manda	26 Apr 1875	1 Jun 1898	
Poline	29 Apr 1905	24 Jul 1905	
PHILLIPS-Annie	14 Feb 1907	16 May 1921	
Calvin	8 Jan 1866	17 May 1896	
Cloan	15 Sep 1907	25 Feb 1933	
David R.	20 Apr 1856	10 Feb 1892	
Pearl	Born & died	2 Feb 1894	
J. M.	20 Dec 1846	27 Dec 1908	
PRYOR-Clyde	29 Mar 1906	5 Aug 1907	
RENEAU-Bell	30 Feb 1884	30 Dec 1917	

ROBERTS-Halcombe	1 Sep 1897	15 Dec 1897
J. C.	11 Jul 1890	3 May 1895
Walter Royal	25 Apr 1903	27 Jun 1903
SMITH-Catherine Bear	7 May 1830	21 Apr 1916
David	4 Dec 1895	6 May 1895
Delin	29 Dec 1859	5 Dec 1928
Cora Mae	1 Nov 1869	20 Dec 1929
Hannah Jane	1 May 1852	9 Dec 1929
Jacob B.	20 May 1848	12 Sep 1895
Jennie	25 Oct 1878	23 Apr 1895
John	15 Nov 1820	22 Feb 1905
Johnie H.	29 Aug 1895	17 Jul 1896
Julia A.	25 Apr 1856	13 Feb 1903
Paul	4 Aug 1886	2 Apr 1903
Susan	2 Mar 1818	7 Oct 1900
William Hardin	2 Mar 1854	4 Aug 1934
Virginia	17 Feb 1853	17 Jun 1896
STOKLEY-Dorothy	5 Apr	23 Sep 1887
John Burnett	Died	1 Sep 1890 44y
SWANN-Alfred R.	24 Sep 1843	9 Apr 1926
John S.	9 Mar 1895	7 Feb 1897
Sarah	29 Apr 1902	30 Jan 1919
THOMAS-Callie	29 Feb 1868	1 Dec 1903
Eliza	16 Dec 1863	16 Feb 1911
George	26 Dec 1863	12 Jan 1906
G. F.	30 Dec 1865	21 May 1934
Hattie M.	16 Jan 1876	22 Dec 1896
Jacob A.	26 Nov 1880	25 Sep 1930
James A.	4 Aug 1872	24 Sep 1892
J. C.	6 May 1849	7 May 1927
J. C.	15 May 1831	27 Dec 1908
Lacy F.	21 Aug 1902	11 Oct 1902
Mary	5 Aug 1871	NOD
Mattie L.	24 Aug 1886	NOD
Nancy	24 Nov 1831	11 Mar 1898
Reba	20 Aug 1905	5 Sep 1912
Susan	12 Mar 1849	20 Mar 1920
TURNER-Ella	8 Feb 1892	10 Nov 1903
WALKER-Samuel T.	23 Nov 1835	24 Jul 1898
WIDNER-Lawrence	14 Oct 1893	27 Jun 1911
R. C.	Oct 1852	Jul 1927
Y. W.	1847	1913
WILLIAMS-Bewsie L.	26 Jun 1893	20 Jan 1897
Charles	28 Jun 1890	11 Aug 1895
Joseph R.	1 Feb 1891	31 Jan 1894
Maggie	12 May 1908	Jun 1909
Samuel Rufus	29 Aug 1862	20 Feb 1894
WOOD-Julie	6 Feb 1911	16 Feb 1911

KELLY CEMETERY
(WPA List)

KELLY-K. E.   Died   May 1827

Although this cemetery is under water when Douglas Lake reaches the 954 foot level, TVA did not move the graves. We visited the site during low water in 1986 and found the remains of three or four fieldstones still standing, but we found no evidence of the marked stone of K. E. Kelly. When WPA recorded the stone, Mr. Moreland remarked that the cemetery contained several other markers which could not be read. TVA recorded the cemetery as containing 7 graves, three of which were marekd with uninscribed fieldstones. In 1937 the cemetery site was owned by Dr. J. C. Anderson, but was better known as the John Sehorn farm. Mrs. McKinley Large remembers that the cemetery was vine-covered and overgrown in the days before Douglas Lake. There is no lushness to it today, no sign of tree or grass. The mud and silt of the dry lake bed leave it looking much like a desert or the surface of the moon.

This cemetery was described by TVA in 1941 as having been "abandoned for years and it is stated that years ago the cemetery was of considerable size but all graves except the 7 have been cultivated over. We are unable to identify any graves or locate any surviving relatives. Older residents in the community state that they have never heard the name of any person buried here and it is either a slave burial plot or the burial plot of the early settlers along the river. We are unable to find any person interested in the removal of these graves and they will remain undistrubed."

TVA did not move the Kelly Cemetery. The three fieldstones in the foreground and the one in the middle to the far right are all that remain. These stones can be seen only when the lake is very low.

BOB LANE CEMETERY

(TVA List)

The site of this cemetery is now covered by Douglas Lake. According to TVA records, there were four burials in this cemetery, none of them marked with an inscribed monument. The burials were identified by TVA as follows:

Name	Died	Age	Reinterment Cemetery
ELDRIDGE-Charlie	Unknown	Unknown	Phillips
HEADRICK-Infant	Unknown	Unknown	French Broad Ch. of Brethern
LANE-Infant	1904	Unknown	Phillips
STUART-Infant	Unknown	Unknown	French Broad Ch. of Brethern

This cemetery was not copied by WPA in 1937.

MOORE CEMETERY

Though this cemetery is now a sad sight, it once commanded one of the loveliest views in the county. In her book A.A. Moore Family, Maud Moore Snyder, writing of her ancestress, Martha Allen Moore, said, "She was buried above the house on the bluff, overlooking the river, island, and mountains, being the first person buried in this place.

Into this idyllic setting came Douglas Dam, changing the landscape until only the mountains remain as they were 150 years ago. TVA did not identify any of the burials in this cemetery and did not remove them from the harm of the floodwaters. The spot is visible when the lake is low, but the fluctuation of the water level for these many years has caused an erosion of the soil so that the exact site cannot now be located. Mr. Sam Henderson remembers this cemetery as it was and with his help we were able to visit the site and pinpoint the approximate location.

According to Leonard Moore, the following are buried here in unmarked graves:

MOORE-Chaney
    Jared

MOORE or McCORKLE CEMETERY

The following list is from the WPA transcription made in 1937:

McCORKLE-Lucy D. Moore	22 Feb 1860	9 Dec 1901	
MOORE-Andrew M.	Died	9 Sep 1854	36y 10m 5d
Elisha	Died	18 Aug 1834	41y 6m 4d
Mary	9 Feb 1795	14 Apr 1859	
Margaret A. Cowan	16 Mar 1828	22 Aug 1886	
Mrs. I. W.	Died	24 Aug 1854	34y 8m 8d
William A.	25 Dec 1815	15 Mar 1895	

This cemetery, referred to as McCorkle by WPA, was listed as Moore by TVA records. The list below was made by TVA when Douglas Dam was built in 1942. All graves were reintered in Jarnagin Cemetery in Hamblen County, Tennessee.

Name	Died	Age
McCORKLE-Lucy Moore	1901	41y
MOORE-Andrew M.	1854	36y
Elisha	1834	41y
Margaret Cowan	1886	586
Mary	1859	64y
Mary J. W.	1854	34y
William A. Jr.	1937	71y
William A. Sr.	1895	80y

When Douglas Dam was built these stones were moved from the Old Shady Grove Methodist Cemetery to the new Shady Grove Methodist. Many of these rough fieldstones were inscribed, though very difficult to read. The oldest marked stone in Jefferson County, that of Josiah Leath, Sr. who died in 1787, was among these graves.

SHADY GROVE METHODIST CHURCH

(WPA List)

This cemetery was transcribed by the WPA project in 1937. Mr. F. W. Moreland remarked that there were several burials, but only one was marked. The cemetery site is now under Douglas Lake. The following grave was transcribed by WPA:

LEEPER-Henry   27 Jun 1817 27 Dec 1845

SHADY GROVE METHODIST CHURCH

(TVA Removal List)

TVA moved the cemetery in 1942. Their records show there were 148 burials, all of which were reintered in the present Shady Grove Cemetery. Many of the graves were marked with rough-cut, handhewn fieldstones, and several had hand-cut inscriptions. These stones may be seen today in the Shady Grove Cemetery . TVA recorded the following information on burials:

Name	Died	Age
DOHERTY-Priscilla	Unknown	65
William	1819	Unknown
GAUT-Margaret	1831	30y
HENRY-Elizabeth	1838	47y
Jane	1836	53y
Jim A.	1837	16y
Mart. T.	1887	5y
LEEPER-Henry M.	1843	26y
LEETH-Josiah	1787	Unknown
Patsey	1820	Unknown
MURPHY-Hugh	1897	Unknown
Rachel	Unknown	Unknown
INDIAN BOY	Unknown	13 months

Also buried here, though unidentified by TVA is Gen. George Doherty (1749-1833), who served in the Revolutionary War under John Sevier, General Greene, and Francis Marion. Doherty was a State of Franklin supporter.   His grave was moved in 1942 to the new Shady Grove Methodist Church Cemetery. Goodspeed's History of Tennessee, published in 1887, said, "His grave, in a very neglected condition may be seen not far from where he lived."

The grave of William Doherty who died 2 Oct 1819

TVA identified this grave as "Doherty Grave."

FIELDSTONES IN OLD SHADY GROVE METHODIST

(All photos this page are courtesy of TVA)

The graves of Atsey Leeth (left) who died 26 Aug 1827, and Josiah Leeth (right), who died 26 Aug 1787.

UNIDENTIFIED

This cemetery was located 3000 feet from the right bank of the French Broad River at river mile 56.8. In TVA records it is referred to as "Bush Slave" because it was on the property of Bush Brothers and Company when Douglas Dam was built in 1941. There were 5 "very old stones." TVA could not identify any burials in the cemetery nor locate anyone who could identify any of the graves. Older residents of the community believed the burials to be those of slaves. The graves were left undistrubed. They are above lake level, but access to the site has been impaired.

UNIDENTIFIED

This lone grave was supposedly located near river mile 65.0. TVA could not locate the grave, but reported that according to legend it was the grave of an "unknown person buried near the spring." TVA stated that if the grave existed it would remain undisturbed. The grave was supposed to be on property owned by the Anderson family and was referred to by TVA as "Anderson" Cemetery.

UNIDENTIFIED

TVA referred to this cemetery as "Fox Private," named for the family who owned the land at the time Douglas Dam was built in 1941. It was described as containing "12 graves, no monuments and is very old and has been abandoned for years." TVA was unable to identify any graves or locate any surviving relatives of the deceased. The oldest residents of the community at the time Douglas Dam was being built said the graves were believed to be those of slaves buried over 100 years ago. Because of its location, this cemetery could possibly be the Gaut family cemetery which we have been unable to locate (see Gaut, Dandridge Section). TVA did not move these graves.

WHITE PINE SECTION

Russell Snodgrass was shot while trying to save his horses from raiding soldiers during the Civil War. His family's bitterness over the killing is reflected in the inscription, "Died by the hands of assassins."

Early settlement in the White Pine section was on the French Broad River and along the old Indian Warpath, which followed Long Creek.

Among the first churches in the area were Beth-Car (1787-1792), Westminster Presbyterian (1787) and Friendship Baptist.

WHITE PINE SECTION

WHITE PINE SECTION

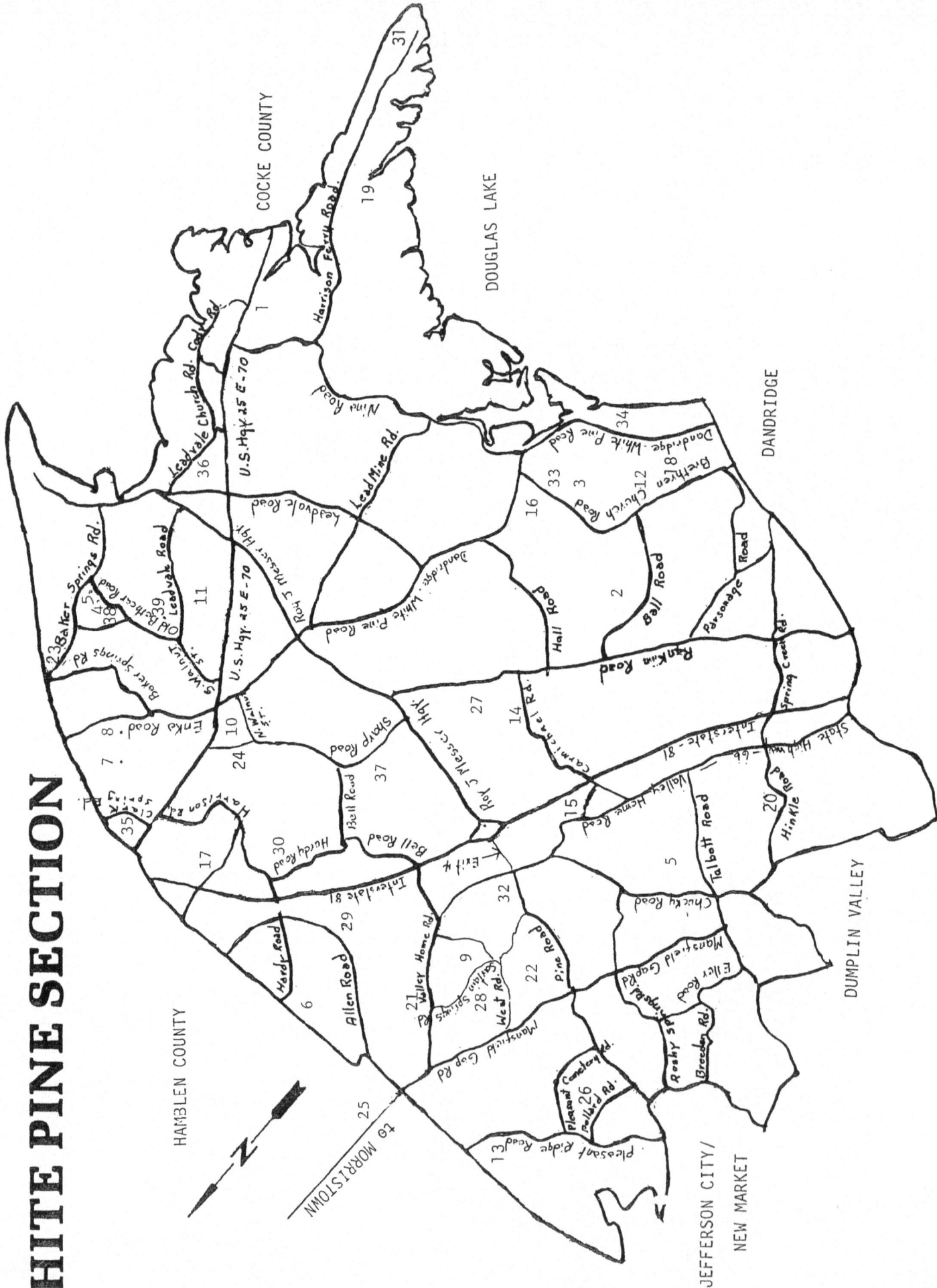

HAMBLEN COUNTY

COCKE COUNTY

DOUGLAS LAKE

DANDRIDGE

JEFFERSON CITY/
NEW MARKET

DUMPLIN VALLEY

to MORRISTOWN

N

ARNOLD CEMETERY

ARNOLD-James G.)   25 May 1885 17 Aug 1972 Married 21 Mar 1909
  Dora Ann   )   26 Dec 1882 16 Mar 1979

In addition to the above, Judy Marie Vanhoose informed us that her youngest sister
is buried here in an unmarked grave:

ARNOLD-Sue Ann   Born & died 16 Jan 1960 d/o Milburn James & Irene Arnold

This small family cemetery is fenced and well cared for. To reach it, begin at
the bridge over the French Broad River on Highway 25E. Drive toward White Pine
for 2.2 miles. The cemetery is on the left in front of a white house.

BALL CEMETERY

Although nothing remains of this cemetery, we are fortunate that it was copied
by the WPA in 1937. The only stone recorded is listed below. The cemetery is
remembered by McKinley Large, who says that there were once several stones, which
with the passage of time gradually disappeared as the area was cultivated. The
stone marking the grave of James Williford is now in the French Broad Church
of the Brethern Cemetery.

WILLIFORD-James   No dates   Co. A 9th Tenn. Cav.

To reach the original site of this grave, take Exit 424 from I-40. Drive
toward Dandridge a short distance to the intersection with US25W-70. Turn
right onto US25W-70 toward Dandridge. Drive 0.5 mile and turn right. Drive
0.1 mile and turn right onto Brethern Church Road. Drive 1.6 mile and turn
left onto Ball Road. The cemetery was located to the right near the crest of
the hill.

BOVINE GRAVE

Turcree Mark Nan, though a cow, has a regular "people" tombstone. According
to her owner, J. M. Leckie, "Tootie" was a registered Holstein who gave 264,000
pounds of milk in her lifetime, a local record.

Her name, in itself, has a story to tell. Turcree is the name of the farm.
Mark was the name of the sire, and Nan the name of the mother.

Some may think it strange that we include the grave of Turcree Mark Nan in
this book, but we feel it is worth a mention. Years from now someone may happen
upon this stone and spend hours poring over area records to find a family with
the surname "Nan," or else try to fit this cow into the family tree.

Mr. Leckie is a kindly man with a fondness for his many animals which include
cows, tens of cats and a one-eyed dog. He has a second cow he plans to bury here
once it goes to the great pasture in the sky.

To reach this grave, begin at Exit 424 on I-40. Drive 2.3 miles toward White
Pine on State 113. Turn left onto Brethern Church Rd. Drive 0.5 mile. The
stone is on the left about 100 feet from the road.

BETH-CAR METHODIST CHURCH CEMETERY

ANDERSON-Sarah E. Mims	1 Oct 1860	23 Apr 1893	w/o John
ARWOOD-William	13 Feb 1852	11 Mar 1934	
Lucinda	1872	1943	
BACKSLEY-John A.	1842	11 Mar 1929	Co. B 8th TN Inf; 87y
BAKER-I. S.)	1820	1901	Erected in the year 1920
Casandria F.)	1823	1889	by C.H. Baker in memory of
Emma C.)	1849	1889	his father's family
Mary E.)	1850	1911	deceased.
James S.)	1851	1858	
Florence B.)	1852	1859	
Bell M.)	1853	1862	
Alice J.)	1859	1912	
Nettie J.)	1860	1901	
Joseph	4 Feb 1802	11 Jun 1880	
Sibilla	1810	20 Apr 1880	
BAXLEY-Maggie Belle	30 Apr 1876	4 Feb 1932	
Virginia Mae	7 Feb 1911	13 Oct 1913	d/o Wm. & M. B.
William Sherman	1 Jun 1871	2 Jan 1953	Erected by members of the Leadvale Baptist Church to a loyal servant of God -- 1962.
BELL-George A.	10 Jun 1923	28 Sep 1924	s/o Archer & Bonnie
BEWLEY-Jesse M.	14 Mar 1846	8 Jan 1868	
Isaac W.	26 Jul 1852	5 Jan 1864	
Malinda H.	9 Mar 1812	21 Jun 1871	
BOYD-Jennie Franklin	6 Nov 1861	9 Jul 1863	d/o J.M. & J.J.
BRITT-Charlie J.	1899	1977	Pvt. US Army WWII
Georgia Bell	18 Mar 1929	15 Mar 1946	
CALFEE-John Henry)	1825	1892	
Eliza Burrus)	1829	1892	w/o J. H.
CARWILE-Laura B.	4 Feb 1884	11 Mar 1920	w/o C. V.
CLARK-Little Robert B.	21 Nov 1894	25 Jun 1895	s/o J.C. & A.F.
CURTIS-Archie	18 Apr 1850	29 Mar 1915	
Bolling	30 Jul 1816	20 Jan 1892	
Nancy Shell	7 Oct 1818	(broken)	w/o B.
George J.	8 Jan 1884	24 Aug 1900	s/o N.D. & N.M.
DALTON-H. H.	1881	1909	
Nancy C.	15 Jul 1868	6 Aug 1919	
Thelbert C.	13 Apr 1879	9 Nov 1953	
Ola	No dates		
DANIEL-Ernest L.	9 Feb 1927	14 Mar 1927	s/o J.P. & E.A.
Emma A.	30 Nov 1902	21 Mar 1928	w/o John P.
Nora Lee	6 May 1898	6 Feb 1924	
Randall Lynn	13 May 1924	11 Jun 1925	
Seargeant C. L.	1894	1919	7th Div 56 Inf Co. C
DENISON-Mary M.	22 Apr 1849	29 Nov 1893	w/o Joseph
DUNN-C. E.	12 --- ----	23 Jan 1891	Born in Forestville, N.(C?) (broken)
EDINGTON-William M.)	20 Oct 1840	11 Jul 1917	
Elizabeth C.)	13 Sep 1842	25 Apr 1888	
ELDRIDGE-James C.)	2 Apr 1846	28 Mar 1919	
Sarah F.)	17 Jun 1848	3 Feb 1927	
FAWVER-Mary A.	1 Aug 1813	25 Jul 1895	

Name	Born	Died	Notes
FRANKLIN-I.W.R.	9 Apr 1865	20 Dec 1889	
I.W.R., Sr.	23 Dec 1827	8 Nov 1866	
Lawson D.	19 Jan 1804	8 Apr 1861	
Elizabeth B.	8 Dec 1809	22 Apr 1846	Consort of L.D.; She was an early member of Methodist Episcopal Church.
L. D.	8 Nov 1841	7 Jun 1847	2nd son of L.D. & Elizabeth B.
Robt. O.	1 Dec 1829	16 Mar 1858	
FUNKHOUSER-Abraham B.	30 Oct 1808	21 May 1872	Born Shenandoah Co., Va.; Died Hamblen Co., TN.
Elizabeth	4 Jan 1813	17 Jun 1888	w/o A. B.
Bessie J.	4 Oct 1881	29 Aug 1897	d/o J. & P.H.
John Luther	30 Oct 1872	1 Sep 1873	s/o John W. & Sarah C.
J. W.	8 Sep 1836	3 Aug 1880	
Elizabeth A.)	26 Oct 1840	27 Dec 1921	w/o J.W.
Daniel McKendree)	13 Sep 1878	3 Sep 1905	Their son
Nellie M.	6 Aug 1884	27 Aug 1884	d/o P.A. & J.E.
Sarah C.	Died	25 Mar 1875	35y 6m 20d/ w/o J.W.
GIBSON-Willie Mae	4 Apr 1920	2 Feb 1977	
GREENLEE-Wm. D.	2 Jul 1822	10 Sep 1893	(broken)
Harriet J.	13 Jan 1844	16 Feb 1907	w/o W.D.
GRIFFY-John H.	4 Mar 1873	15 Feb 1880	s/o J. & M.V.
HAGAMAN-Lizzie S. Montgomery	23 Feb 1855	2 Mar 1894	w/o Rev. C.S. Hagaman; Former wife of C. D. Merritt
HAGY-David M.	1852	1926	
HARRIS-Holcombe H.	30 Jun 1890	6 Oct 1895	s/o H.H. & E.M.
HAWKINS-Arris L.)	24 Sep 1875	18 Dec 1896	
Sallie P. Taylor)	6 Nov 1875	5 Nov 1897	w/o A. L.
Infant	OD	19 Jul 1909	i/o W.E. & C.M.
Dr. J. H.	1 Oct 1861	22 Sep 1934	
Nathan F.	4 Dec 1859	16 Nov 1881	20y 11m 12d; s/o P. & V.F.
Phillip)	2 Aug 1828	12 Dec 1896	
Virginia F. Page)	21 Jan 1843	29 Sep 1924	His wife
HICKS-Leedna M.	17 Aug 1882	18 Feb 1884	d/o G. J. & M.L.
Willie G.	Feb 1890	(broken)	s/o G. J. & M.L.
HURST-Cora Ward	19 Jul 1877	21 Dec 1927	w/o Sam H.
LYLE-Martha E.	19 Dec 1838	12 Oct 1868	
McCLANAHAN-Hugh M.	24 Jan 1851	4 Jul 1900	
Susan M.	21 Nov 1847	8 May 1891	w/o H.M.
MARGRAVE-A. J.	1803	(1873?)	(broken)
MERRITT-C. D.	31 Jan 1841	9 Feb 1889	
Carrie Will	20 Feb 1883	3 Mar 1890	
MIMS-Drury I.	2 Nov 1880	14 Aug 1884	s/o M.J. & M.A.(broken)
Loula F.	15 Apr 1877	6 Jul 1877	d/o M.J. & M.A.;2m 20d
Moses J.)	1835	1909	
Mary A.)	1840	1908	
MONTGOMERY-Cal	4 Oct 1881	23 Nov 1884	d/o F.L. & N.S.
Frank L.	28 Apr 1858	10 Sep 1916	
Nena Ross	19 Jan 1857	25 Jul 1938	w/o Frank L.
Rev. William A.	16 Nov 1829	16 Dec 1905	
Caroline Franklin	5 Nov 1831	5 May 1909	w/o W.A.
Dr. Wm. H.	23 Jul 1796	21 Mar 1873	
Sarah Jarnagin	10 Nov 1796	17 Aug 1867	w/o Wm. H.; my mother
William Hamilton	20 Oct 1862	22 Jun 1882	s/o Rev. W.A. & C.E.

MOODY-Gerlad Cooper	31 Jan 1916	3 Dec 1918	s/o William & Edna
Ross D.	1909	1981	(fhm-Westisde Chapel)
William C.	30 Sep 1912	14 May 1970	Tec 5 Co I 323 Unf. WWII
MOORE-Hugh W.	11 Jul 1838	5 Jul 1893	(broken)
Little Jennie	No dates		
Jesse	Died	14 Jan 1851	81y
Martha	Died	1 May 1849	67y
John C.	1 Jan 1871	24 Jan 1852	
Mary J.	25 Nov 1832	26 Aug 1910	(see John G. ROGERS)
Julia Ann	Died	22 May 1850	35y
Lula K. Fox	12 Oct 1882	4 Aug 1932	w/o L.A.
Lida Dickson	10 May 1847	7 Apr 1905	(broken)
Martha R.	5 Jun 1818	7 Jan 1870	
NORWOOD-Infant	Died	7 Dec 1959	aged 13 hours(fhm-Maloy)
OVERHOLT-Helen Miller	Born & died	13 Aug 1915	d/o W.W. & M.E.
Infant	Born & died	7 Jan 1923	d/o J.C. & M.H.
Mildred	Born & died	19 Dec 1916	d/o J.C. & M.H.
PAGE-Rev. Gaberiel F.	4 Nov 1809	20 Jun 1881	
Matilda F. Jones	17 Jun 1818	18 Jun 1903	His wife
PRYOR-Mack)	3 May 1893	18 Mar 1896	
Jessie Elizabeth)	15 Jul 1900	15 Dec 1901	
RANKIN-Col. Creed W.	25 Sep 1821	7 May 1862	
RAULSTON-Mathew)	1742	1800	Va Pvt Capt Mill's Co.
Martha Moore)	1744	1806	Va Militia; Rev. War
REED-Cecil Earl	10 May 1919	7 Feb 1923	
RHEY-Lizzie Moore	18 May 1853	1 Dec 1937	(See John G. ROGERS)
RODGERS-Cynthia Swann	Died	10 Aug 1934	
Frank Lytle	29 Dec 1901	7 Oct 1938	
Isaac W.	21 Mar 1847	20 Apr 1934	
G. B.)	18 Jul 1894	23 Jul 1931	
Mary Moore)	2 Oct 1868	NOD	
Lizzie Moore RHEY)	18 May 1853	1 Dec 1937	
Mary J. MOORE)	25 Nov 1832	26 Aug 1910	
Joseph L.	18 Aug 1853	24 Jan 1951	
Scott Swann	14 Aug 1883	19 Jun 1907	s/o I.W. & C.G.
Seth	Died	27 May 1850	44y 6m 21d
SARTAIN-Katie Lee Baxley	18 Jul 1898	22 Jan 1920	w/o Chas. E.
SHIPLEY-Robert T.	1876	1916	
Smith)	1853	1949	
Elizabeth)	1845	1921	
Wm. H.	21 Jul 1850	23 Feb 1875	
SINARD-Paul P.	1925	1931	
Theordore R.	10 Aug 1903	16 Feb 1977	
SMITH-Benj. P.	Died	27 Oct 1913	68y; Co C 9 Tenn Cav.
D. J.	12 Oct 1895	28 Jun 1911	s/o B.P. & S.A.
D. Walter	19 Oct 1867	21 Oct 1885	s/o E.L. & B.P.
Emma L.	27 Feb 1850	13 Jul 1891	w/o B.P.
Infant	13 Jul 18__	__ Jul 189_	d/o E.L. & B.P. (broken)
Infant	Born & died	28 Sep 1894	d/o B.P. & S.A.
TALLEY-Rev. Benjamin H.	1850	1917	
Freddie F.		1894	
Ona Campbell	1809	1896	In memory of my Grand mother GMTR
THORNBURG-Charles B.	17 May 1879	25 Oct 1888	s/o J.N. & A.J.
Jasper N.)	4 Jul 1838	1 Oct 1906	
Amanda J.)	23 Aug 1836	26 Sep 1906	

WARD-R. W.	10 Jan 1845	1 May 1920	
Mahala	19 Mar 1843	14 Dec 1928	w/o R. W.

In addition to the above, the following stones were found which could not be positively identified:

(Broken) -(Annie H. Hudson)	20 ___ 1892	5 Jul 1893	
E.R.P. Jr.	OD	1901	(located near Talley and Page burials)
(Broken) - Mandy A.	__ Jun ____	8 Mar 19__	w/o J.A. (Footstone had initials M.A.B. Located beside BAXLEY burials)

The following were found by WPA in 1937, but could not be located in 1986:

HUDSON-Annie H.	20 Apr 1892	5 Jul 1893	(See above)
MARGRAVE-Rheda	1802	1870	
TALLEY-Margaret	23 Jun 1891	11 Dec 1911	

According to the History of Beth-Car United Methodist Church and Cemetery, the following is buried here in an unmarked grave:

CRAVEN-Zeverr Montgomery Pike

To reach Beth-Car Church and Cemetery, take Exit 8 from I-81. Drive toward White Pine to the intersection with 25E. Turn toward White Pine and drive 1.5 mile. Turn left onto South Walnut Street. Drive 0.7 mile and turn left. Drive 0.9 mile. Beth-Car Church and Cemetery are on the left.

(Left) Eckel Cemetery. The stone of Rev. Rich[d] Jack, who died 31 July 1831.

(Right) Dedicated to the Baker family, this monument in Beth-Car Cemetery is the largest in the county.

BETH-CAR BLACK CEMETERY

BROWN-George	Died	29 Aug 1892	
CARMICHAEL-Jesse	No dates		Co F 1st US C.H.A.
FARR-Benjamin	3 Mar 1830	15 Jul 1906	
FAUSETT-Corp'l David	No dates		Co D 1st US C.H.A.
FAWCETT-Sarah	Died	10 Jun 1921	74y
FRANKLIN-James	No dates		Co H 1st US C.H.A.
GIBBS-Samuel Oscow	17 Dec 1887	17 Jul 1903	s/o Sarah
HANKINS-Stephen	OD	11 Jan 1894	
HARRIS-Wm.	1848	1904	Co C US C.H.A.
NELSON-Amanda	Died	17 Oct 1912	w/o D.A.; about 67y age
TALLAY-George A.)	5 Nov 1884	26 Dec 1906	s/o G.T. & M.J.
Alexander)	23 Aug 1893	21 Feb 1909	s/o G.T. & M.J.
Manerva J.)	20 Oct 1861	3 Aug 1913	w/o G.T.
Irene May Hasklea)	3 Sep 1900	4 Jul 1912	
Marshall	26 Jun 1891	16 Dec 1911	
TALLEY-Maria	2 Jul 1816	20 Feb 1902	

FOOTSTONE:

L.H.   (buried beside Wm.
                                               Harris)

According to the History of Beth-Car United Methodist Church and Cemetery, the
following slaves are buried here in unmarked graves:

ALLEN-Doc
COURTNEY- Ed
FARR-Ben
HARLES-Mrs. Harriett   d/o Ezell Bogous and
                                               Mime Moore THOMPSON

    Ken
LINDON-Perry
MAGHIE-Ranse
RICE-Anse
TALLEY-Tom

A fence separates this old black cemetery from the Beth-Car Cemetery. Graveyard
vine covers a large area, and although we found only 16 marked graves, depressions
and fieldstones indicate there are 175-200 burials here.

This cemetery is immediately behind the Beth-Car Church and Cemetery. It is in
a wooded area that is overgrown with periwinkle.

We did the White Pine Black
Cemetery on Halloween and were
startled to come upon this
"dummy" lying on a grave!!

CARTER CEMETERY

ADAMS-Ivy L.	9 Apr 1890	15 Apr 1915	
Robert S.	12 Dec 1946	9 Mar 1947	s/o M/M Sam F.
Sam)	3 Jun 1888	8 May 1968	
Ruby)	19 Sep 1907	NOD	
Scott	21 Sep 1862	6 Sep 1933	
Ida	8 Jan 1870	18 Nov 1954	
AMYX-Baby Girl	1970	1970	(fhm-Brooks)
Sam F.	6 Apr 1922	14 Jun 1964	TN PFC 1385 Base Unit AAF WWII
Stoae B.)	1889	NOD	
Stella A.)	1894	1956	
ATCHLEY-Callie A.)	14 Jan 1896	19 Dec 1896	Infant daughters of
Infant)	OD	30 Aug 1891	C. L. & Louisa
AULT-Roger Scott	OD	13 Jun 1931	s/o M/M A.J.
BLACKMAN-Lillie Mae	1897	1985	(fhm-Mayes)
BUCKNER-Mattie	2 Apr 1876	2 Aug 1938	
CALDWELL-Dollie B.	1913	1981	(fhm-Westside Chapel)
CARMICHAEL-Claude E.)	22 Sep 1895	28 Jun 1964	TN Pvt HQ Co 117 Inf WWI
Lexie V.)	7 Oct 1903	18 Dec 1965	
Flo Ella	29 Mar 1916	25 Nov 1929	
John N.	1869	1927	
Lou Carter	1874	1909	
CARTER-Alonzo	28 Jan 1896	10 Oct 1918	s/o D.P. & Mary J.,Pvt. Co. A 131 Inf. Killed in action
Carolina	16 Jan 1878	25 Dec 1963	
Catherin J.	1876	1894	
Charlie Boyd	16 Apr 1894	12 Sep 1940	
David P.	1873	1875	
D. P.	20 Feb 1871	31 Jan 1959	
Mary Midkiff	8 Dec 1875	5 Feb 1944	
Enoch	7 Jul 1836	7 Mar 1905	
N. E.	1 Oct 1838	19 May 1913	w/o Enoch
Ewing)	Died	1863	
Margaret)	Died	1861	w/o Ewing
Henry Houston)	Died	1879	
William	Died	1882	
Ezra L.)	1 Dec 1911	20 Jun 1979	Tec5 US Army WWII
Alice P.)	17 Jun 1920	NOD	Married 28 Oct 1938
George B.	15 Sep 1884	19 Feb 1885	s/o W.A. & P.J.
George E.	1879	1879	
Harl Ramon	12 Jan 1899	4 Sep 1899	s/o D.P. & M.J.
James A.	16 Oct 1872	5 Jun 1946	
Ada A.	24 Sep 1875	6 Mar 1903	w/o J.A. (broken)
James U.S.	26 Jan 1866	20 Oct 1871	s/o Enoch & N.E.
J. C.)	22 Dec 1859	NOD	
S. E.)	27 May 1849	10 Mar 1925	His wife
Lillie J.	22 Jul 1886	10 Oct 1892	d/o W.A. & P.J.
Mary Maize	14 Mar 1930	16 Mar 1930	
Mattie Mae	21 May 1909	20 Nov 1910	d/o J.W. & Bessie
Nancy E.	1867	1867	
N. V. S.	No dates		Co F 9th Tenn Cav
Robert H.	7 Dec 1839	31 May 1900	60y 5m 24d
Serena A. Rimmer	1841	1908	w/o Robert E.
W. A.	17 Oct 1846	24 Jun 1909	
Jane	18 Nov 1846	27 May 1920	

CARTER-Wilburn J.	17 Aug 1892	18 Aug 1935	
William E.)	28 Feb 1868	27 Jun 1940	
Sarah C.)	18 Jan 1865	26 Jan 1943	
CLINE-Blondon Wirt	25 Sep 1899	2 Dec 1947	
CODY-Bob	4 Dec 1897	24 Aug 1917	
Harrison)	17 Jul 1873	22 Apr 1951	
Lizzie)	18 Jan 1876	NOD	
COLLIER-Beatrice G.	25 Apr 1929	6 Jun 1965	
Timothy Mark	OD	12 Jan 1959	Inf s/o Beatrice & Claude
COLLINS-Claude)	1906	1983	
Nancy)	1918	1976	
COLYER-James W.)	17 Mar 1898	26 Dec 1967	
Cora)	27 Mar 1909	NOD	
Niner Ruth	16 May 1929	13 Jul 1935	
COX-Ida Frances Rickard	1910	1940	
CRIDER-Emma Watts	1890	1957	(fhm-Brooks)
FISHER-Anna Fay	6 Mar 1921	22 Nov 1936	
Frances Edith	26 Sep 1915	10 Apr 1986	
Infant	OD	10 Sep 1915	s/o L.F. & Allie
Leonard L.)	1 May 1889	5 Nov 1959	
Allie Bell)	7 Dec 1890	22 Oct 1958	
Ollie Lee	5 Nov 1905	29 May 1984	
GIBBONS-Mattie	12 Feb 1882	28 Mar 1936	
GOODMAN-Frank L.	1921	1986	(fhm-Westside)
Lillian B.	1895	1975	(fhm-Westside)
Raymond H.	1931	1978	(fhm-Westside)
HAMMER-Nelle Adams	13 Mar 1894	19 Feb 1977	
HARBIN-William O.	1924	1974	(fhm-Stubblefield)
HARDY-Earnest	14 Oct 1910	13 Dec 1910	s/o J.T. & O.E.
HAZELWOOD-A. H.	4 Dec 1877	31 Oct 1962	
Mattie A. Smith	1888	1935	w/o A.H.
Geneva	31 May 1914	7 Jan 1915	
Oscar Jr.	1965	1985	(fhm-Wilson)
HEDRICK-Thomas Lee	18 Dec 1947	8 Mar 1948	
HELTON-Effie Jeanette	1950	1971	
Herman)	21 Aug 1925	20 Apr 1977	
Laura B.)	14 Jun 1927	NOD	
Mayford E.	1938	1980	(fhm-Westside)
Robert H.	15 May 1945	1 Oct 1979	Son
HERREN-Lynn Adams	24 May 1900	31 Jan 1938	
HOLT-Tennie Carmichael	26 Apr 1881	27 Oct 1955	
HOPKINS-David Scott	20 Jan 1959	21 Jan 1959	s/o Glenn & Lorine
Hannah Z.	23 May 1907	1 Jan 1910	d/o N.H. & A.B.
Rev. J.C.	1871	1961	
Drucilla ONeal	1876	1962	
Rev. J.T.	13 Dec 1850	8 Aug 1922	married to Miss Ruthy

Williams 21 Apr 1870. He was ordained Missionary
Baptist Minister 44 years.

Ruthy Williams	9 Feb 1850	31 Jan 1924	w/o Rev. J.T.
J. T., Jr.	19 Apr 1914	25 Jun 1914	s/o N.H. & A.B.
Juanita)	25 Jun 1912	12 Aug 1912	
Verna Jane)	23 Jun 1924	20 Jun 1926	
Marshall N.	11 Apr 1897	12 Oct 1918	s/o N.H. & A.B., 17 Co.
			Auto. Repl. Draft Sard.
Melvin Jackson	11 Jun 1934	14 Jun 1934	

HOPKINS-Noah Henry)	16 Jul 1872	16 Jul 1962	
Annie Belle)	23 Jul 1880	26 Dec 1972	(fhm says Annie B. Sartin Hopkins)
Thomas S.	20 Jan 1904	22 Sep 1983	
William A.)	16 May 1873	13 Aug 1927	married 15 Mar 1903
Lizzie McClanahan)	1 Aug 1883	14 Mar 1970	
HORNER-D. W.)	25 Apr 1869	28 Mar 1945	
Maggie J. Henson)	28 Aug 1873	11 Sep 1956	His wife
Haney	1902	1919	
James Bernard "Jimmy"	18 Aug 1946	1 Apr 1985	s/o Hampton & Hazel Sp4 US Army
James Haskell)	22 Sep 1890	29 Apr 1945	
Rosa Mae)	24 Oct 1898	NOD	
Martha White	1892	1919	
HORTON-J. Arthur)	28 Sep 1902	27 Mar 1983	
June Adams)	2 Jun 1910	4 Oct 1972	
John Abner	1854	1928	
Louisa M.	1854	16 Jun 1926	72y
Joseph Wesley Sr.	2 Jan 1892	21 Aug 1976	US Army WWI
W. M.	9 Oct 1878	7 Dec 1952	
Catherine M.	6 Jan 1882	18 Mar 1963	
INMAN-Artie Smith	24 Feb 1896	25 Sep 1920	
Bertha Fay	16 Jun 1916	19 Jan 1918	
Lillie Josephine	16 Jan 1914	10 Nov 1918	
Ralph H.	27 Mar 1891	25 Oct 1942	
JINKS-Francis	2 Apr 1916	15 Jul 1983	(fhm-Stubblefield)
Phil L.	Born & died	4 Jul 1946	
KIMBROUGH-Aaron Monroe)	12 Apr 1859	24 Dec 1951	
Bell Rickard)	14 Oct 1861	17 May 1947	
Alvin Wayne	Born & died	5 Apr 1937	s/o M/M B. H.
Anna Mae	20 Dec 1918	9 Jan 1928	d/o M/M Oscar
Burnace H.	31 Mar 1912	16 Nov 1975	
E. H.	13 Nov 1829	5 Sep 1898	Co G 4 Tenn Cav
Sarah P.	20 Oct 1828	9 Oct 1915	
Hugh	25 Feb 1883	11 Dec 1898	s/o A.M. & A.B. 15y 9m 16d
James Hale)	1 Mar 1868	2 Dec 1947	
Mary L. Skeen)	24 Aug 1872	2 Jul 1941	
James N.	25 Aug 1895	31 Aug 1896	(fieldstone)
M. R.	2 Feb 1833	21 Nov 1907	Co A 9 Cav.
Ellendor J.	4 Jun 1834	26 May 1919	85y
Oscar A.)	3 Feb 1881	2 Nov 1918	37y 9m
Mary Carter)	16 Apr 1889	13 Jun 1966	His wife
Samuel J.	29 Mar 1896	7 Feb 1899	(fieldstone)
KLEPPER-Arthur	17 Apr 1869	11 Nov 1946	
Mary Elizabeth	14 Sep 1868	28 Oct 1929	w/o Arthur
Lee C.)	10 Feb 1900	29 Aug 1873	
Mossie L.)	8 Jul 1909	NOD	
Lee Jr.	21 Sep 1924	20 Apr 1980	
Sue	19 Mar 1907	11 Apr 1924	d/o M/M Arthur
KNIGHT-Jennie M.	7 Aug 1906	19 Feb 1963	w/o J.G.
LAWSON-James L.	1969	1969	(fhm-Brooks)
LEE-Andy J.	8 Feb 1850	3 Oct 1949	
Mary Jane Gentry	18 Jun 1868	27 Aug 1941	
Lettie May	31 May 1896	25 Nov 1898	d/o J.H. & Nep

McCLAIN-Ella Netta	14 Mar 1899	1 Apr 1900	d/o J.H. & C.B.
Ida F.	28 Oct 1868	22 Jan 1897	
McCLANAHAN-David	OD	10 May 1931	infant s/o W.H. & Ann
Howard C.	16 Jun 1912	28 Dec 1930	
Hugh)	4 Mar 1882	20 Dec 1955	
Lillie)	26 Jul 1888	27 Jul 1940	
James	24 Sep 1928	10 Apr 1929	
Tommy Harvey	OD	26 Apr 1940	
Ulyss Simps)	8 Feb 1871	1 Jan 1946	
Sarah Isabelle)	8 Apr 1877	7 Mar 1947	
Virgie	1904	1984	(fhm-Mayes)
Wm. Ray	12 Oct 1911	29 Apr 1912	
McKINEY-Elender	14 Mar 1836	22 Feb 1900	
McKINNEY-Bessie K.	1897	1985	(fhm-Westside Chapel)
Bonnie Deborah	27 Apr 1920	17 Sep 1921	d/o M/M Roy
Rufus)	1884	1970	
Ida)	1886	1950	
Stella Grace	22 Feb 1913	30 Mar 1928	d/o M/M Roy
McNABB-Angelque Denee	4 Jan 1972	16 Jan 1972	
MIDKIFF-John W.	20 Apr 1853	2 Jun 1922	
Oda Bell	9 Oct 1863	20 Aug 1949	
J. Willard	18 Nov 1885	9 Jun 1947	
Roy	21 Jan 1888	12 Jul 1917	
MOORE-James)	4 Feb 1838	4 Aug 1910	
Mary Rickard)	18 Feb 1894	16 Apr 1924	His wife
Luease	19 Apr 1921	26 Jan 1924	d/o W.M. & Elsie
Wade)	10 Jan 1894	7 Dec 1978	
Elsie)	15 Aug 1897	9 Feb 1983	
Willie Earnest	No dates		
MORGAN-Johnny Jr.	13 Aug 1943	13 Mar 1974	
Steve Lynn	18 Apr 1958	16 May 1973	
MOYERS-Samuel P.)	14 Jun 1852	16 Dec 1915	
Mary L.)	17 Sep 1857	3 Nov 1929	
PHAGAN-Earl G.	12 Jun 1924	28 Aug 1924	s/o M/M F.H.
Fred	8 Jul 1875	16 Oct 1953	Tenn Pvt Co G 26 Reg Inf
Thulia Alice	5 Sep 1884	20 Jun 1924	w/o F.H.
James N.	21 May 1911	28 Dec 1977	h/o Ethel SSgt US Army WWII
Ethel McKinney	6 Feb 1906	17 Jan 1977	
John P.	16 Jun 1812	5 Nov 1884	Volunteered in the Indian War 1836
Millia	29 Mar 1817	22 Mar 1898	
RICKARD-Baby	No dates		
Earl	No dates		
Emma	No dates		
James	17 Feb 1835	1917	Erected by W.P.
Malinda	8 Feb 1839	14 Jan 1924	Erected by W.P.
James Cecil	3 Apr 1907	6 Aug 1964	
J. D.	4 Feb 1824	13 Jan 1913	
Rebecca	15 Apr 1836	13 May 1909	w/o J.D.
Kaih W.	6 Sep 1896	29 Mar 1959	Pvt US Army WWI
Kenneth A.Z.	8 Dec 1910	7 Nov 1965	
Mary	2 Apr 1882	2 Apr 1928	Erected by W.P.
Ona	No dates		
Porter Wilmer	8 Mar 1877	7 Jul 1944	Erected by Cora Colyer
Rebecca	5 Nov 1903	9 Mar 1919	d/o W.R. & Mattie
Samuel J.)	1 Dec 1868	22 Feb 1945	
Ina H.)	2 Nov 1878	NOD	

RICKARD-Verina J.	20 Nov 1913	13 Dec 1920	
Wade)	1867	1986	
Marshal)	No dates		Son
W. R.	15 Mar 1867	13 Aug 1925	
ROBINETTE-Sallie	4 Oct 1857	5 Aug 1927	
SARTAIN-Artie M.	22 Dec 1888	23 Nov 1918	w/o F.M.
Ernest Ralph	Born & died	26 Dec 1935	s/o M/M Dewey
Francis M.	15 Jun 1884	30 Apr 1959	
Frank E.	8 Nov 1915	30 May 1919	s/o J.C. & D.H.
Henry D.)	8 Nov 1875	13 Apr 1966	
Julia C.)	20 May 1879	29 Jan 1945	
Herman Eugene	Born & died	20 Mar 1930	s/o M/M Paul
Jack Rondal	Born & died	9 Jan 1936	s/o Mattie & Pete
James Henry	19 Apr 1899	11 Mar 1971	
Lonnie M.	29 Nov 1905	16 Jun 1935	
Pauline Hopkins	18 Jun 1915	29 Dec 1935	w/o Dewey
William M.)	29 Aug 1868	1 Mar 1951	
Mollie A.)	19 May 1872	23 Sep 1943	
SHEPARD-Jim)	17 Oct 1878	27 Jul 1948	
Sallie)	16 Jul 1879	15 Oct 1937	
Lila Whitlock	15 Jul 1900	16 Oct 1940	
Paul Pinky	6 Mar 1916	19 Jun 1973	TN PFC US Army WWII
Roxie	OD	7 Dec 1936	TN Corp 306 Engrs 81 Div
SHEPHERD-Ruby	14 Mar 1913	30 Apr 1913	d/o R. & J.
SHOCKLEY-Ivan Grant	18 Jun 1917	1 Jan 1934	
Willis M.	1 Dec 1890	22 Feb 1978	
Lizzie Adams	17 Apr 1892	20 Oct 1944	
SMITH-Alexander)	16 Oct 1896	3 Jul 1929	
Laura H. Hopkins)	1 Jan 1903	9 Oct 1985	w/o Alexander
Clarence Earl	7 May 1933	27 Dec 1947	Killed in a car wreck at White Pine
Estel T.)	19 Mar 1908	22 Feb 1968	
Bessie M.)	19 Feb 1914	NOD	
Hobert)	4 Mar 1895	17 Jan 1940	
Lillie Mae)	21 Jun 1899	22 Nov 1985	
Isaac R.)	31 Oct 1859	16 May 1941	
Sallie Rickard)	30 Apr 1863	19 Feb 1946	His wife
Isaac Scott	27 Apr 1920	25 Nov 1921	
J. Frank)	12 Jan 1871	21 May 1960	
Susan R.)	7 Sep 1872	22 Mar 1915	
Thomas	3 Apr 1836	21 Dec 1913	
Martha A. Stansberry	27 Aug 1842	27 Feb 1909	w/o Thomas
Wade)	31 Aug 1899	NOD	
Martha J.)	27 May 1901	25 Jun 1981	
William J.)	30 Jun 1876	9 Jun 1930	
Martha J. Gibbons)	16 Jun 1874	30 Dec 1954	
Noah W.A.	7 May 1928	13 May 1928	
SULLIVAN-Noah B. Jr.	31 May 1884	22 May 1932	
SUNDERLEND-Thomas	Died	3 Aug 1872	s/o S.W. & M.J. 1y 2m 26d
TEMPLIN-William M.)	26 Mar 1869	5 Jul 1925	
Laura V.)	13 Jan 1870	25 Dec 1958	
TUNNELL-Mary Ellen	1924	1928	
WAYMIER-Maggie Adams	28 Feb 1904	16 Mar 1936	
WEST-Alger	9 Mar 1893	12 Mar 1961	TN PFC US Army WWI
Bob	1 Sep 1886	2 Feb 1971	
Ethel	1 Jul 1896	4 Oct 1932	w/o Robert
Georgia Mae	28 Sep 1938	5 Nov 1938	

WEST-W. F.)	31 Dec 1864	3 Sep 1948	
Nancy E.)	2 Mar 1866	10 May 1945	
WHITE-Alice Smith	1869	1936	
Arthur Jr.	24 Jan 1922	2 Jan 1926	
Barsha Hartsell	3 Nov 1900	25 Mar 1933	
Ben L.	2 Sep 1888	6 Jul 1953	
Carrie J. Hazlewood	30 Jul 1893	1 Mar 1920	w/o Ben L.
Billy J.)	No dates		Girls of M/M J.W.
Mary A.)	No dates		(fhm-age 6y 9m)
Charles K.	10 Oct 1983	2 Feb 1984	(fhm-Stubblefield)
Charley	3 Nov 1886	18 Jan 1908	
Ernest Lee	4 Nov 1916	4 Mar 1962	
Ethel J.	2 Apr 1892	22 Jun 1897	
G. Arthur)	1890	1962	
Susan M.)	1896	NOD	
Homer T.	1908	1947	
Isaac A.	1897	1932	
James L.	OD	1925	Infant
James W.	30 Aug 1898	9 Mar 1967	
James W. Jr.	17 Dec 1960	29 May 1979	
Kirk	10 Oct 1983	2 Feb 1984	
Lizzie A.	5 Feb 1890	9 Mar 1904	
Robert A.	22 Jul 1885	4 Nov 1905	
William L.)	15 Jul 1864	1 Mar 1906	
Mary T. Carter)	27 Mar 1866	2 Nov 1931	His wife
Willie M.	22 Jan 1895	11 Mar 1900	(broken)
NO LAST NAME:			
Infant	No dates		(Beside Ben L. White)
Infant	No dates		(Beside Ben L. White)
INITIALS ONLY:			
J.D.R.			(These four markers have
R.R.			no names or dates. They
R.N.R.			are located beside
W.H.R.			Rickard burials.)

In addition to the above, there are 47 burials marked with uninscribed fieldstones.

To reach this cemetery, begin at Exit 4 from I-81. Turn onto Roy J. Messer Highway (away from White Pine) and drive 0.4 miles to to Kimbrough's Crossroads (intersection of Roy J. Messer Hwy. and Valley Home Road). Turn right and drive 2.7 mile on Valley Home Road. Turn right onto Hardy Road. Drive 0.4 miles and turn right. The cemetery is on a hill to the right.

CHILTON CEMETERY

CHILTON-James	Died	30 Oct 1858	62y 7m 6d
Joseph	Died	11 Mar 1858	40y 3m 15d

INITIALS ONLY:

J. T. McK.	Died	1850	(fieldstone)

In addition to the above, there at 15 burials marked with uninscribed fieldstones. The site is unfenced and open to grazing cattle. This old cemetery is on a knoll overlooking the Long Creek Valley.

Adjacent to, but separate from the Chilton Cemetery, are the following graves:

FRANKLIN CEMETERY

FRANKLIN-Arynac	1891	1974	(fhm-Farrar)
James A.	14 Jul 1864	10 Feb 1937	
Walter Luminaus	1901	1972	(fhm-Farrar)

These graves are fenced with an electric fence.

To reach these cemeteries, begin at Exit 8 from I-40. Drive toward White Pine to the intersection with 25E. Turn toward White Pine and drive 1.7 mile, and turn left onto the Enka Road. Drive 1.0 mile. The cemetery is on the left atop a hill.

CIVIL WAR SOLDIER

J.T. Hopkins recalls that old timers passing this site always pointed to a lone grave and remarked that a Civil War soldier was buried there. If anyone knew his identity or if he was Union or Confederate it was never stated. The site is near the ditchline near Sartain Springs Baptist Church, about halfway between a big tree and a drainage tile.

CHURCH-IN-THE-PINES CEMETERY

ACUFF-Henry B.)	20 Oct 1910	27 Mar 1967	
Alice F.)	1 Jan 1918	15 Nov 1978	
John Robert	8 Mar 1965	9 Mar 1965	
ALEXANDER-Cecil)	6 Sep 1936	NOD	
Kathleen)	9 Mar 1941	24 Nov 1976	
Claude R.)	22 Dec 1912	11 Nov 1969	TN ptr2 USNR WWII
Alma G.)	22 Oct 1915	24 Feb 1983	
Ware Ellis	12 Feb 1899	21 May 1907	s/o W.E. & S.E.
W. E.	3 Aug 1869	25 May 1904	
Willie Burl)	7 Sep 1908	2 Oct 1971	Married 15 Jun 1930
Nannie B.)	6 Feb 1912	NOD	
ALLEN-John)	1898	1981	
Beatrice)	1904	1979	
Mary E. Wooliver	8 Mar 1868	21 May 1901	w/o P.C.
ALLISON-Johnathan B.)	4 Jan 1917	10 Mar 1973	
Lancy W.)	11 Jun 1914	19 Oct 1973	
Jonathan M.)	27 Dec 1893	17 Feb 1952	
Docia M.)	22 Apr 1895	15 Jan 1979	
ANDERSON-Frank Mims)	6 Nov 1883	3 Nov 1941	
Mary Kate Inman)	3 Oct 1893	29 Jan 1982	
ARWOOD-Byrle R.)	5 Feb 1908	20 Jan 1964	TN Pvt 79 Inf Trng BN WWII
Pauline B.)	21 Jan 1922	NOD	
John C. "Cal"	6 Apr 1891	18 Jun 1983	
Dora Belle	31 Aug 1897	25 Sep 1966	
Maggie M.	4 May 1887	23 Jan 1968	
ATKINS-Charles C.)	26 Jul 1912	1 Jun 1983	Married 24 Oct 1936
Alice S.)	3 Nov 1913	NOD	
BACON-George W.)	6 Aug 1866	8 May 1940	
Dorcas Katherine)	21 Feb 1884	2 Sep 1944	
BAILEY-Belle	21 Mar 1880	12 Mar 1966	
Elvern J.)	12 May 1878	18 Jan 1942	
Vinnie L.)	3 Oct 1881	17 Oct 1941	
Pvt. Guy E.	1922	1943	391 Inf 2nd Bat.
H. A.	No dates		
James H.)	7 Sep 1914	20 Oct 1948	
Jennie N.)	18 Mar 1916	NOD	
Landon H.	13 Oct 1898	30 Dec 1978	
Eula Grace	7 Jan 1898	17 May 1982	
Sarah A.	29 Aug 1857	5 Feb 1895	w/o D.A.
BAIRD-Linnie M. Humpston	20 Jan 1889	29 Jun 1918	w/o James E.
BAKER-Joseph	20 Feb 1861	16 Feb 1944	
BALLARD-Angela	Born & died	17 Apr 1982	d/o M/M James
Clayton I.)	11 Aug 1877	20 Jan 1963	
Fannie E. Bond)	9 Mar 1887	12 May 1921	
Clayton I., Jr.	31 Mar 1911	4 Nov 1983	
Henry A.)	25 Apr 1913	NOD	
Margaret Wice)	10 Apr 1916	NOD	
BALES-Harvey	27 May 1844	9 Jun 1924	Co M 1st TN Cav
BARNES-James A.)	6 Oct 1902	7 Jun 1959	
Myrtle M.)	29 Mar 1908	NOD	
Raymond	20 Mar 1928	26 Sep 1980	
BARTLEY-Mildred Alleyne	16 May 1897	25 Aug 1897	d/o E.E. & Lena B.
BAUGUS-Edna Ruth	1923	1984	(fhm-Smith)
BAXLEY-Robert E.	21 Jan 1896	8 Feb 1976	

BEAVER-Azzie "Mamie"	23 Sep 1881	9 Jun 1958	
BELL-Lantie J.)	1907	1957	
Edith I.)	1912	1975	
Rhea Calvin)	3 Jan 1883	24 Aug 1965	
Minnie Walker)	7 Jun 1881	27 Nov 1974	
Samuel B.)	19 Jul 1849	27 Feb 1914	Father
Emma C. Blackburn)	23 Aug 1851	25 Mar 1938	Mother
John C.)	22 Dec 1884	12 Oct 1951	
Eva J.)	10 Sep 1884	8 Jul 1978	
Rolf R.)	8 Sep 1890	29 Jun 1981	
Margaret G.)	25 Oct 1902	16 Jul 1980	
Thomas M.)	30 Oct 1879	30 Aug 1910	Son
Anna Ernestine)	29 Nov 1893	8 Apr 1919	Daughter
BERRY-Joe J.	1917	1984	Pvt US Army WWII
BETTIS-Bradley)	30 Nov 1840	20 Mar 1914	
Priscilla C.)	28 Jan 1841	15 Feb 1926	His wife
Rosa B.	19 Jul 1882	9 Sep 1888	
BEWLEY-William Emmerson, MD)	21 Jul 1870	9 Mar 1909	
Mary Louise)	6 Mar 1875	5 Dec 1956	
BEZOLD-Charles R.	31 May 1888	5 Dec 1974	
Eula Calfee	9 Jun 1894	11 May 1980	
BIBLE-lloyd Edgar)	4 Apr 1889	2 Apr 1938	
Fannie Etta)	13 Feb 1893	16 Sep 1942	
Christine)	Born & died	20 May 1926	
Maxie S.)	20 Mar 1912	21 Sep 1926	
Rex D.)	8Feb 1908	30 Sep 1977	
Neva M.)	9 May 1911	23 Nov 1974	
Robert Croft)	31 Aug 1861	6 Sep 1945	
Lillie Haun)	22 Jun 1868	3 Jul 1938	
Helen Hicks	6 Aug 1919	8 Oct 1954	
Roland R.	1894	1935	
BIDDLE-C. A.)	24 Jan 1847	20 Jun 1920	Father; married 11 Apr 1866
M. A.)	1 Nov 1849	25 Jul 1905	Mother
Charles M.)	26 Nov 1878	31 Jul 1942	
Mary E.)	30 Sep 1882	11 Mar 1917	
Charles Mac Jr.)	19 Oct 1919	28 Aug 1965	
Jennie J.)	29 Dec 1888	5 Oct 1976	
Glea "J.C."	20 Nov 1896	2 Aug 1974	
James S.)	3 Dec 1857	8 Jun 1955	
Thulia I.)	8 Aug 1867	4 Sep 1929	
Melvin C.)	30 Aug 1865	17 Oct 1922	
Lida Belle)	19 Mar 1873	9 Feb 1918	
R. C.	22 Jun 1830	7 Jan 1903	
William S.)	5 Sep 1822	12 Dec 1914	
Catherine E. Coldwell)	2 Aug 1832	10 Jun 1906	His wife
BIRD-C. H.)	27 Jan 1854	11 Nov 1926	
Mary L. Broyles)	18 Oct 1857	6 Aug 1929	His wife
BLACK-Arthur M.)	18 Jan 1876	6 Feb 1965	Cpl Co K, 4 Rgt Tenn Inf, Spanish-American War
Charles Robert	26 Feb 1887	24 Aug 1890	s/o J.C. & Belle
Infant	18 Jun 1890	6 Aug 1890	s/o J.C. & Belle
John C.	1 Oct 1860	24 Sep 1904	
Mary E.	21 Apr 1849	11 Oct 1893	
Robert C.	1826	1901	
Addie	1838	1912	

BLACKBURN-Thomas Snoddy)	28 Aug 1823	13 Mar 1903	
Mary L.)	22 Aug 1829	7 Oct 1917	
BOATMAN-Phyllis A.	OD	23 Jun 1939	
BOLLING-Maude Wright	4 Jun 1901	24 Jun 1976	
Wendell Gene	20 Feb 1967	29 Jul 1980	
BOWEN-Rev. J. W.	26 Jun 1842	28 Nov 1894	
BOYER-Sharon Turner	1 Oct 1958	12 Apr 1978	
Terry Scott	23 Mar 1957	12 Apr 1978	
BRACKETT-Jessie O.	Died	27 Nov 1934	74y
BRADLEY-James H.)	21 Jun 1873	21 May 1905	
Annie E.)	4 May 1882	16 Nov 1911	His wife
BRADY-Arthur B.)	11 Feb 1911	NOD	
Lula B.)	21 Jul 1908	23 May 1976	
Freddie Joe	1955	1955	s/o Roy & Ruby
John T.	5 Jan 1909	NOD	
Paul J.)	15 Aug 1936	NOD	
Laverne Ward)	7 Nov 1936	NOD	
Roy)	16 Sep 1918	NOD	
Ruby J.)	30 Aug 1922	NOD	
BRIGGS-Dearl I.)	16 Mar 1921	7 Dec 1981	
Mildred M.)	15 Aug 1926	NOD	
Elwood)	21 Jul 1916	15 Jan 1978	
Bernice)	1 Oct 1923	13 Oct 1983	
BRIMER-Houston	20 Mar 1836	1 Jun 1914	
Elizabeth	9 Oct 1832	5 Dec 1911	w/o Houston
Martha Caroline	20 Dec 1848	27 May 1925	
BRITT-Ellen Ward	1918	1958	
Louis Wayne	23 Aug 1949	19 Jan 1950	
Ralph R.)	9 Feb 1906	16 May 1976	
Lexie I.)	8 Jan 1910	31 Aug 1970	
Veda Alene	4 Jun 1925	30 Jan 1983	
Wm. Clyde)	22 Apr 1907	19 Aug 1981	
Janie Pearl)	5 Dec 1907	2 Jul 1983	
BROOKER-John R.)	1911	NOD	
Hulda E.)	1913	1979	
BROWN-Elisha Foster	1918	1985	PFC US Army WWII
Isaac)	17 May 1893	19 May 1976	
Dovie)	10 Jun 1894	9 Nov 1985	
Mont	7 Aug 1917	25 Jul 1970	
BROYLES-Linda Faye	6 Feb 1948	8 Feb 1948	d/o M/M Clarence
BURCHETT-Maurice C.)	10 Apr 1916	NOD	
Millie J.)	23 Jun 1910	NOD	
Maurice Eugene)	28 Aug 1943	26 Jun 1969	
BURGIN-Martin L.)	25 Feb 1903	NOD	
Virginia A.)	15 Aug 1903±	3 Apr 1982	
BURLING-Alice E.	2 Feb 1891	6 Sep 1930	
Edward)	21 Nov 1835	12 Feb 1916	
Susie A. Steiner)	7 Ocg 1854	20 May 1933	His wife
CAIN-Lidyia	1874	1937	
CALDWELL-Catherine P.	5 Nov 1835	8 Apr 1920	
Lula Geisler	9 Sep 1872	31 Aug 1902	w/o J. E.
Susie Burt	26 Nov 1861	22 Dec 1952	
CALFEE-Casey B.	7 Oct 1878	26 Aug 1954	Co G 3 Regt Tenn Inf
			Spanish-American War
Charles P.)	17 Sep 1883	11 Jun 1954	
Gypsy B.)	3 Apr 1899	11 Jun 1980	
Howard W.)	4 Oct 1906	NOD	
Rubye L.)	4 Oct 1906	NOD	

CALFEE-John Herny		1888	1959	
Wilbur Kite)	7 Mar 1889	23 Jul 1950	
Daisy Stuart)	20 Nov 1888	2 Oct 1981	
Gertrude S. PEPPER)	1 Jan 1901	4 Jan 1979	
William)	13 May 1865	8 Dec 1931	
Louise)	16 Jul 1867	19 Oct 1937	
CAMERON-Millard	25 Feb 1918	28 Jul 1944	TN Pvt 134 Inf 35 Div WWII
CANTRELL-Johnny	10 Jun 1951	16 Jul 1969	
CARDEN-Essie Mae	15 Aug 1906	1 Apr 1974	
CARMICHAEL-Frank S., Sr.)	10 Dec 1896	18 Dec 1973	
Dovie Mae)	20 May 1897	21 Aug 1945	
Jamie)	19 May 1902	30 Sep 1968	
John)	23 FEb 1925	6 Nov 1946	
Paul)	16 Nov 1923	8 Aug 1942	
CARROLL-Jennings B.)	10 Jan 1933	20 Apr 1984	
Rita J.)	2 Apr 1934	NOD	
CARSON-Frank C.	24 Dec 1883	25 Jul 1892	s/o J.H. & L.F.
Carrie D.	30 Nov 1885	(illegible)	d/o J.H. & L.F. (broken)
J. H.	12 Sep 1851	27 Sep 1894	
Father)	1852	1929	
Mother)	1855	1903	
Ella I.)	1856	1929	
Ida Kate)	1900	1901	
Mary E.)	29 Dec 1882	6 Sep 1964	
Willie Henderson)	1893	1903	
Georgia C. JONES)	12 Aug 1889	26 May 1967	
Lola S. JONES)	22 Nov 1878	19 Jan 1946	
Maxey Carson JONES)	31 Aug 1891	20 Dec 1918	w/o I.S.
William H. CRAWFORD)	16 Apr 1858	9 Jan 1943	
Cora CRAWFORD)	2 Apr 1877	16 Aug 1919	
William Isaac	24 Jun 1880	13 Oct 1948	
Golda T.	4 Oct 1904	10 Sep 1984	
CARTER-John J.	17 Feb 1887	5 Sep 1964	
Dovie E. Miller	17 Aug 1890	12 Jun 1959	w/o J.J.
CASE-Iva Woods	13 Feb 1889	23 Jun 1915	
CHANDLER-Boyd	23 May 1917	13 Mar 1977	
CLARK-Annie Louise	24 Mar 1898	12 Jun 1985	
Baxter G.	1868	1949	
Minnie B.	1874	1966	
I. W.	24 May 1805	25 Nov 1882	
Jonas C.)	30 May 1868	10 Oct 1938	
Annie F.)	23 Jan 1869	14 Jun 1954	
William Andrew	6 Sep 1889	24 Feb 1948	Ark. Sgt 1Cl Air Ser WWII
Kate	1892	1976	
Mary N.	19 Jan 1901	10 Apr 1976	
CLICK-Bruce M.)	5 Mar 1880	6 Sep 1964	
Ella S.)	15 Jan 1886	25 Sep 1974	
Jake A.	17 Jun 1914	4 Apr 1933	s/o B.M.
CLINE-Charles V.)	23 Mar 1869	20 Mar 1935	
Eula L. Henkle)	7 Jun 1886	16 Jul 1927	
Brunella A. Biddle	27 Jan 1868	20 Oct 1907	w/o Ch. V; 39y 8m 23d married 22 Jan 1896
Dr. P. L.)	28 Sep 1839	16 Jan 1917	
Amanda Neff)	11 Mar 1845	5 Jul 1923	
Mary Louise	Born & died	19 Jun 1951	d/o M/M Charles A.
CODY-Emmitt	7 Apr 1907	3 Jun 1979	
Linda Grindstaff	14 Mar 1907	27 Mar 1954	w/o Emitt

CODY-Ida Bell	4 Feb 1954	5 Feb 1954	
Jake W., Jr.	27 May 1954	16 Jul 1980	
COGDELL-Eva May Rines	27 Jan 1911	2 Jul 1951	
J. N.	23 Aug 1878	23 Feb 1949	
Lou	18 Dec 1879	1 Jan 1955	
COLBOCH-William Henry	20 Sep 1850	1 Apr 1912	
William Lee)	20 May 1893	4 Jul 1923	
Bessie Maude)	13 Jun 1895	NOD	
COLLINS-Carroll R.)	14 Feb 1923	11 Jan 1983	
Empcie B.)	8 Dec 1923	NOD	
Floyd H.)	15 Feb 1912	NOD	
Mary E.)	23 Nov 1915	NOD	
Ira G.	1880	1943	
Retta A.	1892	1944	
James W. P.)	15 Jan 1882	6 Dec 1963	
Zora France)	15 Jun 1881	18 Feb 1955	
Jess Lee)	2 Mar 1906	14 Oct 1967	
Lexie K.)	25 Nov 1908	NOD	
Minnie Witt	29 Feb 1896	27 Jan 1966	
Virdie Suttles	10 Feb 1899	27 Dec 1971	
COOPER-Delie M.	9 Nov 1875	4 Jun 1894	
William M.)	Died	3 Jun 1897	54y
Nancy A. Woods)	19 Nov 1832	11 Feb 1901	w/o Wm. M.
CORBETT-William J.)	2 Aug 1828	9 Apr 1907	
Mary E.)	1 May 1833	16 Nov 1909	
COURTNEY-Andrew Lafayette)	22 Jul 1856	20 Mar 1906	
Harriet Rowena)	7 Sep 1863	7 Feb 1950	
McFarland	7 Sep 1863	7 Feb 1950	His wife
Mary Ola	30 Dec 1884	29 Dec 1886	d/o A. L. & H.R.
Norma J.	13 Jul 1932	1 Feb 1978	(see Paul L. Holtzclaw)
COWAN-Dorcas A.	4 Apr 1859	17 Oct 1888	
Ella Helm	1869	1964	
Fred B.	7 Jun 1884	1 Jan 1954	
Nina Blackburn	4 Mar 1892	10 Sep 1963	
Infant	OD	10 Aug 1927	s/o P.H. & Ruth
Infant	OD	7 Mar 1931	s/o F.B. & Nina
Dr. James Boyd	26 Jan 1899	21 Dec 1969	
Joseph Stonewall	8 Oct 1886	22 Jun 1888	
Pwrw H.	1895	1948	
Ruth Allen	1898	1948	
Peter H.	9 Mar 1854	5 Feb 1920	
COWDEN-Hershel L.)	1908	1975	
Stella R.)	1898	1981	
COX-Claude J.)	1890	1975	
Betty C.)	1894	1973	
Emily F.	2 Apr 1877	13 Aug 1931	
Grace	10 Aug 1907	17 Mar 1914	d/o N.N. & J.R.
N. N.)	7 Dec 1857	27 Nov 1922	
Julia REbecca)	11 Jan 1862	12 Apr 1941	
CRAWFORD-William H.)	16 Apr 1858	9 Jan 1943	(see Frank C. CARSON)
Cora)	2 Apr 1877	16 Aug 1919	
CROCKETT-Charlie	18 Sep 1914	5 Apr 1976	
King H.)	4 Jan 1883	18 Jul 1943	
Lucretia E.)	23 Mar 1889	NOD	
CROXDALE-Amber Nicole	Died	9 Mar 1986	d/o Howard & Janet CROXDALE granddaughter of John & Margaret HOLT

CUMMINGS-Joseph G.)	23 Jan 1905	30 Dec 1977	
Ada s.)	2 Feb 1909	17 Aug 1983	
DALTON-Ernest T.	9 May 1918	30 May 1983	S1 US Navy WWII
Virgie L.	22 Nov 1924	22 Sep 1973	
DAVIS-Beecher Lee Jr.	28 Aug 1972	22 Sep 1973	
Donna	31 Dec 1966	28 Jun 1978	d/o Kenneth & Barbara
Mary A.)	13 Mar 1889	30 Mar 1913	w/o J.F.
Myrtle M.)	1 May 1901	3 Jul 1901	And children
Teddy E.)	16 May 1912	14 Apr 1913	
T. A.	6 May 1835	20 Sep 1887	
DEAN-Clyde)	1 Aug 1911	NOD	Married 1933
Bertha M.)	1 Nov 1904	26 Sep 1971	
Walter M.)	1890	1978	
Mattie St. John)	1890	1968	
DEBORD-Clarence Edward	11 Aug 1911	10 Nov 1983	PFC US Army WWII
Freddy E.	5 Feb 1961	2 Oct 1974	
Jessie Lee	26 Feb 1885	7 Jun 1962	
Mattie Alder	13 Jul 1886	24 Dec 1954	
DEERING-Billy	26 Jan 1926	18 Dec 1953	
Clara B.	7 Jan 1887	17 Aug 1969	
Clyde H.)	1895	1982	
Shirley L.)	1909	1982	
Ernest Wilson	22 Dec 1910	29 Sep 1978	
George B.)	5 Sep 1859	23 Jun 1934	
Lillie A.)	12 Aug 1878	24 Dec 1965	
Grover C.)	3 Apr 1885	17 Jun 1975	
Anna F.)	2 Sep 1894	22 Apr 1970	
Guy F.)	9 Dec 1910	NOD	
Fina M.)	16 Dec 1899	5 Jun 1981	
Will L.	11 Jul 1881	16 Jun 1951	
DENISTON-Leonard L.	15 Jan 1924	20 Feb 1945	Ill S/SGT 860 AAF Bomb Squad WWII
Phyllis Sue	No dates		3y
William A.)	15 Sep 1880	17 Jan 1961	
Lottie M.)	23 Oct 1913	11 Jan 1985	
DENTON-Audrey M.	24 Jan 1924	10 Dec 1940	
Carrie E.	1894	1975	
Clarence C.)	1898	1962	
Flossie McG.)	1905	1981	
Hubert)	7 Feb 1896	21 Oct 1975	
Ruby H.)	22 Mar 1900	NOD	
John Ponder)	8 Jul 1873	13 Mar 1955	
Florence Turner)	16 Jun 1869	12 Jan 1950	
J. H.	21 Sep 1849	21 Nov 1900	
DORAN-David W.	13 Mar 1852	16 Aug 1887	
Nellie Linton	29 Nov 1881	25 Feb 1884	d/o D.W. & S.L.
DOWNS-Brent Quinton)	26 Feb 1942	4 Oct 1971	A1C US af Vietnam
Janie Ann Justice)	14 Jul 1941	NOD	
DRISKILL-Bessie P.	23 Aug 1894	19 Jun 1907	d/o C.P. & C.J.
Charles P.	3 Aug 1856	29 Jul 1914	
Catherine J. Swan	23 Jan 1854	9 Aug 1908	w/o C.P.
Daniel	6 Jul 1822	24 Oct 1895	
D. L.	3 Aug 1884	26 Aug 1886	
D. P.	26 Nov 1858	6 Sep 1889	
Drew A.	1886	1887	
D. Z.	5 Sep 1851	20 Jul 1921	

DRISKILL-Edwin R.	9 Aug 1891	10 Aug 1909	
Ida C.	29 Jul 1870	15 Aug 1888	d/o R.A. & S.A.
Infant	No dates		Baby
Mattie E.	11 Jul 1874	14 Jul 1888	d/o R.A. & S.A.
Moses Alexander)	1845	1902	
Katherine Stuart)	1854	1933	
R. A.)	1842	1932	
Joanna)	1870	NOD	
Adaline Moyers	18 May 1844	7 Jun 1916	w/o R.A.
Reps E.	15 Jun 1880	31 Jan 1909	s/o R.A. & S.A.
Vennie)	1875	1893	
Mattie Rogers)	1854	1893	
Walter	3 Mar 1882	10 Jun 1888	
DROKE-Jacobus DeVault	9 Aug 1857	23 Jun 1902	Principal of Edwards Academy 1896-1901; President of Lane University 1901-1902
DRUMMOND-Mary E.	21 Jan 1843	11 Feb 1919	
DYER-Ollie M.	1861	1938	w/o S.M.
EGLESTON-Davis Jacobs)	1842	1890	
Mary Elizabeth)	1852	NOD	
ELDRIDGE-Alvin D.)	30 Jun 1907	7 Mar 1977	
Nova Elizabeth)	22 Jul 1908	15 May 1974	
James W.	1889	1961	Pvt US Marine Corps 17 Jul 1917-23 Dec 1919
Lewis D.)	4 Oct 1879	11 May 1966	
Mary Elizabeth)	17 Apr 1867	19 Feb 1953	
ELLIOTT-George E.)	23 Feb 1890	8 Dec 1978	Married 8 Jan 1911
Lula J.)	18 May 1896	25 Dec 1975	
ELLIS-John G.)	7 Jul 1909	7 Jan 1969	
Lizzie Gentry)	22 Sep 1907	22 Apr 1964	
Pvt. John J.	20 Jul 1928	18 Aug 1948	
M. J.)	1859	1937	
Lizzie A.)	1865	1939	
ELMORE-Cora E.	30 Oct 1882	21 Nov 1899	d/o J.M. & H.L.
EVANS-John)	4 Apr 1896	31 Oct 1976	
Myrtle Lee)	10 Mar 1900	2 Apr 1984	
Lou	1866	1947	
Willie R.)	23 Sep 1917	NOD	Married 6 Apr 1973
Una V.)	13 Oct 1926	NOD	
EVERHART-Guy)	11 Mar 1898	11 Dec 1967	
Charlotte)	10 Jun 1902	NOD	
FAIN-Dewitt	21 Jan 1857	30 Dec 1928	
FARMER-Edith	12 Jul 1894	22 Jul 1900	6y 10d
FELKNOR-Audley R.)	16 Jul 1888	30 Apr 1970	Wed 29 Jun 1917
Harriet Lester)	24 Jun 1889	15 Aug 1962	
Shadrach J.)	30 Oct 1842	1 Jun 1919	
Martha C.)	19 Aug 1849	15 Mar 1913	
J. Alexander)	26 Feb 1874	24 Nov 1958	
Elizabeth)	15 Oct 1870	19 May 1942	
W. A.	1844	1919	
Sytha E.	1849	1916	
FIELDS-Emma K.	5 Jan 1883	28 Jun 1973	
FISHER-Mary F.	24 Jun 1855	2 May 1888	w/o D.L.; Born Harrison Co., Ohio; died White Pine, Tennessee
Mary McCollum	20 Dec 1825	22 Sep 1900	w/o Henry

FISHER-Vaughn Lee)	1892	1968	
Alphia Mae)	1902	NOD	
FOWLER-Infant	No dates		i/o Linda & Ronnie
FOX-E. Gus	1888	1969	
Leda S.)	1891	NOD	
Howard)	11 Apr 1898	NOD	
Zena Reed)	22 Jul 1889	29 Nov 1968	
James William)	1876	1958	
Eva Moyers)	1880	1947	
Joyce E.	1940	1961	
Robert M.	9 Mar 1886	20 Aug 1938	
Susan Elizabeth	30 Jan 1903	14 Jul 1976	
T. A.	17 Mar 1857	NOD	
Penelopy	28 Feb 1858	6 Dec 1920	w/o T.A.
Thos. B.	1837	1 Dec 1904	
Ulyss)	10 Apr 1909	2 Dec 1974	
Nellie Smith)	18 Jan 1892	21 Jan 1958	
FRANCE-Barbara Jean	17 Feb 1935	15 Jul 1979	(see Jess James KNIGHT)
FRANKLIN-Albert G.	3 Jul 1830	21 Feb 1898	
Rutha A. Clevenger	18 Oct 1835	19 Oct 1902	w/o Albert G.
Lewis G.	9 Mar 1876	29 Mar 1907	
FRAZER-Henry Clarke)	5 Jan 1899	13 Dec 1976	
Alice G.)	28 Mar 1903	2 Nov 1965	
FRAZIER-A. E.	13 Feb 1848	25 Aug 1911	
Earl H.	15 Mar 1915	27 Jan 1983	S/Sgt US Army WWII
FREE-Mary Sue	20 May 1924	17 Oct 1971	
Roy Lawson	27 Apr 1897	6 Nov 1984	
Ethel Caldwell	24 May 1889	19 Apr 1959	
FREELS-Rev. Elbert A.)	6 Apr 1877	22 Jun 1945	
Anna B.)	16 Dec 1878	5 Dec 1963	
FRY-Baby Girl	Born & died	11 Jun 1886	d/o Emmett & Ida (broken)
Catherine S.	5 May 1824	27 Jan 1896	
George W.	15 Jun 1812	10 Sep 1896	
Neva Gertrude	10 Jul 1889	8 Jul 1890	d/o J.E. & I.E.
Sarah Alice	5 Nov 1858	17 Aug 1934	
Thomas	1830	1907	
Julie A. Scruggs	1848	1935	w/o Thomas
Mamie E.	1875	1937	
FRYE-Cindy)	15 May 1967	7 Jul 1971	
Nancy C.)	OD	11 Sep 1944	Infant
Robert J.)	1905	1976	Wed 9 Oct 1943
Tessie M.)	1907	1982	
Thomas S.	4 Nov 1897	2 Jan 1967	
FUGATE-Lou Verna	12 Mar 1925	NOD	
FUNKHOUSER-Porter A.)	19 Nov 1856	30 Jan 1935	
Emma Mims)	9 Nov 1858	3 Sep 1946	
Mary E.)	5 Jan 1889	25 May 1977	
GANDY-Dixie G. Fry	1895	1932	w/o Edgar E.
GANN-John S.	8 Feb 1876	25 Jun 1934	
Ida Mae	2 Oct 1903	9 Aug 1904	d/o J.S. & L.P.C.
GARRIS-Bob)	19 Oct 1896	15 Oct 1971	
Zola M.)	16 Oct 1900	1 Aug 1931	
Roy	OD	9 Jul 1903	
Eddie	OD	31 Aug 1905	
Fred	13 Aug 1907	1 Jan 1923	
Kate W.	31 Oct 1893	11 Jul 1982	

Name	Birth	Death	Notes
GARRIS-John B.)	1870	1941	
Elizabeth)	1871	1923	
Ralph Wayne	22 Apr 1925	18 Jun 1926	s/o J.P. & Zola
GILDON-Mark Joseph	1 Oct 1879	13 Jun 1955	
Flora Kate Britt	27 Dec 1884	28 Jul 1974	
GILMORE-Gran	13 Oct 1892	12 Jan 1961	TN Sgt US Army WWI
GLOSIP-John F.	Died	25 Jul 1886	77y (broken)
GOAN-Alexander F.)	1883	1920	
Betta)	1881	1929	
Louis "Buss")	1909	1944	C-M-M-M At rest in the Sea
John B.)	1885	1963	
Alonzo David	15 Sep 1878	25 Jul 1903	
Andrew McFerrin	1887	1973	
Daniel Amos	19 Aug 1881	14 Apr 1910	
Frank Bercaw	15 Feb 1885	14 Feb 1953	
Martin Baker	1913	1985	(fhm-Farrar)
Mary Holloway	5 Aug 1850	10 Nov 1914	
Robert M.)	29 Jan 1879	11 Nov 1923	
Annie M.)	17 Nov 1877	8 Nov 1918	
John Rufus)	19 Nov 1907	21 Jun 1968	
Donald L. Jr.)	24 Jul 1937	3 Feb 1976	
James Robert)	23 Mar 1914	20 Apr 1976	BCM US Navy WWII
Rufus Inman)	2 Apr 1869	11 Jul 1960	
Robert)	10 Oct 1835	9 Feb 1922	
GOOCH-Bertie May	5 Jun 1909	25 Nov 1916	d/o J.D. & Katie
Helen	30 Sep 1912	2 Jun 1924	
Hooper Lee	1 Apr 1898	1 Oct 1960	TN Pvt Co F 118 Inf WWI
John D.	5 May 1874	31 Jan 1921	
Myrtle Moyers	15 Apr 1901	25 Jan 1981	
GOODLETT-Infant	OD	Sep 1904	7d; s/o Charley & Letha
Kathreen	18 Jan 1902	28 Apr 1902	d/o Charley & letha
GOODMAN-Dorcus Walters	1893	1931	w/o Howard W. (See Rev. John WALTERS)
GOUGE-William A.)	1891	1971	
Carrie J.)	1910	1964	
GREENE-Earl F.)	13 Apr 1913	22 Feb 1978	
Margaret H.)	22 Jan 1917	NOD	
GREER-Mayme Hudson	7 Sep 1894	15 Jan 1939	w/o Joe M., Jr.
GREGG-Maude R.	10 Apr 1910	20 Apr 1973	
HALE-S. Eugene)	7 Mar 1910	NOD	
Eleanor Bell)	20 Jan 1915	15 Jun 1977	
HAMILTON-Samuel S.)	8 Jul 1873	2 Jul 1946	
Rettie Gulley)	10 May 1873	2 Sep 1964	
HAMMOND-Paul D.)	4 Nov 1906	15 Apr 1971	
Nellie Gooch)	17 Nov 1906	18 Oct 1930	
HANEY-Shufford	4 Jun 1892	17 Jun 1966	TN Pvt Co G 2 Div WWI
HARDIN-Georgia Mae	20 Feb 1898	23 Nov 1965	
Harry William)	19 Jul 1893	9 May 1954	TN PFC Co E 338 Inf WWI
Janie Elizabeth)	27 Aug 1890	5 Aug 1975	
HARDY-Frank Lynn	Born & died	11 Mar 1947	s/o M/M C.F.
H. F.	1855	1940	
Mrs. C. E.	1853	1936	w/o H.F.
James Edward	OD	1926	Infant s/o M/M W. T.
Phillip Lee	21 Jun 1947	23 Jun 1947	s/o M/M Floyd E.
Wm. Clifford	16 Feb 1910	24 Nov 1965	
W. T.	1884	1978	h/o Minnie A. Hooper
Minnie A. Hooper	1885	1934	w/o W.T.
HARMON-Lutie White	Died	17 Mar 1913	

HARRISON-Charles Alfred	2 Mar 1915	14 May 1925	
Eliza Jane	10 Jul 1912	23 Mar 1928	
Fred M.)	30 Jul 1867	25 Sep 1943	
Jennie Brown)	2 Dec 1882	21 Jul 1944	
James L.	7 Apr 1872	17 Oct 1955	
Johnnie McNabb	28 Aug 1882	8 Mar 1980	
John Brown	24 Apr 1912	3 Sep 1965	
James H.	7 Feb 1861	26 Jan 1934	
Peggy Lynn	27 Jul 1925	18 Oct 1951	
HAUN-Edmund Clay	20 Jan 1883	1 Jun 1912	
John E.	1 Jan 1849	7 Jul 1901	
HAWK-Infant	No dates		d/o M/M J. B.
HAWKINS-Lee Carlton)	1 Jan 1891	23 Mar 1974	
Ester)	23 Jan 1894	1 Sep 1975	
Maud	10 Dec 1897	10 Aug 1919	w/o J.P.
William E.)	18 Sep 1867	5 Apr 1951	
Carrie M.)	12 May 1870	30 Oct 1945	
HAZELWOOD-A. C.	29 May 1849	NOD	
Alley G.	16 Aug 1846	9 Jan 1921	w/o A.C.
Ellen C.	1864	1950	
HEADRICK-Wilburn Harrel)	28 Jun 1918	27 Mar 1967	
Viola Knight)	23 Apr 1922	NOD	
HEATHERLY-John W.)	22 Mar 1895	8 Sep 1976	
Ann H.)	27 Jan 1897	21 Feb 1972	
Joe E.	26 Feb 1932	30 Apr 1951	
HELM-Bernice	28 Nov 1898	6 Mar 1899	d/o W.B. & T.I.
Bessie L. Wise	1882	1908	
George B.	19 Dec 1886	24 May 1949	TN Pvt 115 Field Arty 27 Div WWI
Wm. B., MD)	9 Oct 1857	7 Jul 1931	Married 24 May 1882
Thula J. Snodgrass)	9 Dec 1861	24 Feb 1909	w/o Dr. W.B.
Cornie Bales)	13 May 1879	25 Sep 1976	w/o Dr. W.B.; married 7 Jun 1911
HENRY-Hubert)	18 Jun 1909	6 Dec 1975	
Dorothy R.)	30 May 1916	NOD	
John M.)	30 May 1860	17 Mar 1947	
Mary J.)	27 May 1861	11 Apr 1934	
HENSLEY-J.W.)	27 FEb 1838	10 Mar 1919	
Mary A.)	11 Nov 1828	15 Jun 1913	His wife
W. H.	19 Mar 1849	16 Dec 1911	
HICKEY-Charles L.)	30 Mar 1913	3 Oct 1954	
Mable)	19 Feb 1916	23 Jul 1966	
J. W.	16 Oct 1885	11 May 1913	w/o W.T. & M.A.
W. Taylor)	17 Oct 1855	26 Dec 1934	
Elvira A.)	2 Feb 1857	7 Jun 1939	
HICKS-Clarence E.)	1898	1966	
Mary Ada)	1900	1966	
Earl E.	29 Jun 1924	26 May 1974	S2 US Navy
HIGGINS-Elbert Lee	14 Dec 1891	29 Mar 1975	Pvt US Army WWI
Lena White	18 Feb 1888	29 May 1927	
Eliza Rebecca	18 Nov 1864	26 Jan 1955	
Etheridge	10 FEb 1915	12 Mar 1944	
HOLBERT-Jessie Ray)	8 Jun 1922	26 Dec 1979	Pvg US Army WWII
Rose Viola)	16 Aug 1922	NOD	
Sam	18 Oct 1896	4 Nov 1979	Pvt US Army WWI (military stone says died 7 Nov 1979)
Bertie Mae	12 Nov 1897	29 Dec 1945	

Name	Birth	Death	Notes
HOLDWAY-Elizabeth R.	25 Apr 1893	4 Dec 1980	Aunt Lizzie
Sarah Catherine	1867	1942	
HOLLAND-Jane McNabb	31 May 1846	3 Feb 1934	
HOLLOWAY-Howard)	1892	1972	
Mary)	1893	NOD	
James E.	2 Jan 1870	7 Mar 1923	
Fannie H.	30 Mar 1870	15 Jan 1954	
Lorena	23 Mar 1908	1 Jan 1913	
William A.)	1 Apr 1903	17 Jun 1977	
Fannie A.)	8 May 1913	NOD	
William A.	12 Mar 1835	26 May 1902	
Amanda	1836	1920	
HOLT-Arnold)	4 Mar 1899	12 Jun 1957	TN Pvt 43 Chem Lab Co WWII
Ruby J.)	15 Jun 1909	NOD	
Baby	No dates		
Connie)	14 Sep 1908	NOD	
Bonnie M.)	6 Dec 1911	NOD	
John Ruble)	11 Sep 1912	1 Jul 1979	
Margaret K.)	8 Jan 1912	NOD	
HOLTZCLAW-Paul L., Sr.)	15 May 1902	9 Sep 1981	
Emma L. McCoig)	1898	1955	w/o P. L.
Jack A.)	23 May 1933	12 Jun 1946	
Paul L.)	28 May 1924	NOD	
Norma J. Courtney)	13 Jul 1932	1 Feb 1978	
HOOPER-Ira Elmer	14 Sep 1876	10 Mar 1938	
William M.	5 Jan 1839	9 Feb 1894	
HORNER-Anna Lois	28 Mar 1901	21 Jul 1901	d/o E.M. & M.A.
Eddie F.	13 Oct 1901	2 May 1902	s/o F.M. & B.C.
Rev. Edwin)	27 Jun 1844	28 Oct 1916	
Emaline J. Skeen)	7 Sep 1845	29 May 1931	His wife
Herman T.)	29 Jul 1907	28 Jan 1968	
Pansey L.)	29 Oct 1917	NOD	
J. C.	2 Oct 1867	20 Jun 1887	
Larkin J.)	1873	1943	
Bertie H.)	1881	1963	
Lillie C.	26 May 1920	NOD	
Martha Driskill	4 Aug 1869	10 May 1910	
Mary Ruth	2 Sep 1894	5 Aug 1895	d/o E.M. & M.A.
Thomas Nelson	23 Feb 1851	4 Feb 1923	
Ethel E.	5 Sep 1872	9 Jan 1932	
Will T.)	22 Jul 1875	17 Mar 1934	
Alice S.)	12 May 1875	11 Aug 1948	
HORTON-Freeman H.)	7 Jun 1893	4 Jan 1978	
Sarah K.)	2 Mar 1891	2 Feb 1966	
Nicholas M. "Nick")	2 Jan 1919	3 Nov 1983	Brother; US Army WWII
Blanche)	4 Mar 1917	NOD	
HOUK-Sarah Jane P.	28 May 1904	19 Mar 1980	
HUBBARD-Don	27 Jun 1947	8 Feb 1960	
George)	28 Nov 1904	22 Apr 1985	
Nellie F.)	7 May 1906	NOD	
Robert)	5 May 1906	NOD	
Nellie S.)	11 Jan 1914	NOD	
HUFFAKER-Ruby N.	1 Feb 1892	4 Dec 1979	
HUDSON-Edd	1891	1942	
Charlisie M.	1888	1939	
Elizabeth H.	23 Dec 1918	22 Feb 1980	
Joseph M.	20 Jun 1856	13 Mar 1939	

Name	Birth	Death	Notes
HUDSON-Joseph M.	20 Jun 1856	13 Mar 1939	
Margaret E.	22 Jan 1868	23 Jan 1929	
HULL-Ernest W.)	17 Aug 1904	6 Aug 1973	
Flora M.)	25 Mar 1906	NOD	
HUMBIRD-James J.)	1894	1957	
Anna Cline)	1874	1961	
HUMPSTON-Almeda	22 May 1857	20 Feb 1942	
Chas. E.	29 Jun 1885	30 Nov 1919	
Queen Abbie Witt	10 Sep 1887	12 Aug 1916	w/o C.E.
Howard Keith)	28 Jan 1905	6 Jul 1969	
L. Katherine)	18 Aug 1912	NOD	
J. L.	2 Jun 1865	12 Nov 1949	
Lynn	24 Jan 1912	17 Jan 1916	s/o W.E. & H.I.
Mary B.	17 May 1875	24 Apr 1964	
Mary Jo	26 Oct 1907	17 Feb 1984	
R. A.	8 May 1859	9 Dec 1935	
Lucy T. Owen	20 Oct 1864	15 Aug 1916	w/o R.A.
William E.	12 Jun 1875	29 Mar 1946	
Harriette	13 Apr 1879	28 Jul 1951	
William T.)	21 Jan 1887	23 Jan 1979	
Lucille T.)	14 Feb 1895	17 Nov 1979	
HUNGATE-Alice	20 Jan 1891	12 Aug 1891	d/o E.W. & A.P.
Edgar W., M.D.	13 May 1845	28 Jan 1914	
Alice Purdy	18 Apr 1857	29 Jan 1891	w/o E.W.; Born Edwardsport, Ind.; died White Pine, Tennessee
Florence Lee	28 Oct 1870	19 Aug 1946	
Infant	28 Jun 1902	12 Jul 1902	s/o Dr. E.W. & F.L.
HYLEMAN-John A.	20 Apr 1916	26 Jan 1964	TN PFC Co M 473 Inf WWII
INMAN-Andrew Jackson	4 Jul 1869	20 Sep 1926	
Elizabeth Driskill	16 Apr 1867	10 Aug 1922	
Rufus Lancy	20 May 1892	5 Nov 1946	
Samuel	23 FEb 1872	20 Jul 1933	
Lucy Fowler	13 Oct 1872	14 Jun 1956	
IVY-Benjamin Ruble	1 Jan 1912	12 Jul 1951	Brother
Daryl D.	12 Dec 1955	14 Oct 1977	Sgt US Army
Edison	8 Feb 1917	26 Nov 1982	PFC US Army WWII
Janet Daphine	9 Aug 1955	1 Sep 1956	d/o Glenn & Vergie
Orville Ray	23 Oct 1925	30 Jan 1984	PFC US Army WWII
Roosevelt	7 Mar 1902	18 FEb 1980	Pap Paw
Ada	28 Feb 1903	7 Aug 1982	Ma Maw
JACKSON-Ray	27 Mar 1931	24 Jul 1985	
JARRETT-Gary W.)	30 Nov 1948	NOD	
Dorothy S.)	8 Aug 1926	11 Apr 1969	
JESSEE-Martha Fraley	19 Jan 1851	5 Aug 1927	w/o Samuel P.
JOHNSON-William D.)	24 Mar 1917	1 Jan 1980	
Charlsie E.)	16 Oct 1921	NOD	
JOHNSTON-Hugh)	7 Jan 1905	9 Nov 1966	
Jessie)	2 May 1901	2 May 1970	
JONES-Bronell	12 Apr 1940	3 May 1985	
Ruth A.	3 Aug 1939	NOD	
Georgia C.	12 Aug 1889	26 May 1967	(See CARSON)
Hollis Guy	19 Dec 1926	9 Jul 1971	TN PFC SVC Co 187 Glider Inf WWII
Jos.	No dates		Co L 1st Tenn Cav
Lola S.	22 Nov 1878	19 Jan 1946	(See CARSON)
Maxie Carson	31 Aug 1891	20 Dec 1918	w/o I.S. (See CARSON)
William A.)	22 Aug 1903	15 Apr 1984	Married 24 Dec 1932
Mildred T. "Polly")	17 Sep 1912	NOD	

JONES-William P.)	11 Jun 1861	29 Sep 1932	
Nellie Davis)	30 Nov 1862	3 Apr 1925	
Clyde S.)	1 Oct 1889	21 Aug 1958	
KEIRSEY-Hiram	15 Sep 1886	10 Feb 1972	Our Loving Grandparents
Rentie	5 Jan 1891	10 Jan 1971	
KELLER-Donald Gus	25 Feb 1950	24 Feb 1971	PFC US Army Vietnam
Gus	18 Mar 1921	11 Apr 1970	TN PFC 373 Gen Hosp WWII
Gloria Jean	28 May 1926	4 Feb 1972	
Henry Frank	9 Mar 1946	26 Jun 1966	
KELLY-Callie Elizabeth	25 May 1929	24 Oct 1968	
KELLEY-William H.)	21 Mar 1909	8 Oct 1978	Married 15 Jun 1929
Maude)	18 Jan 1909	NOD	
KENNEDY-john E.)	4 Aug 1914	6 Feb 1976	
Mary C.)	20 Jan 1909	NOD	
KILGORE-George K.	1870	1965	
Laura B.	1871	1952	
Maxie R.	21 Jun 1906	30 Sep 1981	
Minnie	17 Sep 1892	12 Sep 1976	
KIMBROUGH-Jack)	16 Feb 1900	27 Jun 1979	
Charlsie Sexton)	3 Aug 1903	20 Jan 1946	
Luther)	6 Aug 1878	22 Jan 1961	
Bertha C.)	15 Oct 1895	26 Oct 1954	
William C.	11 Jul 1924	11 Aug 1944	TN Pvt 116 Inf WWII
KINNICK-Infant	(illegible)		
Iva Anderson	20 Nov 1904	14 Apr 1937	
J. V.	3 Oct 1860	19 May 1937	
Della Hooper	21 Jan 1871	24 Oct 1948	
Margaret Heins	27 Sep 1911	12 Dec 1983	
M. E.	30 Oct 1860	1 May 1895	w/o J.V.
William	9 Dec 1899	31 Oct 1917	
Mary T.	(dates illegible)		
KNIGHT-Gregory J.)	14 Aug 1958	14 May 1977	
James Luther)	5 Feb 1922	10 Sep 1970	TN SC2 US Navy WWII
Jess James)	6 Jan 1911	6 Aug 1963	
Mae)	6 Jan 1919	NOD	
Jess Jr.)	10 May 1933	29 May 1959	s/o Jess & Mae
James Monroe)	3 Dec 1937	16 Jul 1978	s/o Jess & Mae
Barbara Jean FRANCE)	17 Feb 1935	15 Jul 1979	
Johnnie W.)	20 Nov 1899	7 Jan 1952	
Etta)	No dates		
Martha Holt	10 Mar 1878	4 Jun 1953	
Walter C.)	4 Sep 1897	12 Jun 1958	
Bessie L.)	21 Jan 1898	20 Jun 1972	
KNOWLING-Thomas Scott	30 Oct 1966	28 Aug 1979	
William M.)	12 May 1881	22 Feb 1944	
Elsie Dora)	18 Nov 1887	28 Apr 1937	
KOZACEK-Richard Mark	5 Dec 1972	7 Feb 1973	
KREIS-Bruna Driskill)	1886	1978	
Katherine Swan)	1905	1948	
LANCE-Kathryn	1883	1972	
LANDRUM-Edward T.	26 Jul 1907	15 Oct 1969	
E. R.)	5 Oct 1874	30 Dec 1940	
Lizzie S.)	4 Mar 1878	2 Aug 1954	
LANE-Hazel Margarette	10 Jun 1911	9 Aug 1914	
Herbert T.)	9 Oct 1882	14 Apr 1938	
Ethel Haun)	28 Oct 1890	4 Nov 1985	
Mamie	10 Jun 1886	15 Feb 1920	w/o H. A.
Lowell Eugene	4 Jun 1942	2 Dec 1983	Pvt US Army

```
LANE-Mack J.      )          19 Aug 1918  11 Sep 1981
   Thelma C.      )          18 Aug 1920  NOD
   Mamie                     10 Jun 1886  15 Feb 1920  w/o H.A.
   Mary Ruth                      1922         1986    (fhm-Farrar)
   Mitchell                       1907    NOD
   Hazel C.                       1914         1985
LARES-Francis Edward          4 Jan 1897  14 Dec 1982
   Bertha M. Fox            23 Sep 1900   8 Dec 1964  w/o Francis E.
   William F.               23 Aug 1930   1 Mar 1970  Cpl TN HQ 25 Inf Div Korea
LARROWE-Don C.)               2 Feb 1910  15 Mar 1984
   Agnes M.      )          22 May 1907   NOD
LECKEY-Eunice Cox            13 Apr 1900   7 Feb 1953
LEE-Walter Duncan)           15 Nov 1909   5 Dec 1980
   Gladys Lee     )         26 Aug 1913   NOD
LEMONS-Robert E.             15 Sep 1869  28 Feb 1939
   Alice Widener             23 Nov 1871  10 Jun 1942
LEWIS-Clark T.)              17 Oct 1935   NOD
   Lula Bell    )            3 Sep 1935   7 Jun 1980
   Henry H.     )           20 Oct 1889   5 Mar 1954
   Gladys W.)                4 Jun 1906  26 Oct 1955
LINE-Bell B.                 14 Nov 1867  27 Feb 1941
   Mildred I.               20 Feb 1902   8 Jun 1903  d/o J.A. & Myrtle
   Myrtle B.                22 Sep 1885  10 Jul 1909  w/o J.A.
LINEBAUGH-Mary J.            17 Jan 1833  23 Jun 1902
LINN-Miss Eliza             15 Oct 1839   3 Nov 1887  48y 19d
LISTER-Robert F.                  1887         1930
   William C.               30 Sep 1887   8 Aug 1944
LITZ-Arthur Walton )         18 Nov 1898  13 Sep 1975
   Lucile Courtney )         12 Nov 1894  25 Mar 1982
LOOPE-G. Dewey          )     8 Apr 1908   NOD
   Eunice G. Hopper    )     11 Jun 1911   3 Sep 1975
LOWE-John W.                 28 Apr 1872   2 Jun 1946
LOY-Morton  )                     1888         1961
   Zella H. )                     1906    NOD
LUSTER-Larry Dale           22 Sep 1959  31 Dec 1980  "Coach Luster"
McCLANAHAN-Harry M.)         29 Mar 1897  14 Jun 1980
   Bunah A.          )       20 Jul 1889  19 May 1946
McCOIG-Albert L.)             5 Aug 1888   8 Aug 1979  Married 27 Oct 1910
   Abigail R.    )           9 Sep 1891   NOD
   Austin G.          )           1905         1967   Doctor of Divinity - Methodist
                                                      Minister 33 years.

   Priscilla M.       )     No dates
   Charles B.                     1907         1957
   Rose W.                        1912    NOD
   Charles Fred Jr.         27 Dec 1954   2 Sep 1975  A1C US Air Force Vietnam
   Ernest M. )              15 Nov 1895   8 Aug 1966  TN Pvt Co K 46 Inf WWI
   Lillie M. )                    1902    NOD
   Ray N.)                  28 Jun 1909  20 May 1977
   Ola M.)                  22 Apr 1908   NOD
McDANEL-Frank Blackstone     22 Oct 1867  27 Feb 1947
McDANNEL-Charles E. Sr.       9 Aug 1863  16 Jan 1942
   Emma G. Roberts)         31 Jul 1868  27 May 1896  w/o F. B.
   Imogene Corinne)         23 Apr 1896  11 Jul 1896  d/o F.B. & E.G.B.
   John L.      )            8 Feb 1835   9 Jul 1915
   Margaret M.)             22 Feb 1840  15 Feb 1913  His wife
   Mary Virginia Henninger Died      5 Jan 1936  w/o F. B.
```

McFARLAND-B.A.)	29 Jul 1820	13 Jan 1887	
Mary)	24 Aug 1835	9 Aug 1886	
McGARITY-Anna Beth	27 Jan 1919	28 Jun 1978	
McGUIRE-Eugenia E.	14 Oct 1885	9 Jul 1900	d/o M.F. & S.A.
Bernice K.	8 Jun 1894	8 Aug 1894	d/o R.C. & B.C.
Hugh M.)	18 Dec 1873	20 Oct 1924	
Marie D.)	29 Dec 1873	17 Oct 1946	
Marshall Franklin	1858	1910	
Robert C.	5 Dec 1867	22 Jan 1899	31y 1m 17d; died at St. Paul, VA
Bernice C.	2 Dec 1876	30 Jul 1894	w/o R.C.
Silas M.)	12 Aug 1828	8 Oct 1896	A Ruling Elder of the Presbyterian Church for 40 years.
Margaret A.)	12 Feb 1834	23 Jul 1924	A Faithful Member of the Presbyterian Church for 73 years.
Sallie A. Eckel	27 Dec 1862	14 Dec 1897	Married to M.F. McGuire 8 Nov 1882
McKINNEY-Robert J.)	25 Jul 1906	NOD	
Geneva B.)	10 Oct 1911	21 Dec 1983	
McLEAN-Verlon M.)	3 Aug 1929	31 Dec 1983	
Elvalee)	4 Apr 1928	8 Apr 1982	
McMAHAN-John E.)	1910	NOD	
Elsie L.)	1911	NOD	
MADDOX- Elbert C.)	6 Jan 1872	15 Nov 1936	
Kate Collins)	29 Sep 1892	16 Aug 1965	
MALOY-Andrew)	14 Dec 1866	2 Jun 1905	
Sarah)	5 Apr 1874	15 Feb 1947	
Dewey)	8 Jul 1899	17 Oct 1970	
Georgia)	4 Jan 1904	NOD	
MANARD-Julia A.	Died	20 Nov 1904	
MARSH-G. V.)	2 Dec 1891	24 Sep 1968	
Mary Elizabeth)	18 Sep 1913	21 Aug 1983	
MARSHALL-Bryle W.)	1 Apr 1928	NOD	
Thomas R.)	23 Aug 1923	1 Sep 1967	
MARTIN-A. A.)	16 Jun 1872	20 Jan 1946	
Bettie)	7 Mar 1875	28 May 1947	
Floyd)	No dates		Husband
Laura)	No dates		Wife
Arthur G. Sr.)	15 Jan 1881	31 Oct 1948	
Lucille Stuart)	18 Aug 1891	2 Jan 1983	
Dr. Arthur G. Jr.)	16 Mar 1915	20 Nov 1983	
Tidy)	26 Oct 1854	30 Sep 1962	
MASENGILL-Frank	4 Mar 1907	17 Apr 1918	s/o E.M. & T.C.
MATTHEWS-Beatrice Deering	2 Jul 1902	8 Apr 1927	
Edna L.	27 Aug 1925	NOD	
Rosa Lee	2 Jul 1902	16 Oct 1903	d/o J.E. & S.E.
MATTOX-Wilson	Died	26 Jan 1927	57y
Sarah Louise	11 Jan 1867	18 Mar 1957	
MERRILL-Melvin James	17 May 1961	27 Apr 1984	
MESSER-Claude)	26 May 1886	27 Mar 1968	
Minnie M.)	5 Sep 1885	12 Oct 1969	
Arnold)	2 Jan 1925	14 Nov 1951	
Roy J.)	6 Nov 1902	NOD	
Florence M.)	17 Jan 1900	13 Nov 1959	
MILLER-Abraham)	3 Oct 1833	14 Dec 1883	
Belinda Mater)	5 Jan 1835	24 Feb 1902	w/o Abraham
Joshua Morris)	29 Mar 1852	2 Apr 1941	
Margaret Deatherage)	21 Jul 1858	7 Mar 1914	

MILLER-Joshua Morris)	29 Mar 1852	2 Apr 1941	
Annie Almeda)	24 Nov 1904	17 Jun 1979	
Mamie Virginia	1 Jan 1888	23 Mar 1897	
Sallie Lou	28 Sep 1884	7 Apr 1885	
William Andrew	25 Jul 1882	5 Aug 1933	
MITCHELL-Fred)	15 Jun 1916	NOD	
Katherine)	5 Dec 1938	NOD	
James F.)	1 Oct 1879	11 Sep 1945	
Sarah Caudill)	4 Jul 1903	9 Oct 1984	
Rev. J. S.)	1873	1945	
Lula J.)	1873	1934	
Myrtle H.)	1898	1975	
MOORE-John Wesley Sr.)	7 Aug 1899	2 Aug 1978	SC1 US Navy WWI
Ola M.)	29 Mar 1909	NOD	
Oscar E.)	16 Jun 1898	12 May 1937	
Omey E.)	7 Apr 1898	28 Jun 1935	
Virginia Idol	8 Jun 1920	10 Nov 1925	d/o Oscar & Omie
MORGAN-Mary Ann	5 Dec 1869	12 Aug 1938	
MORIE-Frank R.)	5 Dec 1895	25 Dec 1978	Married 25 Jun 1925
Florence M.)	27 Jan 1901	14 Jan 1986	
Raymond G.	16 Aug 1947	26 Jun 1971	TN Sp4 US Army Vietnam
MORRIS-Bessie Goan	18 Sep 1887	3 Feb 1917	
MOSER-Caroline M. Snoddy	12 Aug 1828	30 Oct 1908	w/o J.W.
William)	14 May 1855	26 Jan 1900	s/o Samuel & Mary
Kathern Ann Chilton)	22 Feb 1856	17 Mar 1951	
Mary Moser SHARP)	8 Aug 1812	20 Nov 1882	Mother of William Moser
MOSS-Irvin	4 May 1898	18 Nov 1961	
Jess)	22 Aug 1913	15 Nov 1960	
Mabel)	10 Feb 1914	NOD	
MOYER-Ulas E.)	10 Sep 1880	14 Dec 1944	
Katie)	14 Jun 1873	NOD	
Clinton T.)	1 Dec 1907	7 Aug 1973	TN Pvt US Army WWII
Bessie R.)	31 Jul 1914	NOD	
Frank Hensley)	7 Jun 1897	23 Nov 1950	
Ruby Broyles)	No dates		
MOYERS-Alice May ¦	12 Feb 1894	23 Mar 1895	d/o J.C. & M.A.
Ben Earl	14 Mar 1887	22 Dec 1923	
Buenos C.	19 Mar 1908	28 Oct 1909	s/o T.M. & F.L.
Clerance H.	30 Jan 1924	7 Nov 1927	
D. Alex)	1858	1927	
Mary E.)	1856	1927	
Enoch C.)	31 Aug 1886	18 Dec 1931	
Leota S.)	16 Jun 1895	27 Aug 1970	
George R.	30 Mar 1858	6 Feb 1887	
Hannah H.	22 Sep 1852	21 Dec 1886	w/o G.R. (broken)
Herbert L.	1899	1962	
Lillian V.	1909	1971	
Herbert Wayne	Born & died	6 Jul 1931	s/o M/M H.L.
Irene Leota	26 Jul 1918	9 Nov 1956	
James J.)	11 Feb 1864	18 Jan 1943	
Ella M.)	20 Mar 1869	9 Sep 1948	
James M.)	1 Jul 1832	10 Oct 1898	
Malinda Spickard)	2 Jul 1839	16 Dec 1911	His wife
Jessie A.	1879	1962	
Joe C.)	1867	1937	
Mollie A.)	1874	1962	
Joy Lee	11 Dec 1931	13 Feb 1937	
Kenneth Wayne	17 Aug 1961	7 Dec 1961	

MOYERS-Leonard R.	4 Feb 1848	3 Dec 1893	
Lloyd C.	1907	1964	
Viola Blevins	1909	1984	
Lucy	21 May 1870	27 Feb 1939	
Mose Roadman)	1886	1966	
Lillie W.)	1888	1978	
Ollie A.	11 Aug 1877	14 Oct 1939	Sister
O. P. R.)	11 Feb 1859	6 Oct 1915	
Margaret)	19 Sep 1862	19 Aug 1919	His wife
Raymond	13 Feb 1901	23 Dec 1930	
Robert Earl	1903	1986	(fhm-Farrar)
Ross L.	16 May 1901	29 Jun 1959	Alabama PFC 21 Base HQ & AB Sq. AAF WWI & WWII
Rufus C.	1902	1971	(fhm-Brooks)
Warren W.	25 Jul 1876	29 Dec 1951	
Bertie Fox	15 Jul 1882	10 Apr 1958	
William B.	5 Jan 1850	26 Aug 1920	Father
Ellen Hensley	14 Feb 1857	30 Jan 1883	w/o W.B.
MULLINAX-Annie M.	24 Nov 1888	12 Nov 1943	
MUSICK-Judy Anne	25 May 1948	17 Jan 1974	
MYERS-Moses R.	No dates		Co F 13th Tenn Cav
Amanda	14 Aug 1841	16 Jan 1910	w/o M.R.
A. J. Boley	27 Jul 1872	13 Aug 1904	Married to R.M. MYERS 29 Nov 1893
NEWGENT-Harry Scott	28 Sep 1884	13 Jan 1987	s/o A.J. & A.E. 2y 3m 16d
NEWMAN-Joseph P.)	3 Jul 1875	4 Mar 1965	
Miranda)	7 Aug 1877	23 Dec 1943	
NICHOLS-Benjamin M.	23 Jul 1882	30 Jul 1882	
James F.	25 Dec 1847	20 Apr 1926	
E. R. N.	8 Apr 1855	7 Mar 1889	w/o J.F.; Garrett's Mother
E. Ross)	18 Jan 1888	27 Sep 1964	
Annie)	19 Nov 1888	11 Dec 1956	
J. Henry	20 Jun 1854	30 Mar 1923	
Adelaide McFarland	28 Jan 1861	22 Jan 1936	
Leo Wilson	2 Apr 1890	25 Dec 1982	
Otway L.	12 Aug 1886	31 Dec 1886	
Sarah Adaline	2 Aug 1852	13 Jun 1924	
Love I.	11 Apr 1890	21 Sep 1970	
William F.)	24 Dec 1883	9 Feb 1966	
Amanda A.)	No dates		
W. P.	17 Nov 1821	2 Apr 1911	
Mary V.	13 Oct 1815	6 Feb 1884	
W. P. A.	26 May 1849	15 Aug 1896	s/o W.P. & Mary V.
NOE-Samuel Rufus)	1880	1965	
Ethel Mae)	1888	1968	
NOLEN-Robert Landon)	25 Apr 1906	16 May 1986	
Julia Rines)	19 Feb 1911	20 Aug 1984	
NOONKESSER-Noah)	6 Jul 1878	27 May 1949	
Bessie Sims)	25 Aug 1890	11 Mar 1959	
ODOM-Ralph P.	9 Oct 1916	10 May 1973	Married 3 Jul 1937
Linnie R.	13 Jul 1920	NOD	
OLLIS-Alvin W.)	12 Mar 1907	NOD	
Mayme P.)	29 Apr 1914	NOD	
Alvin W. Jr.	13 Jun 1947	14 Jun 1947	s/o M/M Alvin
OSBORNE-Jesse C.)	27 Jun 1882	4 Apr 1944	
Maude P.)	10 Oct 1894	16 Feb 1970	
J. P.)	17 Oct 1921	NOD	Wed 10 Nov 1949
Birdie E.)	4 Aug 1925	1 Sep 1983	

OSBORNE-William L. "Fate")	25 Mar 1887	14 May 1970	TN pvt 230 PWS Esc Co ASC WWI
Maggie S.	29 Apr 1898	12 Dec 1979	
OWEN-Arthur J.)	1884	1954	
Georgia D.)	1889	NOD	
Frank T.	8 Aug 1873	28 May 1903	Born Witt's Foundry, TN
			Killed at Bridgeport, TN
Dr. Luther H.	27 Jul 1889	28 Mar 1917	
Rufus Morgan)	1856	1942	
Lydia Frances)	1873	1944	
Thomas J.	11 Jan 1862	15 Dec 1891	
Eppie	22 Dec 1866	5 Apr 1890	w/o Thomas J.
W. J.)	16 Apr 1810	13 Feb 1892	81y 9m 27d
Mary J.)	8 Feb 1828	11 Jun 1884	w/o W.J.; d/o James & L.
			TAYLOR; 56y 4m 3d
PACK-Gary Lee	OD	2 Aug 1948	
James P.)	24 Oct 1860	2 Aug 1923	
Alice W.)	9 Aug 1875	8 Mar 1948	
J. Earl)	3 Sep 1909	10 Jan 1978	
Zula B.)	10 May 1909	24 Mar 1978	
PARKER-Claude S.)	27 Oct 1898	14 Jan 1941	TN pvt 120 Inf 30 Div
Mary B.)	10 Mar 1904	1 Jun 1980	
Claude Woodrow	23 May 1925	20 Jun 1945	TN Seaman 2C USNR
Katherine	1939	1982	(fhm-Farrar)
Robert E.	15 Jun 1931	22 Dec 1984	US Army Inf Div Korea 1949-50
Walter Cummings	16 Oct 1886	14 Sep 1940	
Willie C.	29 Feb 1892	6 May 1959	
PARKS-Carrie E.	7 Feb 1932	NOD	
Della E.	22 Nov 1889	4 Nov 1980	
PAPPER-Gertrude S.	1 Jan 1901	4 Jan 1979	(See Wilbur CALFEE)
PHILLIPS-Dave A.)	2 Sep 1882	19 Mar 1957	
Martha Lou)	2 Sep 1887	8 Jan 1972	
PLESS-Henry S.	5 Nov 1857	4 Jun 1931	
Addie B.	1 Apr 1871	11 Feb 1950	
Lee P.)	27 Dec 1871	23 Jun 1945	
Daisy L.)	22 Dec 1880	1 Nov 1967	
Lula E. Biddle	2 Sep 1869	21 Aug 1907	Married L.P. Pless 21 Aug 1896
William P.)	26 Feb 1832	23 oct 1919	
Nancy Lavina)	22 Oct 1836	6 May 1926	
PONDER-J. Grayson)	1880	1958	
Kathern H.)	1893	1976	
PRATT-Francis M.	19 Feb 1909	13 Jun 1974	
PRICE-Barlow Lee)	12 Jan 1913	29 Apr 1915	Son
Infant)	OD	13 Feb 1924	d/o G.C. & L.V.
Geo. "Clint")	1889	1953	
Louvenia F.)	1893	1967	
Ralph)	21 Apr 1891	16 Aug 1965	
Emma Ellis)	16 Sep 1894	6 Sep 1983	
PRYOR-Vincion R.	8 Mar 1829	24 May 1920	
Sarah J.	25 Sep 1838	27 Dec 1920	
RAY-Oscar Samuel "Pete"	1917	1986	(fhm-Farrar)
REED-Clinton R.)	3 Jul 1911	NOD	
Mary K.)	13 Apr 1916	24 Apr 1969	
David Emmitt	29 Dec 1958	21 May 1979	MS3 US Navy
Burl	1906	1933	s/o Tom & Jennie
John W.)	16 Jun 1896	8 Jun 1969	(2nd stone says born 1882)
Lillie Mae Dawson)	29 Apr 1896	25 Feb 1980	

REED-Maggie Ward	17 Jan 1893	13 Jan 1966	
Ralph E.	1913	1930	s/o Tom & Jennie
Tom)	1877	1930	
Jennie C.)	1878	1963	
Youncie Lane	1898	1968	(fhm)
RENEAU-Christopher S.	1966	1967	(fhm)
Elmer R.)	13 Sep 1911	9 Dec 1978	Married 13 Jun 1942; Pvt US Army WWII
Hazel R.)	29 Mar 1923	NOD	
William O.)	29 Aug 1886	14 Dec 1967	
Matilda C.)	14 Feb 1892	24 Jan 1968	
REYNOLDS-Daniel Leazer	24 Apr 1854	10 Jul 1928	
Ella Stevens	31 Oct 1864	5 Jul 1938	w/o D.L.
Daniel Leazer	3 May 1889	9 Mar 1972	
Joseph Stevens	20 Jan 1929	8 Mar 1937	
RHEA-Joseph Edward	10 Sep 1909	12 Feb 1959	TN cM1 USNR WWII
Elsie Edith	31 May 1911	18 Nov 1967	
Mack Clevland)	15 Sep 1884	11 Sep 1940	
Elsie B. Jessee)	3 Mar 1885	8 Oct 1978	
RIGGS-Darthula Jane	14 Mar 1840	8 Nov 1885	w/o E.J.
Ida M.	29 May 1885	4 Oct 1885	d/o E.J. & D.J.
RIMMER-Eliza C.	31 Mar 1898	28 Jun 1954	
RINER-J. S.)	17 Mar 1887	6 Jan 1976	
Mary Anna)	30 Nov 1888	11 Aug 1967	
RINES-Albert)	8 Nov 1879	31 May 1967	
Lou P)	28 Jun 1880	9 Jun 1940	
Charlie	5 Feb 1912	25 Aug 1948	TN Pvt Med Dep WWii
Clifford L.	14 Feb 1922	29 Dec 1984	Tec5 US army WWII
Rev. Haskel)	1 Dec 1913	14 Jun 1964	
Pearl Holt)	9 Jun 1915	3 Jan 1964	
Johnny Wayne	20 Mar 1945	2 Jan 1964	
Mack)	1897	NOD	
Elizabeth)	1906	1985	
Patricia)	1942	NOD	
Mack Jr.	15 Nov 1926	24 Jun 1983	
Ross	1923	1981	US Army WWII
ROACH-Ada	1909	1985	76y (fhm-Rose)
ROBERTS-Johnny	OD	2 Jan 1954	Inf s/o Bill & Ruby
ROBERTSON-lillard B.)	1924	NOD	
Letha)	1925	NOD	
ROMINES-Jack B.)	1933	NOD	
Bobby J.)	1933	NOD	
ROSENBALM-Henry H.)	18 Feb 1913	NOD	
Dean Rines)	25 Apr 1918	20 Aug 1974	
ROUSE-Oliver H.P.)	15 Apr 1840	11 Aug 1898	
Julia A.)	28 Apr 1859	17 Jun 1921	
RUTHERFORD-Wilma Jean	17 Mar 1947	18 Mar 1947	
SAMPLES-Johnnie R.)	2 May 1927	NOD	
Laura Mae)	8 Aug 1920	23 Mar 1974	
SAMS-James W.	21 Jan 1867	2 Feb 1944	
SAMUEL-Edward Milton Jr.	Od	5 Jan 1941	Inf s/o Georgia & Milton
SARTAIN-Alfred T. Sr.)	16 Oct 1886	28 Mar 1956	
Gypsy W.)	15 Oct 1895	19 Jan 1967	
Alfred T. Jr.)	29 Oct 1932	3 Jan 1933	
Arthur Alvin	16 Jul 1937	22 Nov 1978	US Navy
Cecil W.	25 Mar 1908	19 Mar 1967	TN PFC US marine Corp Res WWII

```
SARTAIN-Clara              17 Aug 1887     3 Aug 1961
   Dewey A.    )           30 Mar 1914    NOD
   Virgie M.   )           13 Jan 1914    NOD
   Homer Lee Sr.           14 Jun 1940     7 Feb 1984     Served US Army 1962-64
   Jack J.      )          28 Dec 1913    21 Feb 1985
   Bessie       )           6 Mar 1917    NOD
   Billy Wayne  )               1944          1944
   Jewell Dean  )               1941          1941
   Samuel Hubert)               1939          1939
   Jesse F. )              12 Sep 1901    25 Nov 1975
   Nannie H.)              27 Jul 1903    NOD
   Jessie M.              27 Jan 1887    22 Apr 1956
   John Robert)            23 Jan 1895    19 May 1981     US Army WWI
   Mabel B.    )           14 Sep 1901    NOD             Married 23 Jun 1932
   Robert T.)              12 Feb 1876    27 Sep 1966
   Lucy H.   )             15 Jun 1884     7 Oct 1961
   Roy William            19 Jul 1952    27 Aug 1955
   Ruben Murphy    )        7 Dec 1906    NOD
   Rosa Mae Sinard)         5 Mar 1910    NOD
   Samuel Murpy   )        18 Oct 1882    13 Dec 1958
   J. Cordelia    )        19 May 1887    20 Nov 1967
   William Thomas  )            1868          1951
   Rodah Bigham    )       14 Oct 1870    14 Oct 1953
   W. Robert )             1 Nov 1926     NOD
   Mary Agnes)             26 Jul 1932    NOD
SARTIN-Albert Hutson        1 May 1853     4 Apr 1915
   James H.)                2 Dec 1912    NOD
   Anna E. )              15 Dec 1915    NOD
   Willie D.     )         23 Dec 1889    23 Aug 1924
   Martha Ellen )         18 Aug 1894    17 Oct 1925     His wife
SATTERFIELD-B. C.          11 Sep 1833    12 Dec 1911
   Martha E. Biddle        1 Mar 1832    23 Jun 1895     w/o B.C.
   Edda Roberts           30 May 1875    13 Aug 1896     w/o W.C.
   Cora Stokely           23 Dec 1872    16 May 1900     w/o T.E.
SAVILLE-B.H.                    1872          1926
   Cecil                  15 Jun 1914     1 Jul 1914
   Everett                 5 Dec 1905    25 Mar 1906
   John F.     )          23 May 1839     4 May 1918
   Margaret R.)            3 Apr 1840    30 Mar 1911     w/o Jno. F.
   Willard F.             16 Sep 1880    27 Apr 1952     Pvt 32 TN Inf SP AM War
   Nannie Lister          14 Oct 1880     7 Jul 1914
SCHELL-Rev. Fred F.)       29 Jan 1878     5 Jun 1972     Married 1 Mar 1911
   Louise Felknor )       28 Jul 1881    18 Sep 1971
SCOTT-Baby                 No dates
SCRUGGS-James A.                1854          1933
SEAL-Milford C.)           27 Nov 1904     2 Feb 1960
   Pauline B. )            7 Aug 1904     6 Feb 1979
SEALS-R. H.                 4 Apr 1929    13 May 1986     (fhm-Stubblefield)
SHARP-Fred R.    )         14 May 1886    23 Dec 1966
   Byrd Piercy )          15 Jun 1900     5 Jul 1969     w/o Fred R.
   Nellie Irene)           6 Jan 1882    11 Jan 1967
   Julia Deda              9 Sep 1889     4 Jun 1890     d/o R.P. & M.A.
   Robert P.              22 Apr 1852     2 Sep 1898
   Mary A. Caldwell       19 Sep 1849    23 Dec 1930     w/o R.P.
   Mary Moser              8 Aug 1812    20 Nov 1882     Mother of William MOSER
```

```
SHAVER-Edd H. )                       1908           1983
   Kathleen T.)                       1912           1975
   Elick                     19 Mar 1871   24 Dec 1963
   Rosa Bell                 19 Jun 1877   11 Jun 1956
   Hobert M.    )            7 Sep 1896   31 Aug 1969   Married 9 May 1915
   Alice Dawson )           22 Jun 1896   10 Sep 1967
   Tom A. )                 28 Apr 1900   19 Jun 1977
   Ruth E.)                 24 Nov 1905   NOD
SHEFFEY-Roy T.              15 Nov 1890   20 Dec 1926
   W. Omer                          1883           1953
SHERFEY-J. A.        )      24 Jul 1850    3 Sep 1929
   Nancy Ruth Archer)       21 Sep 1845   21 Dec 1912   His wife
   Lawrence J.              16 Feb 1873   27 Sep 1907   s/o J.A. & N.R. 34y 7m 11d
   Sallie K.                Died          23 Oct 1918   d/o J.A. & N.R.
SHIELDS-Mary A.              9 Dec 1829    5 Sep 1911
SHIPLEY-Lafayette A.)       15 Aug 1881   26 Oct 1963
   Laura Belle      )       25 May 1889   29 Jun 1967
SINARD-Charlotte E.         11 Dec 1933    5 Nov 1934   Daughter
   Earl      )              22 Feb 1904   11 Jan 1974
   Hannah B.)                3 Nov 1908   NOD
   James C.                  4 Apr 1902   22 Mar 1966   Father
   James Michael            20 Jun 1961   21 Jun 1980   Son
   Robert C.                14 Mar 1928    6 Jul 1932   Son
   Robert F.)                6 May 1886   27 Jul 1968
   Daisy     )              23 Dec 1884    8 Feb 1962
   S. Dale                  28 Sep 1949    1 Jun 1979
   Willard                  10 Jan 1919   12 Sep 1950   TN SSgt 184 Inf 7 Inf Div WWII
SMELCER-Robert L. Jr.)      15 Mar 1956   NOD
   Kathryn                  20 Jul 1933   19 Mar 1956
SMITH-Anvil )               23 Feb 1893   28 Jun 1961
   Anna Sue )               24 Jul 1895   NOD
   Arlie V.   )              7 May 1909   15 Apr 1978
   Cressie A. )             24 Feb 1914   NOD
   Arnold Carroll           14 Oct 1945    7 Nov 1945   s/o M/M Carroll
   Ausber Ulys              10 Aug 1888   13 Oct 1908   s/o J.A. & Ellen
   B. Carlene               28 Jul 1957    4 Nov 1959   d/o C.L. & Peggy
   Benjamin Harrison)       26 Aug 1888   27 Feb 1947
   Mary Inman        )       1 Feb 1894   17 Aug 1966
   Willie Frank      )      25 May 1934    1 Aug 1954
   Pless      )             27 Dec 1880   27 Aug 1967
   Lizzie Fox)              15 Jul 1883   23 Apr 1964
   Charles Porter   )       27 Sep 1880   17 Jan 1949
   Bessie Lee Bettis)       15 Apr 1885   17 Jan 1953
   Dan T.)                  29 Feb 1880    6 Apr 1960
   Lena  )                  31 Jan 1884   15 Jun 1952
   Della                           1900           1938   w/o Will; age 38
   F. Ray   )               18 Dec 1900    9 Sep 1984
   Mary Love)               No dates
   Mollie J.)               25 Oct 1870    1 Nov 1954
   Herman F.  )             24 Jan 1905   NOD
   Alma M.    )              1 Mar 1911   NOD
   Howard                   21 Oct 1903   28 May 1904   s/o Pless & Elizabeth
   J. A.)                    4 Aug 1855   18 Aug 1937
   Ellen)                   21 Nov 1867   23 Jan 1936   His wife
   James H.                 22 Jan 1848   18 Oct 1912
   James Thomas             23 Jan 1909   26 Nov 1910   s/o W. L. & I.E.
```

SMITH-Julia D.	4 Apr 1906	NOD	
Kenneth H.	5 Nov 1913	27 Jan 1980	
Orville E.	14 Jul 1929	19 Apr 1974	Sp3 US Army
Theodore R.)	24 Aug 1901	12 Dec 1982	Married 54y
Myrtle J.)	10 Sep 1906	NOD	
Tom Moore	1862	1927	
Elizabeth Rebecca	1867	1937	
Volena	22 Oct 1928	30 May 1930	s/o M/M Herman
Walter Lafayette)	4 May 1881	23 Dec 1957	
Ida Elizabeth)	6 May 1877	1 Mar 1956	
SNEED-Marvin Earl	17 Dec 1942	3 Nov 1982	Beloved son & brother
SNODDY-Gideon	4 Oct 1826	4 Aug 1906	
Mary Elizabeth	26 May 1891	6 Feb 1962	
Robert Newton)	28 May 1839	16 Nov 1906	
Susan S. Witt)	5 Jul 1852	19 Feb 1947	His wife
Thomas E.)	25 Feb 1844	5 Jul 1917	
Maria Riddle)	21 Aug 1848	7 Nov 1910	His wife
Virginia Pearl	1 Mar 1876	19 Dec 1947	
(name broken)	7 Sep 1882	19 Oct 1890	d/o R. N. & S.S.(broken)
SNODGRASS-Ada	22 Sep 1884	4 Apr 1962	
Alvie Thomas	29 May 1891	2 Feb 1981	
Ann Eliza	1863	21 Nov 1947	
Azinetta I.	1 Sep 1884	16 Jul 1899	d/o G.R. & L. V.
Erma Selma	22 Oct 1892	17 Sep 1906	d/o J.W. & Emma L.
James B.	12 Sep 1880	22 Sep 1903	
J. W.)	1859	1940	
Emma 1. Holloway)	1967	1911	His wife
Mada L.)	8 Jan 1888	12 Jul 1967	Twins
Myrtle I.)	8 Jan 1888	10 May 1983	
SOUTHERLAND-Jesse	1887	1935	
Lillie Tindell	1896	1922	w/o Jesse
SPENCER-Earl Benton	Died	6 Jul 1957	
Etter Mae	13 Aug 1928	25 Nov 1933	d/o M/M E.B.
Hugh Carpenter	12 Mar 1923	4 Aug 1968	TN tec5 35 Gen Hosp WWII
Madge C.	27 Jun 1900	8 Apr 1972	
Shirley Jean	19 Oct 1943	26 Dec 1943	d/o M/M E.B.
SPICKARD-Isaac H.)	1887	1966	
Lucy Bull)	1887	1959	
Jacob)	15 Aug 1831	16 Sep 1926	
Ruth Eliza Cannady)	18 Feb 1844	9 Jan 1913	
J. M.	No dates		Co L 8th Cav
SPRADLIN-Larry E.	1962	1986	(fhm-Farrar)
SPRINKLE-L. Marion)	9 Sep 1863	18 May 1949	
Mary E.)	1 Oct 1866	5 Sep 1935	
Howard E.)	27 May 1906	27 Apr 1944	
Robbie M.)	24 Jul 1899	21 Nov 1969	
SQUIBB-Myrtle May	16 May 1877	3 Apr 1903	
STALCUP-Georgia R.	16 Oct 1901	30 May 1968	
STARNES-Donald A.	19 Dec 1914	5 Apr 1979	PFC US Army WWII
Jama Richa	OD	12 Sep 1982	Mother's baby
STEINER-Henry	28 Dec 1849	11 Feb 1916	
Rev. Joel)	Died	5 Dec 1909	85y 9m 22d
Urith Parish)	Died	22 Mar 1896	72y 4m 22d
STEPP-Seldon)	5 Sep 1902	8 Mar 1955	
Anna V. Cogdell)	23 Jun 1911	18 Feb 1977	

```
STEWART-Chas. T.              2 Nov 1841   26 Sep 1926
   James I.                  26 Mar 1853   28 Mar 1927
   Julia T.                  20 Jul 1848   31 Mar 1938
   Samuel H.)                15 Feb 1816   20 Sep 1910
   Susie A. )                15 Mar 1819    2 Dec 1909    His wife
STRANGE-Fred H.)              1 Apr 1903   NOD
   Myrtle C.   )            15 Nov 1905   22 Jan 1978
   Bobbie M.   )            19 Jul 1934   NOD
   Grace M.                 18 Oct 1909   17 Nov 1956
   W. S. "Jack")            5 Jun 1928    9 Apr 1984
   Mary M.     )            17 Dec 1931   NOD
STRAUB-Dora Deane Goan        4 Apr 1875   14 May 1929
STRINGFIELD-Sytha A.         21 Nov 1843   23 Feb 1911    w/o J.H.
STREET-Fonzer)               12 Apr 1883    4 May 1965
   Bessie    )               4 Jun 1887   11 Jun 1928
STUART-George Mc             16 Feb 1826    1 Dec 1910
   George Mell)              5 Jul 1864    10 Sep 1950
   Bell Butler)             13 Feb 1865   24 Dec 1944
   Emert C.   )                    1889          1940
   Geo. Stanley             24 Nov 1886   29 Jul 1975
   Guy Madison    )         25 Oct 1888   10 Nov 1959
   Myrtle Humpston)         20 May 1891   NOD
   Kenneth M.)              21 Oct 1895   12 Apr 1983
   Blanche C.)               2 Sep 1897   29 Oct 1983
   Samuel H.      )                1856          1936
   Effie Kelley )                  1867          1947
SURRETT-Clayton B.)          13 Sep 1910    3 Mar 1969
   Elsie B.       )          7 Nov 1906   NOD
   Fred R.)                  1 May 1901    7 Nov 1956
   Mary F.)                  5 Sep 1903   NOD
   Sherman S.)              29 Nov 1895    9 May 1983
   Beulah    )              24 Jun 1898   12 Sep 1978
   W. C.)                          1874          1938
   M. K.)                          1873          1941
   William A.                6 Nov 1926   30 Jun 1974
SURRETTE-Mary A.              6 Jan 1843   19 Jul 1907
SUTTLES-Charles Herbert  )   10 Dec 1901    9 Apr 1965
   Virdie Suttles COLLINS ) 10 Feb 1899   27 Dec 1971
   Ruthey                    9 Mar 1860   16 Feb 1942
TALLEY-Arvel Lowell          10 Jan 1920   21 Jan 1959    TN Tec5 Co D 253 Inf WWII
   Hattie M.                 7 May 1885   12 Jan 1911    w/o E. P.
TATE-Henry L.      )         12 Jun 1886   19 Dec 1955
   Flora V.       )          3 Aug 1887    1 Feb 1971
   Edward Burgin )          10 Dec 1918   30 Apr 1965    TN Tec4 US Army WWII
   Jodie Lee     )          11 Jun 1907    2 Sep 1966
TAYLOR-Rev. Charles Judson)  18 Dec 1903   14 Feb 1985
   Mary Nell Ross        )   9 Apr 1912   NOD
   James O.      )          14 Jan 1865   28 May 1949
   Laura Hoskins)           16 Dec 1866   26 Jul 1942
   John H. )                       1896          1968
   Lula Lee)                       1893          1979
   Robert M.                31 Oct 1915    3 Apr 1936
   Willard Elbert)          21 Jan 1891   15 Aug 1946
   Willie Ellis  )          16 Dec 1890   22 Apr 1965
```

TEMPLIN-Isaac C.)	1889	1961	
Pearlie B.)	1895	NOD	
THOMAS-Sherry Lynn	OD	5 Aug 1963	Inf d/o Randle & Patricia
THOMPSON-Andrew.	17 Dec 1831	21 Jun 1905	
Dorcas Long	Died	2 Sep 1878	Age 78y
John P.	21 Jan 1889	25 Nov 1950	
Stella Mae	4 Jul 1885	1 Apr 1952	
Joseph A.	24 Nov 1891	10 Jan 1892	
Nannie B.	17 Oct 1860	1 Feb 1927	
Oliver C.	16 Oct 1898	31 Dec 1899	
Willie L.	17 Jan 1893	26 Aug 1900	
THORP-A. D.)	17 May 1914	16 Nov 1980	Married 13 Aug 1933
Mattie G.)	20 Apr 1917	NOD	
TINDLE-William A.)	6 May 1865	NOD	
Mary E.)	25 May 1870	4 Jan 1923	
Jesse Evert	5 Sep 1912	26 Jul 1971	TN Tec5 Co D 800 Mil Pol WWII
TOBY-Glennie Mae	22 Jan 1905	14 Dec 1968	
TURNER-Connie)	1 May 1904	8 Sep 1972	
Pearl)	5 Jun 1903	5 Jan 1969	
William Ben)	21 Nov 1922	NOD	
Edith Duckett)	29 Mar 1931	8 Jan 1981	
ULLSTROM-Arne)	11 Jan 1908	5 May 1979	
Lempie J.)	11 Dec 1908	NOD	
VARNER-Hugh U.	12 Feb 1894	27 Dec 1930	Co C 329 Inf U.S.A.
Minnie Lee	17 Mar 1895	26 Nov 1975	
VINYARD-Henry Ott)	30 May 1891	21 Aug 1963	
Ida Black)	28 Nov 1891	5 May 1980	
WALKER-Clyde Allen	24 Nov 1884	14 Jul 1960	
Cecilia Reynolds	1 Jul 1892	19 Nov 1983	
Frank T.	30 Nov 1878	17 Jun 1905	s/o J.E. & H.N.
Gladys Alicetine	10 Jan 1894	25 May 1959	
Hal Stokely	22 Dec 1919	17 Jul 1980	
Dr. James H.	3 Nov 1863	4 Jan 1930	
Iantha E. Biddle	7 Jan 1866	7 Aug 1904	w/o Dr. J.H.
Ida Elizabeth	22 Dec 1874	14 Apr 1969	
James H., Jr.	11 Jan 1914	5 Aug 1919	s/o Dr. & Mrs. Ida
John E.)	29 Mar 1850	8 Dec 1927	
Helen Stokely)	3 Apr 1854	25 Jun 1912	His wife
Mary Lois	5 Dec 1903	10 Aug 1904	d/o Dr. J.H. & Iantha E.
Perry Stevenson	25 Aug 1941	9 Mar 1974	
Walter Stokley	28 Aug 1876	31 Jul 1914	
Wendell Haynes	18 Sep 1904	26 Jul 1905	s/o F.T. & D.L.
WALL-Alvin C.	1915	1963	
Edward Kyle	30 Jun 1912	12 Jan 1967	
Guy H.	15 Sep 1919	NOD	
Fannie J.	30 Nov 1916	NOD	
Kate G.	13 May 1879	18 Apr 1962	
Mollie Solomon	16 Jul 1866	12 Apr 1953	
Sankey D.	1883	1950	
Dora M. Campbell	1895	1923	
Thomas J.	10 Feb 1914	29 Oct 1982	
Arlevia W.	22 Sep 1920	NOD	
WALTERS-Rev. John M.)	8 Apr 1850	14 Nov 1934	
Lula Franklin)	29 Dec 1858	1 Sep 1927	
Robert McBee)	25 May 1886	28 Jan 1909	s/o J.M. & L.R.
John M.)	10 Jul 1885	27 Jun 1972	
William M.	19 Oct 1826	6 Mar 1895	A Confederate Soldier

WARD-Elizabeth S.	30 Oct 1883	28 Mar 1957	
Elsie M.	14 Jul 1912	29 Oct 1938	
Julia A.	10 Apr 1844	13 Jan 1900	w/o Enoch
Maudie Carmichael	22 Jul 1897	6 May 1929	
Roger Dale	31 Jul 1944	10 Feb 1986	
William	1896	1938	Father; age 42
WARREN-Ernie Carroll	2 Jun 1950	4 May 1954	s/o M/M Edgar
James E.	1 Feb 1918	16 Nov 1980	
WASHAM-Sarah	9 Sep 1837	25 Jun 1912	w/o J.T. (Sunken)
WATSON-Robert H.)	26 Aug 1915	4 Jan 1985	
Rosie L.)	25 Aug 1940	NOD	
WAYMIER-Alexander L.	18 Jan 1897	8 Sep 1942	
James S.)	14 Jun 1868	24 May 1929	
Cordelia)	26 Jun 1876	11 May 1957	
WELLS-Jennie T.	Died	4 Jun 1888	w/o J.P.; 29y 17d
WELSH-Anna Hensley	2 Jul 1876	27 Dec 1922	
Wallace Hensley	23 Nov 1899	10 Apr 1950	SA US Navy WWI
Gertrude	7 Dec 1897	19 Mar 1898	d/o S.T. & A.B.
WHEELER-George W.)	8 Mar 1893	21 Apr 1975	
Nell C.)	22 Oct 1898	8 Oct 1972	
Charles A.)	14 May 1896	27 Jan 1947	
PFC Robert Y.)	19 Oct 1925	16 Mar 1945	Co L US Inf 63 Div; Killed in in Germany with 7th Army
Walter Minnis)	24 Apr 1866	13 Sep 1946	
Martha Jane)	25 Sep 1868	12 Apr 1955	
William J.)	18 Nov 1889	20 Aug 1979	
Bonnie H.)	31 Jul 1893	24 Jul 1926	
Loucille N.)	7 Jul 1902	30 Jan 1970	
William J. Jr.)	1 Apr 1919	19 Apr 1919	
WHITE-Callie Manard	OD	19 Dec 1921	
Clifford D.)	12 Oct 1899	NOD	
Dovie R.)	4 Jan 1899	16 Sep 1976	
Cyrus M.	Died	18 Jul 1904	
Elwood	24 Dec 1902	5 Dec 1984	81y (fhm-Brown)
Grace B.	3 Aug 1890	19 Feb 1965	
James L.)	23 Nov 1840	11 Nov 1930	
Mary C.)	8 Dec 1843	2 Dec 1915	w/o James L.
Myrtice	14 Apr 1896	16 Dec 1911	d/o R.S. Belle
Nannie H.	3 Apr 1914	NOD	
Richard "Fate"	14 Aug 1882	30 Dec 1961	
Nannie S.	2 Mar 1882	9 Jan 1915	w/o Richard L.
Mattie Haun	29 Mar 1889	11 May 1969	
Robert S.	11 Aug 1867	22 Feb 1909	
Belle McGuire	14 Nov 1869	28 Mar 1931	w/o Robert S.
Sallie H.	7 Dec 1903	29 Mar 1952	
T. F.	13 Sep 1848	9 Apr 1898	
Walter W. Sr.	Died	1 Jul 1958	
Rev. William Austen	21 Apr 1886	16 Jun 1966	Methodist Minister for 50 years
WIDENER-Charles L. Sr.)	25 Apr 1874	7 Dec 1956	
Ida B.)	30 Jun 1884	14 Mar 1977	
Charles Lee III)	12 Aug 1943	19 Aug 1943	
Maurice S.)	OD	2 Aug 1944	Inf s/o M/M Charlie
WIGGINS-Bergin W.)	1 Jul 1907	22 Apr 1977	married 5 Sep 1926
Ella W.)	26 Mar 1909	27 Sep 1985	
WIGINGTON-James H.)	23 Feb 1841	1 Aug 1907	
Emily J. Coleman)	2 Oct 1840	9 Jun 1904	His wife
George W.	13 Apr 1874	5 Apr 1917	

WILDER-Tennie T.	13 Dec 1915	8 Jul 1963	
WILLIAMS-Ben M.)	29 May 1865	29 Nov 1941	
William E.)	28 Mar 1867	9 Jun 1945	
Rev. C. W.)	5 May 1876	NOD	
Roe Driskill)	8 Nov 1872	22 Feb 1926	w/o Rev. C.W.
Flint)	26 Jul 1899	9 Feb 1979	
Hazel Holt)	22 May 1909	NOD	
Jessie Bell	20 Nov 1881	16 Aug 1970	
Henry Senter	21 Jun 1882	3 Aug 1970	
J. Buford	1912	1972	(fhm-Brooks)
Jennie Roe	6 Feb 1892	22 Jul 1914	d/o J.R. & M.J.
J. R.)	22 Feb 1863	25 Feb 1916	
Minnie)	18 Sep 1868	18 Jun 1924	His wife
Onnie Lee	15 May 1901	20 Mar 1984	
Ruble)	30 Jan 1915	21 Jun 1974	
Aileen)	31 May 1944	NOD	
Yewell R.)	1879	1967	
Georgia Zimmerman)	1881	1939	
Gertrude O.	1905	1985	
WILLIS-John L.)	3 May 1924	NOD	
Eula M.)	15 May 1929	NOD	
Howard W.)	10 Jul 1949	4 Jun 1971	
WILSON-Hal)	1898	1963	
Ruth)	1907	NOD	
James M.)	1831	1894	Father
Sarah Martha)	1854	1934	Mother
James B.)	1919	1924	
Joseph Barton)	1874	1935	Father
Rella N.)	1885	1972	Mother
Lon O. Jr.	OD	20 May 1939	Infant
Lon O.)	18 Oct 1906	NOD	
Aileen B.)	27 Jan 1909	NOD	
Norene L.	8 Dec 1923	25 Feb 1978	
Oscar)	17 Jul 1896	NOD	
Nellie Lee)	10 Oct 1905	27 Jul 1976	
WINSTEAD-Daniel S.)	1877	1959	
Abigail)	1880	1963	
WISE-Hugh L.)	1846	1912	
Lina A.)	1850	1914	
WITT-Abraham	24 Oct 1821	18 Jul 1892	
Mary J.	1835	29 May 1896	w/o A. (broken - repaired)
Almer H.)	15 Nov 1883	29 Jul 1934	
Mary E.)	5 Jul 1878	24 Nov 1944	
Oscar Floyd)	7 Apr 1882	5 Oct 1936	
Sarah Bailey)	31 Sep 1877	9 Jul 1936	
Rettie L.	19 Dec 1874	26 Nov 1902	d/o D.M. & A.T.
Rhoda Emily	22 Dec 1877	6 Apr 1962	
WOOD-Ethel	28 Aug 1890	26 Feb 1915	w/o Ed
WOODS-Anna B.	19 Jan 1919	8 Dec 1946	
Bernice	10 Mar 1898	12 Oct 1906	
Carl C.)	2 Sep 1902	17 Nov 1976	
Gladys C.)	5 May 1909	NOD	
Charles C.)	12 Oct 1859	13 May 1926	
Mary A.)	7 Sep 1859	2 Jun 1931	
Chas. Richard	11 Nov 1924	25 Dec 1946	
David Blair)	28 Jun 1900	28 Jun 1964	
Phronia Berry)	5 Mar 1904	30 Jul 1945	
Carolyn Sue)	18 Jan 1945	20 Jan 1945	

WOODS-Dora Amanda	5 May 1925	4 Aug 1971	
Doris E. "Pug"	22 Nov 1946	23 Nov 1983	
Eugene Lee	11 Mar 1932	12 Mar 1932	s/o C.C. & Gladys
H. C.	9 Jan 1867	12 Dec 1904	
Carrie	7 Dec 1868	27 May 1958	
Homer Clyde)	25 Jul 1892	16 Feb 1972	
Lennie V.)	26 Jan 1894	11 Dec 1980	
Hubert)	10 Oct 1894	6 Dec 1979	
Leona)	27 Mar 1895	18 Dec 1966	
Infant	Born & died	31 May 1891	s/o C.C. & M.A.
James W.	1 Jun 1864	1 Aug 1935	
Ida Fry	2 Jul 1866	20 Jan 1901	
Lynn	13 Feb 1889	9 Dec 1911	s/o C.C. & M.A.
Mary Emily	1835	1889	
Robert L.	8 Dec 1886	14 Feb 1890	s/o C.C. & M.A.
W. B.	30 Dec 1896	25 Dec 1946	
Lydia Shorter	25 Feb 1901	25 Dec 1946	
WOODY-James Mack	17 Nov 1917	7 Dec 1973	
WOLIVER-Alex	No dates		Co K 1st Ill L.A.
Maggie Ida May	4 Jan 1915	6 Mar 1915	
WORLEY-Sandra Renee	22 Oct 1959	24 Mar 1974	
WYRICK-Parlen W.)	1 Jan 1875	26 Jul 1957	
Nancy J. McMillian)	19 Aug 1874	11 Aug 1923	w/o P.W.
A. E.)	4 Nov 1895	14 Jan 1964	
Carrie Wall)	31 May 1895	27 Dec 1937	w/o A.E.
Chas. Curtis)	14 Dec 1900	19 May 1916	
YATES-Ferd T.	10 Apr 1854	24 Oct 1936	82y
Eva	8 Mar 1860	7 Jul 1934	w/o Ferd T.
Hugh T. Sr.)		23 Nov 1966	
	29 May 1882	23 Nov 1966	
Margaret Elizabeth McNabb)			
	11 Jan 1887	4 Dec 1951	
Mary Ellen Yates YOUNES)			
	25 Nov 1923	28 Oct 1960	
Ralph L.	23 Jun 1899	2 Nov 1901	s/o F.T. & E.V.
YOUNES-Mary Ellen Yates	25 Nov 1923	28 Oct 1960	(See Hugh T. YATES, SR.)
ZIMMERMANN-Marvin Christian	3 Apr 1885	22 Dec 1943	
Maude Reynolds	30 Jun 1887	7 Feb 1941	
S. I.)	8 Mar 1848	31 Aug 1903	
J. G.)	2 Dec 1828	27 May 1901	
ZOLLARS-Charles M.	15 Nov 1813	13 Aug 1889	
Ermal	10 Jun 1892	20 Jul 1923	
Ella L.	21 Mar 1885	6 Nov 1960	
Kate	1875	1953	
Ora A.)	5 Mar 1888	5 Apr 1931	
Bertie C.)	19 Sep 1891	17 Mar 1968	
R. P.	1867	1916	
Dola J. Davis	10 Aug 1868	10 May 1904	w/o R.P.; 35y 9m
NO LAST NAME-Ada I.	No dates		

To reach this large cemetery, begin at Exit 8 on I-81. Drive toward White Pine to the intersection with 25E. Turn toward White Pine and drive 1.5 miles. The Church-in-the-Pines is on the right.

COLEMAN CEMETERY

BARNETTE-Robert	10 Feb 1942	17 Dec 1974	(fhm-badly faded)
BEASLEY-Jarvis Edgar	29 May 1978	29 May 1978	
CARMICHAEL-William M.	1900	1971	(fhm-Farrar)
COLEMAN-Carl S.)	13 Aug 1928	NOD	
Dorothy H.)	5 Oct 1928	4 Oct 1979	
James L.	9 Oct 1926	14 Oct 1959	Cpl 556 Air Svc GP
			AAF WWII
Patrick Todd	5 Nov 1963	7 Nov 1963	s/o Carl & Dot
Ruby C.D.	No dates		
CURETON-Tilda	8 Apr 1912	NOD	w/o Clarence
DAVIS-Patricia Evon	12 Apr 1941	5 Feb 1975	
EDINGTON-Sallie	6 May 1883	9 Jan 1938	
HARBIN-Larry E.	1951	1970	(fhm-Brooks)
HAYES-Charles A.)	17 Feb 1911	27 Feb 1970	
Ida Parker)	2 Apr 1911	NOD	
Frank	31 Jan 1949	24 May 1970	
HAYS-J.D.	26 Jan 1931	4 Sep 1936	
HENDERSON-Rachel L.	1980	1980	(fhm-Westside)
HILL-Bertha Lou	28 Apr 1894	9 Jan 1984	
HINKLE-Sarah Parker	1873	1956	
JACKSON-Tony Eugene	2 Jun 1972	3 Sep 1978	
JONES-Jess Lee	1 Jan 1893	30 Mar 1976	
KEIRSEY-Arthur J.	1908	1975	
William S.	22 Apr 1946	20 Aug 1972	
KIMBROUGH-Bill	1914	1949	
LINER-Oscar Clemon	1895	1984	(fhm-Farrar)
LOYD-Mary	1908	1982	73y (fhm-Brown)
MANTOOTH-Leonard	10 Nov 1958	5 Aug 1980	
MULLIS-Janet M.	1979	1979	(fhm-Westside)
MUSICK-Delphia H.	29 Jan 1929	NOD	
MYERS-Tony Lee	26 Apr 1963	10 Aug 1985	
PARKER-Billy Allen	16 Dec 1940	28 Sep 1941	
Briscoe H.	26 Dec 1915	11 Sep 1972	TN Cpl US Marine WWII
Elbert A.)	13 Apr 1913	15 Apr 1976	
Essie Mae)	17 Nov 1919	5 Apr 1967	Mother of Clyde, William,
			& Shelby
Emanuel)	6 May 1914	NOD	
Lucille)	25 Jun 1907	14 Apr 1983	
Esau E.	11 Mar 1903	13 May 1957	
Callie E.	28 Feb 1900	26 Jul 1977	
John A.	Aug	24 Dec 1936	(broken)
Biddie Viola	11 Jan 1894	29 Dec 1936	
Gladys Irene	Born & died	24 Oct 1947	
Jacob Romey	1 May 1932	22 Jan 1955	
Romey J.	2 Jun 1906	21 Nov 1975	
William Girlen	Died	6 Oct 1966	(fhm)
RAY-Doris	8 Jul 1951	8 Jul 1951	Twin
REED-Clyde	15 May 1912	10 Apr 1939	
Dorothy Jean	6 Jan 1939	2 Dec 1939	
Estel)	6 Aug 1905	31 Jul 1973	
Lucille)	1 Oct 1904	NOD	
Lee Daniel	5 Apr 1937	15 Nov 1937	
RINES-Lilly Rose	1937	1982	(fhm-Farrar)
Terry Lynn	25 Mar 1957	10 Nov 1979	
SINARD-Andy B.)	1905	NOD	
Sarah J.)	1910	1983	

SINARD-Sherry Faye	OD	16 Jan 1966	
Walter	8 Oct 1898	17 Jun 1949	
UNDERWOOD-Audrey	1937	1946	Daughter
Fred A.	1900	1948	Father
WARDEN-William	1905	1981	75y (fhm-Maloy)
Mrs. Fanny Kay	1911	1980	78y (fhm-Maloy)
WARREN-Medra Parker	5 Mar 1942	4 Apr 1942	

To reach this site, begin at Exit 8 from I-81. Drive toward White Pine to the intersection with 25E. Turn toward White Pine and drive 1.9 mile. Turn left onto South Walnut Street. Drive 0.9 mile. The cemetery is on the right.

COLLIER CEMETERY

COLLIER-Laura J.	7 Nov 1858	11 Sep 1878	w/o William; d/o W.R. & Jane VINSON; 19y 10m 4d

This stone once stood near the garden on the Lem Hall farm, but is now in a field on the opposite side of the road from its original location. To reach this cemetery, take exit 424 from I-40. Drive toward Dandridge a short distance to the intersection of US25-70. Turn right onto US25W-70. Drive toward Dandridge 0.5 miles and turn right. Drive 0.1 miles and turn right onto Brethern Church Road. Drive 1.6 miles. The stone was once located near the house on the left, but is now on the right about 50 yards from the road and near a large gully.

The pieces of this stone were found scattered about Couch Cemetery. Reassembled, they look like a jigsaw puzzle. The cemetery appears to have been vandalized.

COUCH CEMETERY

COUCH-David A.)	27 Mar 1853	31 May 1923	
Darthula Reams)	23 May 1857	10 Mar 1926	
Eugene P.	27 Nov 1895	24 Aug 1950	
Infant	No dates		i/o Peter & Elizabeth
Infant	No dates		i/o Peter & Elizabeth
J. J.)	4 Jul 1850	6 Feb 1910	
Mollie E. Mann)	26 Nov 1856	9 Nov 1940	
Mary	27 Dec 1851	19 Jul 1906	d/o Peter & Elizabeth
Peter	-- --- ----	-- --- ----	(broken; pieces missing)
Elizabeth	Jul 1829	14 Aug 1900	w/o Peter (broken into 10 pieces)
KIDWELL-Rachel M.	Died	25 Jul 1858	d/o S.H. & M.A. 1y 11m 14d
PATTERSON-W. L.	11 May 1833	20 Jan 1920	
Sarah	23 May 1835	23 Nov 1904	w/o W. L. 69y 6m
SMITH-Sallie Couch	5 Aug 1859	21 May 1931	w/o G.A. (broken 6 pieces pieces)

All of the above burials, with the exceptions of the two Couch infants and Rachel Kidwell, are inside a wrought-iron fence. We have seldom seen such destruction in a cemetery as in this one. Many of the stones were broken into pieces and the fragments scattered about the cemetery. It was necessary to search through the undergrowth and rubbish to locate missing pieces of stones. The tombstones had to be fitted together like working a jigsaw puzzle. Couch appears to have been a sizeable cemetery. Nine uninscribed fieldstones were outside the fenced area, and three more were inside the fence.

To reach this cemetery, take exit 4 from I-81. Turn onto Roy J. Messer Highway and drive away from White Pine 0.4 mile to Kimbrough Crossroads. Turn right onto Valley Home and drive 2.7 miles. Turn left onto Alpha-Valley Home Road. Drive 0.7 mile. Turn left onto Pleasant Ridge Road. Drive 0.5 mile. The cemetery is to the right near the top of the hill.

CRIDER CEMETERY

CRIDER-Isaac	Died	4 Jul 1847	47y 5m 10d

The Isaac Crider burial is the only marked grave. Another burial is marked only with an uninscribed fieldstone, and perhaps a third is marked with a pile of large stones. A large holly tree grows in the cemetery. The Isaac Crider grave is unusual because the entire grave is covered with large, shaped stone blocks.

To reach Crider Cemetery, take Exit 4 from I-81. Turn south toward White Pine and drive 0.8 mile. Turn right onto Rankin Road and drive 1.3 mile. Turn right and drive 0.5 mile. The cemetery is under a tree atop the hill in the field to the right.

EBENEZER METHODIST CEMETERY

AILEY-C. E.	6 Jul 1918	29 Mar 1920	d/o R.W. & E.C.
C. L.	23 May 1916	4 Jun 1916	
James Orville	2 Sep 1921	11 Feb 1928	s/o R.W. & E.C.
ANDERSON-Claude O.)	8 Jul 1883	21 Oct 1951	
Viola K. Mills)	24 Feb 1888	17 Sep 1964	
BACON-Sarah Ann	Died	3 Jan 1855	Consort of James 24y 1m 27d
BAILEY-Mary	30 Oct 1823	22 Feb 1905	w/o David
Robert Windford	OD	28 Nov 1932	
BAKER-Frank)	29 Mar 1908	14 Jul 1984	
Pauline S.)	11 Mar 1914	OD	
BASS-Royce Larry	25 Oct 1943	30 Mar 1944	
BELL-Jacob	7 Mar 1808	29 Aug 1890	
Mary M.	22 Feb 1817	3 Aug 1895	w/o Jacob
Marshal N.)	15 Jun 1850	29 Mar 1879	
Araminta J.)	12 Mar 1852	24 May 1877	
BETTIS-C.E.	No dates		13 Batty U.S. Field Art.
Emily K.	15 Mar 1864	22 Apr 1864	i/o S. & L.A.
Harriet J.	Died	21 Sep 1848	26y
Infant	No dates		i/o S. & K.
Infant	No dates		i/o S. & K.
Infant	Born & died	8 Oct 1869	d/o W.H. & M.E. (broken)
John	27 Sep 1819	16 Oct 1883	s/o William & Mary 64y 19d
Catharine	18 Aug 1818	10 Aug 1857	w/o John (broken)
A. A.	3 Jun 1833	19 Jan 1892	w/o John
John D.	Died	7 Oct 1861	6y 5m 20d
John E.	2 Jun 1862	5 Nov 1883	
John E.	Died	4 Dec 1861	6y 9m 14d
Julia D. Peerman	1 Aug 1851	25 Feb 1871	w/o R.J.
James A.	Died	13 Mar 1856	8y 2m 19d
Leroy S.	22 Aug 1866	26 Jun 1870	
Linda E.	Died	24 Oct 1861	4y 10m 12d
Lucinda J.	Died	28 Sep 1861	8y 1m 3d
Maria J.	22 Jun 1862	17 Mar 1876	d/o W.H. & M.E.
Mariah A.D.C.	Died	19 Sep 1861	17y 4m 28d
Martha J.	Died	4 Oct 1861	12y 21d
Melvin H.	Died	24 Feb 1858	s/o S. & L.A. 2m 15d
Sarah A.	24 Apr 1855	9 Oct 1866	d/o W.H. & M.E.
Simeon)	19 Sep 1819	1 Jun 1865	Returning from Rock Island Prison, his grave was made in the Mississippi River.
Louisa A.)	27 Apr 1830	30 Jul 1879	w/o Simeon
Kiziah	Died	18 Sep 1852	28y
Purlina F.	13 Apr 1863	26 Apr 1863	i/o S. & L.A.
W. H.	4 Dec 1826	21 Jun 1891	64y 6m 17d; h/o M.E.
M. E.	19 Oct 1830	27 Dec 1910	w/o W.H.
William	Died	20 Jun 1857	71y
Mariah W.	Died	29 Mar 1854	59y
Rev. W.W.)	1846	1925	
Addie)	1848	1932	
BIDDLE-Infant	OD	4 Jul 1919	s/o Rueben E. & Maude Ellen

BOLES-Pheby	16 Mar 1782	19 Apr 1834	59y; (fieldstone)
Sarah	(chipped)	3 Mar 184_	(fieldstone - chipped)
William	Died	28 Oct __8	(fieldstone - broken)
BOWMAN-C. L.	1863	1930	
Frank	No dates		
Garnett A.	1904	1940	
J. W.	8 Aug 1866	28 Oct 1915	
Minnie	18	1905	(as written)
Samuel Westley	No dates		(fieldstone)
BREEDEN-Lorry C.	14 May 1824	31 May 1851	
Loftis L.	6 May 1905	21 Sep 1907	s/o W. R. & N. L.
BURCHFIELD-Infant	OD	1967	(fhm)
Infant	1956	1956	(fhm-Horton)
BUSLER-Elizabeth	Died	15 Jul 1867	w/o Henry; 76y 2m 3d
CAMERON-Porter)	5 Feb 1892	17 Oct 1961	"P. J."
Martha Jane)	21 Jul 1886	30 Apr 1969	
Thurman H.)	10 Jun 1914	24 Apr 1981	
Marie C.)	25 Feb 1916	NOD	
Harmon Lindy)	18 Jul 1935	17 Mar 1957	
CANNON-E. J.	23 May 1863	21 Sep 1936	
Lula Katherine	1884	1974	
Sheely	14 Jul 1905	11 Jun 1949	TN Pvt Co A 53 Armd. Engr. WWII
CARMICHAEL-Ben Nona)	12 Feb 1874	14 Jun 1909	
Bertie Mills)	20 Jan 1879	29 Jun 1951	
Clifford Herman	24 Sep 1902	26 Apr 1921	s/o W.H. & C.A.; 18y 7m 2d
Dale E.	20 Jul 1954	18 Jun 1974	s/o O.D. & Ethel
James Hale	10 Sep 1842	20 Aug 1918	
Mary Jane	12 Apr 1851	28 Aug 1919	
John	No dates		3 day old s/o Will & Cora
Mary Jane	No dates		w/o James Hale Carmichael Aged about 30 years
Pearl Thomas	6 Feb 1915	18 Nov 1937	w/o O.D.
Robert H.)	29 May 1903	NOD	married 20 Jul 1924
Mattie E.)	10 Jul 1900	12 Feb 1979	
William H.)	20 Sep 1879	28 Jan 1959	
Cora)	5 Mar 1879	11 Feb 1939	
CARTER-Benjamin Morten)	16 Apr 1889	16 Sep 1928	
Henrietta Smith)	9 Dec 1893	3 May 1984	
CLUCK-A. W.	13 Jan 1818	30 Jun 1842	
Col. Benj.	12 Jul 1812	4 Apr 1876	
B. F.	19 Sep 1840	12 Feb 1908	Erected by Margaret Cluck
Daniel	Died	17 Jul 1862	Aged about 70y
Jane	Died	1 Feb 1878	77y
Eveline	No dates		d/o Wm. & Mary
James M.	26 Jun 1847	19 Nov 1909	
H. J.	30 Mar 1828	13 Apr 1885	(broken)
M. L.	27 Sep 1863	26 Aug 1876	
Margaret A.	28 Dec 1835	15 Oct 1913	
N. B.	22 Mar 1850	22 Oct 1861	s/o Col B. & Mary E.
Peter	1 Feb 1775	17 Feb 1845	70y (fieldstone)
Susanah	Died	26 Jun 1832	55y (fieldstone)
Raustis C.	19 May 1857	22 Jul 1925	
Richard K.)	1866	1943	
Mary I.)	1871	1949	

CLUCK-Sarah J.   5 Oct 1837   11 Jun 1907
   Willard   No dates   s/o Wm. & Mary
   William   10 Jun 1803   14 Apr 1887
   Mary   15 Sep 1818   26 Jun 1895
COLBOCH-Anna   19 May 1788   31 Jun 1861   w/o John
   Infant   OD   18 Feb 1863   d/o Isaac & Barbary
   Isaac   )   8 May 1819   20 Jun 1896
   Barbara)   22 Feb 1823   7 Dec 1899   w/o Isaac
   Liza Estell   25 Apr 1900   20 Aug 1901   d/o E.R. & N.V.
   Samuel   21 Nov 1812   13 Oct 1882   70y 11m 22d
   Elizabeth Bettis   12 Aug 1831   7 May 1912   w/o Samuel
   Sarah C.   5 Sep 1852   25 --- 18--   10y 9m 20d; d/o Isaac
                                                                & Barbary (broken)

COLLIER-Anderson   30 Dec 1882   25 Oct 1883
   Arvel   19 Mar 1857   2 May 1974
   Donald Ray   29 Jan 1936   19 Feb 1936
   Elbert   17 Jun 1855   25 Sep 1875
   Houston A.   May 1865   Jan 1923
   Maggie L.   11 Jan 1884   19 Jul 1900   d/o M.C. & L.D.
   Mary Katheryn   1 Oct 1938   23 Jul 1956
   M. C.   7 Mar 1855   20 Aug 1905   w/o L. D.
   Myrtle A.   26 Apr 1893   25 Apr 1894   d/o W. L. & M. A.
   Oval   )   6 May 1902   4 Oct 1975
   Emma Lee)   23 Jul 1904   14 Mar 1972
   Print   7 Dec 1884   8 Aug 1965
   Samuel   19 Feb 1835   10 Aug 1917
   Caroline   25 Oct 1831   18 Aug 1896   w/o S. I.
   Simeon   25 Jun 1867   21 Sep 1888
   William H.)   14 Jun 1909   18 Sep 1957
   Lottie H.)   26 May 1908   NOD
   W. L.   12 Mar 1850   15 Jan 1933
   Mary A.   15 Dec 1858   8 Sep 1922   w/o W. L.
COTTER-Emily I.   15 Aug 1847   15 May 1884   w/o William; 36y 8m
COURTNEY-Mary Ellen Walker   10 Apr 1913   6 Jul 1984
COX-Kenneth Randall   23 May 1961   21 Jun 1980
CRESWELL-Bonnie Ruth   27 Sep 1929   28 Feb 1935
   Carroll M.)   25 Jul 1891   1 Dec 1963
   Ethel R.   )   24 May 1895   2 Jan 1981
   Edward E.)   9 Nov 1881   9 Dec 1956
   Polly   )   14 Jan 1881   12 Feb 1969
   Rev. A. F.)   3 Feb 1848   10 Jun 1897   Father
   Ella   )   28 Mar 1863   29 Apr 1941   Mother
   Carrie   )   10 Feb 1884   Nov 1895   Sister
CRIDER-Jacob   Died   27 Apr 1838   80y
DAWSON-Baby   OD   1937   Baby of M/M Leonard
   Leonard)   1910   1970
   Aileen)   1916   NOD
   Ola Mae   Died   4 Sep 1984   d/o Samuel K. & Laura E.
   Roy L.)   12 Sep 1912   3 May 1975
   Ruby L.)   25 May 1917   NOD
EASTERLY-John R.   Died   10 Sep 1849   9m 13d
ECKEL-Infant   Born & died   21 Sep 18--   d/o P. & M.A.H. (broken)
FREE-Hal Swan   6 Jul 1901   8 Jun 1932
   James Allen   24 Oct 1893   6 Aug 1907
   James W.   )   24 Jun 1869   30 Jan 1935
   Evelyn McKay)   9 Jan 1870   26 Apr 1942

FREE-Sarah Jane	1838	1928	
FRY-Gerald Escoe	18 Apr 1904	9 Aug 1909	s/o H.L. & R.C.
John Bible	Died	16 May 1905	Co A 124 Ird Inf
			72y 4m 1d
FRYE-Nannie G.	1845	15 Feb 1916	w/o J.B.
GARBER-Lizzie D.	17 Oct 1873	26 Sep 1892	
Virginia Lee	30 Jul 1895	12 Oct 1895	d/o J.M. & M.E.
GIBBONS-V.C. Kimbrough	26 Feb 1867	17 Mar 1896	w/o H.H.
GILLIAM-Pauline	16 Apr 1915	1 Sep 1917	d/o J.R. & Iva
GILBERT-Mary E.	1895	1982	d/o Simmie & Margaret
			Alafair Duty GILBERT
HAMILTON-Hilton	1865	1929	
Jane Collier	1870	1938	w/o Hilton
HART-Benjamin M.)	1886	1964	
Frances M.)	1896	1980	
HARVILLE-Wiley "Pop"	9 Jun 1909	10 Jun 1964	
HENSON-Carl B.	18 Jul 1923	10 Oct 1938	
L.	No dates		(fieldstone)
Marian)	22 Jan 1889	23 Jan 1889	Twin son & daughter of
Mildred)			John & Ellen
Mollie	Died	22 Dec 1896	26y
Oda)	No dates		
Thula)			
Pleasant Luther)	3 May 1877	23 Feb 1951	
Eddie Riga McGlamery)	23 Dec 1877	31 Jul 1902	
Frances Massengill)	22 Jul 1884	11 Nov 1968	
W. P.	7 May 1827	23 Jun 1900	
Nancy A.	14 Feb 1837	21 Aug 1922	w/o W. P.
Wm. H.	15 Oct 1860	17 Jun 1862	
HICKMAN-Hannah	1868	1942	Mother
Lonzo)	4 Apr 1897	12 May 1963	
Ethel)	30 Mar 1900	6 Jun 1976	
Margaret	1886	1938	Sister
Willie	1899	1962	Brother
HIGHTOWER-J.H.)	14 Mar 1841	28 Jan 1901	
Cathern)	24 Feb 1845	28 Jan 1902	
HINKLE-A.A.)	24 Nov 1852	24 Oct 1933	
Louisa I.)	23 Sep 1854	12 Apr 1927	His wife
Blanche Richardson	12 Feb 1892	12 Apr 1918	w/o Roy
Crickie I.	15 Jan 1876	15 Dec 1926	
Daisie	2 Feb 1897	15 May 1898	d/o W.S. & E.L.
George Newburn	27 Feb 1878	28 Aug 1884	6y 6m 1d; s/o A.A. & L.I.
Harold Jesse	26 Jul 1917	30 Aug 1947	
James Wayne	6 Sep 1914	18 Dec 1916	s/o R.B. & A.B.
William S.)	23 Mar 1872	24 Feb 1956	
Ellen Loretta)	12 Aug 1975	12 Oct 1939	
HOPKINS-Cleo Henson	16 May 1900	24 May 1974	
Henry)	14 Feb 1906	NOD	
Viola Smith)	9 Mar 1908	9 Nov 1963	
HORNER-James Scott	15 Aug 1929	30 Jan 1959	TN Pvt US Army
Thomas Dewey	28 Oct 1944	22 Dec 1944	
William Roy	21 Nov 1892	1 Jan 1969	TN Pvt Co C 156 Depot
			Brig WWI
William Roy Jr.	22 Nov 1927	19 Nov 1944	
HOWARD-Claude T.)	9 Mar 1906	21 Jan 1979	Married 21 Dec 1930
Lura D.)	28 Dec 1908	NOD	

Name	Born	Died	Notes
HURST-Robert R.	7 Jan 1950	9 Sep 1971	TN Sp4 US Army Vietnam
JACOBS-Daughter	13 Aug 1830	-- --- ----	(Surface chipped)
Jacob	Died	27 Aug 1858	57y 5m 20d
Maria E.	19 Jul 1849	23 Mar 1862	
Mary Jane	Died	23 Aug 1833	d/o Lydia & John L. 1y 2m 8d
S.	No dates		
Samuel	7 Jul 1794	16 Dec 1880	86y 5m 7d
Sarah Crider	18 Nov 1795	27 Dec 1848	Consort of Samuel
Wesley F.)	15 Oct 1837	24 Aug 1899	
Mary E.)	21 Oct 1842	18 Jan 1931	
JARNAGIN-James Shelton	31 Aug 1926	16 Jul 1939	
JARNIGAN-Clyde	13 Jun 1883	20 Mar 1950	
Mattie	27 Jan 1887	25 Feb 1929	
W. L.	19 Mar 1834	8 Jan 1938	
JONES-Silviry	Died	29 Jan 1838	7m 9d
KEIRSEY-James C.	9 Dec 1915	5 May 1966	
KIDWELL-Caroline	26 Sep 1821	7 Nov 1846	25y (fieldstone)
KIMBROUGH-Arthur	30 Mar 1872	11 Nov 1942	
Benjamin H.	4 Nov 1869	28 Aug 1870	
Benony	Died	17 Jul 1856	(fieldstone)
Claude W.	1916	1981	Pvt US Army WWII
Drucilla	Died	17 Mar 1866	26y 9m (fieldstone)
John A.	29 Feb 1868	24 Sep 1870	
John A.	Died	21 Dec 18(72?)	(fieldstone-year illegible)
J. T.	2 Nov 1833	3 Aug 1915	
Martha E.	15 Oct 1839	18 Jan 1924	
Lethia	1886	1965	(handmade-also fhm-Fielden)
S.A.E.	29 Oct 1886	26 Nov 1887	
Wesley	Died	10 Sep 1862	(fieldstone)
William H.	6 May 1872	16 Nov 1902	
KNIGHT-William)	23 Jun 1852	21 Jun 1910	
Mary D. Haun)	8 Dec 1851	13 Dec 1944	His wife
KNOWLING-Andrew Jackson)	13 Jun 1856	10 Feb 1917	
Louisa Mills)	5 Mar 1856	3 Jun 1936	
Floyd M.)	1897	1966	
Eula P.)	1896	NOD	
Mable Burton	24 Mar 1902	7 Dec 1920	w/o F. M.
LANCASTER-Eugene)	1 Aug 1902	28 Mar 1939	
Carrie Gibbons)	29 Jun 1909	20 Jan 1977	His wife
Gertie A.	10 Feb 1887	9 Aug 1924	
James)	26 Dec 1859	11 Aug 1936	
Mary E.)	25 Jul 1865	13 Jun 1941	"Mollie"
Reva Inman	30 Sep 1900	14 Jun 1928	
Willie	3 Oct 1884	1 Jul 1887	s/o J.E. & M.E.
LANDRUM-Margaret Beatrice	Born & died	21 Dec 1909	d/o E.R. & L.S.
Robert M.	Died	4 Jul 1848	45y 2m 28d (broken)
Purlina	Died	28 Nov 1850	44y 3m 1d; Consort of R.M.
LANE-Nora M.	3 Oct 1882	2 Dec 1907	w/o W. J.
Frank B.	17 Sep 1901	3 Dec 1901	s/o W.J. & N.M.
LANGDON-Rachel	No dates		About 100y (fieldstone)
LARGE-Jeffery Lynn	Born & died	1 Jan 1964	
LAWSON-Ellen M.	Died	24 Nov 1878	21y 3m
LINE-Nancy E.	24 Mar 1863	24 May 1863	d/o John & Adaline E.
Wiley	17 Jan 1801	9 Aug 1873	72y 6m 22d

LINK-Elizabeth	9 Feb 1852	18 Jan 1922	
LOVE-Dewey E.)	27 Jul 1917	28 Apr 1961	
Sarah Grant)	30 Dec 1906	NOD	
Martha Adale	14 Jan 1944	29 Sep 1944	d/o M/M Dewey
LYLE-Rev. Daniel	Died	13 May 1856	65y 3m 10d; Rev. of the M.E. Church
Mary M.	20 Mar 1784	5 May 1830	w/o Rev. Daniel
Lucinda	1810	19 Apr 1875	w/o Rev. Daniel
Sarah	Died	20 Nov 1861	16y 7m 12d
(broken)	1830		(large stone; broken; date could be born or died)
McGUIRE-Mary	Died	10 Oct 1861	5y 8m 29d
Infant	Died	23 Mar 1861	5m 14d; i/o P.J. & S.
Michael A.	(broken)		s/o John & Catherine
MANNING-Jasper	19 Jul 1821	15 Jul 1868	s/o David & Anna
Jane	22 Dec 1821	25 Feb 1889	w/o Jasper
Joseph A.)	1852	1935	
Katharine H.)	1869	1947	
Moses Ann	25 Dec 1860	17 Nov 1899	w/o Joseph; 39y 10m 22d
Ross Thurman	1 Nov 1907	14 Nov 1907	s/o J.A. & Katharine
Willie Love	Born & died	21 Dec 1895	s/o W.C. & G.A.
MARTAIN-Infant	No dates		1m 3d;s/o J.H. & E.L.
MARTIN-George M.	11 Mar 1882	4 May 1898	s/o R.M. & M.F.
James W.	3 Jun 1872	14 May 1874	s/o R. M. & M.F.
J. H.)	7 Mar 1852	8 May 1932	
Ellen)	12 Jul 1849	10 Jun 1919	
Sam)	27 Oct 1877	28 Mar 1952	
Leta)	15 Jun 1879	25 Jan 1936	
MILLER-Alvan	17 May 1939	7 Nov 1945	s/o M/M G.G.
Garland G.)	10 Aug 1896	26 Jul 1939	
Virgie)	1 Sep 1909	NOD	
MILLS-George W.)	10 May 1856	8 Jun 1905	
Laura E.)	13 Apr 1860	5 Feb 1936	
Infant	Born & died	21 Apr 1902	s/o M.M. & N.A.
J. H.)	4 Jul 1862	20 Jun 1914	
Ida E.)	14 Aug 1867	27 Feb 1896	His wife
J. T.	5 Jun 1860	14 Jul 1863	
Moses M.)	1868	1935	
Nancy A.)	1867	1952	
W. R.	27 Feb 1873	20 Jul 1873	
Robert	18 Sep 1820	2 May 1895	Co C 9th Tenn Cav
Harriet C. Peerman	16 Jan 1834	6 Nov 1913	w/o Robert
Robert W.	1832	1897	
Nancy C.	1837	1902	
Samuel	6 Nov 1851	11 Nov 1864	
MOORE-George S.)	4 Dec 1901	4 Sep 1974	
Gussie S.)	30 May 1901	NOD	
Infant)	Born & died	7 Dec 1914	infants of M/M O.B.
Infant)	Born & died	28 Aug 1917	
L. P.	2 Mar 1889	17 Apr 1889	s/o S.R. & M.J.
Otha B.)	17 Jun 1892	22 May 1972	
Annis S.)	11 Apr 1893	25 Apr 1971	
S. A.	1 Sep 1909	17 Jan 1912	s/o S.R. & M.J.
S. R.)	24 May 1867	13 Nov 1944	
Jane Reneau)	4 Mar 1869	24 Jan 1954	

NEWMAN-Child   OD   7 Oct 1898   child of G.E. & Mollie
    Child   OD   7 Dec 1902   child of G.E. & Mollie
    Child   OD   12 Mar 1900   child of G.E. & Mollie
    Child   OD   1 Jun 1906   child of G.E. & Mollie
    Child   OD   17 Oct 1912   child of G.E. & Mollie
    Mollie Henson   Died   22 Dec 1896   w/o G.E.
OWEN-Mary E.M. Dade   8 May 1835   19 Nov 1880   w/o J.P.
PROFFITT-John M.   22 Jan 1914   22 Dec 1984
REEVES-H. J.   17 May 1830   12 Jul 1905   75y 1m 25d
    S. I. R.   20 Jan 1831   11 Nov 1898   w/o H.J.
    James R.)   1865   1866
    John W.)   1861   1863
    Nancy A.)   1856   1863
RICHARDS-Hugh J.   )   3 Dec 1884   28 Sep 1927
    Lucinda Tunnell)   21 Aug 1881   29 Nov 1868
RICHARDSON-Emerson   22 Jan 1897   17 May 1925
    William   12 Jan 1839   19 Apr 1907
RIGGS-Jesse   28 Sep 1805   29 Jun 1886
    S. M.   Died   2 Jul 1890   aged about 84y
RIMMER-Rebecca A.   5 Nov 1862   25 Feb 1864
ROBERTS-J.B.R.   17 Feb 1869   9 Nov 1871   s/o W.E. & M.E.
    Jennie Biddle   12 Sep 1888   12 Nov 1982
    Mattie   20 Sep 1877   24 Feb 1913   d/o W.E. & M.E.
    Dr. Wm. E.   28 Nov 1848   11 Mar 1925
    Mary E. Bettis   4 Sep 1848   28 Sep 1926   w/o Dr. Wm. E.
ROBESON-Hubert J.)   1899   1976   married 13 Oct 1923
    Jessie Mae   )   1905   1966
ROGERS-J. J.   )   1 Feb 1869   31 Mar 1942
    Carline Henson)   12 Feb 1871   29 Aug 1954
    Charlie)   21 Sep 1893   26 Feb 1972
    Ollie W.)   19 May 1889   16 Oct 1966
    Grace Agnes   7 Feb 1926   14 Feb 1926   d/o Frank & Opal
    James Glen   9 Jul 1917   NOD   WWII Veteran
    Hazel   22 Feb 1920   NOD
    Jesse K.)   6 Dec 1891   29 Jul 1952
    Naomi S.)   4 Aug 1893   24 Apr 1978
SARTAIN-Emett A.)   1866   1931
    Ida A.   )   1871   1952
    Rufus O.   5 Jul 1891   7 Mar 1919   Pvt A.R. Depot 319 QM
                                                        Corps; s/o E. A. & I. A.

    Ruby Grace   6 Sep 1906   26 Sep 1906   d/o E.A. & I. A.
SCOTT-Bonnie Skeen   8 Jan 1906   5 Feb 1963
SCRUGGS-Elizabeth   20 Sep 1841   22 May 1846   4y 8m (fieldstone)
SHARP-Rev. James B.   Died   4 Sep 1824   34y 10m 29d
    Lockey M.   Died   21 Jan 1880   w/o James B.; 87y 2m 14d
SKEEN-Infant   Died   20 Apr 1915   s/o M. F. & G. M.
    Infant   OD   31 Mar 1918   d/o M/M P.W.
    Marshal H.)   23 Jul 1884   3 Jan 1953
    Flora M.)   11 Jul 1890   7 Jul 1977
    Melvin Franklin   )   14 Oct 1874   16 Feb 1929
    Cora Myrtle Bettis)   7 Sep 1880   22 Jun 1960
    P. W.)   1889   1961
    Lula M.)   1898   1984
    Samuel Thomas   )   28 Feb 1879   7 Mar 1951
    Clementine Breeden)   28 Mar 1878   6 Jan 1967
    Ulas E.)   9 Feb 1904   3 Dec 1969
    Myrtle G.)   25 Feb 1904   NOD

SMITH-Clyde L.)	23 Mar 1902	6 Feb 1985	
Hattie M.)	19 Jun 1903	NOD	
George A.)	1872	1932	
Florence F.)	1873	1905	His wife
Gilbert N.)	22 Mar 1879	3 Jun 1940	
Bertha A.)	9 Oct 1883	4 Feb 1913	
Hubert)	11 Oct 1897	8 Aug 1960	
Rosa)	20 Oct 1898	NOD	
Infant	OD	Jul 1905	s/o M/M Porter
I. D.	9 Aug 1878	3 Jun 1879	s/o L. & E.
Lelia Cleo	12 Dec 1898	5 Feb 1901	2y 1m 23d;d/o G.A. & F.E.
Willie May	9 Dec 1893	27 Sep 1894	
W. M.)	1867	1908	
Laura A.)	1868	1935	
SOLOMON-Albert A.J.	6 Oct 1858	OD(born)	11d
Jim	1881	1940	
Nancy Jarnigan	1880	1932	
TALBOTT-Infant	Died	22 Sep 1899	i/o W.O. & I.M.
TALLEY-Napolian	20 Jan 1872	25 Feb 1889	
THOMAS-John M.)	30 Nov 1864	28 Nov 1944	
Melissa Hart)	7 Jan 1876	26 Dec 1961	
TUNNELL-Dana H.)	4 Jul 1899	7 Nov 1964	married 6 Apr 1919
Violet)	18 Jul 1901	NOD	
John P.	6 Mar 1893	8 Mar 1966	
Roger Lee	5 Apr 1948	7 Sep 1948	s/o M/M Wayne
Wesley	27 Feb 1860	23 Mar 1945	
Malinda F.	5 Dec 1861	25 Mar 1940	
WALKER-A. F. Jr.	30 Jan 1913	17 Jul 1914	s/o A.F. & H.C.
Annie L.	27 Feb 1875	3 Jul 1965	
David	21 Feb 1870	27 May 1919	
Sydna Winsted	12 May 1875	18 Jun 1916	w/o David; Our sister
Frank William	22 Dec 1907	18 Dec 1957	
Haynes)	14 Apr 1814	4 Mar 1901	
Louisa)	9 Mar 1818	30 Mar 1903	w/o Haynes
Charley H.)	23 Nov 1860	15 Oct 1926	
Lucinda B.)	23 Nov 1855	14 Feb 1945	
Irlene Il.)	20 Feb 1893	27 Dec 1965	
Hugh Elbert)	26 Aug 1881	12 Apr 1971	
Annie Creswell)	7 Aug 1885	25 Sep 1962	
James E.)	30 Aug 1834	16 May 1911	
Nancy A.)	19 Nov 1831	26 May 1907	His wife
John	Died	12 Feb 1856	70y
Priscilla	Died	31 Oct 1847	Consort of John;54y 8m 7d
John Monroe	14 Aug 1855	6 Feb 1938	
Joseph Samuel	12 Apr 1868	18 Feb 1949	
Maude	No dates		15d; d/o C.H. & L.H.
Paul N.	15 Apr 1908	14 Jan 1909	s/o H.E. & Annie
T.C.)	22 Mar 1838	21 Sep 1919	
Mary S. Neff)	25 Nov 1837	5 May 1912	His wife
Willie D.	12 Apr 1868	23 Mar 1890	s/o T.C. & Mary S. 21y 11m 11d
W. P.	7 May 1827	23 Jun 1900	
Nancy A.	14 Feb 1837	21 Aug 1922	
William C.	2 Apr 1868	3 Nov 1902	s/o J.E. & N.A.;34y 7m 1d
WATSON-Roy Newman	27 Aug 1934	3 Aug 1983	Pvt US Army

WEBB-Ben H.)	26 Feb 1890	21 Jan 1942	
Dicie Reese)	1 Apr 1888	12 May 1974	
Bernard	11 Aug 1917	5 Jun 1925	s/o Ben & Dicie
WEST-J. Clifford)	2 Feb 1911	23 Feb 1983	
Mary Ruth)	7 Oct 1919	14 Oct 1985	
WILKINS-Freeman	1814	1893	
WILLIFORD-Abe H.)	21 Feb 1878	3 Feb 1960	
Hannah)	2 Nov 1892	28 Mar 1957	
Clark D.)	No dates		
Margaret E.)	No dates		
Ruffus	1898	1899	
Sarah Ann	2 Oct 1828	19 Oct 1910	w/o Simeon
WILSON-William Nathan	1851	1926	
WINSTEAD-George)	1879	1963	
Sallie)	1877	1917	
M.	4 Oct 1843	3 May 1929	
Elizabeth	13 Sep 1849	25 Nov 1905	w/o M.
John	29 Apr 1902	4 Mar 1904	s/o George & Sallie
Mattie L. Gilliam	19 Jul 1880	19 Mar 1947	
Woodrow W.	7 Sep 1913	24 Feb 1960	
WITT-Wm. Crockett)	1855	1908	
Decatur)	1880	1901	
Wm. F.)	1883	1900	
Hughey Otto)	1885	1900	
WOODS-William Jefferson	No dates		
Liza Kimbrough	No dates		

In this old cemetery many burials are marked with fieldstones. Some of these
were aged and very difficult to decipher. Others were inscribed with initials
only. We are including these here. Perhaps they will have some meaning to
someone familiar with the families.

PHILIPS-Benjamin	18 Oct 1837	5 Jan 1840(4?)	(fieldstone;upside down)
(No last name)-Susan	18 Mar 1805	22 Dec 1843	(beside PHILIPS;fieldstone)
Cordelia C.K.	28 Jan 1873	25 Jan 1894	(by Kimbroughs)

INITIALS:

M.J.			(beside Samuel Jacobs)
B.F.K.	19 Sep 187_	23 Sep 1883	(broken fieldstone)
W.R.K.	Died	8 Oct 1869	16d; (fieldstone)
J.L.	Died	26 Feb 1844	(fieldstone)
W.L.	Died	25 Feb 1844	(fieldstone)
S.M.			(near Mills)
R.L.M.			
M.A.M.			
R.L.M.			
J.G.P.			
W.W.	Died	9 Jul 1877	(fieldstone)
P.W.	Died	187_	
CAR CHA			(illegible)

This neat, well maintained cemetery is located at Ebenezer Methodist Church. To
reach the site, take Exit 4 from I-81 onto Roy Messer Highway. Turn north to Kimbrough
Cross Roads   0.4 miles. Turn left onto State Route 66 (Valley Home Road). Drive
1.0 miles and turn left. The cemetery is 0.1 miles ahead on the left.

Immediate care is needed if these beautiful old fieldstones in Ebenezer Methodist Church Cemetery are to be preserved. Left, "Silviry C. Jones died 29 Jan 1838, age 7 months, 9 days." Right, "Sarah Crider, 18 Nov 1795-27 Dec 1848, consort of Samuel."

Ebenezer Methodist. Fieldstone of Peter Cluck, 1 Feb 1775-17 Feb 1845.

This elaborate stone in Church-in the-Pines Cemetery marks the grave of Alice Purdy Hungate, w/o E. W.

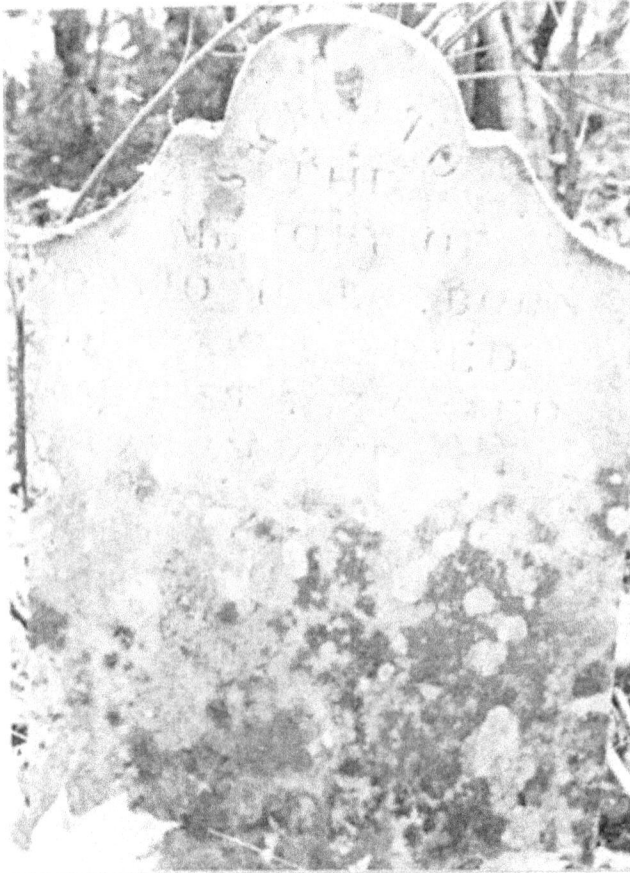

These matching stones were found in a badly overgrown section of Friendship Primitive Baptist Cemetery. Left, "David Moyers, 7 Oct 1766-4 Aug 1836." Right, "Margaret H. Gray Hale, 11 Jul 1773-27 Nov 1856, wife of 1st David Moyers, 2nd Richard Hale."

The grave of Turcree Mark Nan, champion cow of J. M. Leckie

This photo of the Isaac Crider grave was made in 1986. We revisited the site in April, 1988 and found that the stones had been removed. The inscribed fieldstone remains on the site.

ECKEL CEMETERY

Name	Born	Died	Notes
BLACKBURN-Infant	Born & died	4 Oct 1881	s/o Joseph & A. E.
Infant	Born & died	6 Nov 1883	s/o Jos. & A. E.
John	1 Jun 1894	4 Dec 1899	s/o J.F. & J.; 5y 6m 4d
John Fain)	30 Jan 1846	19 Sep 1920	
Julia Eckel)	28 Aug 1851	24 Jun 1921	
Julia	27 May 1891	18 Jun 1894	d/o J.F. & J.
Lucy	10 Jan 1886	18 Sep 1886	d/o J.F. & J.
Peter Samuel	16 Nov 1887	7 Jun 1950	
CARSON-Emelia Eckel	Died	29 Jun 1841	Consort of Samuel
Samuel	7 Sep 1768	21 Mar 1850	81y 6m 14d
ECKEL-Catherine	Died	29 Dec 1868	89y 6m 22d
John	Died	23 May 1887	died at Leadville, Colorado; Co C 4th Tenn Cav
Peter P.	27 Feb 1854	27 Oct 1938	
Peter)	1 Jul 1812	3 Dec 1885	
Mary A. H.)	2 Mar 1819	6 Oct 1888	
Thomas R.	Died	11 Oct 1895	76y 8m 10d
Harriet N.	28 Nov 1830	8 Nov 1889	59y lacking 20 days w/o T. R.
Maria J.	26 Sep 1830	17 Apr 1860	29y 6m 22d; Consort of Thomas R.
William H.	Died	2 Jan 1895	79y 1m 21d
Priscilla R.	Died	20 Sep 1874	54y 10m 6d
FELKNOR-George S.)	4 Nov 1856	7 Oct 1901	
Sarah E.)	2 Jun 1860	5 Apr 1935	
Nellie May	Died	29 Jul 1890	1m 29d; d/o G.S. & S.E.
GRAHAM-William	6 --- 1826	-- --- ----	(broken)
JACKS-Rev. Richd.	Died	31 Jul 1831	
MOULTON-E. P.)	22 Dec 1820	13 Nov 1892	
Hannah)	5 Mar 1821	11 Jul 1884	w/o E. P.
WAKER-Infant	No dates		d/o R. & C.
Infant	No dates		s/o R. & C.
WALKER-Maria	4 Mar 1803	6 Oct 1864	

The following stones were in a row with the stone of Rev. Richd. Jacks and are all the same style.

E. J.	OD	1824
E. F. J.	Died	1823
Lydia J.	OD	1824
Milton D. J.	OD	1824
Thomas J.	OD	1824

To reach this cemetery, begin at Exit 8 on I-81. Drive toward White Pine to the intersection with 25E. Turn toward White Pine and drive 1.8 mile and turn right onto Main St. Drive 3.9 miles. Eckel cemetery is atop the hill to the right.

FRIENDSHIP PRIMITIVE BAPTIST CHURCH CEMETERY

ANDERSON-Frederic Hale)	7 Feb 1886	27 Mar 1886	Children of W.H. & M.D.
Elmer Ernest)	11 Oct 1887	4 Feb 1888	
Mary David	8 Dec 1861	10 Nov 1906	w/o W.H.
ATCHLEY C. Boid	13 Apr 1886	4 Jul 1889	s/o Dr. J.C. & M.
CLINE-A. J.	No dates		Co. D 4th TN Inf
FLASHER-Nancy	Died	9 Nov 1898	79y
HALE-Margaret H. Gray	11 Jul 1773	27 Nov 1856	83y 4m 16d, w/o 1st David MOYERS; 2nd Richard Hale
KIDWELL-Joshua J.)	30 Dec 1827	8 Jul 1902	Deacon
Maria J.)	5 Sep 1830	NOD	w/o J.J.
KNIGHT-Arch	7 Jun 1836	21 May 1920	83y 11m 14d
LIVINGSTON-Joseph Lindsay	26 Mar 1877	27 Dec 1893	s/o L.W. & M.J.
Martha J.	18 Mar 1844	6 Jun 1891	w/o L.W.
Thos. P.	23 Mar 1871	26 Dec 1880	s/o L.W. & M.J.
McBEE-Emily	12 Aug 1824	3 May 1890	
Samuel	8 Oct 1822	11 Jun 1889	(broken)
MILLER-Samuel	Died	26 May 1833	28y 5m 18d
MOSER-Nancy J.	26 Oct 1845	6 Jun 1881	w/o John
MOYERS-David	7 Oct 1766	4 Aug 1836	69y 9m 27d
NANNEY-Mattie Willie	24 Mar 1893	10 Aug 1894	d/o J.P. & S.J.
Susan J.	28 Feb 1866	19 Jan 1894	w/o J.P.
OWEN-Barbara A. McBee	22 Jan 1853	19 Jul 1902	w/o R.G.
Eddie Clevie)	12 May 1894	16 Dec 1894	Children of R.G. & B.A.
Fronia Mc)	3 May 1888	8 Oct 1889	
Herbert L.)	21 Dec 1883	17 Jul 1887	
PROVENCE-Catharine Josephene	Died	13 May 1854	15d; d/o M.J. & A.T.M.
Infant	Born & died	20 May 1848	d/o A.T.M. & M.J.
RANDOLPH-Henry	4 Jul 1778	15 Feb 1848	Pastor of the Primitive Baptist Church at Friendship. Tribute of affection erected by his friends.
SMITH-Bonnie May	27 Dec 1903	29 May 1905	d/o T.L. & M.J.
Carrie	12 Nov 1875	23 Jul 1892	Sister
Elmer F.	8 Oct 1882	5 Jul 1905	
John)	22 Oct 1844	7 Apr 1927	82y
Maggie E.)	4 Mar 1849	15 Jul 1904	His wife 55 years
Mattie E.	24 Aug 1859	11 Jun 1890	
John R.	21 Sep 1904	1 Oct 1904	
J. W.	18 Feb 1880	12 Jun 1931	
Lillie	26 Nov 1877	30 Sep 1918	
Mattie A.	17 Nov 1842	16 Feb 1890	(broken)
Maude E.	22 Aug 1899	26 Feb 1905	
Wm. Montgomery	25 Jul 1847	27 Jun 1880	(broken)
Prissie Elizabeth	(27 Jun)1852*	(14 Apr)1920*	(broken)*( )dates from WPA
Thomas	1 Feb 1852	30 May 1919	
Martha Washington	3 Feb 1855	13 Feb 1947	
T. L.	28 Sep 1871	20 Jan 1919	
William	25 Mar 1802	1 Oct 1888	86y 6m 9d
Martha	7 Sep 1813	20 Oct 1889	(broken)
William A.	20 Aug 1873	15 Jul 1904	
WALKER-Mary C.	Died	31 Dec 1857	d/o J. & R.E.; 18d
WELCH-Patrick	Died	18 Feb 1874	(broken)
Rutha			(broken-dates missing)
WITT-Daniel M.)	15 Sep 1851	7 Aug 1912	
Alice T.)	30 Jan 1857	3 Oct 1940	
Hubert	28 May 1894	29 May 1894	s/o D.M. & A.T.
Plesant	12 Jun 1892	23 Aug 1893	s/o D.M. & A.T.

WITT-Pleasant A.	18 Feb 1800	1 Feb 1872	Elder of the Primitive Baptist Church
Elizabeth	24 Apr 1801	26 Jan 1870	w/o C.H.
Rhoda Anderson	1 Nov 1823	20 Apr 1867	
Ollie Leona	18 Jul 1872	10 Jul 1873	d/o C.H. & Nancy M
Isaac N.	18 Dec 1858	4 Sep 1859	s/o C.H. & Rody

NO LAST NAME-Festus)   17 Aug 1885   25 Aug 1890   Twins (located between
  Maude   )   Smith burials)

INITIALS ONLY:

D.K.C.	No dates	Fieldstone
P.B.C.	No dates	Fieldstone
T.C.	(only date) 30 Jan 1845	
T.D.	Died (2?)9 Jun 1840	

This historic cemetery is now overgrown with trees, grass, and weeds. There are many fieldstones and depressions in the ground indicating unmarked burials. To reach the site, begin at Exit 4 of I-81. Turn onto Roy J. Messer Highway and drive toward Kimbroughs Crossroads 0.4 miles. Turn right onto Valley Home Road. Drive 2.7 miles and turn right onto Hardy Road. Drive 3.3 miles. Turn left. (The road is a sharp angle). Drive 0.2 mile and turn right onto the gravel road leading to the cemetery.

Gentry Family Burying Place

The Gentry Family Burying Place is mentioned in the late Jefferson County Historian Rev. Reuell B. Pritchett's CENTENNIAL BOOK of the French Broad Church of the Brethern, published in 1975. Rev. Pritchett said there were two Civil War soldiers buried here and describes it as being "on the Gentry, Carson, Owens, Rodeffer, Fisher and now the Reuell B. Pritchett farm." We have not been able to locate this cemetery, and it is our understanding that it no longer exists.

To reach the approximate location of this cemetery, begin at Exit 424 of I-40. Drive 2.3 miles toward White Pine on State 113. Turn left onto Brethern Church Rd. Drive 2.1 miles. The cemetery was located somewhere to the left.

GRAHAM CHAPEL CEMETERY

ALLEN-Catherine C.	Jul 1868	4 Aug 1870	
Daniel	Died	4 Oct 1870	42y
Nancy J.	18 Sep 1856	14 Sep 1870	
BEAR-Mae	9 Jun 1895	29 Nov 1937	
BRADY-Roy Lee	1939	1939	s/o Roy & Ruby
CARSON-Conway)	1882	1939	
Lucy)	1885	1930	
James M.)	9 Jun 1886	22 Feb 1924	
Dora D.)	13 Dec 1884	14 Nov 1961	
Joseph)	19 Apr 1844	21 Jan 1907	
Catherine)	16 Apr 1854	NOD	
Joseph	1907	1910	(fhm-Stubblefield)
No name	No dates		(fhm-Stubblefield)
CARTER-Elizabeth H. Evans	26 Dec 1816	29 Jun 1863	w/o Wm.
DENISTON-Barbara Jean	No dates		3 months
Althea Elizabeth	31 Jan 1888	29 Dec 1926	w/o A. A.
Cpl. Neil W.	19 Oct 1913	13 Aug 1941	Brother
FOX-Nellie Moss	1 Jul 1918	11 Sep 1982	
GANN-Debbie K.	1870	1908	
HARRISON-Charles A.	5 Jan 1859	8 Oct 1891	
Frank F.	26 Apr 1866	OD(Born)	s/o J.B. & E.J.; age 6d
James Rogers)	28 Nov 1826	9 Aug 1913	
Eliza J. Hunter)	24 Aug 1831	3 Sep 1910	
Robert	17 Jun 1908	22 Jul 1908	
Sarah E.	6 Nov 1856	30 Jan 1875	d/o J.B. & E.J.
IVY-Edgar	5 May 1912	8 Jun 1946	Grandson
George Mack	24 Feb 1874	6 Nov 1946	Father
Martha Lily	9 Oct 1873	30 Jun 1944	Mother
Joe Lee	2 Sep 1900	22 Dec 1918	Brother
JONES-Charlie	17 Jul 1927	26 Mar 1985	57y (fhm-Manes)
George G., Jr.	1972	1977	(fhm-Westside Chapel)
Sam H.	1898	1976	Pvt US Army
Ernestine Holt	11 Apr 1902	20 Apr 1963	
Wiley	20 Apr 1876	9 Oct 1941	
Mandy	15 Mar 1883	9 Aug 1935	
William T.	12 Feb 1912	1 Feb 1983	
Rosa Mae	13 Oct 1914	8 Mar 1984	
KNIGHT-John	Died	24 May 1943	71y (fhm-Stetzer)
LAIN-James H.	15 Feb 1886	24 Feb 1907	s/o W.A. & E.J.
LANE-Alexander	Born & died	11 Nov 1902	s/o F.A. & S.V.
Betty Delores	11 Jan 1938	11 Jan 1938	d/o George &athalea
Francis A.	26 Jan 1881	26 Jul 1904	
Gracie Leoma	15 Nov 1903	25 May 1904	d/o R.M. & M.B.
Inez	Died	17 Mar 1900	77y
Patricia Ann	16 Apr 1942	18 May 1942	d/o George & Athalea
Robert Earl	6 Nov 1900	9 Jun 1901	s/o R.M. & M.B.
Sam A.	6 Mar ----	7 Sep 19--	(broken)
Wesley)	1882	1935	
Martha)	1883	1942	
Wm. A.	Died	23 Jun 1931	84y 7m 27d
Eliza Jane	28 Aug 1847	27 May 1904	w/o W.A.
McCOIG-Carl William	25 Sep 1902	31 Jul 1967	TN Cox USNR WWII

McCOIG—Gilbert Austin)	31 Oct 1904	9 Jan 1985	
Sarah Frances Lane)	30 May 1904	13 Jun 1941	
MAETIN—James Gregory)	28 Mar 1875	11 Jan 1924	
Martha Dona)	2 Jul 1880	NOD	
MOORE—Janie R.	No dates		21 years on earth
MOSS—Theodore	13 Mar 1905	20 Apr 1905	
Olie May	10 Feb 1904	20 Mar 1904	
NOONKESSER—David	3 Mar 1848	16 Dec 1921	
Ida Belle Sims	17 Jun 1887	11 Apr 1912	w/o D.N.
Sarah Victoria	18 Oct 1880	18 Dec 1924	
PRESLEY—Vanie A. Lane	14 Jan 1846	24 Apr 1900	w/o M.M.
RINES—Bart	26 Feb 1902	13 Dec 1904	2y 9m 17d
Boyd "Doc"	2 Jan 1906	24 Nov 1983	
Burnace Faye	19 Apr 1936	8 Dec 1937	d/o M/M J.W.
Calvin	Died	14 Jul 1940	
Iva Mae	Died	5 Dec 1944	
Emett)	20 Jan 1881	13 Dec 1937	
Ida Lou)	7 Nov 1882	6 Sep 1937	
Flocey	2 Jan 1906	21 May 1907	16 4m 19d
Mitchell	3 Apr 1908	20 Apr 1923	s/o J.C. & I.M.
Wm. Jackson)	1 Dec 1873	10 Aug 1941	
Cora Lee)	16 Feb 1873	13 Jun 1952	
SMITH—Maria	7 Nov 1846	18 Feb 1906	
Sherman	15 Apr 1868	1 Mar 1946	Uncle
STRANGE—Frances L.	12 Apr 1914	28 Aug 1914	d/o Geo. & E. M.
George M.	30 May 1868	27 Jul 1940	
Letisha A.	22 Apr 1876	2 Oct 1908	w/o Geo.; 32y 5m 10d
Emma Noonkesser	2 Jun 1871	5 Jun 1941	w/o Geo. "aunt Em"
Tim	4 Apr 1881	15 Sep 1935	
William A.	10 Sep 1875	29 Mar 1935	
TAYLOR—Allen M.	2 Jul 1889	21 Nov 1889	
A. P.	26 Sep 1865	21 Aug 1885	
Luther	Died	16 Jul 1877	8d
Parmenas	18 Jan 1821	29 Sep 1898	
Sarah A.	Died	25 Feb 1893	w/o P.; 69y 2m 8d
Robert L.	12 Sep 1882	13 Sep 1883	s/o L.W. & M.D.
TUNNELL—Matilda C.	10 May 1893	16 Nov 1918	w/o W.H.
WALLIN—Dallas P.	1922	1922	
Frank)	11 May 1880	31 Oct 1922	
Minnie)	14 Jun 1880	29 Apr 1937	
WHITE—Jane Eliza	6 Apr 1873	2 May 1898	w/o J.S.
WILLIAMS—Bessie J.	10 Mar 1890	12 May 1890	d/o W.E. & M.E.
Charles H.	16 Oct 1888	23 Jun 1946	
Curtis Andrew	24 Feb 1929	5 Mar 1973	
John H.)	13 Jul 1892	5 Sep 1961	
Dora Jones)	5 May 1896	NOD	
Nancy E.	16 Nov 1870	15 Aug 1939	
Tilman	1892	1939	
WISE—Samuel A.	27 Sep 1907	1 Dec 1907	

INITIALS ONLY:

N.C.	No dates
S.E.H.	No dates

Mr. Fred Strange, age 82 in 1985) identified the following who are buried here in unmarked graves:

STRANGE-John Alfred	Died	ca. 1945	s/o Fred & Myrtle
Ruby Novella	Died	Feb 1923	d/o Fred & Myrtle
Wesley	Died	ca. 1905	Grandfather of Fred Strange
Elizabeth Lane			w/o Wesley

According to Frank Moss the following are buried here in unmarked graves:

MOSS-George	Died	1918	Father of Frank Moss
Mary Slover	Died	1919	w/o George

Graham Chapel Methodist Church once stood near this cemetery. In a fenced wooded area behind the cemetery are uninscribed fieldstones and grave-size depressions. We were told these were slave burials.

Take exit 424 from I-40 and turn and drive toward White Pine on State 113 for 2.1 miles. Turn right at Nina Baptist Church and drive 3.0 miles. Turn right onto Harrison Ferry Road. Drive 1.8 mile and turn right into what seems to be a private drive. The drive deadends at a house. The cemetery is to the back and to the right of the house.

This lovely stone in Friendship Primitive Baptist Cemetery was erected by his friends as a "tribute of affection" to the memory of Henry Randolph, an early pastor of the church.

As tangled as it looks, this is one of the clearer areas in the Friendship Primitive Baptist Cemetery. Irises and an illegible funeral home marker mark this unidentified grave.

HINKLE CEMETERY

HANES-Ellen	4 Mar 1808	5 Apr 1881	73y 1m 1d
HAYNES-Jane	10 Feb 1813	13 Feb 1850	euy 3d
Louisa J.	26 Jan 1850	28 Aug 1850	d/o W.C. & J.
William C.	Died	22 Mar 1853	28y 7m 4d
JETT-Lucy E.	5 Nov 1866	30 Apr 1867	d/o C.M. & Parmeli
LOVE-Elizabeth	25 Dec 1843	4 Sep 1880	d/o James & Catharine
James	4 Feb 1806	4 Nov 1885	
Catharine Lacy	6 May 1813	11 Jan 1873	w/o James
Martha	7 Dec 1850	13 Oct 1861	d/o James & Catharine
Mary	2 May 1840	10 Jun 1890	d/o James & Catharine
McCUISTION-James	20 Dec 1796	3 Oct 1871	74y 9m 2d (broken)
Wm. D. M.	8 May 1825	12 Oct 1872	(broken)
MANSFIELD-Joseph)	26 Feb 1830	20 Sep 1855	s/o T. & C.
Thomas M.)	14 Jan 1839	27 Apr 1865	Lost in Mississippi River; s/o T. & C.
Mary P.)	14 Oct 1868	29 Oct 1868	d/o Wm. E. & S.A.
Infant)	Born & died	18 Mar 1862	d/o Wm. E. & S.A.
NICHOLSON-Catherine B.	Died	24 Feb 1854	46y 5m 18d
Jeremiah	Died	7 Apr 1848	72y 8m
Rebecca	Died	28 Dec 1832	58y 10m 23d; Consort of Jer.
Margery G.	Died	28 Jun 1834	31y 4m 26d
SARTIN-Albert Olen	9 Aug 1896	2 Dec 1896	
Anna May	10 Dec 1893	27 Jan 1894	
Mary Virginia Martin	10 Oct 1859	9 Aug 1896	w/o Albert H.

This small cemetery is overgrown. To reach the site, begin at Exit 417 from
I-40. Turn south toward Dandridge on State Highway 92. Drive 1.7 mile to the
intersection with US25W-70. Bear left onto 25W-70. From this intersection
drive 1.4 mile and turn left onto State Route 66 (Valley Home Road). Drive
5.4 miles and turn left onto Hinkle Road. Drive 0.5 mile. The cemetery
is on top of the hill to the right.

LAME CEMETERY

LAME-Jno.	No dates	Co M 8th Tenn Cav.

INITIALS ONLY:

M. A.	Dc 1795	Au 1825	(fieldstone)

In addition to the above there are two, perhaps three, other burials marked with
uninscribed fieldstones.

To reach this site, begin at Exit 4 from I-81. Turn onto Roy J. Messer Highway
and drive away from White Pine 0.4 mile to Kimbrough Crossroads. Turn
right onto State 66 (Valley Home Road) and drive 1.7 mile. The graves are
beneath a tree in the field to the right behind and to the left of a white
house.

MILLER CEMETERY

BAKER-C. B.	1 May 1873	7 May 1940	
Henry I.)	2 Apr 1876	16 Oct 1936	
Ollie Large)	30 May 1895	NOD	His wife
John Gideon)	31 Mar 1838	8 Jan 1919	
Happy Jane Mann)	16 Aug 1841	23 Jul 1893	His wife
Walter W.)	26 Apr 1871	22 Jan 1937	
Mary Hart)	14 Jan 1872	18 Jan 1960	
BELL-Elizabeth	29 Mar 1795	15 Jun 1833	
BETTIS-Bradley	Died	11 Sep 1840	53y 9m 4d
Frances	Died	11 Sep 1840	56y 11m 26d
Infant	No dates		i/o Bradley & Frances
Martha	Died	Apr 1829	18y
CARMON-James	Dec(eased)		(fieldstone - appears to be unfinished)
Jane	Died	29 Ju 1837	(fieldstone)
CLINE-S. L.	No dates		(fieldstone)
LINE-Shadrach	Died	6 Jan 1860	5m 15d
MANN-H. C.	13 Aug 1843	23 Dec 1936	
MASSENGILL-Stella	1916	1984	(fhm-Farrar)
MILLER-Abraham	Died	11 Mar 1879	85y
Elizabeth	Died	22 Aug 1889	w/o A.; 82y
Arlie Annie	10 May 1868	1870	
J. A.)	25 Mar 1846	25 May 1898	Co A 9th Tenn Cav
Margaret C.)	1 Apr 1850	6 Sep 1889	w/o J.A.
J. F.	15 Jun 1865	27 Aug 1883	
Lucy	17 Nov 1888	30 Nov 1896	
Shadrach S.	Died	19 Oct 1864	s/o A. & E.; 22y 6m 7d
Rev. W. A.)	4 Mar 1836	22 Jul 1916	
Eliza J.)	20 May 1842	NOD	His wife
SITZLER-John	28 May 1814	29 Sep 1889	
STIGHLER-Mahaley	1822	16 Jun 1895	
WALKER-Albert J.	7 Jun 1874	29 May 1877	2y 11m 22d; s/o J.E. & N.A.
Anderson	16 Feb 1840	10 Feb 1843	(fieldstone)
Mary C.	5 Jan 1859	14 Jun 1877	18y 5m 9d

The following are fieldstones and are printed here exactly as they were read.
We have printed these inscriptions, not in columns, but up and down as they are
on the stones. The D and DE probably indicate "deceased."

E.W. D	M. W.	C. W. DE	---------(surface
Oct 7th	D Au 11	Ap 1st	1826 flaked)
1800	1805	1826	M

```
LE    (or BE) (matches writing on
----ON       Jane CARMON stone)
Apr 18--
```

This cemetery is somewhat overgrown, but not terribly so. To reach it, take
Exit 4 from I-81. Turn onto Roy J. Messer Highway and drive away from White
Pine toward Kimbrough Crossroads 0.4 mile. Go through the Crossroads and drive
0.9 mile. The cemetery is on the right.

MOORE CEMETERY

MOORE-John Lauriston   6 Jun 1842   5 Aug 1862

This cemetery was copied in July, 1937 as part of the WPA transcription of Jefferson County cemeteries. In addition to the above stone, one other stone was found at that time. This stone, listed below, could not be found in February, 1986. We found no evidence of other graves.

MOORE-Alexander Smith   6 Feb 1851 19 Sep 1853

This cemetery is in a pasture field near the road. To reach it, begin at Exit 8 from I-81. Drive toward White Pine to the intersection with 25E. Turn toward White Pine and drive 1.7 mile. Turn left onto Enka Road. Drive 1.9 mile and turn right onto Leepers Ferry Road. Drive 0.8 mile and turn right onto Powers Rd. Drive 0.5 mi and turn left onto a gravel road. Drive 0.4 mile. The cemetery is in a field on the left.

MOYERS CEMETERY

MOYERS-E.	No dates	(fieldstone)
J. S.	No dates	Co C 9th Tenn Cav
M. B.	No dates	(fieldstone)
Nellie E.	19 Jan 1884 8 Apr 1884	d/o N.W. & M.E.
W. R.	No dates	Co C 9th Tenn Cav
--------h	No dates	Fieldstone
TURNER-Julia C.	7 Oct 1840 15 Dec 1879	w/o W.P.
(Broken)	missing -- --- 1886	(This stone is broken and the top portion missing. The death year is all that remains.)

According to Mr. Wall who lives near this site, the following is buried here in an unmarked grave:

DAIVS-first name unknown   father of Rosa Davis

This cemetery contains over 30 burials marked only with uninscribed fieldstones. The site was once fenced, but now only the fence posts remain. Groundhogs have set up housekeeping in the southeast corner and unsightly holes now dot that section of the cemetery.

To reach this cemetery, begin at Exit 8 from I-81. Drive toward White Pine to the intersection with 25E. Turn toward White Pine and drive 1.5 miles and turn right onto North Walnut Street. Drive 0.2 mile. The cemetery is in a grove of grees to the right, above Long Creek.

MOUNT CARMEL CEMETERY

LEWIS-Mary   22 Apr 1829 29 Apr 1880

In addition to the above, there were four burials marked with uninscribed field-stones. It is impossible to estimate the number of graves here. The land adjacent has been cultivated and it is at the edge of the church parking lot. To reach the site, take Exit 4 from Interstate 81. Drive north 0.4 miles to State Route 66. Turn right and drive 2.9 miles. The cemetery is on the right at Valley Home Baptist Church.

PLEASANT RIDGE BAPTIST CEMETERY

AESQUE-David K.	9 Sep 1939	15 Dec 1948	
BEGLEY-Arlena Pollard	20 May 1889	6 Apr 1975	
Arthur Edd	12 May 1916	8 Dec 1983	
Lowell Jacob	26 Aug 1932	NOD	
Virginia Mable	2 Jun 1918	1 Mar 1920	
BISHOP-Ronnie E.	1955	1978	(fhm-Westside Chapel)
BROWN-Margaret I.	7 Nov 1882	29 Mar 1966	
CODY-Albert M.)	12 Jul 1916	NOD	
Hazel Louise)	23 Feb 1917	30 Jul 1959	Wife
Ernest Eugene)	15 Dec 1938	25 May 1941	
Ruble Henderson)	25 Jan 1936	27 Jul 1936	
Tommy Carrol)	10 Mar 1940	26 Mar 1980	
James Deroy)	4 May 1937	13 Jul 1937	
COTTER-Infant)	1974	1974	daughters of M/M
Infant)	1970	1970	Frankie
DILLINGER-Bill)	29 May 1913	NOD	married 16 Oct 1934
Ada M.)	2 Sep 1903	21 Jan 1964	
J. D.	29 Apr 1936	15 Sep 1936	s/o Bill & Ada
GIBBONS-Joyce Winifred	12 Jul 1946	17 Jul 1946	
INGRAM-Bud L.)	11 Feb 1860	13 Jan 1933	
Margaret Emma)	17 Jan 1863	15 Jul 1952	
Tom C.)	21 Aug 1879	2 Sep 1957	
Berlie C.)	12 Apr 1901	9 Apr 1977	
LEAVINS-Hazel Lorean	17 Oct 1955	21 Oct 1955	
LEWIS-Alfred S.)	22 Apr 1907	9 Jun 1978	
Alma)	7 Jul 1911	7 Feb 1937	
Jahava B.)	No dates		
LOVE-Harding)	28 Mar 1920	NOD	
Haner Pollard)	29 Nov 1918	27 Dec 1950	
LOWE-Frank D.)	1914	1966	
Alice L.)	1910	NOD	
MESSER-David S.)	18 Mar 1909	27 Jun 1970	
Edith P.)	11 Mar 1913	NOD	
Glenn Cecil	29 Jan 1953	27 Nov 1982	
John	1865	1954	
Lucy W.	1863	1946	
Perry R.	1894	1971	
MYERS-Joe R.)	11 Sep 1905	26 Jan 1961	
Minnie L.)	16 Oct 1906	NOD	
POLLARD-Daisy E.	1909	1983	(fhm-Mayes-Brooks)
Elmer T.	1925	1979	(fhm-Mayes-Brooks)
Harden)	20 Aug 1884	29 Sep 1974	
Ora)	9 Jun 1889	30 Jul 1949	
Lloyd E.	1901	1968	(fhm-Brooks)
Tadlock)	2 Jul 1897	14 Aug 1959	
Bertie Watkins)	4 Dec 1895	25 Jan 1935	
REED-Perry	1957	1981	(fhm-Westside Chapel)
RICKARD-Curt R.)	1 Dec 1903	9 Mar 1971	
Mamie E.)	13 Sep 1905	NOD	
Edmond)	29 Dec 1901	4 Aug 1984	
Willie W.)	17 Mar 1900	29 May 1954	
M. E.	OD	17 Mar 1937	d/o M/M Edmond
T. G.	20 Apr 1926	23 Apr 1926	
ROGERS-Lina	1904	1969	
R. J.	1932	1985	(fhm-Westside Chapel)

ROGERS-Robert J.)	10 Jun 1894	NOD	
Luevena)	10 Apr 1892	7 Sep 1936	
Tammy Louise	24 Apr 1966	21 Aug 1966	
RYNES-Wilburn	26 Dec 1919	15 Apr 1921	s/o D.R. & M.R.
William F.)	2 Sep 1894	29 Mar 1963	
Mae)	13 Jun 1904	NOD	
Wilson)	1 Aug 1872	3 Jan 1939	
Parlie)	28 Sep 1843	3 Feb 1933	
SILVER-Victor Bruce	17 Apr 1971	18 Apr 1971	
SOUTHERLAND-Ella P.	22 Feb 1903	11 Dec 1928	
Infant	10 Jun 1942	12 Jun 1942	d/o M/M W. A.
James F.)	15 Feb 1922	NOD	
Alice F.)	6 Jul 1925	14 Mar 1982	
Minnie Jane	9 Jun 1959	6 Aug 1959	
Samuel M.)	29 Aug 1874	22 Jul 1952	
Laura E.)	4 Feb 1884	13 Apr 1968	
SWANN-Bobby Lee	1948	1985	(fhm-Farrar)
WEST-Harold D.)	1914	NOD	
Edith L.)	1915	1968	
Infants	OD	19 Feb 1937	Twin d/o Harold & Edith
WESTON-William L.)	18 May 1928	NOD	
Mary E.)	8 Aug 1925	27 Dec 1973	
WHALEY-Shirley	No dates		Infant of F. & G.
Walter A.	16 Jan 1889	8 Jan 1944	
WOODS- Ronald J.)	21 Mar 1944	8 Sep 1978	married 21 Jan 1964
Lorene C.)	7 Jan 1946	NOD	

In addition to the above, there are 6 burials marked with uninscribed fieldstones.
To reach this cemetery, begin at Exit 4 from I-81. Turn onto Roy J. Messer Highway
and drive away from White Pine, toward Kimbroughs Crossroads, 0.4 miles to the
intersection with Valley Home Road (St. 66). Turn right onto Valley Home Road
and drive 2.7 miles and turn left onto Alpha-Valley Home Road. Drive 0.7 mile and
turn left onto Pleasant Ridge Road. Drive 1.8 mile. The cemetery is on the left.

The fieldstone of John C. Bell,
23 Sep 1843-16 Apr 1869, in
Westminster Presbyterian Cemetery

This double stone marks the graves of
Rev. Andrew Blackburn and Gen. Alexander
Blackburn in Westminster Presbyterian
Cemetery.

SARTAIN CEMETERY

CARTER-Lada F. Sartain	16 Jan 1887	17 Jul 1929	w/o J.J.
CROSS-T.H.	Died	1 May 1880	(handmade)
HOWELL-Virnie	17 Jun 1887	11 Nov 1920	Mother
HUMPSTON-Martha J.	28 Feb 1835	30 Nov 1880	w/o John W.
McCLAHAN-N. R.	Died	2 May 1892	(handmade)
SARAIN-Albat M.	Died	20 May 1873	(handmade)
SARTAIN	Died	2 Jul 1882	(handmade)
David M.	1844	1923	Co. C 9th Tenn Cav US
John D.	Died	22 Nov 1875	(handmade)
John W.)	22 Feb 1838	9 Jan 1928	Co. C 9th Tenn Cav
Hannah E. Mills)	1 Nov 1846	27 Dec 1928	His wife
Margaret Lavina	8 Feb 1870	28 Oct 1873	d/o J.W. & H.E.
Mary L. A.	Died	19 Mar 1891	(handmade)
Milley	Died	8 Jul 1871	(handmade)
SARTIN-James P.	16 Oct 1873	6 Feb 1909	
TINDELL-Charles	16 Apr 1838	12 Jul 1906	
(NAME BROKEN)	Died	20 Mar 1878	(handmade; may be J. R. Sartain)

To reach this cemetery, begin at Exit 4 from I-81. Turn south toward White Pine and drive 0.8 mile. Turn right onto Rankin Road and drive 1.0 mile. Sartain Cemetery is on the hill to the right.

SARTAIN SPRINGS CEMETERY

HATLEY-Frances M.)	16 Feb 1910	5 May 1985	
Edsie T. ROGERS)	8 Feb 1929	NOD	
HOPKINS-William M.)	5 Feb 1905	12 Jan 1972	
Mary Pearl)	21 Jul 1905	17 Feb 1973	
KNIGHT-Clarence L.)	10 Apr 1920	29 Sep 1975	
Grace L.)	13 Jun 1919	NOD	
MOORE-Leon	10 Apr 1936	7 Dec 1982	
ROGERS-Edsle T.	8 Feb 1929	NOD	(See Frances M. HATLEY)
SARTAIN-Paul R.)	18 Feb 1905	14 Jul 1973	married 9 Jun 1929
Vina Hopkins)	2 Jul 1909	6 Feb 1978	
SOUTHERLAND-Roy	26 Apr 1922	25 Jul 1977	

This neat, well-kept cemetery is located beside Sartain Springs Missionary Baptist Church. To reach this site, take exit 4 from I-81 and drive 0.4 miles north. Turn right onto State Highway 66 and drive 1.0 miles. Turn left and drive 0.4 miles. The church and cemetery are on the right.

SKEEN CEMETERY

CALDWELL-Vivia May	15 Sep 1897	3 Feb 1904	d/o Will & Minnie
KNOWLIN-Darah Elizabeth Skeen	6 Dec 1877	Oct 1938	Aunt Lizzie
LEADFORD-Infant	Born & died	3 Apr 1871	s/o W. S. & M. E.
William S.)	Oct 1850	27 Jun 1908	
Minerva E.)	15 Apr 1843	NOD	
SKEEN-C. H.)	13 Jul 1839	19 Jul 1919	
Martha L.)			
J. A.)	14 Jan 1821	31 Aug 1864	
Mahaley J.)	6 Oct 1822	6 Aug 1899	w/o J. A.
J. E.	No dates		Q. M. Sgt 1st TN Cav
Sarah Cannon	5 Oct 1816	21 Oct 1881	w/o J.E. (broken)
John	Died	19 Dec 1854	5m 21d
John F.	8 May 1870	20 Jul 1889	s/o C.H. & Martha L.
John W.	16 Sep 1854	16 Jun 1861	s/o J.A. & M.J.
Marcellus	Died	2 Jan 1872	Infant s/o M. & N.J.
Marcellus C.)	31 Mar 1850	6 Jan 1923	
Nancy J. McDonald)	11 Sep 1845	12 Oct 1920	His wife
Mary L.	Died	13 Jun 1861	18y 1m 3d
Moses	1 Oct 1851	9 Jun 1861	s/o J.A. & M.J.
Moses)	21 Aug 1798	9 Nov 1885	87y 3m 19d
Susannah Haynes)	17 Jul 1795	17 Jul 1874	79y; w/o Moses; Parents of 11 children; erected by J.E. Skeen
Sallie A.	16 Dec 1875	10 Jul 1894	d/o C.H. & Martha L.
Sarah C.	Died	4 Jul 1861	8y 8m (broken)
Taylor	5 Feb 1850	11 Jun 1861	s/o J.A. & M.J.
INITIALS:			
J.S.	11 A. 1761	A. 1836	(large fieldstone)

This cemetery is fenced and cared for. To reach the site, begin at Exit 4 on I-81. Turn onto Roy J. Messer Highway and drive 0.4 mile away from White Pine to Kimbroughs Crossroads. Turn right onto Valley Home Road (State 66) and drive 2.7 miles and turn right onto Hardy Road. Drive 2.0 miles and turn right onto Allen Road. Drive 0.4 miles. The cemetery is to the left on a hill behind a brick house.

Our first visit to Westminster Presbyterian Cemetery was a mad scramble through briars, bushes, and tall weeds. We were delighted to find, on our second visit, that the cemetery was being cleaned.

SNODGRASS CEMETERY

SNODGRASS-Catharine E.	12 Feb 1858	14 Mar 1862	(broken)
Rosey B.	3 Jul 1880	25 Feb 1885	(overturned)
Russell	3 Jul 1808	8 Jul 1863	55y 5d; Died by the Hands of Assassins
Jane	20 Sep 1818	12 Jul 1887	68y 9m 22d
Tennessee	16 Jul 1860	1 Apr 1862	

This cemetery is located at the intersection of Hardy and Harrison Roads. To reach the site, take Exit 4 from Interstate 81, and drive 0.4 miles to the intersection of State 66. Turn right and drive 2.7 miles to Hardy Road. Drive 2.6 miles. The cemetery is located in the barn lot to the right. In addition to the above stones there are six burials marked with uninscribed field stones.

TAYLOR CEMETERY

LAREW-Darthula J.	Died	26 Jun 1854	3y 3m 28d d/o C.W. & S.H.
TAYLOR-Ann W.	Died	20 Apr 1844	1m 16d
Alfred D.		8 Sep 1858	(broken)
Jane R.	Died	2 Oct 1847	18y 2m 12d
Leeroy	Died	14 Aug 185(6?)	33y 8m 12d
Laura	17 Aug 1862		d/o S. B. & M (broken)
Parmenas	4 Apr 1753	20 Feb 1827	73y 10m 23d; Col. NC Militia Revolutionary War - War of 1812 (2 stones; original says died 28 Feb 1827)
Peter H.	Died	13 Feb 1847	22y 11m 18d
William	Died	18 Aug 1834	54y 5m 6d
Willis	Died	30 Oct 1836	16y 3m 26d
_____	Died	9 Jul 1869	(broken)
THOMPSON-John S.	28 Aug 1915	7 May 1972	Minn. Capt US Army WWII, Korea

This old cemetery was restored and fenced by descendants of Parmenas Taylor and is cared for by members of the Thompson family who now own the site.

Take exit 424 from I-40 and turn and drive toward White Pine on State 113 for 2.1 miles. Turn right at Nina Baptist Church and drive 3.0 miles. Turn right onto Harrison Ferry Road and drive until it deadends at a farm. The cemetery is to the left behind a barn.

Though a visitor to this site would see no evidence of burials, this graveyard was recalled by at least two people we interviewed. Mr. J.T. Hopkins always heard there were Civil War soldiers buried here. Mr. Cathey, who lives near the site, says he has been told that two Civil War soldiers and two members of a Kimbrough family are buried here.

To reach this graveyard, begin at Exit 4 from I-81. Turn onto Roy J. Messer Highway and drive away from White Pine toward Kimbroughs Crossroads 0.4 mile. The graves are behind the white house on the northeast corner of the Crossroads.

UNIDENTIFIED

According to the CENTENNIAL BOOK of the French Broad Church of the Brethern, written by the late Jefferson County historian Rev. Reuell B. Pritchett in 1975, a few Civil War soldiers are buried in this graveyard. Rev. Pritchett describes the location as "on the old Webb farm, now the John Hill farm." This cemetery is also recalled by John CHilton, age 71, who grew up in the area. He believes this to be a black cemetery.

To reach this site, begin at Exit 424 on I-40. Drive 2.3 miles toward White Pine on State 113. Turn left onto Brethern Church Rd. Drive 0.4 mile. The approximate site of this graveyard is to the left, several hundred yards from the road, near the present fence line.

UNIDENTIFIED

This cemetery is mentioned in the CENTENNIAL BOOK of the French Broad Church of the Brethern, written in 1975 by the late Jefferson County historian Reuell B. Pritchett. He describes it as "up the big ditch on the Dewey Turner farm where cattle have destroyed what stones were grave markers." We have no information as to the number of graves or the identity of anyone buried here.

To reach the approximate location of this cemetery, begin at Exit 424 on I-40. Drive 1.6 miles toward White Pine on State 113. The exact site of this cemetery is not known, but the Turner ditch is to the left and crosses the road near this point.

UNIDENTIFIED

A couple of years ago Mary Helen Fox pointed out this small cemetery to Debbie Lutz and told her that her (Ms. Fox's) relatives were buried here. Unfortunately, since that time the stones have disappeared. The area where this cemetery was located has recently been cleared and bulldozed, and in the spring of 1988 we could not find any trace of the four or five stones which Miss Lutz remembers seeing. Ms. Fox has moved to Morristown and we have been unable to locate her.

Begin at Exit 8 from I-81. Drive toward White Pine 0.4 mile. Turn left onto Spring Road and drive 0.4 miles. The cemetery was to the left.

Westminster Presbyterian Church, founded in 1787, is one of the oldest in the county. The destruction of its earliest cemetery can be regarded as a loss to historians and genealogists alike.

On March 8, 1802, John Neely sold for $150.00 to Westminster Presbyterian Congregation, represented by its ruling elders, John Blackburn, Samuel Patton, Thomas Snoddy, Shadrich Inman, Joseph Snodgrass, William Horn, William Snodgrass, and William McClanahan, land on the French Broad River which included "a meeting house and grave yard and all houses buildings." From this we can infer that the old cemetery certainly was in existence by 1802 and probably much earlier.

In 1837 the church moved to a new site located on Long Creek on Sharp Road and started a new cemetery. According to interviews with various folks in the area, sometime in the 1920's a person who lived near the old graveyard decided it was an eyesore and should be done away with. We have been told he took up the stones and piled them in a corner of the lot, telling relatives of the deceased if they wanted the markers they should come and get them. Some of the stones were relocated in Jarnigan Cemetery in Morristown. Others lay there for years and no one has been able to tell us of their final fate.

The cemetery has been described to us by those who remember it as about one acre in size and having 25-30 bought markers, plus several fieldstones.

This site of the first Westminster Presbyterian Church and cemetery is now occupied by the Leadvale Baptist Church. The cemetery stretched to the back of the present-day Baptist church and we have been informed that a few graves are underneath the church's new education building.

Although we can assume that many of the early members of the Westminster Presbyterian Church are buried here, we regret to say that we cannot state with any certainty the name of any one individual in this graveyard.

To reach the site of this cemetery, begin at the bridge over the French Broad River on State 25E and drive toward White Pine for 2.7 miles. Turn right onto Leadvale Church Road. Drive 0.6 mile. The cemetery was behind the present-day Leadvale Baptist Church.

Beth-Car Black Cemetery. The stone of Civil War soldier "Corpl David Fausett, Co. D, 1 U.S.C.H.A."

BACON-Walter	24 Aug 1870	28 Apr 1892	s/o J. & S.D.
BELL-Calvin H.	14 Feb 1821	30 Dec 1908	
Annie Eliza Biddle	22 Apr 1827	25 Mar 1896	Married C.H. Bell 7 Jan 1847
Edmund)	15 Dec 1809	24 Dec 1893	
Isabelle)	12 Oct 1814	19 Jul 1851	Consort of Edmund
Ann)	22 Feb 1817	3 Jan 1894	w/o Edmund
Ezeca___	4 Dec 1845	Mar 1870	(broken) 25y 3m
John C.	23 Sep 1843	16 Apr 1869	26y 5m 23d
Louie J.	21 Aug 1865	14 Mar 1917	
Malinda	1860	1933	
Marcas C.	30 Dec 1830	1 Aug 1856	
R. C.)	21 Jun 1851	20 Sep 1891	Ruling Elder in Presbyterian Church
Jenie)	18 Oct 1857	3 Aug 1883	w/o R. C.
Ruth S.	5 Jul 1815	2 May 1848	w/o Jacob
BIDDLE-Eliza J.	28 May 1825	24 Aug 1890	
F. T.	4 Mar 1876	8 Sep 1897	
Isabella A.	3 Jul 1817	6 Dec 1888	
Dr. J. H.)	9 May 1824	24 Sep 1892	
Julia A.)	27 Mar 1841	20 Oct 1886	
Malinda L.	11 Apr 1836	7 Mar 1867	30y 10m 23d w/o R.C.
Margaret A.	7 Dec 1819	27 Jul 1892	
Robert W.	Died	7 Jun 1858	2y 1m 12d; s/o R.C. & M.L.
Sam'l	Died	12 Dec 1863	73y
Margaret	Died	17 Jul 1855	60y 10m 22d; Consort of S.
Serrenia A.	Died	22 Jul 1886	64y 11m 19d
Sintha A.	28 Feb 1828	9 Dec 1893	
BISHOP-Phoebe E.	Died	14 Oct 1900	About 70 years
BLACKBURN-Gen. Alexander)	Died	10 Feb 1846	41y (has two stones)
Rev. Andrew)	Died	22 Aug 1859	31y 10m 24d
Gen. A.	23 Feb 1805	10 Feb 1846	Ruling Elder Presbyterian Church at Westminster
Ella S.	8 Nov 1866	26 Jul 1868	d/o Wm. E. & S. J.
Iantha E.	16 Jul 1849	3 Nov 1854	d/o J. H. & I. E.
James	2 Oct 1782	13 Nov 1860	Ruling Elder Westminster Church for over 40 years
Catharine	24 Oct 1784	5 Sep 1867	Consort of James
James M.	29 Jan 1849	15 Oct 1849	s/o T. S. & M. L.
John A.	20 Oct 1852	12 Dec 1852	s/o J. H. & I. E.
Lucy Jane	18 Nov 1855	OD (born)	d/o A. & A. E. 2y 2m
M. J. J.	28 Mar 1868	19 May 1868	d/o T. S. & M. L.
William H.	30 Oct 1859	2 May 1864	s/o J. H. & I. E.
Wm. Minnis	8 Nov 1861	22 Dec 1861	s/o T. S. & M. L.
BROWNING-Verna	12 Mar 1882	8 Dec 1884	d/o J. B.S. & S. F.
CALDWELL-David	1 Feb 1802	21 May 1855	Ruling Elder of Presbyter- ian Church at Westminister
Mary	1 Oct 1808	5 May 1848	Consort of David
Harriet E.	22 Feb 1834	30 Jan 1838	
Narcissa	3 Jan 1831	22 Jul 1860	d/o Samuel & Sally
Samuel	Died	15 Feb 1863	58y 10m 29d
CALFEE-John C.	11 Nov 1920	14 Nov 1920	
CARSON-Ann E.	Died	14 Nov 1861	6y 3m 7d; d/o B. & S.
Anne	7 Aug 1855	14 Nov 1861	d/o B. & S.
Benjamin	15 Dec 1820	30 Jun 1881	
Carrie L.	Died	6 Nov 1862	6y 7m 18d

CARSON-Clarence C.	1 Jun 1875	12 Oct 1875	s/o J.R.N. & E.J.
Cyntha J.	30 Nov 1850	6 Aug 1852	d/o R.H. & H.E.
Elijah	Died	29 May 1863	55y 6m 29d
Eliza J.	Died	28 Dec 1863	18y 10m 26d
Horace M.	2 Jun 1857	1 Mar 1864	s/o B. & S.
Infant	Born & died	21 Apr 1875	s/o T. H. & L. D.
Infant	19 Sep 1863	19 Sep 1863	d/o R. H. & H. E.
Infant	Died	15 Oct 1849	s/o E. & C.N.; 3w
James A.	22 Oct 1852	7 Mar 1864	s/o B. & S.
John	31 Jan 1774	6 Feb 1850	76y 6d
Mary	30 Sep 1781	7 Nov 1857	76y 1m 7d; Consort of John
Margaret M.	3 Jan 1857	13 Apr 1859	d/o R.H. & H. E.
Parthena I.	1 May 1859	29 Jul 1859	d/o R.H. & H. E.
Porter J.	27 Oct 1842	24 Feb 1864	s/o B. & S.
Robert H.)	31 Jan 1824	27 Oct 1898	
Harriet E. Rankin)	11 Feb 1826	9 Nov 1889	w/o Robert H.
Robert H.	12 Jul 1844	24 Jul 1844	s/o E. & S.
CHAPMAN-Bettie Rugel	15 Nov 1864	1 Aug 1889	w/o G.F.
Infant	No dates		s/o J.C. & M.A.
COLDWELL-Minnie	15 Jan 1886	19 Jun 1887	d/o J.M. & Susie
Sally	30 Sep 1808	7 Dec 1892	w/o Samuel
COPELAND-James M.	13 Mar 1831	13 Dec 1893	
Sithy Elizabeth	18 FEb 1831	20 Nov 1915	
DICKEY-Ann Elizabeth	5 Jun 1880	11 May 1881	
Thomas L.	24 Oct 1854	17 Feb 1893	
Thomas J.	16 Aug 1878	3 Mar 1900	21y 6m 17d
DOUGHTY-Infant	31 May 1887	28 Jun 1887	s/o William S. & Maggie
Infant	20 Sep 1892	29 Oct 1892	d/o Wm. & Maggie
ECKEL-Geo. S.	Died	13 Jul 1886	77y 7m 1d
Jane W.	Died	15 Jan 1873	55y 8m 12d
Geo. S. Jr.	18 Jul 1853	25 Nov 1891	
Infant	Died	23 Jul 1852	d/o G.S. & J.W.; 24d
Infant	Died	22 May 1840	s/o G.S. & J.W.; 7d
Joseph P.	Died	27 Mar 1870	22y 6m 22d
Susan M.	Died	31 Oct 1863	13y 4m 17d
FELKNOR-Alexander)	20 Oct 1818	7 Mar 1904	
Anna Chilton Goan)	2 Apr 1815	29 Jan 1891	His wife
Anna	1834	1929	(sunken dates WPA list)
Infant	10 Dec 1877	OD (born)	d/o S. J. & M.C.
FRANKLIN-Cora J.	29 Aug 1875	OD (born)	1d; d/o Geo. & J.E.
Julia E.	26 Nov 1853	18 Sep 1878	24y 8m 22d; w/o Geo.
GARRIS-Rhodella	9 Oct 1868	15 Apr 1869	d/o Wm. & Nancy
GASS-Emily	7 Dec 1837	15 Aug 1899	w/o Powell W.
GOAN -Daniel H.	15 May 1812	10 Oct 1852	
Elizabeth	4 Jul 1816	25 Jan 1896	w/o Daniel
Florence S.	17 Mar 1880	25 Jan 1894	d/o O.R. & M.E.
Martha A.	3 Mar 1843	9 Aug 1893	w/o Robert
Mary Ann	19 Oct 1837	21 Jul 1855	d/o Daniel & Elizabeth
Sarah Jane	10 Nov 1839	19 Jul 1855	d/o Daniel & Elizabeth
HALE-George F.	13 Aug 1846	13 May 1917	
Elizabeth	28 Feb 1846	5 Jul 1921	
HELM-David P.)	27 Dec 1819	29 Apr 1865	
Nancy M.)	16 Aug 1830	28 Nov 1906	w/o David P. Helm & W. F. GARRIS
Dr. Henry	No dates		
Matilda C.	No dates		
Susan	21 May 1859	28 Mar 1860	d/o David & Nancy

HOLLOWAY-Amos	Died	30 Dec 1865	63y 2m 18d
Mary D.	15 Apr 1812	25 Jul 1887	75y 3m 10d; Consort of Amos
David A.	25 Mar 1868	OD (born)	5d; s/o Wm. A. & Amanda
Mary H.	16 Jun 1862	15 Apr 1871	d/o W. A. & Amanda
HORNER-Louie M. Rugel	1 Mar 1860	13 Apr 1894	w/o H.
HUNTER-Catherine	Died	6 Oct 1864	64y 10m 6d
Issabella	Died	11 Jan 1877	66y 6m 15d
James	28 Jan 1768	1 Sep 1847	Ruling Elder of Presbyterian Church at Westminster
Isabella	Apr 1769	8 Dec 1843	Consort of James
Jane	26 Apr 1798	21 Sep 1848	
Letty	21 Nov 1801	6 Dec 1857	
Polly	26 Apr 1804	22 Jun 1852	
IRVIN-Jane	3 Feb 1822	21 Mar 1867	45y 28d
P. J.	9 Jun 1856	19 Jul 1856	
JOLLEY-William H.	18 Oct 1828	1 Jan 1888	(broken)
KIMBROUGH-Samuel J.	2 Nov 1857	2 Jan 1892	
LEEPER-Caroline Snapp	6 Jan 1815	22 Jul 1891	w/o Elijah CARSON and Lewis F. LEEPER
McNEAL-Fannie M.	20 Sep 1853	7 Jun 1885	d/o Rev. J. & E.M.
Rev. James	10 Feb 1821	18 Nov 1892	
Elen M.	22 Mar 1825	19 Sep 1885	w/o Rev. James
MILLS-Gambel	No dates		(fieldstone)
A.A.B.	died	3 Dec 1861	
M.	No dates		(fieldstone)
T.	No dates		(fieldstone)
NELSON-L. C.	12 Apr 1845	10 Nov 1851	(fieldstone)
REAMS-Mahala I.	30 Apr 1859	11 Nov 1863	(fieldstone)
REED-Robert	7 Apr 1841	7 Feb 1930	
Will	7 Jul 1890	Oct 1912	22y
RITCHIE-Henry J.)	7 Feb 1827	2 Oct 1893	(2 stones; old stone says Ritchey and gives death as 27 Oct)
Amanda Jett)	2 Sep 1833	6 Jan 1904	w/o Henry J.
ROACH-Enos M.	25 Feb 1844	20 Oct 1893	49y 7m 25d
Mary A.	13 Apr 1851	NOD	w/o E.M. Roach; also J. A. VINYARD
RUGEL-Dr. F.)	24 Dec 1806	31 Jan 1879	Born Wurtemburg Germany
Laura C.)	4 Aug 1824	20 Jan 1903	
Infant	19 Oct 1843	OD (born)	s/o F. & L.C.
Infant	10 Aug 1850	25 Aug 1850	d/o F. & L.C.
Infant	8 May 1855	19 May 1855	s/o F. & L.C.
Josephine	23 Mar 1856	3 Jul 1865	d/o F. & L.C.
SARTAIN-William Clarence	18 May 1932	14 Aug 1933	
SCROGGS-Jane H.	29 Jan 1815	9 Oct 1847	32y 8m 10d
SINARD-Rossie	23 Feb 1906	1 Sep 1923	s/o R.F. & Dasy
SNODDY-Cary	12 Nov 1814	18 Jan 1852	Ruling Elder of the Presbyterian Church at Westminister
Sarah Rebecca	9 Jun 1820	19 Jul 1876	56y 6m 10d; w/o Cary
Frank Lee	15 Apr 1878	12 Jul 1878	s/o Rev. A.C. & S.A.
Infant	6 Jun 1879	6 Jun 1879	s/o R.N. & S.S.
Jane	28 Jul 1798	6 Apr 1880	81y 8m 8d
John D.	25 Nov 1795	2 Jun 1870	74y 6m 7d
John L.	14 Aug 1832	22 Mar 1863	30y 7m 8d
Sarah A.	1 Apr 1852	18 Jul 1878	w/o Rev. A.C.
Willie	2 Oct 1873	29 May 1874	s/o T.E. & Maria; 7m 26d
Walter M.	13 Feb 1877	9 Nov 1879	s/o Rev. A. C. & S. A.

STALCUP-N.A.	Died	31 Aug 1877	w/o C.T.
STRAIN-Nancy A.	15 Mar 1791	26 Jun 1880	89y 3m 11d; w/o Robert W.

She attached herself to the Presbyterian Church very young and remained a consistant upright member through life.

STRINGFIELD-Pearly	20 Sep 1879	17 Jan 1880	d/o J.H. & S.R.
SUTTLES-Floyd	4 Jun 1893	19 Mar 1923	
TAYLOR-Edna L.	6 Jan 1878	18 May 1878	d/o W. B. & M.L.
Mary L.	21 Feb 1855	3 Apr 1879	w/o W. B.
TOMPKINS-Staphen)	1833	27 Sep 1915	
Eliza Reed)	1863	15 Mar 1924	
TRIBUE-D.J.	23 Jun 1818	18 May 1881	
WALKER-Kate I.	4 Jan 1848	21 Apr 1878	30y 3m 17d; w/o Samuel
WILSON-Melville Wyly	Died	3 Apr 1878	19y
WOODS-Alfred J.	Died	23 Aug 1840	34y 9m 13d
WREN-S. J.)	2 Jan 1832	31 Mar 1894	Co C 8th Tenn Cav
Manervy Biddle)	20 Sep 1830	10 Sep 1900	w/o S.J.

The following footstones were found with only initials on them:

R. C.
B. C.
M. A. L.
S. B. S. (fieldstone)

In the WPA list in 1937 the following stone was found, but could not be located in 1986:

WILSON-Jane M.   16 Feb 1807 23 May 1880

When we first visited this cemetery, it was terribly overgrown. We returned a few months later to again tackle the tangle of briars and weeds. We were pleasantly surprised to see that it had been cleaned. We would like to congratulate whoever is responsible for this and offer our hearty thanks. We were able to recover several stones which we had been unble to see on our previous visit.

To reach the site, begin at Exit 4 from I-81. Turn onto Roy J. Messer Highway and drive toward White Pine 1.3 mile. Turn left onto Sharp Road. Drive 0.6 mile. The fenced cemetery is on the left.

Of beautiful pink marble, the stones of Bernice C. and Robert C. McGuire in Church of the Pines Cemetery resemble giant chess pawns.

WHITE PINE CEMETERY (BLACK)

BRIGON-Mariah	27 May 1846	26 May 1931	
CHANDLER-Sam	18 Sep 1872	NOD	
Josie Magbee	1 Jan 1878	12 Jun 1941	w/o Sam
CONWAY-Annie C.	16 Oct 1879	26 Nov 1964	
CURRY-E. C.	1892	1930	(broken)
JOHNSON-Lubertha Mae	1897	1957	
LEEPER-Annie	Born & died	Dec 1932	
Authur	Born & died	Dec 1932	
Charlie	1891	1978	Mech US Army WWI
Roy H.	3 Apr 1888	22 Jan 1983	
Edith West	10 Apr 1894	23 Oct 1973	w/o H. Roy
Roy Jr.	16 Apr 1922	1 Jan 1924	s/o Roy & Edith
Taylor R.	15 May 1910	20 Jan 1924	s/o Roy & Edith
LYLE-Clarence P.	4 Apr 1920	28 Jan 1940	
Frances L.	30 Sep 1917	25 Mar 1935	
Willie Ross	3 Jun 1925	24 Jul 1925	
MOORE-Amanda	1 Feb 1871	26 May 1931	w/o G. P.
Aurbury Lee	4 Jul 1955	16 Jan 1983	
Douglas	20 Sep 1942	24 Oct 1974	
Williard	25 May 1915	14 Mar 1974	
PORTER-Lula	11 Jul 1873	7 Jul 1919	
RICHARDSON-Mattie B.	Died	16 Nov 1920	
RIGGS-S. A.	21 Mar 1857	26 Aug 1920	
RUFFIN-Annie Okadel	23 Sep 1916	12 Mar 1974	w/o Milton
STEWARD-Charlie	1872	1963	
Willie Kate	5 Sep 1885	13 Dec 1948	
THOMPSON-Emma	Died	3 Jan 1927	w/o J. R.
Hannah	No dates		Age about 70; Mother
Minnie L.	7 Jan 1886	2 May 1949	w/o J. L.
WATKINS-Nat	2 Jun 1855	2 Dec 1929	
WILSON-Albert)	No dates		Father and Mother of
Lou)	No dates		George Wilson
George	1870	1951	
Lillie G.	Aug 1885	20 Jun 1920	

There are 27 burials in this cemetery marked with uninscribed fieldstones. Depressions in the ground indicate many more burials.

To reach this site, begin at Exit 8 on I-81. Drive toward White Pine to the intersection with 25E. Turn toward White Pine and drive 1.9 mile. Turn left onto South Walnut Street. Drive 0.7 mile and turn left. Drive 0.7 mile. The cemetery is on the left.

White Pine Colored

We found no marked stones in this cemetery, but only grave-shaped depressions and funeral home markers indicated there were burials here. It is located in a thicket and the ground is covered with leaves.

INDEXES

The **PRIMARY INDEX** is the surname index only to those names which were interpreted
by the transcribers as the surnames of the deceased. These surnames are usually
in the left hand column, but in a few instances a burial may be listed in the text.
Since other surnames were included in the "**Comments**" field, a **SECONDARY INDEX**
was created to make available that information. A more careful search of the page
listed will be necessary to derive any benefit from the secondary index. The
secondary index includes maiden names of wives which appear on the tombstones.

SECONDARY INDEX